INSIGHT GUIDES

BALTIC STATES
Estonia·Latvia·Lithuania

DISCOVERY
CHANNEL

APA PUBLICATIONS
Part of the Langenscheidt Publishing Group

L

INSIGHT GUIDE
BALTIC STATES
Estonia·Latvia·Lithuania

Editorial
Editor **Roger Williams**
Art Director **Klaus Geisler**
Picture Editor **Hilary Genin**
Cartography Editor **Zoë Goodwin**
Production **Kenneth Chan**
Editorial Director **Brian Bell**

Distribution
UK & Ireland
GeoCenter International Ltd
Meridian House, Churchill Way West
Basingstoke, Hampshire RG21 6YR
Fax: (44) 1256 817988

United States
Langenscheidt Publishers, Inc.
36–36 33rd Street 4th Floor
Long Island City, NY 11106
Fax: 1 (718) 784 0640

Australia
Universal Publishers
1 Waterloo Road
Macquarie Park, NSW 2113
Fax: (61) 2 9888 9074

New Zealand
Hema Maps New Zealand Ltd (HNZ)
Unit D, 24 Ra ORA Drive
East Tamaki, Auckland
Fax: (64) 9 273 6479

Worldwide
**Apa Publications GmbH & Co.
Verlag KG (Singapore branch)**
38 Joo Koon Road, Singapore 628990
Tel: (65) 6865 1600. Fax: (65) 6861 6438

Printing
Insight Print Services (Pte) Ltd
38 Joo Koon Road, Singapore 628990
Tel: (65) 6865 1600. Fax: (65) 6861 6438

©2007 **Apa Publications GmbH & Co.
Verlag KG (Singapore branch)**
All Rights Reserved

*First Edition 1992
Third Edition 2005
Updated 2007*

CONTACTING THE EDITORS
We would appreciate it if readers
would alert us to errors or out-
dated information by writing to:
**Insight Guides, P.O. Box 7910,
London SE1 1WE, England.
Fax: (44) 20 7403 0290.**
insight@apaguide.co.uk

www.insightguides.com
In North America:
www.insighttravelguides.com

ABOUT THIS BOOK

The first Insight Guide pioneered the use of creative full-colour photography in travel guides in 1970. Since then, we have expanded our range to cater for our readers' need not only for reliable information about their chosen destination but also for a real understanding of the culture and workings of that destination. Now, when the internet can supply inexhaustible (but not always reliable) facts, our books marry text and pictures to provide those much more elusive qualities: knowledge and discernment. To achieve this, they rely heavily on the authority of locally based writers and photographers.

How to use this book

The book is carefully structured both to convey a proper understanding of Estonia, Latvia and Lithuania and to guide readers through their sights and activities:

◆ To understand the Baltic states today, it is important to know about their past. The first section of Features, with a yellow band at the top of each page, covers the countries' history of occupation and its people, with essays on culture, nature and food. These lively, authoritative essays are all written by specialists.

◆ The main Places section, with a blue band at the top of the page, covers each country and their history since independence. There is then a full run-down of all the attractions worth seeing. Principal places of interest are co-ordinated by number with full-colour maps.

◆ The Travel Tips listings section, colour-coded in red, provides a convenient point of reference for

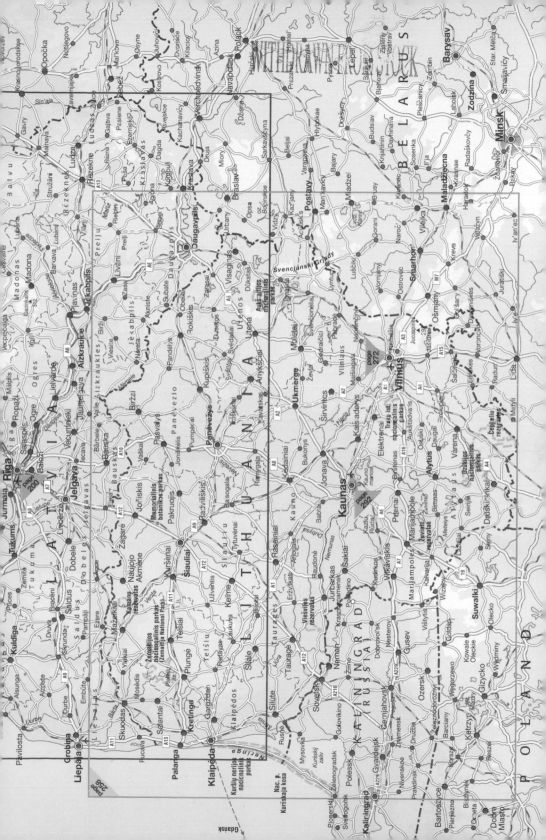

ABOVE: granny and granary, Tallinn Open-Air Museum. **BELOW:** Baltic lynx.

information on travel, accommodation, restaurants, activities and festivals. Travel Tips information may be located quickly by using the index printed on the back cover flap – and the flaps also serve as bookmarks.
◆ Photographs are chosen not only to illustrate landscape and attractions but also to convey the moods of the countries and the activities of their people.

The contributors

This edition was produced by **Roger Williams**, who compiled the original edition, one of the first guides to the then newly independent countries. New material has been produced and kept up to date by the correspon-

dents of the Baltics' very successful *In Your Pocket* listings magazines: **Steve Q Roman** in Tallinn, **Martins Zaprauskis** in Rīga, and **Lara Belonogoff** in Vilnius. **Eva Staltmane** of the Latvian Tourist office in London has been immensely helpful, supplying the chapter on saunas. The Lithuanian Embassy in London helped spot errors and Baltic travel expert **Nell Taylor** kindly checked the text.

Among the original contributors were: **Rowlinson Carter**, who provided the history; **Lesley Chamberlain**, author of *The Food of Russia*; **Edward Lucas**, then the London *Independent's* Eastern Europe Correspondent; **Anatol Lieven**, *The Times* correspondent; **Juris Lorencs** of the World Federation of Free Latvians; and **Valdis Muktapavels**, Latvia's leading authority on music.

Their essays have been updated and enhanced with the help of **Clare Thomson**, author of *The Singing Revolution* and **Tim Oscher** of *The Baltic Times*, who contributed new essays on Nature and Outdoor Activities.

Photography for the original edition was undertaken by **Lyle Lawson**, quite a feat at a time when colour film was hard to find in the Baltics and there were no local guidebooks for reference.

For this edition, many new photographs were commissioned from Insight Guides regulars **Anna Mockford** and **Nick Bonetti**. Picture research was undertaken by **Jenny Kraus**.

The book was proofread by **Sylvia Suddes**, steered through a maze of computers by **Sylvia George** and **Mary Pickles**, and was indexed by **Elizabeth Cook**.

Map Legend

– ·· –	International Boundary
– – – –	Province Boundary
⊖	Border Crossing
– · –	National Park/Reserve
– –	Ferry Route
✈ ✦	Airport: International/ Regional
🚌	Bus Station
❶	Tourist Information
✉	Post Office
✝ ✝ ✝	Church/Ruins
✝	Monastery
☾	Mosque
✡	Synagogue
🏰	Castle/Ruins
🏠	Mansion/stately home
∴	Archaeological Site
∩	Cave
🜚	Statue/Monument
★	Place of Interest

The main places of interest in the Places section are coordinated by number with a full-colour map (e.g. ❶), and a symbol at the top of every right-hand page tells you where to find the map.

INSIGHT GUIDE
BALTIC STATES
ESTONIA·LATVIA·LITHUANIA

CONTENTS

Beach party,
Estonia

THE BEST OF THE BALTIC STATES

From saunas and sandy beaches to stunning old world architecture and fascinating open-air museums, the three Baltic countries have a great deal to offer, both in the towns and in the countryside

SPAS AND SAUNAS

- **Scandic Rannahotell** Have a sauna in this elegant Functionalist hotel in the spa resort of Pärnu, long known for its mud baths and health cures *See page 147.*
- **Fra Mare** Best-equipped spa hotel in Haapsalu, the famous 19th and early 20th-century spa resort frequented by Tchaikovsky. *See page 150.*
- **Kemeri Hotel** Newly renovated, this is a flagship hotel in Latvia's "riviera" at Jūrmala, where

people have been taking the cure for two centuries. *See page 215.*
- **Druskininkai** There are eight sanitoria and balneotherapies in Lithuania's premier spa town famous for its saline waters and mud treatments. *See page 313.*
- **Hotel Palanga** The latest, 5-star spa hotel in this lively resort that has several spa establishments. *See page 321.*
- *See Spas and Saunas chapter, page 62.*

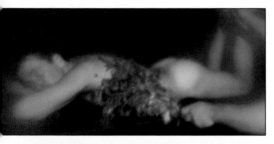

BIRD LIFEBIRD LIFE

- **Vilsandi National Park** Covering 150 Estonian islets, this is a hatching ground for many European species. *See page 182.*
- **Matsalu National Park** A range of habitats attracts waders, terns and white-tailed eagles. *See page 149.*
- **Lake Engure Nature Reserve** Every year around 50,000 birds visit the 18-km (12-mile) long lake, which has a

floating orthinological station. *See page 238.*
- **Pape Natue Park** Supported by the World Wildlife Fund, this is the best place to see migrating birds – and bats – in Latvia. *See page 228.*
- **Nemunas Delta Regional Park** Base of the Ventė Horn Ornithological ringing station and an important stop on migration routes. *See page 347.*
- *For Top 10 nature sites, see page 66.*

WHEN TO VISIT

- **Spring** Arrival of the storks, and wild flowers in abundance.
- **Midsummer** The Balts' favourite. Singing, dancing, imbibing everywhere.
- **Autumn** Bird migrations, flax and wheat harvests, music festivals.
- **Christmas** Faitrytale, snowy cities with markets, lights and concerts.

WORLD HERITAGE CITIES

● **Tallinn**
The Old Town of Estonia's capital was added to Unesco's list of World Heritage Sites in 1997 as "an outstanding and exceptionally complete and well preserved example of a medieval northern European trading city". *See page 111.*

● **Rīga**
The Historic Centre of Latvia's capital was listed in 1997 for "the quality and quantity of its Art Nouveau/Jugendstil architecture, which is unparalleled anywhere in the world, and its 19th century architecture in wood". *See page 199.*

● **Vilnius**
Lithuania's capital was listed in 1994 for its "impressive complex of Gothic, Renaissance, Baroque and classical buildings as well as its medieval layout and natural setting". *See page 271.*

ABOVE: The Three Sisters, medieval dwelling houses, helped to put Tallinn's Old Town on UNESCO's World Heritage list. **LEFT:** Lithuania's sandy shores have also been made a UNESCO World Heritage Site.

BEST BEACHES

● **Pärnu**
White sands and a ladies-only beach bring Estonians to the "summer capital".
See page 147.

● **Jūrmala**
With some 30 km (21 miles) of sandy beach, Jūrmala has been dubbed the "Baltic Riviera".
See page 215.

● **Ventspils**
Great family beach with lots of activities for children.
See page 227.

● **Palanga**
A romantic spot to watch the sun set.
See page 321.

● **Nida**
Feel the UNESCO-rated sands betweeen your toes. *See page 325.*

MUSEUMS & GALLERIES

● **Viinistu Art Museum,**
The largest private collection of Estonian painting was acquired by the former financial manager of pop group Abba and is now housed in the fishing village's canning factory. *See page 169.*

● **Museum of the History of Rīga and Navigation**
The first museum in the Baltics, opened in 1773, is the best, and has little to do with navigation. It's full of interest about the city's rich past, with paintings, furniture and decorative arts.
See page 206.

● **Devils Museum,**
Kaunas, Lithuania's second city, has the country's best museums. This is the most curious.
See page 297.

RIGHT: Rīga in the 17th century (detail), from the Rīga Museum of Navigation and History.

CRAFTS & MARKETS

- **Wall of Sweaters,** Tallinn's Knitwear Market on Müürivahe Street along the Old Town Wall is a great place for souvenirs, from socks to shawls, knitted mostly by elderly women. *See page 122.*
- **Central Market** One of the wonders of Rīga is this market, housed in five Zeppelin hangars. Get a taste of the Baltics here. *See page 210.*
- **Latgale ceramics** The eastern region of Latvia is known for its pottery workshops; visit them in Rēzekne and other nearby towns and villages. *See page 235.*
- **Kaziukas (St Casimir's Day)** On 4 March tens of thousands of people descend on Vilnius for the country's biggest fair, with crafts from all over the country. *See page 356.*
- **Panevezys Art Gallery** Showcase for the 2,400 members of Lithuania's Union of Art Masters is a special exhibition here each May. *See page 303.*
- **Flower Market, Vilnius** You can buy flowers at the market on Basanavicius Street any time day or night. *See page 363.*
- **Amber** There are a number of jewellery outlets in Palanga, the home of the Amber Museum. *See page 321.*

FAMILY ATTRACTIONS

- **Open-Air Museums** These provide highly entertaining days out for the family, showing how people once lived, with staff in traditional costume, workshops and sometimes music laid on. *See page 126 (Tallinn), 213 (Rīga) and 298 (Rumšiškės).*
- **Gauja National Park** Centred on the town of Sigulda, this is Latvia's big recreation area, with canoeing, boating, biking and horse riding. *See page 243.*
- **Gulbene railway** Take a trip on the narrow-gauge railway to see the lakeside castle at Alūksne. *See page 250.*
- **Grutas Parkas** A bizarre memorial park with Soviet statuary gives a glimpse of a previous generation's world. *See page 315.*
- **Puppet theatres** All three capitals have puppet theatres. Performances are in the local languages but are easy to follow, action-packed and colourful. *See page 360.*
- **Zoos** Perennial favourites, with wild animals and children's corners, in Tallinn, Rīga and Kaunas. *See page 360.*

LEFT: craft market in Tallinn Town Hall Square.
TOP: windmill in Lithuania's open-air museum.

CASTLES AND MANOR HOUSES

● **Kadriorg Palace**
Built near Tallinn by
Peter the Great, now
housing art treasures.
See page 124.

● **Kuressaare**
The only surviving
medieval stone castle
in the Baltics, situated
on the island of
Saaremaa.
See page 157.

● **Palmse Manor**
A magnificent
18th-century manor
house containing
Empire furniture and
set in lovely grounds.
See page 167.

● **Sigulda Castle**
Built in the early 13th
century , Sigulda was
a focal point of
Latvia's National
Awakening.
See page 243.

● **Rundāle Palace**
The Duke of
Courland's fabulous
130-room palace,
where the cream of
Russian and German
Society were
entertained.
See page 240.

● **Trakai Castle**
Built just outside
Vilnius in the 14th
century by Grand
Duke Vytautas, the
lakeside castle
embodies Lithuania's
glorious past.
See page 286.

● **Raudondvaris Castle**
The Castle Route
along the Nemunas
river, the former
Lithuanian border, is
lined with red-brick
fortified manors.
See page 301.

ABOVE: Trakai castle, the former capital of Lithuania.
BELOW LEFT: Transport for human cargo at the Tornkalns.

PILGRIMAGE SITES

● **Pühajärv Oak**
The largest and oldest
oak in Estonia is said
to have magic
powers. *See page 138.*

● **Virgin of Aglona**
This venerated
Byzantine figure is
the object of Latvia's
largest pilgrimage, on
the annual Feast of
the Assumption
(15 August). *See page
234.*

● **Madonna of the
Gates of Dawn**
Thousands of Poles
and Lithuanians come
every year to pray

before Vilnius's
dazzling icon.
See page 278.

● **The Ninth Fort**
A haunting memorial
to 30,000 Jews who
were shot in this
19th-century fort that
became the burial
ground for the victims
of Kaunas's ghetto.
See page 298.

● **Hill of Crosses**
An astonishing act of
faith has led to this
forest of devotional
crosses near the
town of Šiauliai. *See
page 330.*

THE JEWISH STORY

The Baltic States hold many reminders
of the slaughter of Jews who lived in
the Baltic states or who were
transported here to be murdered as
part of the Nazis' "final solution".

In Vilnius, the pre-war "Jerusalem of
Lithuania" and a centre for Yiddish
publishing, 150,000 perished. The site
of the former ghetto is explained in
street maps, while the **Vilna Gaon
Jewish State Museum** and the

Museum of the Holocaust (see page
281) give more detail. The **Yiddish
Studies Centre** in Vilnius University
helps trace ancestors (see page 280).

In Riga, 100,000 died. **Jews in
Latvia** is a museum that tells their story
(see page 209). The ruins of the **Great
Synagogue** (see page 211) serve to
recall its incineration in 1941 with
dozens of people still inside.

A visit to the concentration camps,

Salaspils in Latvia or the **Ninth Fort**
in Lithuania (pages 215 and 298), give
a glimpse of the horrors perpetrated.

Reminders also exist of Soviet
tyranny. The wagon pictured above was
one used by the KGB in 1941 and 1949
to deport 15,000 men, women and
children to remote corners of the Soviet
Union. Now in the Tornkalns railway
station, Riga, it forms part of the city's
Occupation Museum (see page 201).

THE BALTIC PEOPLES

The European Union, NATO and the Eurovision Song Contest have all helped three disparate peoples find their new identities

The people of the three Baltic nations are as different from each other as the Poles are from the Norwegians, or the Irish from the Dutch, but for more than a decade after independence they had in common one characteristic: a tendency for self-absorption, accompanied by a constant need to discuss their plight. In part, this trait was a result of being from small countries but, more importantly, it was the result of the systematic, and partially successful, attempt by Russia to exterminate them, leaving many with a strong sense of doubt as to their own worth, and to the worth of their countries on the world stage.

If repression had been any harsher, Estonians, Latvians and Lithuanians might have met the same fate as the Ingrians, Kalmuks, Tatars and other small nations who got in Stalin's way. As it was, the debasement of the language and national culture through Russification and Sovietisation left a deep-rooted scar on the collective psyche. The relative size and perceived insignificance of their emerging countries at first inflicted an inferiority complex, as they frequently tended to assume – rightly – that the world was largely ignorant of both their countries and their needs. This was also a legacy of Soviet rule, during which national identity was placed firmly in second place to the supposedly superior language and culture of Russia.

New-found confidence

By the start of the new millennium, however, the world had sharpened its focus on the former Soviet countries as they headed towards Europe's orbit. They began to make a name for themselves, from winning and staging the Eurovision Song Contest (a dubious honour, but certainly a way of becoming noticed) and gaining medals at the Olympics to EU and NATO membership, which to most Balts was the final sign that their Soviet

PRECEDING PAGES: island boating, Estonia; National Festival Parade; Pärnu beach pub on the Bay of Riga. **LEFT:** winter music, Latvia. **RIGHT:** Latvian football fan on midsummer's eve.

days were dead and buried and the endless soul-searching about their future was at an end.

Having a shared recent past has done little to diminish national differences. For instance, Lithuanians remain stereotypically the most outgoing people from the three countries, and are perhaps the most nationalistic. A memory of the Grand Duchy that ran from the Baltic to the Black Sea still exerts a profound influence over people. Sometimes the result is attractive: national self-confidence gives Lithuanians a zeal to succeed and regain their rightful place among what they consider to be Europe's "real" countries. The desire not to be outstripped economically by Poland, their historical partner and sometime coloniser, is deep.

"The world may not know much about us, but it should" is a deeply ingrained attitude – though anyone who follows basketball will know its stars well. This "think big" *Weltanschauung* meshes neatly with a continuing fixation with the USA, the Promised Land to which many tens of thousands of Lithuanians have emigrated over the past hundred years. Despite its distance, the USA remains a dominant cultural influence: televised NBA basketball games attract an avid following, while the American ambassador's comings and goings are front-page news.

Conversely, Lithuanians tend to be remarkably uninterested in their neighbours. Few could name the prime ministers of major neighbours such as Poland, Sweden or Belarus. The idea, therefore, that economic or political self-interest should lead to a close engagement with such countries is regarded with amused indifference,

renowned Lithuanian political commentator remarked during the scandal surrounding President Rolandas Paksas, who was impeached for awarding Lithuanian citizenship to a rich Russian financial backer, "We used to joke about how Lithuanians couldn't defend themselves against a few million Russians. Now we joke about how we can't defend ourselves against a few Russians and their millions."

Solid stock

The stereotype goes that the Latvian national character lies somewhere in between the reserved Estonians and the outgoing Lithuani-

or, in the case of Poland, with suspicion and defensiveness.

Lithuanians like talking about Baltic co-operation, but they are generally much less enthusiastic about following it up in practice. Despite close linguistic ties with their Baltic cousins, the Latvians, Lithuanians treat their northern neighbours rather as Americans treat Canadians: benignly and with sweeping ignorance. Contacts between Estonians and Lithuanians, when they happen, seem to be the warmest, with the austere Nordic character of the former complementing the exuberance of the latter. But all three Baltic republics share a certain shrewd scepticism in their humour. One

ans, but this really doesn't begin to do them justice. The German, Protestant influence, as in Estonia, results in a solid, reliable work ethic that has largely survived the effects of communism. Slow starters, Latvians initially lagged behind their Baltic neighbours in economic reform. Now they have easily overtaken Lithuania in attracting investment from abroad, and on several scores are doing even better than Estonia, which was first out of the traps to race ahead as the unquestioned star performer.

Much of Latvia's booming private economy is run by Russian-speakers, a principal cause of the uneasy ethnic balance that is a more sensitive issue here than in the other countries. Native Latvians are still outnumbered today by Russian-speaking people in Rīga and Daugavpils.

Latvians' roots are traditionally in the countryside – something apparent in everything from folk art to the national cuisine. But while the Latvians treasure their rustic roots, they have also taken to their new way of life with aplomb. Most work hard in their determination to make a better life for themselves and it is perfectly common for young people to hold down a demanding full-time job, study for a higher degree, attend language lessons and go to the gym, while still maintaining a full social life.

Latvians' good nature is sometimes said to be their undoing. Whereas the Estonians maintained a stony inner resistance to Russification, this process advanced far further in Latvia: mixed marriages were more frequent, and national consciousness seemed the weakest in the Baltics when the independence struggle began in the late 1980s. Whereas Lithuanians make up 80 percent of the population of their country, Latvians are in a bare majority (just under 60 percent at the last count) in theirs – which adds a bitter edge to the question of naturalising the hundreds of thousands of post-war settlers, many of whom have taken up their entitlement for Latvian citizenship.

Not to be forgotten among the Latvians are the Livs, a handful of descendants of the original coastal tribe, who like the Estonians speak a Finno-Ugric language. Latvians have a special respect for this almost extinct race and its mystical link with the past.

Linguistic differences

The difference between Estonians and their Baltic neighbours – and indeed most of Europe – is well illustrated by the language. Whereas Latvian and Lithuanian have some elements in common, Estonian, with its unfamiliar vocabulary, chirruping intonation, ultra-complex grammar and distinctive word order, is as impenetrable to most European ears as Hungarian or Finnish. This is not surprising: Estonians, like these two nations, are members of the Finno-

POPULATION DECLINE
In the first decade after independence all three countries suffered a decline in population, taking their numbers back to where they were before the intense Russification of the 1970s.

Ugric ethnic family, whose origins lie deep in the marshes of Siberia. Despite substantial influences from their Swedish, Danish, German and Russian rulers over the past six centuries, Estonians prize their bloodline – sometimes comically: "War is an Indo-European phenomenon," one visitor was startled to hear. "It's because of your settlement pattern: you live in villages, while we prefer solitary forest clearings."

Equally incongruously, the Estonians' Finno-Ugric near neighbours, the Finns, are regarded

rather disparagingly, frequently referred to as "moose". Of course, there have long been close ties between the two countries. During Soviet times Estonians could not be prevented from tuning into Finnish television, and Finland's helping hand in the early days if independence was invaluable. But the long-standing tradition of boatloads of Finns turning up in Tallinn for a weekend of heavy drinking is as strong as ever, and for many Estonians, this is the image they have of their neighbours.

Estonians have had many years to brood on the misfortune that has soured their history. Just as Lithuanians like to tell you that their country is at the geographical centre of Europe, that

LEFT: Lithuanian woodcarver.
RIGHT: picking berries in Latvia.

their language is archaic and their folk art extraordinary, and just as Latvians will point out that in the pre-war years of their first independence they were one of Europe's great dairy exporters, so Estonians relish any chance to explain that their country was, before the war, more prosperous than Finland.

Estonia has its face set squarely towards Helsinki and Stockholm. The majority of young, economically active Estonians have visited one or both of these cities. Unlike Lithuanians or Latvians, whose emigrations are far more dispersed – Ireland is an especially popular destination in recent years – in other hemi-

spheres, one of the most active Estonian diasporas lies just across the Baltic Sea, in Sweden. Estonians are only too aware of the importance of their Scandinavian neighbours: indeed, many Estonians would be glad to shed their "Baltic" tag altogether and are more likely to describe themselves as being Scandinavian. However, even if Estonia does consider itself the "least" Baltic of the three states, no Estonian would deny that their country is historically inextricable from both Latvia and Lithuania.

Estonia sometimes chooses to see itself as more Scandinavian simply to differentiate itself from its southern neighbours. It is not a rational attitude to geo-politics that distinguishes the

Estonian national character, but rather its degree of reserve, which is in stark contrast to the other Baltic states. Staying for more than a few days in Vilnius, for example, a foreigner is likely to be invited into a Lithuanian household, stuffed with food, offered presents, taken on guided tours, introduced to family, friends and pets, and generally made to feel at home. In Latvia the visitor will find hospitality, too, though the atmosphere will be more relaxed and not quite so intense. Invited to a house, you will not escape without sampling home produce, some of which may be pressed on you to take away.

More hugs and kisses

Estonians, however, have mastered the art of being impeccably polite without being friendly, and an invitation to an Estonian home is rare. Friendship, an Estonian may tell you, is for life, and it would not be right for a new acquaintance to be invited into their home when they know that sooner or later he or she will go away. Though the idea that real friendship is like a precious cordial which should only be offered to one's nearest and dearest can be offensive and off-putting to foreigners, it must be said that Estonians are not truly selfish or unfriendly. Once the friendship is actually made, it is solid and lasting.

But, as with so much else in the Baltics, old habits are changing, especially with the young and more widely travelled generation. Whereas public displays of affection were once disdainfully regarded as a "Russian thing", young Estonians increasingly kiss each other on the cheeks or hug by way of greeting each other and generally behave like most other Europeans in public settings.

Despite their differences, Estonians, Latvians and Lithuanians are united by a love of nature and the outdoors. Admittedly, they enjoy it in different ways. Lithuanians will drive their car to a beauty spot and blast their surroundings with pop music, whereas Latvians will organise lavish barbecues or swimming parties. Estonians tend to regard such habits with horror, going to great lengths to find a truly solitary spot where they can sit in silence with their loved ones – or, even better, entirely alone. ❑

LEFT: newlyweds at the lucky Shiskin Tree, Estonia.
RIGHT: a ballerina in Tallinn.

Decisive Dates

6000 BC Finno-Ugric peoples from southeast Europe reach Estonia.

2500 BC Indo-European culture arrives to merge with indigenous population in Latvia and Lithuania. Kurs, Semigallians, Letgallians, Sels and Finno-Ugric Livs established.

AD 1000–1200 Estonian tribes beat off Russian (Slav) attacks.

9th–10th centuries Vikings on the coast utilise trade routes to Byzantium and the Caspian Sea via the River Daugava.

1009 The name Lithuania appears in written form for the first time.

1201 German crusaders establish a bishopric in the Liv settlement at Rīga under Albrecht of Bremen. It becomes the basis for the Baltic conquest.

1207 Livonia (Terra Mariana) is recognised as part of the Holy Roman Empire, with Rīga as its capital.

1219 Danes take Tallinn.

1230 Mindaugas unites the Grand Duchy of Lithuania. He adopts Christianity and is crowned King of Lithuania (1252).

1236 Latvian and Lithuanian forces defeat crusaders at Saulė.

1237 The German crusaders' Order of the Knights of the Sword changes its name to the Livonian Order.

1280 Semigallian tribes fail in their attack on Rīga and retreat to Lithuania.

1282 Rīga joins Hanseatic League; Tallinn joins three years later.

1316 Under Duke Gediminas, the founder of Vilnius and the Jogaila dynasty, the struggle against Teutonic knights continues and Lithuanian expansion begins.

1343 Estonian rebellion on St George's night fails to bring lasting independence, but leads to Danes selling duchy of Estonia to the Teutonic Order.

1386 Lithuania and Poland are united in marriage between Duke Jogaila and Queen Jadwiga. They remain united until 1795.

1410 Dukes Vytautas and Jogaila defeat the Teutonic Order in the Battle of Tannenberg (Grünwald).

1520s The Reformation establishes Lutheranism in Latvia and Estonia.

1558–83 Livonian Wars between Sweden and Russia result in Livonia being divided up (1562). Northern Estonia comes under Swedish rule, southern Estonia under Polish rule. Duchies under Polish suzerainty established in Kurzeme (Courland) and Pārdaugava in Latvia. The German bishop of Piltene (Latvia) and Oesel (Saaremaa Island) sells land to Denmark.

1579 Vilnius University founded by Jesuits.

1581–1621 Rīga swears loyalty to Stephan Bathory, king of Poland and Lithuania, who introduces Counter-Reformation.

1600–29 Polish-Swedish War leaves Estonia and northern Latvia in Swedish hands; southern Latvia and Lithuania in Poland's.

1632 Tartu University founded.

1642–82 Flowering of Courland under Duke Jēkabs.

1694 St Peter's steeple, Rīga, the tallest in the world, is completed.

1700–21 Great Northern War between Charles XII of Sweden and Peter the Great results in Russian victory. Russia occupies Estonia and Latvia. The first poem to be written in Estonian, by Kasu Hans, is about the Russian destruction of Tartu (1708).

1712 Martha Skavronska, a peasant from Latvia, marries Peter the Great and 12 years later is crowned Catherine, Empress of Russia.

1768 Rundāle Palace, Latvia, is completed.

1795 Lithuania becomes part of the Russian Empire. Lithuania Minor (now Kalliningrad) falls to Germany.

1812 Napoleon marches through Lithuania, on his way to Moscow, raising hopes of freedom from Russia.

1832 Vilnius University is closed down by Russians following attempts to restore independence.

1860–85 The era of National Awakening. The abolition of serfdom combines with new educational opportunities and leads to a great literary and artistic movement.

1864 A 40-year ban on the printing of books in Lithuanian begins.

1869 The first national singing festival is held in Estonia.

1872 The first strike is organised by women workers in Narva.

1885 An era of intense Russification begins following unsuccessful uprisings against Russia; local languages displaced.

1905 The first socialist revolution demands independence. Manors are burned and hundreds of citizens executed.

1914–18 World War I. War is waged on three fronts, between Germans and white and red Russians. Bolsheviks seize power in bloodless coup in Estonia, but are unable to maintain control. Germany occupies Latvia and Lithuania.

1918 The Republic of Estonia is declared in Tallinn, Latvia in Rīga. The German Army moves in, and manors and power are given back to German aristocracy. Germany loses the war and the Soviets move in. With some allied help, the Soviets are fought back.

1920 Independence is achieved, for the first time in Estonia and Latvia, and for Lithuania the first time since the Grand Duchy. Poland, also newly independent, seizes Vilnius.

1923 Lithuania reclaims Klaipėda.

1933 Darius and Girėnas fly across the Atlantic.

1934 Bloodless coup in Estonia. Parliament is dismissed in Latvia.

1939 When the Hitler–Stalin Pact puts Estonia and Latvia under the Soviet sphere of influence, Soviet soldiers arrive. Baltic Germans are ordered back to Germany, and German troops occupy Klaipėda (Memel).

1940–41 Red Army terror rages. Thousands are deported or shot.

LEFT: tomb of a crusader bishop in Dundaga castle, Latvia. **RIGHT:** America's President George W. Bush and Lithuania's President Valdas Adamkas confer at the NATO summit in Prague in 2002.

1941–44 German occupation of Baltics. Concentration camps are set up. Many Jews are exterminated, especially in Vilnius. Russians and Germans fight over Baltic soil.

1944 The Soviets reoccupy Baltics and turn them into Soviet republics. The Stalinist era begins. Mass reprisals, deportation to Siberia.

1952 The armed resistance to Soviet occupation is finally crushed.

1988 Opposition parties are established.

1989 A 430-mile (690-km) human chain, from Tallinn to Vilnius, links up in protest in the "Singing Revolution".

1991 Soviet intervention results in 14 people

killed at TV tower, Vilnius; five die in Rīga. Republics finally restored to independence.

1993 Pope Paul II pays a visit to Lithuania's Hill of Crosses.

1994 Russian troops pull out. The *Estonia* ferry, operating between Tallinn and Helsinki, sinks, with a loss of 852 lives.

2001 Estonia wins the Eurovision Song Contest and hosts the competition the following year, when Latvia wins.

2002 Rolandas Paksas, president of Lithuania, is impeached.

2004 All three countries become members of NATO and the European Union.

2008–09 Baltic states hope to adopt the euro. ❑

OCCUPATION AND ASPIRATION

For eight centuries Estonia and Latvia lived under occupation, while the duchy of Lithuania flourished in a union with Poland

One of the most perplexing problems facing the Paris peace conference in 1919 was what to do about the Baltic provinces of tsarist Russia which the Bolsheviks, not without a fight, had consented to let go. Lithuania had once ruled the largest empire in Europe. It was somewhat overwhelmed by Poland before both were swallowed, almost but not quite whole, by Russia in the 18th century. Estonia and what was put forward to the peace conference as an independent state which called itself Latvia were, by any historical or political criteria, equally elusive.

Nevertheless, three independent states were internationally recognised under these names, although first the Bolsheviks and then Stalin made it plain that it was not a situation that could be tolerated forever. Their independence was sentenced to death by the Nazi-Soviet Pact just before World War II. The pact implied that the Baltic states would be parcelled out between the two, but it was overtaken by events with Hitler's invasion of the Soviet Union.

The three states were incorporated into the Soviet Union in 1940 and at the end of the war they were reconquered, and though there were some minor concessions to autonomy, they became virtual Russian provinces once again.

Russia's grand designs

Among few other peoples did the Soviet mill grind finer than in Estonia, Latvia and Lithuania. They occupied a special place in Soviet strategy, an updated version of Peter the Great's "window to the West", which began with the founding of St Petersburg but envisaged expansion southward to maximise Russia's access to the Baltic, often referred to as the "Northern Mediterranean". Like its southern counterpart, it had a coastline over which the adjacent nations were ready to fight for every inch. Russia had initially been held to ransom by Ger-

man Balts who controlled the Estonian and Latvian ports, and Peter the Great was determined that it would never happen again, a view with which the Soviet regime totally concurred. Lithuania was regarded in exactly the same light, and it was agents of the tsar, long before any thought of Soviet Man, who vowed to

obliterate all signs of national Baltic identities. The Russification of the Baltic provinces in the 19th century was so successful that when the matter of their independence came up at the Paris peace conference one question asked was sublimely naive: "Who are these people and whence did they come?" For three nations buried so deep in the history of others that their identities were long presumed to have been lost, they have surprisingly robust tales to tell.

The countries also have common bonds. With their backs to the Baltic Sea, they have been hemmed in by the great powers of Sweden, Denmark, Germany and Russia, who have interfered in their affairs for 800 years. In fact,

LEFT: the end of occupation – a painting in Lithuania's parliament building of a 1991 rally in Vilnius.
RIGHT: starting the occupation, Teutonic knights.

the peoples of the three countries come from two distinct groups, neither Slavic like the Russians nor Teutonic like the Germans. In the north were the Finno-Ugric tribes of Estonia and the Livs of Latvia, of whom only a handful remain. Latvia was otherwise peopled by Letts who, like Lithuanians, were Indo-European Balts whose language has some similarities with Sanskrit. For instance, the words for "god", "day" and "son" in Lithuanian are *dievas*, *diena* and *sunus* and *devas*, *dina* and

ALL AT SEA

The Latin *Mare Balticum* is known as the West Sea by Estonians and the East Sea by Scandanvians and Germans. English, Lithuanian, Latvian and Romance language speakers call it the Baltic Sea.

and others wanted it. This gem, made of fossilised pine resin, made its way to ancient Egypt and Greece.

Among those taking this trade route were the Vikings, and it was their leader, Vladimir I, who first united the Slavic Russians and made a capital on the Dnieper at Kiev. When the Scandinavians settled down on the Baltic coast, they did so in Estonia: *Taani Linn* (Tallinn) is Estonian for Danish town. By then the real conquering force of the Baltics was beginning to dig in. The

sunu in Sanskrit. In Estonian, which has similarities with Hungarian, those words are *jumal*, *poeg* and *päev*. But it was a long time before the languages, with their extended alphabets and complex word endings, were written down.

Religion follows trade

Baltic peoples also took longer than the rest of Europe to embrace Christianity, preferring their sacred oaks and thunderous gods. Some of the earliest Christian teaching came from Orthodox traders from the east. The trade routes were well established, up the River Daugava and down the Dnieper to the Black Sea. Amber was the singular commodity the Balts possessed,

German crusaders appeared in 1201 in Rīga where they installed a bishopric for Albrecht of Bremen. From there, they set down roots of a ruling class in all three countries that lasted into the 20th century.

This elite arrived in religious orders, which fought among themselves as much as they fought against those who opposed them. There were the ministerials of the archbishop, the burghers of the city and the Knights of the Sword, who became Knights of the Livonian Order. The country of Livonia that they created put the different peoples of Latvia and Estonia under the same authority and established a healthy and lucrative environment for the

Hanseatic League's merchants, the German trading confederation that followed in their wake. Their architecture, of half-timbered *Fachwerk*, and storehouses with gables stepped as high as those beside Amsterdam's canals, spread from Klaipėda and Kaunas to Rīga to Tallinn.

Lithuania, however, was not so easily brought to heel, and it frequently joined forces with the Kuronian and Semigallian Letts in clashes with the German knights. By the middle of the 13th century the Lithuanian tribes had been unified under Mindaugas who briefly adopted Christianity so the Pope, in 1252, could crown him king.

grandson married the Polish queen and the two houses were united for the next 400 years.

Jesuit builders

Poland brought a strong Catholic influence to Lithuania, and the Jesuits arrived to build their schools and fancy baroque churches, while the Reformation whipped through the Germanic northern Baltic lands in a trice, converting everyone overnight. In the brief period when half of Latvia became a Polish principality, everyone converted back to Catholicism. The Balts had little say in this matter as in everything else. Compulsory church attendance made them in-

When the German knights opposed him, he reverted to his pagan beliefs, and stood his ground against the knights. In 1325 the Lithuanian ruler Gediminas allied himself to the Poles who had similar problems with the Teutonic knights.

This union also gave Poland access to the sea, which was crucial to the success of its empire-building ambitions. At its height the duchy was one of Europe's largest countries, stretching from the Baltic to the Black Sea. Gediminas's

LEFT: the Danes' capture of Tallinn.
ABOVE LEFT: Catherine the Great showed concern for Baltic serfs.
ABOVE RIGHT: Peter the Great prized the coast highly.

different as to how the service was conducted.

The local inhabitants were denied virtually every privilege and for centuries were not permitted to build houses of stone nor live within the city walls. Membership of the greater guilds was forbidden; even semi-skilled workers, such as millers and weavers, were brought in from abroad. The ruling society was impenetrable. In Estonia and Latvia the German descendants of the knights ruled; in Lithuania there was a rigid aristocracy of Poles. This survived even the break up of Livonia by the Swedes during the mid-16th century.

The Swedish period is sometimes looked on as an enlightened one, in spite of wars against

Poland, then Russia. But there was more talk than action. In Tallinn in 1601 Charles IX demanded peasant children be sent to school and learn a trade. "We further want them to be allowed, without hindrance, to have themselves put to use as they like, because to keep children as slaves is not done in Christendom and has been discontinued there for many years." Despite noble intentions, however, his words fell on deaf ears.

Serfs exchanged for dogs

Further upheaval followed in the 18th century. When Charles XI threatened to take away more

droit de seigneur. Serfdom was not finally abolished until the middle of the 19th century.

In the 18th century the idea of nationhood was fomented by teachers such as J.G. Herder, but it wasn't until the 19th century and the Romantic movements, with towering poets and intellects such as Lithuania's Adam Mickiewicz, that the idea really started gaining ground. There was much lost time to catch up on. The more enlightened German landlords did their best to make amends, starting schools and themselves learning the local languages perhaps for the first time. Tartu University, near the Latvian border, was the intellectual force

than 80 percent of the domains occupied by the descendants of the Teutonic knights, these German Balts called him a "peasant king" and turned to their other enemy for help. Russia was soon in charge and thereafter took control of Lithuania as well. In 1764 Catherine the Great visited Estonia and Latvia and found serfs still being sold or exchanged for horses or dogs, and fugitives branded and even mutilated. Little became of her demands for change. In 1771 public auctions of serfs became illegal, but there are records of auctions for years afterwards, while in Lithuania a noble who killed a serf faced only a fine. The barons remained powerful, making laws and practising their

IMPOSSIBLE DECISIONS

One recent event confirms the impossible choices people had to make at the start of World War II. In the village of Lihula in Estonia a former dissident who had become mayor allowed a statue of a soldier in German (Nazi) uniform to be erected. Though disagreeing with Nazi ideology, many veterans see the Germans as delaying Stalin's return and providing a breather in which to try to re-establish independence as well as allowing people to escape abroad. Many of this dwindling band of "freedom fighters" spent years in Soviet labour camps and argue that if Soviet army monuments can remain, the Germans should have one, too. The mayor was told to take it down.

behind the National Awakening in both Estonia and Latvia. However, Lithuania suffered a setback with the closing of its university in 1832, followed by a ban on printing Lithuanian books, punishment for uprisings against the tsar. Paradoxically, throughout the Baltics there was as much Russification towards the end of the century as there was national fervour. Discontent with the unenlightened tsars broke out into the Russian Revolution of 1905. It was an horrifically violent time that affected all the Baltic states, where many were delighted to torch the grand manors and other buildings of the ruling class. The destruction sparked was

The final injustice was the permanent imposition of Soviet rule and Stalinist terror. Anyone a visitor meets today in the Baltics is likely to have a relation who was sent to Siberia or shot.

The period between the two world wars saw the extraordinary flowering of three quite separate cultures, each coming into their own as nation states. From 1918 to 1939 the land belonged to the people of the Baltics for the first time for more than seven centuries. The German Balts were sent home, first through land reforms, and in the end by Hitler who, under his pact with Stalin, ordered them out. There was great hardship to overcome, but the

the start of a savage century. The two world wars were particularly fiercely fought.

The retreating Red Army scorched its way homeward at the end of World War I, leaving the land in ruins. After World War II, only a few dozen people crawled from the rubble of major ports such as Klaipėda, Ventspils and Narva. Vilnius, the Jerusalem of Lithuania, witnessed the wholesale extermination of the 50,000 Jewish population.

economies, based on agriculture, grew to match those in the West. Political life was not all roses, but at least it was their own.

This golden age of political autonomy was an era that the Balts looked back to for 50 years thereafter. Only in the late 1980s did they turn away from the past and start to build a new future for themselves. The struggle for independence during this period cost many lives, but secured for Estonia, Latvia and Lithuania the freedom of self-determination and a future over which they were to have control. ❑

● *For the story of the three nations since their independence, see the Places sections of the relevant country chapters.*

LEFT: conscription of Estonians into the Russian Army in the 19th century.

ABOVE: Hitler leads German troops in the occupation of Klaipėda (Memel), Lithuania, on 23 March 1939.

LIFE TODAY

*Life is busy, though not stressful, and there's an optimism in the air,
but more money for health and education would help*

The vote by the three Baltic countries to become members of the European Union in 2004 had an enormous effect on national pride. It was final proof that they had surfaced from the great crushing boulder of the Soviet Union into the light of the democratic West. Personal self-confidence and self-esteem was restored.

Though some groups, such as farmers, feared that they may lose out by the move, the vote was for more than just economic benefits and national security – the Russians are still deeply mistrusted. Membership was the final confirmation that they truly belonged to the European family of nations.

In order to accede to the European Union, the countries had been made to demonstrate that they were both socially and economically fit. The intervening decade had been far from easy. They were years characterised by divisive political in-fighting, institutionalised corruption, rampant crime, high prices and appalling wages, all of which contributed to a general sense of malaise.

The worst nightmares following independence are, however, now in the past and the most pressing remaining social problems are being addressed. The mafia and other sundry crooks, always in the vanguard of capitalism's advance, are generally under control, and those who have spent their lives involved in crime and corruption are too old to change their ways and are simply starting to die out. The press is free. There are fewer political parties, and those that remain are more clearly defined. The word "social" or "socialist" no longer means a party is automatically associated with the USSR.

In many different areas hard work has paid off. A civic pride has revitalised old buildings and kept the streets clean and litter-free, making a necessarily dignified backdrop to progress

(though civic responsibility, of course, was always one of the Soviets' strengths). Many people have more than one job – not always paid legally – and will often tell you how busy they are, yet the word "stress" is almost unknown. Despite this new-found dynamism, there is a pleasantly relaxed rhythm about day-

to-day life, even in the cities, where the line between work and leisure is often blurred.

Health and education

There is still need for improvement, particularly in the basic services of education, healthcare and transport, and there is hope that EU membership will help to finish the work already begun. The public healthcare systems in the main work well. Hygiene is strict, medical supplies are no longer a problem. Scandinavians book into Estonia for cosmetic surgery and modern dentistry attracts Finnish dental tourists. Elsewhere, however, there are occasional horror stories of misdiagnoses and other

PRECEDING PAGES: goodbye Lenin, Rīga, 1991.
LEFT: wood, a main export of all three counties, being loaded at Tallinn. **RIGHT:** a mobile generation.

mishaps, while a culture of "bribing" medical staff with small gifts and money to ensure a decent standard of treatment is the result of appalling wages, and needs to be addressed.

Although woefully under-funded, the education system is good and the literacy rate is high. Many teachers from school right through to university tenaciously cling on to Soviet-style pedagogy, which gives children a sound schooling in maths, literacy, science and all the other important subjects. The job cer-

A TERRIBLE TOLL

In the traumatic first years of independence, the suicide rate in all three countries was high, and Lithuania had the highest rate in the whole world.

The Russian-speaking populations, many of whom can now lay claim by birth to being Balts, has been a thorny issue, resolved in part through EU-influenced legalisation on minority rights. EU laws on minorities also had a bearing on education. But some problems in minority education have not been entirely resolved. Russian-speakers may form cabals and cliques, but they are not an elite, and they must deal with authorities who speak only Estonian, Latvian or Lithuanian. Narva, on the Estonian border with Rus-

tainly gets done, and in fact many ways Balts are better educated than some of their Western counterparts.

The majority of people are fluent in two languages, and a great many are proficient in three. Most Estonians and Latvians are fluent in Russian, a language spoken by some 250 million people. After years of going out of fashion, it is being taken up again by the young. English is taught in almost every school, beginning at an early age, and there are few young people who aren't reasonably fluent. Many older people increasingly choose to study German, French, Spanish and other European languages, either for work or pleasure.

sia, has a 90 percent Russian population and remains the only town hall in the country where Russian is allowed to be officially spoken.

Finance and fitness

If public-sector wages are still critically low, private-sector wages for professionals are relatively good. Many foreign companies have set up in the Baltics, taking advantage of the highly educated workforce and helping to create a modernised and efficient working culture.

Capitalism has not, on the whole, made people particularly greedy. Few people are overly materialistic. While people cherish comfort and certainly enjoy material wealth, most retain a strong sense of what's really important in life, such as family, friends and the need to spend time communing with nature.

The changing seasons are very much a part of the rhythm of their lives, from the arrival of storks in the spring, when ice melts can lead to floods, to the celebration of midsummer, the berry- and mushroom-picking of early autumn and the hunkering down of winter, when skis, skates and sledges provide mobility and fun for several months. Many town dwellers head for the country at weekends, arriving back with baskets full of provisions. Some have bought the allotment plots provided by factories and

However, alcoholism is still a serious problem, despite government legislation to try to tackle the problem, such as banning the sale of alcohol in shops after 10pm in Latvia and some parts of Estonia. Among society's poorest members, there is still a widespread culture of consuming cheap, potent and sometimes lethal home-made alcohol.

There is also concern about the decrease in populations. Public figures have urged procreation as a matter of patriotic duty, and there were jubilant headlines recently in Estonia when a hospital ran out of baby packs. However as the three economies improve and people are more

companies during Soviet times, and many city blocks have cellars in which to store produce.

The average life expectancy for both sexes now stands at 70 in Estonia and 69 in Latvia and Lithuania, and this is forecast to rise considerably over the next few years. Obesity is notable by its absence in all three Baltic countries, perhaps due to the fact that eating habits remain by and large healthy. Many Balts lead an active life. Saunas are regularly taken, and if you are invited to have one, especially in the country, it's an offer worth accepting.

LEFT: clubbing in a disused chemical plant near Tallinn.
ABOVE: summer on the beach, Pärnu.

reluctant to go abroad to find work, this is becoming less of a problem Estonia pioneered the introduction of a flat tax to get the economy off the ground, and the other countries followed suit. After accession to the EU, the rate was lowered to encourage business. There are signs that this is having an effect, and emigration is slowing down. Of the three countries, Estonia has the lowest unemployment and the highest GDP.

Home life

A burgeoning middle class is building homes, taking out mortgages and loans – even for holidays – and joining the debt societies of the West. A mass programme of re-privatising state-owned homes in the years following independence gave them a good start. Property prices were incredibly cheap throughout the 1990s and there were strict state regulations in relation to the purchase of property by foreigners. If you could prove familial ownership of a property prior to the Soviet occupation, you could reclaim the property. Many people who didn't have any claim took advantage of the relatively cheap prices to take on a mortgage.

Property prices in the capital cities have, however, rocketed, thanks in no small part to EU membership and the willingness of some foreigners to pay anything asked. However,

prices are still very low in the provinces and in smaller towns. The mortgage market is steadily growing year on year, especially among young people who want to live independently of their families. The average cost of renting and a mortgage are roughly the same. Many families are increasingly choosing to build larger, more spacious houses in the countryside, from where they then commute to the cities.

You can clearly tell when a new home is nearly complete – oak wreaths are displayed when a building is "topped out". There is little or no inheritance tax, a huge incentive for parents to pass their wealth on.

At home television is a staple entertainment,

although it's sometimes hard to see why. TV is mostly a mixture of kitsch home-grown programmes and US and Russian imports. The national TV stations are so underfunded that they can barely afford to buy the rights to major events such as the World Cup or the Olympics, and all three Baltic states have become obsessed with budget-friendly reality TV shows, such as *Robinson*, in which young people had to eke out an existence on an Estonian island. And there was a national scandal when a young couple had sex on a Lithuanian reality TV show. The young man involved proudly proclaimed that he did it "for Lithuania", while the woman was so vilified in the media for her actions that she moved abroad. Equality of the sexes still has a way to go in this predominantly male culture. Homosexuality is something that is often declared only behind firmly closed doors.

On the wilder side

Lithuania, the most morally conservative of the three countries, is loosening its Catholic ties. While Tallinn and Rīga have a widespread reputation for their wild nightlife, Vilnius isn't far behind. Estonia and Latvia are generally liberal in relation to sex, although there are occasional, Soviet-style lapses, such as Latvia's first-ever streaker, an attractive young woman who held up a football game against Portugal for several minutes as she danced around the pitch. The authorities arrested her and were going to press charges that could have resulted in a prison sentence. Happily, they relented and Strawberry, as she's known, went on to enjoy a successful career in reality TV.

Life has moved on, and there is now even some nostalgia for the Soviet era. Grutas Park, the Soviet "theme park" in Lithuania, has attracted world attention, and Lenin memorabilia has become collectible. Some say that people have short memories, others that it is a sign of normality, of no longer being afraid or ashamed of having been "Soviet". Some miss the fact that people had more time, that friendships were more treasured in that atmosphere of mistrust. Others just like to talk about that "crazy" time with others who understand. ❑

LEFT: typical Soviet-era housing bloc, Latvia.
RIGHT: Haanjamehe Farm, Estonia; rural tourism is a growing part of the economy.

ETHNIC DIVERSITY

With independence come feelings of nationalism that are not always
tolerant. But nothing compares with the impact of the Holocaust

At least since the 13th century, when the German and Scandinavian crusaders arrived to impose Christianity at the point of the sword, the territory of the present Baltic states has been one of mixed settlement. Over the intervening period, apart from the various native peoples who later came together to make

up the Estonians, Latvians and Lithuanians, the area has also been settled by large numbers of Germans, Poles, Jews and Russians.

Centre of Jewry

Jewish settlement began in the 14th century, when Jews were invited into Lithuania by the Grand Duke Vytautas. Precisely because the rulers of Lithuania, and later of Poland-Lithuania, were relatively tolerant towards the Jews, Lithuania became a great centre of world Jewry, and the "Litvaks" one of its most important branches. "Lithuania", as understood by the Jews, embraced the whole area of the former Grand Duchy, including Belarus and parts of

the Ukraine. By the 18th century, its capital, Vilnius (in Yiddish, Vilna or Vilne) was known as "the Jerusalem of Lithuania", because of its large number of synagogues and its many *yeshivas*, or Hebrew schools.

Later that century, Vilnius became a centre of Jewish Orthodox resistance to the Hassidic religious movement then sweeping eastern Europe. Gaon Street in the centre of the city's old town is named after the Gaon or "Genius" of Vilna, the rabbi who led the Orthodox, and whose prayer house stood on that street until it was demolished by the Nazis along with most of the ghetto. Nearby was the Great Synagogue (now a playground), which had the dimensions of a cathedral.

Before the Holocaust, Jews made up 8 percent of the population of what is now Lithuania, and a much larger proportion of Kaunas (Kovno) and Vilnius. Many Lithuanian Jews had also moved to Latvia, and there was a small population of 5,000 or so in Estonia. The Nazis were to wipe out those populations almost completely, exterminating 250,000 in Lithuania alone. Only a few thousand Jews remain in the Baltics today – around 5,200 in Lithuania – and many are emigrating. The Lithuanian-Jewish writer Grigory Kanovitch has warned that if things go on as they are, "there will soon be more Jewish organisations here than there are Jews".

Jewish emigration from the Baltics was much encouraged by the memory of the Holocaust, in which Baltic partisans and volunteers played a major part. Though there was no history of attacks on them prior to the war, the initial massacres in Lithuania were conducted entirely by Lithuanians without direct German involvement. Baltic participation in the Holocaust was due partly to anti-Semitism, but more to the belief that Jews had played a major part in supporting the Soviet regime that was imposed on the Balts in 1940. This was indeed true, but what the Balts who make this charge forget is that the Jewish communists also turned on their Jewish opponents, and that in fact a higher proportion of Jews than Balts was deported to Siberia in 1940–41.

Compared with neighbouring Poland, where the wartime treatment of Jews was equally infamous, there has existed a serious lack of dialogue between Lithuanians and Jews on this subject. The result is that the Lithuanians have only recently come to realise the full extent of their role in the Holocaust. But all three governments have condemned the Holocaust and their countries' participation in it, and have been making efforts to both confront this shameful chapter of their history and atone for it. Holocaust Memorial Days are now marked and the memory of the slaughter is kept alive in many other ways.

Poles' position

The official Polish presence in what is now Lithuania also began in the Middle Ages, with the marriage union of the Lithuanian Grand Duke Jogaila and the Polish princess Jadwiga in 1386. However, for a century and more before that the Lithuanian Grand Dukes had ruled over large numbers of Slavic peoples, many of whom were ultimately to see themselves as Poles.

After the union, many Lithuanians, especially those from the upper classes, also became Poles – a cause of enduring resentment in Lithuania. The Polonisation of Lithuania was helped by the Catholic church, the Polish nobility, and the fact that, as in all the Baltics until the 16th century, there was no written form of their language.

It is hard to point to specific Polish monuments in Vilnius (Wilno, in Polish), because the whole of the old city is in effect such a monument, built by Polish architects, studded with Polish inscriptions and similar to many Polish baroque towns. Czesław Milosz, the Nobel prizewinning writer who lived there until 1941, described it as "narrow cobblestone streets and an orgy of the baroque: almost like a Jesuit city somewhere in the middle of Latin America". Vilnius still retains its character as a Catholic frontier outpost.

Until World War II, Lithuanians were a small minority in Vilnius, with Poles the largest com-

munity, followed by the Jews. Vilnius was the home city of a number of great Polish cultural figures like Milosz and Adam Mickiewicz. The latter's epic, *Pan Tadeusz*, begins with the famous invocation:

> *O Lithuania, my fatherland,*
> *Thou art like health; what praise thou*
>   *shouldst command*
> *Only that man finds who has lost*
>   *thee quite.*

The passage also refers to the Gate of Dawn, the chapel in Vilnius dedicated to Our Lady, which is still a place of pilgrimage for Poles as well as Lithuanians. Worshippers from the two

communities sometimes scuffle there as the Poles coming in for a Polish-language Mass bump into Lithuanians coming out from a Lithuanian-language service.

The heart of Marshal Józef Piłsudski, the ruler of Poland between the wars and himself a Polish-Lithuanian nobleman, is buried in Vilnius's Rasu (Rossa) cemetery beside his mother.

In the 19th century Lithuanian peasants participated in rebellions against Russian imperial rule along with their Polish-speaking landlords. But by World War I Lithuanian nationalists were distinguishing themselves from the Poles, whom they blamed for many of Lithuania's historical problems.

LEFT: the Jewish memorial in Rīga.
RIGHT: the Polish-Lithuanian Nobel laureate Czesław Milosz likened Vilnius to a Jesuit city in Latin America.

After Lithuania and Poland achieved independence from Russia in 1918, the two countries clashed over Vilnius, until in 1921 it was seized by a Polish expeditionary force under General Lucijan Zeligowski. Newly independent Lithuania made the recovery of Vilnius the centrepoint of its foreign policy, and finally received the city back from Stalin in 1940, when he had won it from Poland following the Molotov-Ribbentrop Pact.

The Polish minority in Lithuania dropped

JEWISH REVIVAL

In 2000 the Government of Lithuania agreed to a plan to restore elements of the Jewish ghetto in Vilnius, including the rebuilding of the Great Synagogue.

by more than 50 percent after the Soviet reconquest in 1945, when almost all the Polish intelligentsia and upper classes emigrated to Poland (or were deported to Siberia). It still numbers more than 270,000. Tens of thousands of Poles also live in Latvia, the southern parts of which also used to be part of Poland. However, whereas in Lithuania, fear of Lithuanian nationalism made many Poles support the Soviet communists in the independence struggle in the late 1980s and early 1990s, in Latvia most Poles were pro-independence.

The Lithuanian nationalisation and land-ownership laws have caused considerable tension between Poland and Lithuania. For some time this caused difficulties on the Polish-Lithuanian frontier and hindered trade going to and from the Baltic states.

Relations between Lithuania and Poland tend to be warmer than those between Lithuanians and local Poles. But authorities in Warsaw are making attempts to strengthen what had been, at times, a weak relationship with ethnic Poles in Lithuania.

After several years of haggling over whether Poland needed to "apologise" for seizing Vilnius in 1920, the two countries signed a long-overdue friendship treaty in 1991. The Catholic church, to which many people in Lithuania and Poland belong, has helped to bridge the gap between these two countries, despite the close identification between the church in Lithuania and Lithuanian nationalism. Further progress was made when Lithuania adopted the Law on Ethnic Minorities, and by the year 2000 relations between Warsaw and Vilnius had considerably improved. Since then, co-operation has continued. Of the 109 different nationalities residing in Lithuania today, 7 percent are Poles and a joint Polish-Russian party representing the minorities stood in the 1995 elections.

Russians who remain

Lithuania's problem with the Poles has been fairly minor, however, when compared to those of Estonia and Latvia with the local Russian-speakers, who make up 32 percent and approximately 37 percent of the respective populations. Small communities of Russians had lived in the area since the early Middle Ages, when some Baltic tribes paid tribute to Russian princes. After the conquest by Peter the Great, these were joined by Russian soldiers, merchants and officials. At the end of the 19th century a major influx of Russian workers began. This was interrupted by World War I and the Russian Revolution, which drove considerable numbers of white Russian refugees to the Baltics.

Before 1940, Rīga was the greatest Russian émigré centre after Paris. When Stalin occupied the Baltic states in June 1940, these émigrés were among the first to suffer from the secret police. Newspapers and cultural centres were closed and churches converted for secular purposes. The reconquest of the Baltics by the

Soviet Union in 1944–45 began a process of Russian immigration that drastically altered the region's demography. The great majority of Russians now living in the Baltic area are immigrants from the Soviet period or their descendants.

Unlike Lithuania, which granted citizenship to all of its residents during the early 1990s, the Latvian and Estonian governments decided that its non-citizens would not be allowed such automatic rights. The citizenship law in Latvia and Estonia is based on birth, not on ethnicity, and applies equally to everyone. It provides citizenship to descendants of those who once had citizenship before the Soviet occupation,

the Baltic states, however, all three governments – Latvia's especially – began focusing attention on the minority issue, eager to meet accession standards. In Latvia, new education laws were passed allowing 40 percent of instruction in the minority language in minority schools, which included Ukrainian and Belarus as well as Russian. But 60 percent of teaching was to be done in Latvian. This was a cause of heated reproach from much of Latvia's Russian population, as well as from Moscow, and friction over the subject remains.

The issue is less divisive in Estonia, which has fewer Russian residents (350,800 or 25.6

The withdrawal of Russian troops from the Baltic states in 1994, after a great deal of anxiety and complaint, was a monumental step in relieving social tension. A few thousand Russian civilians had already repatriated back to the Soviet Union, and some tens of thousands have since plumped for Russian citizenship. The rest waited, somewhat passively, in legal limbo, neither wanting to integrate, nor leave the place they had come to regard as home.

Once the European Union spotlight fell on

percent), though at the time of EU entry, Russia still refused to ratify its border. A progressive programme of naturalisation has been backed up by the creation of a large, state-funded Russian cultural centre in Tallinn and a Russian museum in Kadriorg. Meanwhile, public administration employees such as nurses, police and prison officials are required to have a minimum level of Estonian-language ability and, with the exception of Narva, which has a high Russian population, all public adminsitration is in Estonian. Full-time Russian-language education can continue in minority schools until 2007 when 60 percent of the curriculum in secondary schools has to be in Estonian. ❑

LEFT: pre-EU protests by Russian pupils in Rīga over moves to increase lessons in Latvian to 60 percent.
ABOVE: growing up in Russian-speaking Narva.

THE CHURCH AND RELIGION

The variety of Christian and Jewish beliefs practised in the three countries
has helped to define their architecture

Throughout the Baltics, religion is often the defining style of a place, from simple wooden Lutheran churches in the north to lavish baroque masterpieces in the south. Their restoration has been a major part of independence and has helped the old towns of the three capitals become World Heritage Sites. Money from the Vatican, from northern Europe's Lutherans and from the USA's varied sects, who were swift to leap on to communism's grave, has refurbished the fabric and educated the new congregations.

Ever at the mercy of changing spheres of influence, the Baltics have amassed a collection of churches with an extraordinary variety of styles. Their history has also left the countries with some two dozen differing belief codes and has created such a tolerance towards other people and their religions that there are Lutherans who regularly attend Catholic Mass and Catholics who sing in Orthodox choirs. In Tallinn, for example, Methodists and Seventh Day Adventists both share the same church.

Orthodox beginning

With the help of Greek Orthodox Russian merchants, the first teachings of Christ were voiced here in the 11th and 12th centuries but Christianity did not arrive in full force until the early 13th century when the German crusaders subjugated Estonia and Latvia. This belated start meant that the early European ecclesiastic style, Romanesque, was on the decline. Only St George's in Rīga and the remains of Ikskile church on an island on the River Daugava give a glimmer of that expiring style. Church architecture in the Baltics begins with Gothic.

In Estonia the earliest stone churches, built of limestone and dating from the end of the 13th century, are on the islands. These were simple Gothic buildings without towers, and were used for protection. On Saaremaa the churches at

Kaarma and Valjala have interesting murals and the one at Karja has beautiful sculptures.

Lithuania converted to Christianity nearly two centuries after its Baltic neighbours, in 1387. Although nothing remains of Vilnius's first church, it must have echoed the red-brick building of the castle. When St Anne's and the

Bernardine monastery were built in the 15th century, its bricks, like those of the cathedral in Kaunas, would not have looked as out of place as they do today.

The Reformation took hold almost immediately after Martin Luther published his thesis in 1520 and its first centres were Tallinn and Rīga, where sacred paintings began to be destroyed. There is a strong painterly tradition in Baltic churches, on collection chairs, priedieux, pews, galleries, altars, triptychs, tablets and doors. Many churches had decorated walls and ceilings, which were painted over during the Reformation, and in subsequent years. These were mostly done by Balts, and only the

LEFT: Bernt Notke's *Dance of Death* (detail, 1463) in Tallinn's Niguliste church.
RIGHT: carving on the organ in Ugale church, Latvia.

"easel" paintings were produced by foreigners.

In Tallinn, the late 15th-century Baltic painter Bernt Notke, who produced the high altar of Aarhus cathedral, Denmark, and Lübeck cathedral's great cross, was responsible for the folding altar at the Holy Spirit Church (1483), which has more paintings than any other in the Baltics. He also produced the macabre *Dance of Death* painting now in the Niguliste church museum (pictured on previous page). In the middle of the 16th century the newly formed Duchy of Courland sought to

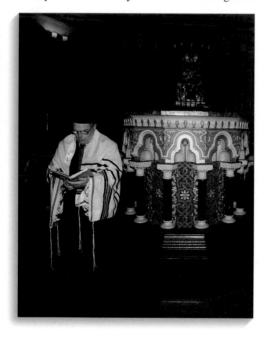

secure its power base by ordering the building of 70 new Lutheran churches.

Catholics sought refuge in the Polish territories of southern and eastern Latvia and Lithuania where the Jesuits began to build their sumptuous churches. Many of Vilnius's 40 Catholic churches are in the highly decorative baroque style. The first, begun in 1604, was dedicated to Lithuania's patron saint, Casimir. Among the finest is the Sts Peter and Paul church, supposedly built on the pagan temple to the goddess Milda. Its Italian sculptors adorned it with more than 2,000 white stucco figures, many of them quite beautiful. The churches, which typically feature a twin-towered facade, show Hispanic influence. In the Latgale region both St Peter's in Daugavpils and the huge, isolated church at Aglona, which attracts pilgrims from all over eastern Europe on the Feast of the Assumption, are in this style.

Catholics were not the only refugees. A split in the Russian church in the 17th century brought an influx of Old Believers to the Baltics and elsewhere. They belong to the *bezpopovci* (without ministers) faction: during Russia's great repressions against the church all trustworthy bishops were eliminated and it was impossible to ordain new priests. Today the world's largest Old Believers congregation, numbering some 20,000, is in the gold-domed Grebenschikova temple in the Moscow district of Rīga. The church's walls are lined with stunning icons depicting only the saints' faces, and services are led by someone from the congregation, elected teachers *(nastavniki)* of the church.

Class distinctions

Though they tend not to last as long, there are still a number of wooden churches throughout the three countries, mostly in Lithuania. The oldest examples date from the middle of the 18th century. The ethnographic museum near Rīga has a typical example. Its figurative carvings and round log walls were all hewn with nothing more refined than an axe. It has a special fancy seat for the local German landlord and the front pews were more elaborately made for German workers; the native peasants were obliged to sit at the back – and were put in the stocks if they failed to attend services.

Because the Lutheran churches in Estonia and Latvia served the interests of the overlords, the Herrnhuters, or United Brethren Church, gained many followers during the 18th and 19th centuries. Services were conducted in farmers' houses or specially built prayer halls, and it became known as "the people's church", with an emphasis on education and religious enlightenment.

The United Brethren's activities diminished during the middle of the 19th century as pressure was put on them by both the Lutheran church and the tsar who won some conversions to Orthodoxy after promising support to farmers against the demands of German land barons.

After Poland failed to gain independence in the 1863 uprising, the tsarist government also came down heavily on Old Believers, whom it looked on as renegades, and Catholics, whom it thought were a threat to the empire.

A huge building programme brought a crop of onion-domed churches including the Orthodox cathedrals of the Holy Theophany of Our Lord in Rīga (1844) and the Alexander Nevski in Tallinn (1900). Many can be seen, abandoned, throughout the countryside today. There are still a few practising Orthodox Latvian and Estonian churches, though commercial links with Moscow have been severed.

churches came under the direct subordination of the Pope.

Jewish populations were well established in the Baltic region, which was one of the world's largest Yiddish language centres. Vilnius, the "Jerusalem" of Lithuania, had 98 synagogues, some of them elaborate wooden buildings, and there were synagogues in nearly every town in the countryside where a large proportion of the shops and small businesses were Jewish-run. Almost the entire population was deported or killed during the Nazi occupation: more than 200,000 died in Vilnius. Estonia was the only country Hitler triumphantly declared *Judenfrei*

Towards the end of the 19th century the first Baptist churches appeared in Estonia and Latvia, and around the beginning of the 20th century Seventh Day Adventists and other Protestant sects arrived. At that time people changed their convictions quite freely and even became involved in the old pagan religions, a romantic revival that was stoked up as a part of the independence movements. After World War I and the break with Russia the countries formed independent Evangelical Lutheran churches, while all the Catholic

(Jew-free). Though some of the synagogue buildings around the countries remain, it is hard to identify them. One or two have re-opened in the capitals to serve the several thousand who have not yet left on their hoped-for emigration. The one in Rīga has been beautifully restored, and optimistic plans to rebuild the Great Synagogue in Vilnius have been mooted.

The church underground

During the Soviet years, all church properties and holdings were nationalised and many churches became concert halls or museums. St Casimir's in Vilnius was turned into a Museum of Atheism, and Rīga's Orthodox cathedral

LEFT: the Jewish synagogue, Vilnius.
ABOVE: the late Pope John Paul II visits Lithuania's Hill of Crosses in 1993.

became a planetarium and cafe. The state continually interfered with the works of the church and those who attended it: their careers were threatened, and their children were banned from higher education.

Even though Soviet rule was harsh, local authorities in the Baltic countries were more lenient and liberal compared with the Soviet heartland. There were many more working churches in Rīga than in Leningrad (St Petersburg), which had nearly three times the population of the former. Because it was easier to register a church and educate children in the Baltics, many Baptists, Adventists, Pentecostals

and other believers emigrated here from Russia, the Ukraine and elsewhere.

The Roman Catholic Seminary in Rīga educated all new priests from the entire Soviet Union, except for Lithuania. Other institutions survived, such as the only Orthodox nunnery in the Soviet Union, at Kuremäe in Estonia. The church battled on, and many priests, evangelists and activists were imprisoned for their work. Estonia lost more than two-thirds of its clergy in the first Soviet years. The Catholics, along with the smaller Protestant churches (Baptist, Adventist and Pentecostal), were most successful in organising their opposition and keeping in touch. A group of Catholic priests

regularly published the underground *Chronicles of the Lithuanian Catholic Church*, which informed the world about repression and human-rights violations. The people, too, remained resilient. The Hill of Crosses, just north of Siauliai on the Kaunas–Rīga highway, was bulldozed by the Soviets three times, but each time the crosses were rebuilt. Now, encouraged by the late Pope John Paul II's visit in 1993, new monasteries are rising beside it.

Changing congregations

Today the Baltics are still centres of religion, with a bishop's chair for the German Evangelical Lutheran church in Rīga, and Vilnius re-established as one of Catholicism's citadels in Europe. People have returned to the church but things have changed. The Lutheran and other Protestant congregations have fallen in the intervening years, and many country churches have only a handful of worshippers. By contrast, the Catholic church, through its diligence, organisation and might, has held its flock. In Latvia, where there are nearly twice as many Lutheran as Catholic churches, the number of baptisms in each is now about the same, around 10,000 a year.

Everywhere there are still signs of the religious mix. In Trakai and Vilnius are two *kenessas*, prayer houses of the Karaites, a surviving Jewish sect of Tatars who arrived in the 14th century at the behest of Grand Duke Vytautas. There are Muslims and Mormons, Uniats and *dievturi*, pagan Latvians whose churches are holy places built around sacred oaks.

Not all the ecclesiastic splendours are on the beaten track. The wonderful Pazaislis monastery should be sought out near Kaunas. One of Rīga's architectural secrets is hidden behind the Academy of Sciences: the 1822 Church of Jesus, the Lutheran bishop's seat, is a wooden octagonal building in the Empire style. The largest wooden church in the country, it measures 27 metres (90 ft) wide and has eight Ionic columns supporting elliptical domes.

When you have seen everything in Estonia, it's worth obtaining a Russian visa and visiting Petchory in the Pskov region. A great fortress wall encircles this 15th-century monastery, which remains an abiding symbol of the Church's struggles and endurance. ❏

LEFT: prayer house of Lithuania's Tatar community.

Timber buildings

The timber buildings of the Baltic countries are one of their principal appeals. Combining both folk art and professional craftsmanship, they are all highly individual, exuding character and style. In its citation of Rīga as a World Heritage Site, Unesco made particular mention of the city's "19th-century architecture in wood".

Wood in the Baltics is more abundant, if less long lasting, than stone. Spruce, pine and oak are the main materials used in buildings that have survived from as far back as the 16th century. Some were constructed on foundations of alder logs, with oak shingle roofs and pine floorboards a foot wide. The oldest existing wooden buildings tend to be churches. None of the elaborate synagogues of Lithuania survive but the country has 265 wooden churches and its roadside shrines, some like fairy-tale castles or dolls' houses, are an art in themselves. It is intriguing to think that the very trees that have always brought out the pagan in Balts should be doing duty supporting so many faiths.

The best places to see wooden folk architecture is in the larger of the open-air ethnographic museums, just outside Tallinn, Rīga and Kaunas. Farmhouses, barns, saunas, windmills and workshops can all be seen in one place. Traditional farmsteads had to cater for the needs of self-sufficient families. They were built to share with livestock and dry storage, and the comfort of their hearths was enhanced with smoking meat or fish. There was not much room left to live in.

Few large farmsteads have survived. In the 19th century, with the drift towards the cities, timber suburbs grew up and though many of these are now dilapidated, they are full of character. Rīga's Moscow district, for example, is starting to attract a young, arty crowd. Across the river is Pārdaugava, a suburb of delightful streets of wooden buildings that are increasingly sought after. Timber houses in other suburbs, such as Tallinn's, are also beginning to be fully appreciated and the restorer's crafts have been revived, often with help and expertise from Scandinavia.

With the 19th-century railways came the burgeoning of resorts. Grand villas grew beside the sea in places such as Pärnu and Narva-Jõesu in Estonia, Jūrmala and Liepāja in Latvia and Palanga and Drusininkai in Lithuania. The saw added

RIGHT: fancy woodwork in Narva Jõessu, Estonia.

finesse that axes could not match, with fancy finials, ballustrades, duckboards, verandas, balconies, towers and turrets, all prettily painted. Among the best known architects-in-wood then was the multi-talented artist Stanislaw Witkiewiecz (1851–1915), inventor of the Zakopane style, whose flights of fancy decorated the villas of Palanga. Railways station, such as the one in Haapsaala that now houses a railway museum, were architectural gems. When the 20th century arrived, prospering cities continued to use wood as a building material. The eclectic European revival styles – classicism, Gothic, baroque – could all be replicated in timber. Among the masters of the craft

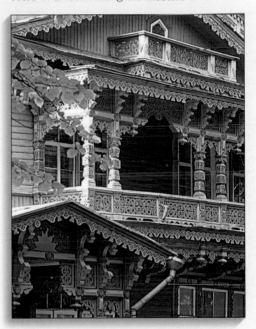

was Alexander Vladovski whose handiwork can be seen in Tallinn's wooden Art Nouveau. Indeed the Art Nouveau movement itself had a strong folkloric, back-to-nature element that suited wooden buildings well.

Many buildings suffered from neglect in Soviet times, as concrete suburbs were built and farms collectivised. Thatched roofs were replaced with corrugated iron, and the rot set in. But renovation in recent years has shown just how attractive these buildings can be, and there is a great enthusiasm to see them restored. Thatch is coming back – and few villages are more picturesque than Altja, on the coast east of Tallinn, where trees and reeds combine in the most harmonious country style. ❑

CULTURE

The contemporary arts scene may sometimes poke fun at the past, but it's
the rich cultural inheritance that makes music and literature so forceful today

Bertolt Brecht wrote: "Unhappy the land that needs heroes." Yet the Baltic states could hardly have survived 50 years of political and cultural subjugation without consolation from folklore and literature. Heroes from old legends embodying the national fate, and those from painting, poetry and music, offered freedom and a refuge to those who felt the Soviet occupation had snatched away their homeland. Theatre, opera and ballet performances were packed – and packed with half-hidden national significance that the censors either ignored or missed.

Writers exploited communist subsidies to keep national pride and independent thought alive. They fostered a climate for independence that was brought to the surface in the 1980s by rock music. Banned under communism, the music united classical composers, politicians and people in a mass gesture of defiance, earning a unique place in Baltic history.

A wave of new experience

Today, almost a generation after the restoration of independence, the state of fear has largely been forgotten, and the topsy turvy Soviet era is remembered with bewilderment, bemusement and even nostalgia, so distant does it seem. Artists no longer need national myths to sustain them. The freedom to travel west as well as east has led to a tidal wave of new influences, and those best able to handle this are often those old enough to have experienced two very different cultural worlds. Artists struggle to balance aesthetic aspirations with the need to stay financially afloat, to secure grants, find agents to promote their work and, in theatre and film, forge co-productions with foreign participation.

Having flirted with politics in the early 1990s, they now question the new accepted values, including national pride. The *Users' Guide to Tallinn*, a brutal spoof on tourism and guidebook writing that also explodes the myth of

LEFT: Tallinn song festival.
RIGHT: Estonian composer Arvo Pärt.

the joyless Soviet era, became a cult classic.

Culture, happily, is not for the few. Theatres, festivals, exhibitons and concerts are well attended, and there is growing realisation from governments that small countries need strong cultural initiatives to earn respect in the wider world. Baltic writers, painters, musicians,

sculptors, composers and philosophers have, historically, been prime movers in public life. Being a musicologist was no bar to Vytautas Landsbergis becoming president of the newly independent Lithuania, nor was a background as a novelist anything but an asset when Lennart Meri became Estonia's first post-war president. The Latvian president, Vaira Vīķe-Freiberga, is well known as a folklorist and literature specialist, a psychologist and linguist.

Roots of literature

Intellectuals and artists have nurtured the idea of independent nationhood since it emerged in the early 19th century, when the three languages began to be recorded in written form. The freedom to write and to express a national sentiment in this manner arrived in a burst of romantic novels and epic verses from which the modern culture took off. Latvian Andrējs Pumpurs told in *Lāčplēsis* the tale of the bear-slayer drowned in the River Daugava, who, on returning to life, will ensure the eternal freedom of his people. Friedrich Kreutzwald fathered the national Estonian epic, *Kalevipoeg*, which ends with the hero trapped in hell but vowing to rise again and build a new Estonia.

Despite a tsarist ban on printed Baltic languages, the lyrics to *Pavarasario balsai* (*Voices*

of Spring, 1885), by a Lithuanian priest, perfectly encapsulated national striving and romantic sentiment. Indeed, priests, doctors and professors played a large part in establishing the region's written cultures, first in German, then later in Estonian, Latvian and Lithuanian. The Baltic peoples could boast early of high-quality European centres of learning and a fertile intellectual ambience. In Lithuania, the Jesuits created Vilnius University in 1579; and in 1632 the Swedes established a university in Tartu, southern Estonia.

Rīga, meanwhile, acquired a cosmopolitan cultural importance. The East Prussian-born Johann Gottfried Herder (1744–1803), author of the idea of folklore, was a popular young preacher at its Dom cathedral, while from 1837–38, Wagner managed the German Opera and Drama Theatre. Today, you can see the delightful Art-Nouveau residence where the philosopher Isaiah Berlin (1909–97) was born.

When the Russians closed Vilnius University, between 1832 and 1905, many culturally active Lithuanians moved to Rīga, while Tartu educated Balts of all origins. Students of the 1850s included Latvian Krišjānis Barons, who collated the Latvian folk songs called *dainas*, and Krišjānis Valdemārs and Juris Alunāns, who founded Latvian theatre. Much Latvian effort went into overcoming perceived German colonial condescension. Budding Estonian culture was less confrontational, and many Germans teaching and studying in Tartu were fascinated with the native language and themes. But for young Estonians the birth of their nation was above all romantic. As Kristjan Jaak Peterson (1801–22), a poet and Tartu graduate living in Rīga, declared:

> *Why should not my country's tongue*
> *Soaring through the gale of song,*
> *Rising to the heights of heaven,*
> *Find its own eternity?*

Peterson's question has remained relevant to the present day. The Baltic languages are no longer oppressed, but the populations are declining, while the post-war émigré communities abroad that have striven to keep those languages alive are dwindling.

Literature led the emerging 19th-century arts, with the novel of social realism, to the fore. In Lithuania, Jonas Biliūnas described peasant life under his own name; more familiar are three assumed names, Julija Žemaite, Juozas Vaižgantas and Antanas Vienuolis. In Estonia, novelist Eduard Vilde and playwright August Kitzberg ploughed a similar furrow, while the brothers Kaudzīte wrote the first Latvian novel, *The Times of the Land Surveyors* (1879).

Exiled genius

Then suddenly, from Latvia, emerged a world-class talent, Jānis Pliekšāns (1865–1929), who assumed the pseudonym of Rainis. A complex, multi-faceted figure, he was a lyrical poet, dramatist, translator (of *Faust*) and political activist. He wrote his best plays in Switzerland, where he fled after his involvement in the 1905 Revolution. *Fire and Night* (1905) is a dramatic statement of the Latvian spirit; The *Sons of Jacob* (1919), based on his own experience, deals with the conflict between art and politics. Jānis Tilbergs's portrait of Rainis in the State Musuem of Art conveys his authority as a national elder and the personal loneliness voiced in his poetry. Modern Latvian literature still rotates around this giant figure, while his wife, Aspazija (1868–1943), a romantic poet and feminist, is also revered. Both are remembered in a museum in their Jūrmala home.

WHAT'S ON

To find out about the latest cultural events, visit the Cultural Institutions in any of the capitals – *see Activities in Travel Tips.*

Latvian literature, always influenced by folk traditions and rustic life, was given a lyrical quality by the terse, philosophical *daina*. The plays of Rūdolfs Blaumanis (1863–1908) also set a high artistic standard. His folk comedy *The Days of the Tailor* in Silmači (1902) is still staged in the open air every midsummer. Affected by his German education and familiarity with the German poets, Jānis Poruks (1871–1911) introduced introspection, melancholy and dreams to Latvian poetry and prose. Kārlis Skalbe (1879–1945), dubbed the Latvian Hans Christian Andersen for his allegorical tales, was also an exquisite poet and short-story teller.

Other notable poets include the symbolist Fricis Bārda (1880–1919), Anna Brigadere (1861–1933) and Aleksandrs Čaks (1901–50), whose Imagist style burst forth with Latvia's 1918 independence and brushed the realities of urban life in Rīga with lyrical excitement.

Lithuanian literature did not develop such early power and variety, which may explain its greater openness to European influences. The literary group Four Winds, formed by Kazys Binkis (1893–1932), was devoted to Futurism; others imitated German Expressionism. Vincas Krėvė-Mickevičius (1882–1954) was a great prose writer and dramatist whose work continued in exile. Having briefly been foreign minister, he fled in 1940, and his epic *The Sons of Heaven and Earth*, was never finished.

The Young Estonia Movement, devoted to raising Estonian literary standards to a European level, flourished in the decade after 1905. The traveller Friedebert Tuglas (1886–1971) brought the world to Estonian readers through

his romantic, exotic stories. A.H. Tammsaare (1878–1940), author of the epic *Truth and Justice*, was influenced by Dostoevsky, Knut Hamsun and Bernard Shaw. He has been called the greatest Estonian prose writer of the 20th century. Find out more about the modest lifestyle of this retiring, reflective man at the tumbledown villa in Kadriorg, Tallinn, where he once lived. A more radical experimental literary group, Siuru, nurtured the poets Jaan Oks (1884–1918) and Marie Under (1883–1977). Under, who spent the Soviet

period in exile, is one of Estonia's most highly regarded poet, along with Betty Alver, whose poetry is generally darker, and whose husband was deported to Siberia.

Romance and mysticism

Foreign influences and rural life stimulated the visual arts and music in the Baltic region. National Romanticism, imported from St Petersburg in the 1900s, ousted academic painting and influenced architecture, taking over from Art Nouveau. When that dreamy style became exhausted, new schools of national painting took over. The Baltic National Romantic style incorporates folk heroes and legends,

LEFT: Estonian writer Jaan Kross.
RIGHT: Latvian violinist Gidon Kramer.

with echoes of Munch, Beardsley, Klimt, Boecklin and Bakst.

In this vein, over Latvia's Vilhelms Purvītis (1872–1945) and Estonia's Konrad Mägi, towers the Lithuanian mystical painter and musician Mikalojus Konstantinas Čiurlionis (1875–1911), a Baltic William Blake. In thin, richly coloured pastels and tempera, he created symbolic landscapes suggesting a mystical universe, with motifs from Lithuanian folklore. He conceived many of his paintings as linked musical movements or as cycles of life and death, day and night. They are extraordinary, pantheistic, poetic distillations of human life.

Čiurlionis's own nature was rich and varied. He travelled widely, wrote for newspapers and almost single-handedly founded the national cultural life before dying at the age of 36. His pictures can be seen, and his music heard, at his own museum in Kaunas.

After Čiurlionis, Lithuanian painting, in the hands of the Kaunas-based Ars Group, grew into a satisfyingly complex art of landscape and portraiture, well informed on European developments and characterised by a rich, dark palette. Emerald green, dark pink, mauve and a touch of yellow evolved into national colours, and a persistent motif was the inclusion of folkloric wooden figures and toys.

The first Estonian school was realist, shaped by Russian and German artistic influence. Impressionism came late, and is best seen in the works of Ants Laikmaa, Alexsander Vardi and Kondrad Mägi. Mägi co-founded the Pallas Art School in Tartu, which produced the highly individual painter Eduard Wiiralt (1898–1954), best known for his graphics, and Jaan Koort, whose deer sculpure stands at the foot of Toompea on Tallinn's Nunne Street. By the end of the 19th century, there was a strong interest in national romanticism and quasi-mythological themes, as in the symbolist-influenced works of Kristjan Raud, who illustrated *Kalevipoeg*. Ado Vabbe is the greatest Estonian Modernist of the early 20th century, while noteworthy Cubists include Karin Luts and Karl Pärsimägi.

Any Baltic visitor interested in painting should head for Latvia, where Vilhelms Purvītis, Janīs Rozentāls (1866–1917) and Jānis Valters (1869–1932) combined European Impressionist, Fauvist and German Expressionist tendencies with their own distinctive approach to landscape and portraiture. Their influence extended to Lithuania and to future generations of Baltic artists. Purvītis, founder of the Rīga Art Academy, depicted the Latvian landscape, but most of his work was burnt in Jelgava during the war; Valters, who studied in Germany, painted landscapes tinged by subjective mood and represented in stark Fauvist colours; Rozentāls's work peaks with his portraiture.

Generally, the Latvian portrait tradition is outstanding. Rozentāls's depiction of his mother and a painting of opera singer Pāvils Gruzdna by Voldemārs Zeltiņš (1879–1905), using Purvītis's pale Latvian colours, lead into the highly coloured avant-garde movement. Artists such as Oto Skulme, Leo Svemps and Jānis Tīdemanis bring this rich period to life.

Notable music

Čiurlionis contributed to modern Lithuanian culture not only through painting, but through music. An intensely active year at the Leipzig Conservatoire produced works still recorded today, including the String Quartet in C minor and the first Lithuanian symphonic composition, *In the Forest*. To a modern ear, the symphonic work often recalls the music of Bruckner, Mahler and Sibelius, but Čiurlionis was a distinct talent in his own right. He later reworked folk songs, wrote choral pieces and organised the national musical life in Vilnius.

From the First National Awakening, all the Baltic cultures developed strong traditions in choral singing. The first operas were written on national themes in the early 20th century, establishing opera as a popular but conservative genre. Baltic symphonic music evolved from the St Petersburg Conservatoire, echoing the memory of Tchaikovsky and Rimsky-Korsakov. Outstanding composers of the era included Latvia's Emīls Dārziņš, best known for his *Melancholy Waltz*, and Estonia's Artur Kapp.

Latvians consider Alfrēds Kalniņš a musical father-figure for his varied work, both romantic and choral. His son Jānis also became a composer, later well known in Canada as John Kalniņš.

In all the arts, there was strong Scandinavian influence between the wars. An equally strong sense of alienation was felt from the Russian soul, the so-called "Asiatic principle". In the applied arts, the Balts excelled in graphic work, textiles and book publishing and illustration.

The aesthetic spirit

All the Baltic cultures reach out to the larger world through theatre, frequently devoting half their repertoire to world classics, with many adaptations also from prose. A strong tradition of open-air performances, with real animals on stage, persists in Latvia, alongside rather verbose poetic theatre. After the war, alien ideology and the expulsion of several key figures cramped the development of the arts. Latvians Anšlavs Eglītis, Zenta Mauriņa and Mārtiņš Zīverts, Lithuanians Antanas Vaiculaitis and Kreve, and Estonian Marie Under continued the best pre-war traditions of theatre, prose and poetry abroad. But many writers died during the war or shortly after.

A literature of suffering and displacement, recounting the mass deportations to Siberia, emerged only in the 1980s, though in 1946, *The Forest of Gods*, by Balys Sruoga, recounted the experience of Lithuanian intellectuals in a German camp with irony and humour. The Estonian Jaan Kross (born 1920), who was imprisoned by the Nazis, spent nine years in Russian labour camps, and his novels and short stories provide poignant accounts of his country's history and of the awful compromises faced by a repeatedly occupied population.

Soviet avant-garde

A new creative generation emerged during the Khrushchev thaw, ready to exploit the advantages of being at the fringe of a centralised empire. The Baltics became the home of the Soviet avant-garde, with productions of Beckett and Ionesco, and in Tallinn in 1969 the daring publication of Russian writer Mikhail Bulgakov's satirical masterpiece *The Master and Margherita*. An uncensored edition of George Orwell's *Nineteen Eighty-Four*

LEFT: *Going to Church* (detail) by Janis Rozentāls.
RIGHT: *Vyties preliudas* (detail) by M.K. Čiurlionis.

appeared in the mid-1980s. The thaw also produced notable opera singers and ballet dancers, including Mikhail Baryshnikov, from Rīga, and anti-establishment poetry. Musicians managed to experiment with atonality and minimalism. The coincidence of modern ideas with folksong was cleverly exploited, as in the haunting compositions of Estonia's Veljo Tormis and the ritualistic rhythms of Lithuania's Bronius Kutavičius. The late Soviet period brought more abstractionism into painting, from Jonas Svazas and Dalia Kosciunaite in Lithuania to Latvia's Maija Tabaka and Ado Lill and Raul Meel in Estonia.

Korčunovas. Lithuanian dramatist Marius Ivaskevicius and Estonia's Andrus Kivirähk both delight in poking fun at national identity while Adolfs Žapiro and Pēteris Petersons are two very active, cosmopolitan figures in Latvian theatre. The National Opera in Rīga is the most dynamic in the Baltic states and contemporary dance now has a dedicated following in all three countries.

Film and video

Estonia has a particularly strong tradition in animated film, with directors such as Priit Pärn scooping prizes at international festivals.

Estonian music is flourishing at home and abroad, thanks to the émigré contemporary composer Arvo Pärt, the former rock musician-turned-avant-garde composer Erki Sven Tüür and a stream of world-class conductors, among them Neeme Järvi and his son, Paavo. The Latvian conductor Mariss Jansons, Lithuanian modernist Osvaldas Balakauskas and Latvian violinist Gidon Kremer also enjoy world renown, while Lithuania's Osvaldas Balakauskas has earned the title of "Lithuanian Messiaen".

Lithuanian theatre, currently favouring radical takes on the classics, has generated several world-class producers, among them Jonas Vaitkus, Juozas Nekročius and Oskaras

Latvia's best-known film director is Laila Pakalniņa, whose work has been screened at Venice and Cannes. Latvia is also renowned for documentaries, a form championed by award-winning directors Ivars Seleckis and Herz Frank. Lithuania's best-known film director is Sarunas Bartas, whose philosophical and minimalist films have won international acclaim. Bigger-budget historical films about the post-1917 fight for independence, the collapse of the first republics and post-war resistance are popular in all three Baltic countries.

Vilnius is home to the excellent Centre for Contemporary Arts, which has a reputation for being one of the most dynamic and innovative of its kind in the Nordic area. In all three countries, video art has taken over from painting. Estonia's Raoul Kurvitz and Jaan Toomik and Lithuania's Deimantas Narkevičius have all contributed to the Venice Biennial. In Lithuania there has been particular focus on social issues and issues of female identity, as in a video by Egle Rakauskaite which investigates the recent experience of Eastern Europeans working in the United States.

Film makers are making their mark, too, not least because the three countries provide exceptional backdrops. The unspoilt towns and countryside are ideal for period dramas.

nians Vytautas Bubnys and Vytautas Martinkus, though very different, show the continuing attraction of folk themes. Critics in Latvia have spoken of the "rebirth of the short story", a form championed by writers Andra Neiburga and Nora Ikstena. Estonia's Jaan Kross and the poet Jaan Kaplinski have an international following and have both been nominated for the Nobel Prize for literature.

Moving on from explorations of the Soviet era, writers such as Estonia's Tõnu Õnnepalu's whose *Border State* explores the experience of a young homosexual in Paris, examine contemporary life and adopt more experimental

Modern literature

Popular present-day writers include Latvian poet and writer Imants Ziedonis and prose-writer Zigmunds Skujiņš. Writers who were censored and repressed during the Soviet era and who have since won wide acclaim include Latvian poet and writer Vizma Belševica, poet Knuts Skujenieks and Lithuania's Juozas Aputis. Traditionally dubbed "land of poetry", prose and innovative essay writing is now flourishing in Lithuania. The novels of Lithua-

styles thanks to exposure to Western trends. Lithuania's Jurga Ivanauskaite has tackled in ironic and provocative fashion contemporary issues such as consumerism, advertising and the dumbing down of culture, while also exploring Buddhism following travels in Tibet. A mystic tendency in Lithuanian literature contrasts with a strong, continuing cult of the grotesque, the absurd and magic realism in Estonia. Inevitably, Baltic literature suffers from a dearth of translation into foreign languages, although extracts are regularly published by the countries' literature centres and cultural institutes, which will happily inform the curious about the latest trends in the arts. ❑

LEFT: Priit Võigemast and Hele Kõre in *Names in Marble*, a film about Estonia's first independence.
ABOVE: watching a video installation, Lithuania.

FOLKLORE

From strange musical instruments and midsummer festivals
to national costumes and sacred trees, the Baltics are steeped in folklore

Folklore is at the very heart of Baltic culture. Indeed, until the 19th century, folklore in effect *was* Baltic culture, because German and Polish rule from the Middle Ages onwards had meant that no real indigenous literary culture had been able to evolve. In the 19th and 20th centuries, the Baltic scholars and writers who developed the new Baltic cultural identity primarily used peasant folklore as their starting point.

Fortunately this folklore was of immense richness, especially in the field of music. Songs appear to have played an important part in the worship of the ancient Baltic gods, and ever since have been at the heart of the Balts' sense of themselves. Almost every village has its own choir, many of a professional standard. State and public occasions often begin with folksongs. As a Latvian *daina*, or folksong, has it:

I was born singing, I grew up singing,
I lived my life singing.
My soul went singing
Into the garden of God's sons.

A visit to a folk performance is recommended for any visitor. Apart from major festivals, performances of one sort or another go on all year round, attracting top performers, and they show no sign of becoming jaded. From the beginning, folklore and the Baltic national movements were mixed up together. The first Estonian and Latvian song festivals, in 1869 and 1873 respectively, were also political events, celebrating the end of serfdom and symbolising the reawakening and unity of the new nations. The republics between 1920 and 1940 turned them into great symbolic events.

The Singing Revolution

Under Soviet rule, these festivals were among the very few ways in which national feeling could be legally displayed, although several of the more patriotic songs were banned and there was some attempt to turn them into paeans for

the likes of Lenin. After Mikhail Gorbachev came to power, these songs were restored, and the various folklore festivals became key symbols of the national independence movements in a process which has been dubbed, especially in Estonia, the "Singing Revolution". It was at the Baltica festival in 1987 that the old national

flags of the former republics were publically displayed together for the first time under Soviet rule and without those responsible being promptly arrested.

The national song festivals are astonishing affairs, with the choirs numbered in thousands and the audiences in tens or even hundreds of thousands – a considerable proportion of the population. A charming element of informality is added by the beautiful costumes and the lovely tradition that, after every song, young girls run on to the stage to present flowers to their favourite conductors.

Folklore was also the key to rediscovering, or reinventing, the beliefs and society of the pagan

LEFT: folk art painting, Lithuania.
RIGHT: Estonian wedding socks from Saaremaa.

Balts which existed before the Christian conquest. These seem to have been based on the idea that the world was itself created partly through song and story-telling:

Once upon a time, the Lord God walked through the world, telling stories and curses, asking riddles...

Modern-day scholars such as the great French-Lithuanian semiologist, Algirdas Julien Greimas, have used surviving folk tales to try to establish the nature of the ancient gods and their worship. Many gods have been rediscovered: Perkūnas or Pērkons, god of thunder, akin to the Slavic Perun and the Scandinavian Thor;

Lithuania were still cutting down sacred oaks in an effort to stop their worship, and until the 20th century some of the ancient spirits lived on in folk tales about forest spirits such as the leprechaun-like kaukai, the aitvarai (who can lead people to hidden treasure) and the barzdukai, a form of bearded gnome. The kaukai were originally neutral spirits who could be won over with gifts. Later, however, they came to be identified with the Christian devil. The Devils Museum in Kaunas, unique in the world, contains a magnificent collection of portrayals of the devil by Lithuanian folk-artists. Unfortunately, this is also to some extent a museum of

Laima and Māra, goddesses of luck (good and bad, because Laima, like some Indian goddesses, also brings the plague); Ausra (the dawn), and many lesser gods and goddesses, some of them figures in their own right, while others are merely subsidiary aspects of the main divinities.

The 14th-century priest Peter of Duisburg wrote that the Balts of his time "worship all of creation... sun, moon, stars, thunder, birds, even four-legged creatures down to the toad. They have their sacred forests, fields and waters, in which they do not dare to cut wood, or work, or fish."

Until the 18th century, Catholic priests in

historical anti-semitism, since most of the devils are meant to be Jewish.

Midsummer frolics

By the 18th century, awareness of the old Baltic religions as such had disappeared or become completely mixed up with Christian beliefs. Thus the great pagan festival of Midsummer Night was renamed St John's Eve, but it has retained many of the old pagan legends and customs, especially those connected with fertility. One of these is that on that particular night and only then, a flowering fern appears, and if a boy and a girl find it together, it will fulfil their heart's desire. Of course, ferns don't actually flower, but the tradition is a good excuse for young couples to go off into the forest at night.

For many centuries, Christian priests and ministers did their best to stamp out much of Baltic folklore, precisely because it embodies so much paganism. The earliest records of Latvian folksongs are provided in evidence for 17th-century witch-trials, and it has been suggested that the "witches" of this period were in fact the linear descendants of the old pagan priests and sorcerers.

In the 1920s and '30s, efforts were made by some people to resurrect the old pagan religions. In Latvia, this took the form of the Dievturība movement, which continues to this day. Because in the 1930s the movement was closely associated with Latvian fascism, it was savagely persecuted under Soviet rule. Its ideology today remains intensely nationalist. "We have always believed that Latvia should be only for the Latvians," one of its leaders has said. "God is a Latvian – or at least, our god is."

Its theology maintains the existence of a single godhead who takes different forms. This, however, is a modern construct derived from the real, but now almost forgotten, ancient pagan religion. The Dievturi number only a few hundred, but their past sufferings and the purity of their folk singing gives them a prestige.

A certain holistic, pagan-influenced mysticism, a willingness to see divinity in all the works of nature, has however characterised all three Baltic cultures up to the present day. This is true both of those authors who hark back directly to the ancient traditions, and those, like the Estonian poet Jaan Kaplinski, who render them into wider, universal terms – in his case, neo-Buddhist.

Romantic tradition

The new attitude to folk-traditions in Europe dates to the later 18th century and the rise of Romanticism. Baltic folklore played a part in this cultural shift, because a key figure in the movement was the German philosopher Johann Gottfried Herder, who was moved by Latvian folksongs and stories when he was a Protestant

> **STIRRING SPEECH**
>
> "Has a people anything dearer than the speech of its fathers? In its speech lies its whole domain, its tradition, history, religion and basis of life, all its heart and soul."
>
> – *Johann Gottfried Herder*

minister and teacher in Rīga in the 1760s. His influence led to generations of research by Baltic German scholars and, in the mid-19th century, the work was taken over by the first generations of native Baltic intelligentsia.

Their first task was the recording and codification of this oral history. In Latvia, this process is linked above all with the name of Krišjanis Barons, who assembled the *dainas*, or Latvian folksongs. The 217,996 items form one of the largest collections of oral folklore in the

world. Following the formation of the independent states after 1918, the governments and universities also set out to collect folk-art.

The Estonian National Museum in Tartu (now returned after being confiscated for 46 years by the Soviet Air Force) houses hundreds of thousands of examples. These give clues to an ancient tradition: for example, beer mugs were decorated with "male" symbols, such as suns and horses.

Lithuania has a particularly rich tradition of folk-carving, which is illustrated by the intricately carved wooden crosses to be found outside many villages. Covered with ancient symbols, these crosses resemble pagan totem

LEFT: festive girls, Estonia.
RIGHT: kanklės player, Lithuania.

poles. The carved crosses on the famous Hill of Crosses at Šiauliai is an apotheosis of Catholic piety and of Lithuanian nationalism, but also of ancient pagan symbolism. Another sight to watch out for in the Lithuanian countryside is Rūpintojelis ("The Thinker"), a mournful figure, now presented as Christ, but much older than Christianity.

However, the task of recovering the meaning of such figures, and the ancient Baltic tradition in general, is an intensely difficult one, both because of the suppressive affect of Christianity, and the effects of modernisation, especially that which took place under Soviet rule.

One of the reasons why many Estonians wish to recover the area of Petseri, or Pecory, captured by Estonia from Russia in 1920 and transferred back by Stalin in 1944, is that the small Setu minority who live there have preserved folk traditions which have been lost in Estonia itself.

The first major guide to Estonian folk stories (as opposed to folksongs, which had been published in various collections) was *Old Estonian Fairy-Tales*, first published in 1866. It is still popular in Estonia, and is held to have contributed to the creation of an Estonian prose-style that is independent of the German models it previously imitated.

In 1861, Kreutzwald published the "national epic" *Kalevipoeg* ("Son of Kalev"), a reworking in verse of stories about a giant hero; the work was intended to help build up a national spirit, and prove to a sceptical world that the Estonian folk tradition was capable of producing an epic – considered at that time to be the highest form of literature. As with the Finnish *Kalevala*, debate has raged over the merits of the work ever since.

Invented gods

The *Kalevipoeg* is still taught in every Estonian school, but otherwise its influence has progressively diminished. This has been far less the case with the Latvian national epic, *Lāčplēsis* ("The Bear-Slayer"), by Andrējs Pumpurs, in which another mythical hero is made a leader of the medieval Latvian resistance against the German invaders. *Lāčplēsis* has since become the theme of a verse play by Jānis Rainis, a rock-opera and several other works. Under the first Latvian republic, the Order of Lāčplēsis was the highest state award, and there are plans to restore this honour. Kangars, the traitor in the epic, has become a generic name for traitors, while Laimdota, Lāčplēsis's beloved, has given her name to boutiques and hairdressers, and Spīdola, the witch, has given her name to ships and yachts.

Pumpurs also gave the ancient Latvians a pantheon of pagan gods, like the classical Olympus – quite unhistorical, but another passport to European respectability in his time. The contemporary habit of giving children "traditional" pagan names, such as Laima or Vytautas (after the Lithuanian medieval Grand Duke), dates from this period.

Today, this rich folkloric tradition is threatened from two directions: the first is by Western mass culture, and second by a danger that the over-use of folklore on official occasions, in schools and so on, may eventually drain it of the joyous spontaneity which kept Baltic folklore alive and part of Baltic life, and not – as so often in the West – either a museum piece or an artificially revived hobby. Now that the repression, which forced people to keep their identity alive, has been lifted, folklore traditions may become diluted. If they do, it will be the price that has to be paid for joining the global capitalist community ❑

LEFT: tying the knot with Lielvārde's belt.

The Singing Tree

Most traditional musical instruments are common throughout the Baltics and Eastern Europe: the goat-horn, whistle, flute, reed, violin, squeeze-box and zither. Other instruments belong to particular regions: the bagpipe in Estonia and Latvia's Protestant part, the hammer dulcimer in Lithuania and Latvia's Catholic part, and the *hiukannel* or bowed harp in the Estonian islands. But one instrument unique to the Baltic lands is a kind of board zither with between five and 12 iron or natural-fibre strings. Its history can be traced with some certainty back at least 3,000 years and its Baltic names have supposedly originated from the proto-Baltic word *kantlés*, meaning "the singing tree": *kantele* in the Finnish language, *kannel* in Estonian, *kândla* in Livonian, *kokles* in Latvian and *kankles* in Lithuanian.

This is a deified instrument and, according to folk beliefs, the tree for its wood must be cut when someone has died but isn't yet buried. In a fairytale, a youth helps an old man who turns out to be God and he rewards the good-hearted lad with this particular instrument.

Thus the Apollonic, heavenly aura and the fine, deeply touching tone quality have made kokles a symbol of national music for Estonians, Latvians and Lithuanians. Unfortunately, the playing of the original instrument has almost died out. At the beginning of the 20th century, kokles developed into a zither of 25 to 33 strings, like a harp. "Modernisation" during the Soviet time resulted in a soprano, alto, tenor and bass kokles family. Folksong arrangements and compositions of questionable musical quality were played and presented as the national music.

A folklore revival in the 1970s and '80s restored an interest in traditional instruments. Many of them, such as the bagpipe, jew's-harp, whistle, flute, reed, horn, clappers and rattles, are made by enthusiasts and played informally. They are used by both solo performers and folklore groups and it is now hard to imagine a celebration of calendar customs, folk-dance parties or folklore festivals without them.

The most important festivals are the summer and winter solstice celebrations and there are large gatherings at such festivals as the Baltica, which

involves all three Baltic republics and sometimes includes Scandinavian countries, too. More local but no less exciting are Skamba, skamba kankliai in Lithuania, and the children's and young people's folklore festival, Pulkā eimu, pulkā teku, in Latvia. There are also a number of festivals associated with individual towns and villages.

In Lithuania visitors should try to listen to *sutartines*, which is endless sonoric meditation, both vocal and instrumental. For a while it seemed this unique ancient polyphonic style had become extinct, but it has been revived by folklore groups. The instrumental version of *sutartines* is played on kankles, pan-pipes, trumpets or horns. Primi-

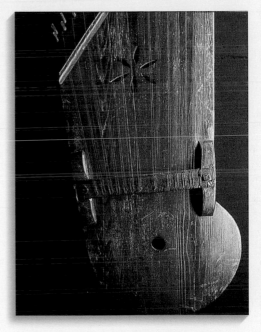

tive musical instruments are usually made by the players themselves. The more sophisticated ones such as the kannel/kokles/kankles, bagpipes, flutes, violins, accordions and zithers are made by a few skilled masters. These instruments are not easy to obtain, though they can be found at fairs and folk-crafts festivals where there is also a good variety of bird-, devil- and animal-shaped clay whistles, usually played by children. The most popular instruments are the accordion and guitar, played at family celebrations and informal parties.

Catholic and Lutheran churches mostly have organs with distinctive characteristics. Rīga Dom's organ is recognised world-wide, while those in rural areas can have their own unique charm. ❑

RIGHT: the deified "singing tree", made with wood cut after someone has died but before their burial.

SAUNAS AND SPAS

The spa culture that has gripped the West could learn something from
the traditional sauna of the Baltics, which has an ancient and respected past

Sauna is the Finnish word for a steam bath, and the practice extends across the northern countries of three continents. In Estonia and Latvia, where winters are cold and long, they have always been a way of life. Now they are going through a revival, and every new home, as well as many new hotels, has one.

This culture, combined with the water cures and mud treatments that for two centuries have been offered in traditional spa resorts – Pärnu in Estonia, Jūrmala in Latvia, and Druskininkai in Lithuania – makes the Baltic states a region of healthy living and offers the visitor the prospect of a healthy and rewarding holiday.

If you are ever invited for a sauna, you should not pass up the opportunity of a very Baltic experience. And if you are not invited, you should seek one out.

In Estonia saunas are called *saun* – there is a Sauna Street and a Sauna Tower in Tallinn – and they can be found everywhere from Sauna Küla (Sauna Village) in a forest 8 km (5 miles)

from Tallinn that can cater for 60 people, to the floating sauna in Saaremaa National Park. They are usually dry steam baths in the Finnish style, though in the current revival there has also been a move back to smoke saunas, in which smoke from a wood fire is allowed to fill the room.

In the traditional Finnish sauna, heat is raised by ladelling water on to heated coals, bringing the room temperature up to around 60–70°C, though Estonians often like it much hotter than that. Sauna rituals consist of steaming and cooling off. Novices are advised to start off gradually, steaming for about seven to 10 minutes, then cooling off and repeating the exercise three to five times. Only then should they start switching.

This light flailing by birch branches, which should begin with strokes and then go on to gentle switching, is a type of massage. It helps blood circulation, increases perspiration, opens pores to help the skin to breathe and cleans out toxins. It is an excellent remedy for muscular pains and a very good way to get rid of extra weight. Either do this switching yourself or ask a friend – it's best to lie on the bench while someone else switches your back, starting from your feet and moving towards your head. Twigs should be soaked in cold water for up to 15 minutes before being used.

Cooling off can be done by taking a shower, relaxing for five minutes in a separate room or swimming in a lake. In winter the hardy roll in the snow. But do take it easy after coming out of a sauna as you might feel a little giddy. Herbal teas or beer are generally a part of the cooling-off process.

Bathhouse of the spirits

In Latvia, where steam bathhouses are as old as time, the sauna is called *pirts*, and, as in Estonia, they are today also undergoing a revival. Every farmstead traditionally had its own *pirts*, located in a quiet spot, often by some kind of water source, a lake or river or pond, for filling the pail for the fire and to cool off afterwards.

Saunas have always been used for hygienic

or medical reasons but *pirts* are also part of a pagan religion. This was the place where Māra, the Latvian goddess of fertility and happiness, lived with lesser spirits – the word *gars* in Latvian means both bathhouse steam and spirit. The *pirts* was where life began and ended, where babies were born and the old passed away.

Every time anybody used the *pirts* they had to say thanks to Māra and the spirits and then, after tidying up, they had to leave a bucket of clean water and new twigs for the spirits to use. On the day before getting married, a young woman and her girlfriends went into a

The main feature of the traditional *pirts* is the oven. Traditionally, a pile of large stones is put over the hole where a fire is made to heat the stones. When the stones are hot enough, the house is cleared of smoke, then the windows and door are closed to keep the heat inside and cold water is thrown on the stones to create steam.

Bathhouse walls were always made from logs but the roof was often made from clay or earth with grass growing on top of it. There were two rooms, a dressing room at the front and a bathing room containing the oven and wooden benches.

sauna to prepare, physically and emotionally, for the wedding.

Women gave birth in *pirts* and there are many rituals and superstitions about assisting pregnant women. One of them, for example, warns not to heat the room with wood from a fir tree – its sparks will result in a quarrelsome child. When a baby was born there was a special celebration called *pirtīžas* when girlfriends helped a young mother to bath the baby. If it was a girl, lime twigs were used, if a boy, oak twigs.

Today, Latvian *pirts* and natural medicine traditions are undergoing a revival. Traditional bathhouses equipped with modern conveniences are once again an inseparable part of any country house or summer cottage, while in the cities public bathhouses are available for groups of friends or companies to hire.

Basic *pirts* rituals are easy to learn but if you are using one for the first time, you might need some guidance from a qualified bath-man or woman, who may also be able to find you the right plants or trees for your health, skin type or mood. The efficacy of the *pirts* depends on the energetic and aromatic properties of the particular twigs. ❑

LEFT: a typical lakeside sauna.
ABOVE: when it comes to switching, enlist a friend.

NATURE AND WILDLIFE

Though lacking in dramatic scenery, the region has some of the most unspoilt spaces in Europe that are wonderful habitats for wildlife

Like their northern neighbours in Scandinavia, people in the Baltics have an espe cially close relationship with nature. Many have a summer house and get away to the countryside during the warm weather as often as they can. A surprisingly strong sense of rural tradition permeates almost every aspect of Baltic culture, from popular music and food to the very way people think. And where many Westerners tend to romanticise nature, people in the Baltics enjoy it in a refreshingly hands-on and non-sentimental way. The average Balt is at ease working in a state-of-the-art office in the city one day and chopping firewood out in the sticks the next.

Estonia

Roughly the same size as Holland, with a tenth of its population, Estonia is relatively under-populated, which helps to make it a truly unspoilt natural habitat. One fifth is covered by peat bogs and because much of the country is unsuitable for agriculture it was spared much of the environmental abuse for which the Soviet Union was so notorious.

There are still vast areas of untouched forest and wetland that provide a haven to all sorts of indigenous wildlife, including wolves, bears, lynxes, otters, beavers, elk, roe deer, eagles and storks. Ten species of rare and protected birds include the golden eagle (250 pairs), white tailed eagle, spotted eagle and eagle owl, as well as the rare black stork.

The country has a long and, in many areas, dramatically beautiful coastline that covers some 3,794 km (2,357 miles), most of which belongs to the more than 1,000 islands. The coast differs from the rough granite seaboard of its northern neighbour, Finland, and the sandy beaches of Latvia to the south. It changes from limestone cliffs in the north to sandy beaches and shelving coastal meadows in the

west. These coastal meadows used to be widespread but today only a few are grazed; the rest have become overgrown with juniper or reed.

During the period when the coast served as part of the Soviet border, most of it was a restricted zone. This helped to preserve it from extensive development. Today, grey seals fre-

quent the undisturbed shores and roughly one fifth of the estimated 7,500 Baltic grey seals tend to keep close to the Estonian coast. During mild and ice-free winters, many give birth to their pups on the small islets.

The country is also a stopover-point for Arctic waterfowl migrating along the East Atlantic Flyway. According to some estimates, up to 50 million water and coastal birds use the abundant coastal wetlands. Many stop here to prepare for the long journey to their Russian Arctic breeding grounds. During the first two weeks of May, every small inlet teems with coots, grebes, ducks, geese and swans.

The biggest coastal wetland is Matsalu, a

LEFT: gathering wild flowers.
RIGHT: moose are found throughout the three countries – motorists should beware.

large bay surrounded by various coastal habitats. During the spring migration, more than 2 million waterfowl pass though Matsalu, primarily long-tailed and other Arctic diving ducks.

Situated on what is called a "boreonemoral" zone, Estonia is a transitional area where the coniferous Euro-Siberian taiga opens into a European zone of deciduous forest. Forests and woodlands cover almost half the country. Historically, most forests were owned by German landlords and churches; today, nearly half the forested land belongs to the state, which considerably facilitates conservation efforts.

Unfortunately, free-market principles are also being recklessly applied in some quarters. In the late Soviet era, when forest operations ceased in spring and early summer, three to four times less timber was felled. Nowadays, timber companies operate all year round for maximum efficiency and illegal logging has been a problem.

A good indicator of the state of Estonia's forests ecosystems is the number of forest-dwelling predators, such as bears, lynx and wolves. There are estimated to be stable numbers of all these at present, with some several hundred lynx, together with up to 200 wolves and more than 500 brown bears. Forests are also home to the flying squirrel, an animal seldom found elsewhere in Europe.

The islands, which make up nearly 10 percent of the country's total territory, really set the country apart from its otherwise similar southern neighbours. The largest of these are Saaremaa and Hiiumaa, both of which are becomingly increasingly popular tourist destinations because of their raw beauty and unchanged way of life. Recently, scientists were overjoyed to discover a completely new species of moss on Hiiumaa. But many of the islands are all but inaccessible in winter when, around January, the surrounding sea freezes over for about three months.

There are four national parks in Estonia, as well as many nature reserves. Two of the most spectacular are Karula and Lahemaa national parks. Karula National Park, near Valka in the south of Estonia, was established in 1993 to protect a unique landscape and its rich natural ecosystem. More than 70 percent of the terri-

TOP 10 NATURE SIGHTS

Lahemaa National Park, Estonia. Set beside the north coast, Lahemaa is a great place to see Estonian nature in all its rugged beauty. *www.lahemaa.ee*

Lake Peipsi, Estonia, The fifth-largest lake in Europe is by far the best for fishing. *www.turism.tartumaa.ee*

Saaremaa Island, Estonia. This natural gem abounds in unusual flora and fauna. *www.saaremaa.ee*

Gauja National Park, Latvia. Around spectacular River Gauja is some wonderful hiking and impressive caves linked to local folklore. *www.sigulda.lv*

Ķemeri National Park, Latvia. Part forest, part swamp, medicinal waters. A birdwatchers' treat. *www.kemeri.gov.lv*

Kolka, Latvia. Unique for many reasons – sublime beaches, remarkable lighthouse, great birdlife. *www.kolka.info/*

Aukštaitija National Park, Lithuania. Nature trails through the many lakes and unspoilt forest. *www.tourism.lt*

The Curonian Spit, Lithuania. Carved out by the wind and Baltic Sea, this is a natural miracle of pine forest and dune. *www.nerija.lt*

Trakai National Park, Lithuania. Close to Vilnius, Trakai is a labyrinth of forest, lakes and villages. www.trakai.lt

Zuvintas State Nature Reserve, Lithuania. A boggy area rich in wildlife known as the "kingdom of birds". *www.jzum.lt*

tory is covered by forest, which varies from dry sandy pine forests to waterlogged swamp forests. This, along with many small lakes and streams, creates an ideal habitat for wildlife, including wolves, moose, otters, beavers, golden eagles and black storks.

Lahemaa (see page 167) is the oldest national park in Estonia and is the best developed for tourism, with a visitors' centre, well marked trails and paths and guided tours. The park has glimmering cliffs, broadleaf primeval forests, stone fields with giant boulders, small coastal lakes and bogs, as well as charming coastal villages, farms and old German manor estates with immaculately landscaped parks.

Latvia

Latvians' love of nature is particularly striking for its, well… naturalness. And it's apparent in everything from the way many people routinely adorn their homes with fresh flowers, to the fact that many Latvian surnames are derived from the names of various trees, flowers, animals and birds.

Latvia has an especially beautiful coastline, which stretches for some 494 km (307 miles) along the Baltic Sea. Locals certainly make good use of the abundance of white sandy beaches during the summer, but you can always find a secluded stretch of beach for yourself if you're prepared to drive that little bit further on from popular tourist spots such as Jūrmala, Saulkrasti and Liepāja. In Soviet times, the resort of Jūrmala, which is just 20 km (13 miles) away from Rīga, was considered one of the most prestigious summer resorts in the entire USSR.

The strict coastal restrictions during Soviet times helped preserve much of the natural beauty of the coastline, as it did in Estonia, and there are still countless picturesque fishing villages strewn right the way along the shores where locals sell smoked fish and other seafood on rickety stalls by the roadside.

Latvia has more than 12,000 rivers that stretch for 38,000 km (23,610 miles), as well as more than 2,000 lakes. The Latgale region, where many of these lakes are found, is known as the "Land of the Blue Lakes".

Nearly all inland waters are pollution-free and ideally suited for swimming and fishing. Although some rivers have had their courses straightened, most large and medium-size rivers retain their natural contours.

Many lakes provide feeding and breeding grounds for numerous bird species. Some of the most ecologically valuable of these are the shallow coastal lagoons situated along the Baltic coast. Places such as Lakes Pape, Liepājas, Engure, Babītes and Kaniera were cut off from the sea long ago and are now fresh water. Rare species of birds, such as the bearded tit, common and little bittern, corn-

crake, hen harrier, and little and spotted crake nest in Lake Pape and its surroundings. The lake and the nearby Nida marsh are important stopovers for bean and white-fronted goose and curlews during migration.

Forests cover some 45 percent of Latvia's territory – compared, for example, with 8 percent in Britain. Most are mixed coniferous and broadleaf, with pine, spruce, birch, aspen and black alder the most common.

About a quarter of Latvia's forests are moist and wetland forests, habitats which have been mostly destroyed in other European countries. These so-called "swamp" forests cover large areas of low-lying ground that are permanently

LEFT: the Baltics are home to around 10 percent of the world's population of storks.
RIGHT: the rarer, shyer, black stork.

or seasonally flooded. Many rare plant and animal species belong here. Home to more than 1,000 pairs of black storks (about 10 percent of the world's population), 500 pairs of the lesser spotted eagle, woodpeckers and innumerable other species, these forests are a dream for bird watchers.

The forests also have a rich supply of berries – wild strawberries, blueberries, raspberries and loganberries. The berry-picking season lasts from late June until late September, the latter also being the time for gathering mushrooms, a

> **HAPPY SALMON**
>
> Latvia is one of the few places in the whole Baltic Sea region where natural salmon spawning still occurs.

troduced into the country in the 20th century and now number an estimated 50,000–80,000.

Marshland makes up almost 5 percent of the country, most of which is unspoilt habitat. There are more than 20 protected plant species within this territory, and at least 15 species of bird that nest here, including the crane, golden plover, black grouse, whimbrel, merlin and peregrine. Marshes are also popular places with berry pickers for the wide and exotic range of berries that grow there, including cranberries, cloudberries, cowberries and bilberries.

favourite pastime – the Latvian word *sēņot* means, "to go mushroom picking".

The most popular mushrooms are the edible boletus (very tasty with sour cream), orange cap boletus, chanterelles and rusulla. Best of all, although there is some inaccessible private property, the vast majority of forests, with a wealth of berries, mushrooms and hazelnuts, is free for everyone to enjoy.

Indigenous Latvian wildlife is similar to its Baltic neighbours. Some 4,000 Eurasian otters live in the rivers. There are an estimated 200–400 wolves at large, as well as 400 lynxes. Beavers, which were hunted to extinction by the end of the 19th century, were successfully rein-

Latvia has made much progress in trying to protect its rich natural heritage since independence. At present 6.8 percent of the country is protected by law. There are five nature reserves, two national parks, and 240 protected areas (nature parks, protected landscape areas, restricted areas and biosphere reserves).

Teiči State Reserve *(see page 248)* is the largest protected marsh in the Baltic and a sight well worth seeing. A raised bog covers most of the territory but there are also 19 lakes, hollows, mineral-soil islands, fens, swamps and natural meadows. It also has the largest concentration of pre-migratory cranes in Latvia. An ancient Russian village of Russian Old Believers (people who adhere to the Russian Orthodox Church as well as old pagan beliefs) still lives on one of the marsh islands. The marsh can only be entered in the company of a guide.

Gauja National Park *(see page 243)* is one of the most spectacular places in Latvia and is named after the Gauja, Latvia's longest river. For 90 km (56 miles) the Gauja flows through a breathtaking valley that is the heart of the park. Nowhere else in Latvia are there so many steep banks, ravines, streams, sandstone and dolomite cliffs, and caves. Most people use the picturesque town of Sigulda as a start-

over a bonfire, the search by couples for the legendary fern blossom and the all-night revelry of singing and dancing (not to mention copious beer-drinking). Latvians don't glorify nature the way some people do. They simply make the best of it.

Lithuania

Roughly the size and population of Ireland, Lithuania lies on the western fringe of the East European Plain that stretches across Belarus and part of Russia. Like its Baltic neighbours, the country is largely flat. Its highest point is at Juozapines, which stands an under-

ing point to explore Gauja National Park.

In all, Latvians' love of nature can be most eloquently summed up by the midsummer festival known as Jāṇi. Held over the night of 23–24 June, Jāṇi derives from a pagan celebration of fertility and is by far the most popular holiday in the country. The cities largely shut down as people head off en masse to the countryside to be with family and friends. Many aspects of the original celebration are still widely practised today, such as jumping

whelming 294 metres (965 ft) above sea level.

Many Lithuanians will proudly tell you that the geographical centre of Europe (54°51' north and 25°19' east) lies in Lithuania, 20 km (12 miles) north of Vilnius – a focal point for EU accession celebrations.

The country was once entirely covered with thick forests and bogs, which provided local tribes with a natural stronghold to resist the crusading Teutonic knights. Today about a third of Lithuania is still covered by forest, most of which is coniferous. In the central and southern parts of the country, small areas of Central European deciduous forests have survived. The forests and wetlands are home to moose,

LEFT: the lynx, a woodland wild cat.
ABOVE: Konik Polski wild horses in Pape Nature Reserve, Latvia.

wolves, lynxes and beavers. The rare mountain hare can be found in marshy bog lands. Birds of prey include the white-tailed eagle, osprey, honey buzzard and lesser-spotted eagle.

Lithuania's glacial history can be seen in the country's extraordinary abundance of rivers, lakes and wetlands. More than 800 rivers, including the 937-km (582-mile) Nemunas, transform the landscape into a liquid latticework and about 3,000 lakes cover some 1.5 percent of the country. Many of these are in pristine condition and are

> **WELL PRESERVED**
>
> Lithuania has five national parks, five nature reserves, 30 regional parks and 750 protected landscape objects.

Although Lithuania is the largest of the Baltic states, it has the shortest coastline at just 99 km (62 miles). Most of it is taken up by the Curonian Spit *(see page 319),* a thin stretch of sand composed mostly of dunes and pine forests that separates the Curonian Lagoon from the Baltic Sea. This precious natural habitat, which is sometimes referred to as Lithuania's "tiny Sahara", is also a national park and enjoys Unesco listed-status as a World Heritage Site. It is, however, currently the focal point of political tension

ideal for swimming. It's even still possible to find your "own" little lake, where few others go, even in the height of summer.

Lake Zuvintas in the south is an important breeding ground and migration resting ground for many different water birds. It is also one of the few breeding grounds for endangered species such as the aquatic warbler and ferruginous duck.

Some 70 percent of Lithuania's wetlands has been lost through overzealous land drainage for agriculture, which began in the 17th century, and much of what remains is seriously affected by all the mineral fertilisers being washed out from fields into the water.

between Lithuania and Russia, which has begun to exploit nearby oil fields in its waters off the enclave of Kaliningrad. The northern part of the lagoon belongs to Lithuania and the southern part to Russia.

Aukštaitijos National Park *(see page 323)* was designated as the country's first national park in 1974, and covers an area of 40,570 hectares (100,250 acres) around Ignalina, Utena and Švenčionys. The park is especially picturesque and perfectly encapsulates the lush, primeval beauty of Lithuanian nature. The majestic Trakai National Park *(see page 286),* which lies 25 km (16 miles) from Vilnius, was designated in 1992 and embraces the historic city of Trakai, together with the forests, lakes and villages in its vicinity.

Between all the various national parks and nature reserves, the sizeable protected natural habitat of Lithuania supports a huge variety of wildlife, including elk, deer, wolves, foxes and wild boar. Bird species include white storks, herons, geese, ducks, swans, eagles and hawks.

Environmental concerns

One of the greatest and certainly most publicised environmental concerns in the Baltics is that of the Ignalina nuclear power plant in

ment, both regional and national, has made huge progress in protecting and restoring the country's natural heritage.

All three Baltic states are also faced with the grave environmental threat posed to the Baltic Sea, which plays such a significant part in the life of all of its people in one way or another.

The low salinity of the Baltic Sea – seawater infused with a substantial amount of fresh water – presents the worst possible living conditions for aquatic organisms.

Few species can survive in the Baltic and they are all particularly vulnerable to ecological change. The Baltic Sea is almost entirely

Lithuania near the Latvian border, which still operates two reactors similar to those at Chernobyl, as well as the chemical and other industries that pollute the air and empty wastes into rivers and lakes. According to calculations by some experts, about one-third of Lithuanian territory is affected by polluted air at any given time. However, the Ignalina plant is due to be closed down by 2009 as part of an agreement reached with the European Union during the accession process, and the govern-

cut off from the North Sea, which means that the same water remains in it for about 30 years, along with all the pollutants and organic matter it contains.

Rivers and streams, stretching all the way from Ukraine to Norway and the Baltic states, have been continuously dumping toxic matter into the Baltic for years, so that today it's one of the world's most threatened marine ecosystems. However, there has been some promising regional intergovernmental action on this front in recent years, and it would seem that although the problem is deep-rooted, serious efforts are now being made to try and undo the immense damage done to the Baltic Sea. ❑

LEFT: hunters on Hiiumaa island, Estonia.
ABOVE: one of several hundred brown bears living in the unspoilt forests.

OUTDOOR ACTIVITIES

The long coast, sleepy rivers and lush national parks
are ideal places to get active and have some recreational fun

Rural tourism and outdoor recreation are two of the fastest-developing areas in the Baltic economy. Estonia, Latvia and Lithuania continue to come up with good reasons for tourists to trek beyond the capital cities for some outdoor fun. The countries' nearly untouched ecosystem is scattered with

der, there is a handful of adrenaline-inducing ways to enjoy it.

Latvia's major playground, Gauja National Park, located in the central town of Sigulda, is a magnet for outdoor adventurers. The Gauja river cuts through the park's ancient valley of sandstone and dolomite cliffs. Bungee jump-

small tourism enterprises, offering activities from hot-air ballooning to river rafting and horse riding on wild mares. Regardless of the sport, and dramatic high ground notwithstanding, the countryside has sufficient diverse beauty to creates a playground for the outdoor enthusiast – and none are more enthusiastic than the Baltic peoples themselves.

Gauja National Park

Latvia has an almost untouched natural ecosystem that covers more than 50 percent of its territory. From rolling plains to a 494-km (307-mile) stretch of coastline, it has a variety of rustic settings. And for each natural won-

ing, water rafting and trail trekking are some of the area's most popular activities. Bungee jumping can, in theory, be executed over any mass of empty space, allowing for proper equipment and safety precautions. Gauja offers two choices for jumpers; from a cable car suspended 43 meters (140 ft) above one of the park's deepest ravines, or from a lower Gauja river bridge. The cable-car has become popular with thrill-seekers, while the cars are also open for the less-extreme sport of sightseeing.

Lacking dramatic white water, river rafting on the slow-moving Gauja is by no means a dangerous affair. In fact, the activity is the most opportune way to enjoy the park's natural splendours with the family. Tourists can rent rafts that accommodate more than 10 people with an accompanying guide, as well as private canoes and boats. Although the Gauja is riddled with small whirlpools, which swimmers are cautioned about, the river has no trace of any four- or five-class rapids, as white caps simply don't exist. Yet, any skilled canoeist can work his or her way to a thrilling amount of speed on the 90-km (55-mile) stretch of river.

Pot-holing and bobsleighing

Avid spelunkers can find the largest cave in the Baltic states – Gūtmanis cave – in the centre of

ticipating in one of the Winter Olympic's most popular sports. The structure is primarily used for professional bobsleigh and luge training and competitions, in which athletes reach speeds of up to 125 kph (78 mph). Amateurs, however, will fly through the concrete track at a much safer speed of 80 kph (50 mph) under the guidance of professionals. The tourist bobsleigh, called Vučko, is open every weekend between October and March and there is also a summer bobsleigh from May to October.

Like almost every state park in the Baltics, Gauja National Park's natural territory is carved with hiking trails, observation points and camp-

Gauja National Park. The cave's natural sand catacombs wind 18.8 metres (62 ft) deep, 12 metres (40 ft) wide and 10 metres (33 ft) high. Local legend tells of a Liv warrior who ordered his beautiful but unfaithful wife to be entombed in the wall of a cliff. The woman's tears turned into a stream of water, carving the massive cave into the sandy bedrock.

Sigulda's most prized recreational feature is the professional bobsleigh track. Open year-round, the 1,420-metre (4,660 ft)-long track allows visitors to live out their dream of par-

ing sites, as well as historic landscapes that include castle ruins and archaeological excavation areas. The main centres for the park are Sigulda and Cēsis.

Water sports

During the summer months, Estonians find little more enjoyment than seaside relaxation. The country's bountiful lakes, endless stretch of shoreline and lush coastal islands create a haven for water lovers. Sailing, canoeing, jet-skiing and other water recreation activities are some of the many ways to enjoy Estonia's aqua playground.

Sailing between the mainland and Estonia's

LEFT: cycling along Pirita Beach, Estonia.
ABOVE: rowing on Lake Galvė, Lithuania.

remarkable 1,520 islands is perhaps the most elegant way to enjoy the country's stunning coast (Arthur Ransome, friend of Lenin and author of *Swallows and Amazons*, recorded his own sailing adventures in Estonia and Latvia in the 1920s). Visitors can splurge on a yacht trip to the island of Kihnu or spend a more casual day in the Bay of Pärnu watching the Baltic sunset over the boats while enjoying wine, cheese and fruit.

There is no shortage of sailing trips along the country's 3,794-km (2,357-mile) shoreline. Sea excursions are so popular, however, that booking should be made at least a few weeks in advance *(for details, see box below)*. For those who prefer boating activities of a more sporty nature, speedboat, jet-ski and wake-board rentals are offered at almost all of Estonia's sea-side resorts, such as Pärnu and Haapsalu. Windsurfing is also a popular coastal activity, and the relatively safe shallow waters are a good place to learn.

Diving is another aqua-sport popular in all three countries. Tallinn, Kipsala Island in Rīga, and Lithuania's Kaunas have diving centres that offer certified courses with trained professionals as well as open-water dives. There is diving in some lakes, too, but the best place for

WHERE TO FIND OUT MORE

Ballooning: Lithuania, Eurocentras, Vilnius, tel: 370 8 527 32702, *www.ballooning.lt*; Lithuania, Nemunaicia, tel: 370 611 20911, *www.orobalionai.lt*.

Diving Latvia, *www.divers.lv*; Kaunas, X-Pro extreme sports centre, tel: 370 377 64390; Tallinn, Diving Club Maremark, tel: 372 601 3446.

Flight and paragliding: Lithuania, Kaunas Flyers Club, tel: 370 251389. Latvia, Altius (hot air ballooning), Riga, (tel: 761 1614, www.altius.lv.

Horse riding: Lithuania, Belmonto horse riding, Vilnius, tel: 370 5260 0236; Rieses village, Vilnius, tel: 370 6982 2135; Latvia, Kavalkade Riders' Club, Jūrmala, tel: 371 941 5916;

Estonia, Sammull farm, Viljandi county, tel: 372 526 9100; Kivisaare riding farm, Harju county, tel: 372 5663 1520.

Sea excursiuons, Estonia, *www.holidayresort.ee* and *www.parnu.ee*.

Sigulda and Gauja National Park *www.sigulda.lv*.

Skydiving *www.dropzone.com*; Lithuania, *www.skydive.lt*; Estonia, *www.skydive.ee*; Latvia, *www.skydive.lv*.

Water activities, Latvia, *www.udensklubs.lv*; Lithuania, *www.palangatic.lt*.

Winter sports: Estonia, *www.otepaa.ee*; Latvia, *www.sigulda.lv* or *www.gaizinkalns.lv*; Lithuania, *www.tourism.lt*.

diving is off the coast, where one can explore the Baltic Sea's deep underwater secrets, including wreck sites.

Extreme and airborne sports

Extreme sports are all the rage in the Baltics. Lithuania has long been keen on daredevil activities, such as the annual ice-horse race on Lake Sartai. With a history as turbulent as theirs, it comes as little surprise that Lithuanians indulge life to its maximum, often throwing caution to the wind.

There is possibly no better way to take in the patchwork Lithuanian countryside than from above. The Kaunas Flyers Club offers delta-plane flights and paragliding – stepping stones in aviation development – for recreational enjoyment. Professional lessons are provided for beginners, though flights depend on weather conditions.

Skydiving has also, as it were, taken off. Founded in 1992 at Pociunai Airfield, the Kaunas Skydiving Club is the oldest parachute club in Lithuania and one of the most popular in the Baltics. The club is open every weekend from March to October and organises more than 5,000 jumps a year. Although the majority of skydivers are familiar to the sport, the club's professional staff offers training for beginners, who can choose a static-line or tandem jump.

Hot-air ballooning is a less intimidating way to enjoy the landscape from the air. A tradition that goes back for years, all three countries have air-balloon festivals that bring a rainbow of floating ornaments to the skies each summer. The rides are an ideal way to enjoy a scenic evening of relaxation, with baskets comfortably carrying up to three people. For a cityscape ballooning trip visit Eurocentras in Vilnius. For a taste of rustic scenery, Nemunaitis village in the Alytus district of Lithuania is the best place to call.

Horse riding

For centuries, horse riding has been perhaps the most traditional and best-enjoyed outdoor activity. Even today, Balts treasure this age-old way of getting around that carries a trail of culture and folklore behind it. The flat lands make hacking easy and whether it's bareback riding along the coastal dunes of Latvia or keeping to the tame wooded paths of Estonia, riding is one of the most romantic ways to enjoy the outdoors. There are numerous stables and riding clubs throughout all three countries that offer lessons for every level.

Winter sports

The polar freeze that strikes northeastern Europe from mid-November, lasting until late March, has earned quite a name for Baltic winters. Yet the long snowy days serve as the perfect excuse to head to the country for some

snowy winter sports and hot mulled wine. Temperatures in all three Baltic states sink to between 0 and –15°C (32–5°F) during the winter. With a generous snowfall, these temperatures create ideal skiing conditions. There are no Alpine peaks – the highest it gets in the Baltics is 318-metre (1,044-ft) Suur Munam gi (Big Egg Hill) in Estonia. Yet that same country's "winter capital", Otepää, has ski jumps and holds the World Cup Cross-Country Skiing Championship each January.

Winter sports such as skiing, snowboarding, hockey, ski-mobiling – even ice fishing – manage to keep Baltic inhabitants entertained all season long. ❑

LEFT: a horse is a good all-weather friend, and the countryside is ideal for hacking.
RIGHT: skiier in Otepää, Estonia's "winter capital".

FOOD

Baltic food is basic and not heavily flavoured, relying on the
natural ingredients of its waterways, farms and back gardens

Baltic cooking today is basically pretty straightforward country fare. The plain, wholesome, unspicy dishes characteristic of all three countries – although especially Latvia and Estonia – demand little artistry, but nevertheless can be very good.

The best place to see what's in the Baltic larder is in Rīga where, if your schedule allows, you should take an hour or two to peruse the disused Zeppelin hangars that house the city's massive – and extremely crowded – market. Scores of indoor stalls tout fresh and fermented dairy products: vast slabs of soft white cheese, harder yellow cheese, bottles of sour cream, yoghurt and cultivated sour milk. In another hall, high-quality fresh pork gleams pink, and many varieties of sausage and ham wait to be sampled. Smoked fish sells at one end of the market, while delicious fresh fruit is on offer at the other.

In summer, baskets are piled high with early apples and pears – small irregular specimens that are not subject to the trading controls that are all too familar in Western Europe; glass tumblers spill over with red and black berries and tiny yellow mirabelle plums. Look out for the different varieties of nuts, the dried fruit, the umbrils of caraway seed drying on the branch, huge bunches of fresh, strong, flat-leaf parsley, pots of honey, barrels of sauerkraut lined up for tasting and trays of fresh, home-made black, brown and white bread. These staple foods, which are brought in by private sellers from the nearby countryside, are the raw materials of traditional Baltic cooking.

Lightly seasoned

These ingredients are usually served at the table with very little seasoning. In the vegetable hall you may smell dill and garlic – but for flavour Latvia mostly relies on fermented milk, smoked fish and cheese, and bacon, with a sprinkling

LEFT: the stalls are piled high in Rīga's huge market, one of the wonders of the Baltics.
RIGHT: garlic and camomile.

here and there of caraway seed, rather than strong herbs and spices. Onions are considered too strong to feature heavily. Lithuanian cooking, partly influenced by the Orient, is the most pungent of the three.

This hint of Oriental spice in Lithuanian cooking is a result of the country's complicated

political past. From the 15th century exiled Crimean Tatars and refugees from the Golden Horde flocked to this powerful state to coexist with Russians, Belarussians and Poles under the leadership of the Polish/Lithuanian noble class. The results today are a half-forgotten legacy of exoticism and luxury, recipes which dare to include black pepper and nutmeg and marjoram. Spices were imported from the East; marjoram was probably brought into the country from Italy, via Catholic Poland.

With independence came a rediscovery of the richness of Estonian, Latvian and Lithuanian traditional country-style cooking. In each of the three capitals, countless traditional restaurants have opened, typically offering heavy butter-doused Lithuanian *cepelinai* and other traditional dishes. However, the best local cooking can usually still be sampled in private homes.

Bread baskets

Excellent natural resources, quality farming and careful husbandry contribute to the goodness of Baltic food. The lush land provides rich harvests of grains and berries, dark forests provide the ideal environment for mushroom growth, fish populate the rivers, lakes and sea, and pig and dairy farming are important industries.

Excellent bread, especially rye bread, comes

hotels and which should not be judged by the dryness and sourness it exudes when left indefinitely exposed to the air. (Don't let this put you off.) Among the white breads are the robust and versatile French *baton*, not at all like its Gallic counterpart, and the creamy-coloured sourdough loaves that are usually home-made and well worth seeking out for their extraordinary muscular texture.

These breads, which are also very popular in Germany, Poland, Russia, Sweden and Finland, are top class, especially now that private producers are offering previously rare wholegrain varieties. More than one Western traveller has

from this northern part of the world, where the hardiest of the cereal crops flourishes even in cold, poor soil. Rye bread, which has a strong rich taste, is enhanced by molasses, made from native-growing sugarbeet, and caraway seed. This bread keeps well and is an ideal accompaniment to the local beer, cheeses and pungent cured meat and fish. One type of pale rye loaf, which has a smooth, shiny, tan-coloured crust, is widely known as Rīga bread and is best eaten when it is fresh and sweet. (Most bakers hang a two-pronged testing fork beside their self-service shelves.)

Other Baltic speciality breads include the plain dark rye variety that is often served in

made a meal out of bread alone, to the consternation of the locals who cry: "But where's the sausage to go with it, or the butter?" (In the Baltics they love their meats and fats.)

Porridge and potatoes

Although porridge used to be a staple food in these parts, porridges made from cooked grain are now rarely seen on menus except on special occasions. The ancient Latvian version, called *putra*, is made of barley (or a mix of barley and potato) and typically served with a ladle of bacon fat, some smoked meat or fish, or perhaps also with milk products, as a main course. In Estonia mixed-grain porridges are sometimes served with milk. There is also a breakfast speciality that is akin to Scottish porridge: *kama*, made of ground toasted grains and raw oats is mixed with yoghurt or milk and eaten with salt or honey. *Kama* is good for upset stomachs.

These gruels make good use of the region's barley, which doesn't have enough leaven in it to be used in the preparation of modern bread. There is another dish that is similar to porridge; this speciality is made of mushy peas and then eaten with bacon fat. Grey field peas eaten with fatty bacon is another local favourite in Latvia.

BEST RESTAURANTS

For a list of the best restaurants in the Baltic States *see Travel Tips, page 347.*

meaning that this potassium-rich foodstuff plays a part in most daily diets. Yeast-leavened wheat dough – the food stuff from which genuine pizza bases are made – is another staple carbohydrate here. On street corners in Tallinn you can buy slightly sweet white dough made from this yeast-leavened wheat, which tastes deliciously fresh.

In Latvia the array of savoury baking is highly enviable. Special treats include cheese- and meat-filled yeast-dough buns and yeast-dough horns stuffed to the brim with minced bacon. If

If a Lithuanian were asked to name his or her favourite dish, it would probably be something prepared with potato. The Baltic Germans introduced this tuber to the Baltics at the start of the 18th century, and the whole region fell for its charms, especially the Lithuanians. Today they eat boiled potatoes with everything from yoghurt to bacon fat, and, like the Poles and the Jews, they are fans of grated potato pancakes. The same grated potato is used to make a variety of filled rissoles, such as *cepelinai*,

pizza makes you think of pasta, look no further than Lithuania, where cooking is strongly influenced by the Russian and Polish fondness for Slavic *tortellini* – another Baltic treat.

Fat feasts

One of the hallmarks of Baltic food is the non-prevalence of protein. Meat and fish, at least in Latvia and Estonia, are traditionally eaten in very small quantities, almost as a dressing or garnish to the bread, pasta or porridge as the focus of a meal. Rich, fatty foods, rather than lean meats, tend to prove most popular at special feasts.

Although fat features so prominently in the Baltic diet, however, it is interesting to note

LEFT: mushrooms are plentiful in the woods.
ABOVE: *Grūdenis* is a thick country stew from Latvia that uses a pig's head.

that traditional food here is rarely fried. Vegetables and carbohydrates are typically boiled first and are then covered later with fat – whether it's in the form of bacon, cheese or, quite simply, butter.

Pork is without doubt the most commonly eaten meat, though quality beef is also available, as well as game, including duck and sometimes hare. (The term pork covers salt pork, sausage and the black pudding – blood sausage – that Estonians traditionally eat every year on Christmas Day.)

In the 15th century Lithuania was highly renowned for its smoked wild boar. Domestic

pig farming was later introduced by the Germans with exceptional results. This pork-production industry was so successful that smoked lean pork from the Baltics, all pink, wrinkled, juicy and tender, is believed to have been the stuff of many a privileged Communist Party banquet. Smoked lean pork is certainly more inviting than the whole wedges of salted pork fat, the dietary mainstay of the labouring male peasant in the early 1900s, which are still classed as a delicacy.

On commercial menus you will come across hot, fresh meat dishes more familiar to the visitor than anything mentioned so far. In many restaurants, meat cutlets, fried escalopes, meat-

balls and boiled and fried sausages are more often than not prepared by foreign chefs.

Fish dishes

If you like fish, you'll find there is much in the way of local delicacies to tempt you here. Local fish preparations, such as smoked saltwater salmon, pickled herring, smoked sprats and smoked eel, rank among the best fish dishes in the world. If you travel around the fishing villages, you will have the chance of sampling locally-smoked fish, while around the inland lake districts you are likely to encounter freshwater fish dishes, notably those using trout, pike and pike-perch.

In Latvia and Lithuania fish is often cooked in bacon fat – a rare case of frying. Russian caviar, which was once the pride of every restaurant menu, is becoming increasingly difficult to find and is now very expensive. More affordable are the Estonian fresh fish soups, which are made with vegetables and then thickened with flour and milk.

Cold dishes

Until early in the 20th century two-thirds of traditional Baltic dishes were those for its cold table. This is something that seems to come especially into its own at breakfast time, when a mix of cheese and meat, as well as vegetables and cream, is served. At other times of the day, the cold table is often supplemented with soup.

Salads are an important part of the cold table. They are usually accompanied by dressings and eaten with bread. One of the culinary highlights of a visit can be a bowl of tomatoes and cucumbers picked straight from a country garden, tossed with fresh dill and parsley and sour cream. Sometimes strips of meat or cheese are used in the same way as raw vegetables to make composite salads for the cold table but often these are covered in bottled flavourings. Unfortunately, they represent only a poor attempt at a quick urban cuisine adapted from the country.

Soups

Although there are old recipes in Lithuania for varieties of beetroot soup along the lines of the Russian/Ukrainian/Polish beetroot-based *borscht*, and for mushroom soup, this liquid dish is most typically found on the menus of cheaper eateries. Lithuanian beetroot soup has a sweet-and-sour base and is usually flavoured with sorrel, a rich source of iron and vitamin C.

Estonian food is generally fairly mild and its soups are no exception. A classic Estonian soup contains milk, dried peas and buckwheat grains and the majority of varieties on this are made with milk and vegetables, or with yoghurt and dill cucumber.

Under German influence, Latvia and Estonia used to make a sweet bread soup out of leftover fruit. Since the bread was probably sour and black the soup was closely related to the sour-sweet kīselis made with summer berries. Beer soups belong to this curious category.

and you should look out for local cheeses while travelling round the country.

Garden produce

The country garden is something that is celebrated in all three states, and it cannot be stressed highly enough how vital a part it plays in Baltic culture. One of the most charming and notable poems in Lithuanian literature – one that is frequently, and many believe quite rightly, compared to Virgil's *Eclogues* – is called *The Seasons*, written by an 18th-century clergyman, Kristijonas Donelaitis. In the kitchen garden, which became popular in

Special occasions

Christmas Day is celebrated with pork dishes in Estonia, goose in Protestant Latvia, and fish and mushrooms in Catholic Lithuania. At midsummer – an important date in the Baltic calendar – the dairy products come into their own.

A special dense yellow country cheese, smoked and flavoured with caraway seeds, is traditionally produced for midsummer (Jāņi, or St John's Day) in Latvia; a similar, spicier cheese is eaten in Lithuania. You can sample both of these varieties in Rīga's Central Market,

LEFT: cold beetroot soup, a summer dish.
ABOVE: strawberries, just one of many forest fruits.

BERRIES FROM THE FORESTS

Blueberries, bilberries, cloudberries, cranberries, lingonberries, raspberries, strawberries, whortleberries… there are a wonderful kaleidescope of berries found in the Baltic forests and bogs. You can come across these in roadside stalls, as well as in restaurants and on the dining table. Try corn pancakes with berries and yoghurt for breakfast, or as pies and tarts or flavoured ice creams. Buy them bottled or in jams in markets and shops. There are juices and country fruit wines, and gins flavoured with berries – including juniper berries, which are often used in cooking. Anyone with a garden will grow berries and currants along with their flowers.

Donelaitis's time, the sweetest tomatoes, ridge cucumbers, courgettes, beets, kohlrabi, potatoes, swede and turnips grow in profusion alongside peas and cabbages and rhubarb. Somewhere near the vegetable garden you will also find apple trees and plum trees and, in an ideal world, a beehive. A guest might enjoy an inspiring summer tea made from baked sour windfall apples sweetened with clear plum jam and macaroons. Nothing is wasted.

Another crop that is increasing in importance in Latvia and Lithuania is sea buckthorn, which produces a juice full of minerals.

Cakes

At the opposite end of the spectrum from the healthy ideal of the country garden is the Baltic sweet trolley. Nowadays, cakes are generally more popular than desserts in the Baltics and there are some excellent specialist chocolate shops. In Lithuania, look out for treecakes and honey cakes. Treecakes are made by adding dough in layers to a rotating wooden pole in front of a hot fire. The result is a cake with many age lines and fungi-like appendages clinging to its outer "bark", where dollops of egg and lemon dough have been added. Despite its peculiar appearance, it is quite delicious.

In cafés, where many varieties of short-breads, shortcrust and flaky pastries, and eclairs are sold, you can't help noticing that Latvians and Estonians have a penchant for eating large amounts of sweet whipped cream with their cakes. Chocolate cafés are the in-thing in Rīga.

Drinks and picnics

Coffee is one dietary feature that distinguishes Russia from the Baltics: coffee is far more prevalent here. Note that both tea and coffee are served without milk. Soft fizzy drinks are widely available here. Mineral water is normally good-quality, although some varieties are pumped full of unpalatable salts and are hence rather unsuccessful at quenching thirst. Note that it is not safe to drink tap water in Rīga – always buy bottled water instead.

If you are in the mood for something stronger, you'll find that the majority of bars and cafés serve beer on tap rather than in bottles. The main breweries (Kalnapilis and Utenos in Lithuania, Aldaris in Latvia and Saku and A le Cocq in Estonia) all have their loyal following. The local brews are available on tap in most restaurants. Varieties range from dark beer to the latest craze of ice beer.

Herbal *eau-de-vie*, Rīga Black Balsam (a dark brew, which tastes like a mixture of treacle and Campari), sweet Lithuanian liqueurs, locally produced Russian vodka and sparkling wines complete the standard alcoholic line-up. You may also find expensive wines from France and less costly but decent vintages from Georgia, Hungary and Romania.

Traditional food is something that many Balts think of as something they make at home, but wouldn't necessarily look for when they go out, hence its scarcity in the restaurant. The best local food is therefore enjoyed in private homes or in the form of a picnic, composed of some of the delicacies offered at a typical Baltic cold table – excellent fresh vegetables, cold meats and tasty, albeit mild cheeses. Although the fare served in long-established hotels may seem rather heavy and fatty to the diet-conscious, health-obsessed Westerner, it can certainly work wonders for an empty stomach.

More imaginitive chefs, however, are beginning to look at ways of using traditional ingredients in a new way. ❑

LEFT: chocolate shop in Vilnius. **RIGHT:** buying treecakes and other festive items in Kazioko market, Vilnius.

The Baltic States

PLACES

The principal sites in this detailed guide to the three countries are clearly cross-referenced by number to the maps

Added together, the three Baltic states, each covering about the same area, are a little larger than England and Wales, or the size of Washington State. They sit side by side on the eastern edge of the Baltic Sea between Poland and the Gulf of Finland. Tallinn, the northernmost capital, is on roughly the same latitude as Scotland's Orkney islands and southern Alaska. Vilnius, capital of Lithuania in the south, shares an approximate latitude with Newcastle and Newfoundland. This means that summer days lengthen into white nights and winter days are grey and short.

Although they have linguistic, cultural and historic differences, the three countries share a similar landscape and coastline. The overwhelming image is one of quiet roads and flat lands, rising in low, rolling hills towards the east, of myriad small rivers and lakes and of forests of the tallest pines. This is one of the most underpopulated regions of Europe. Scattered through it all are ancient hill forts and occasional boulders, "presents from Scandinavia" left by retreating glaciers. Like some of the oldest trees, these have frequently been bestowed with magical properties.

The human landscape is essentially rural, with vast tracts of arable and pasture lands, bogs and forests. Some of the remaining neoclassical manors, built by the occupying Russians, Scandinavians, Germans and Poles, have been converted into restaurants, hotels or cultural centres. In the cities, it is the legacy of these conquerors and their religions that prevail, in particular the Hansa merchants who for centuries monopolised trade. Urban development in Soviet times left the capitals' old towns largely untouched and now, spruced up and inviting, each is a Unesco World Heritage Site.

There is a lot of pride in the home, too. Domestic architecture of two- and three-storey houses built of solid wooden planks is still evident, and many run-down country farms patched up with utilitarian corrugated-iron roofs have been reclaimed and are being revitalised with thatch and shingle. Pride in the countryside and local craftsmanship has resulted in a number of rural museums, as well as museums devoted to folklore, poets and local heroes.

The Baltic Sea's "Amber Coast" is a wonder of endless white pristine beaches backed by dunes and pine forests, which stretch for hundreds of miles. Its rest homes and cure houses, spas and safe swimming beaches have made its resorts popular for millions.

Travelling through these three European countries by public transport is slow but not difficult, and the roads are not always in good repair. But a visit to one country can easily include a day or two in part of another. ❏

PRECEDING PAGES: winter rider, Estonia; summer sands, Curonian Spit, Lithuania.

ESTONIA

*The smallest of the three countries has a fairytale capital
and hundreds of lakes and islands*

The northernmost of the Baltic states is *Eesti Vabariik*, the Republic of Estonia. It is also the smallest, least densely populated of the three countries. On the south side of the Gulf of Finland, its capital, Tallinn, is 53 miles (85 km) from Helsinki and about 130 km (80 miles) from St Petersburg. Finns have long taken advantage of Estonia's proximity and relative cheapness, making the ferry crossing in droves, where a lot of their money is spent on alcohol. Other European visitors have joined their ranks, particularly cruise-ship passengers and weekenders from the UK.

It is easy to see the attraction: Tallinn has the prettiest old town in the Baltics, a medieval enclave set on a hillock above its port. Within the fairy-tale walls and towers and beneath the Gothic spires are winding cobbled lanes leading to the old square. Beside this ensemble, a rapidly developing commercial district is redrawing the city's skyline and giving locals more places to spend their new-found wealth. Some of this wealth comes from hi-tech industries. Tallinn is one of the most switched-on cities in the world.

Estonia has a second city in Tartu in the south, a distinguished university town that brims with student life. The historic, west-coast towns of Pärnu and Haapsalu are popular health resorts, and maintain a pace of life that's decidedly more relaxed than in the capital. A very different scene can be found in the industrial northeast of the country, particularly in the city of Narva, which has a high ethnic Russian population and is struggling to find its place in the new European Union economy. Much of the Russian border is otherwise taken up by Lake Peipsi, the fourth-largest lake in Europe, where a settlement of Old Believers flourishes.

Beyond the urban areas, nearly 40 percent of the country is forested with pine, spruce and junipers, and inhabited by moose, brown bears and beavers. Lahemaa is the largest of four national parks, with a shoreline east of Tallinn. Its rocky outcrops are part of the limestone Baltic Glint that stretches from Scandinavia into Russia. There are also four nature reserves, and Estonia's commitment to the environment keeps beaches clean.

The land is generally flat and unpopulated. Nearly half of it is made up of forests, while marshes, wetlands and peat bogs provide habitats for many unusual plants and wildlife. There are around 1,500 lakes and as many islands. The largest islands, off the west coast, are Hiiumaa and Saaremaa, rural backwaters where the earliest stone churches in the Baltics can be found. More peaceful surroundings are hard to imagine. ❏

PRECEDING PAGES: island family, Saaremaa; Maiasmokk Kohvik, Tallinn's oldest cafe, which opened in 1864. **LEFT:** Pärnu beach

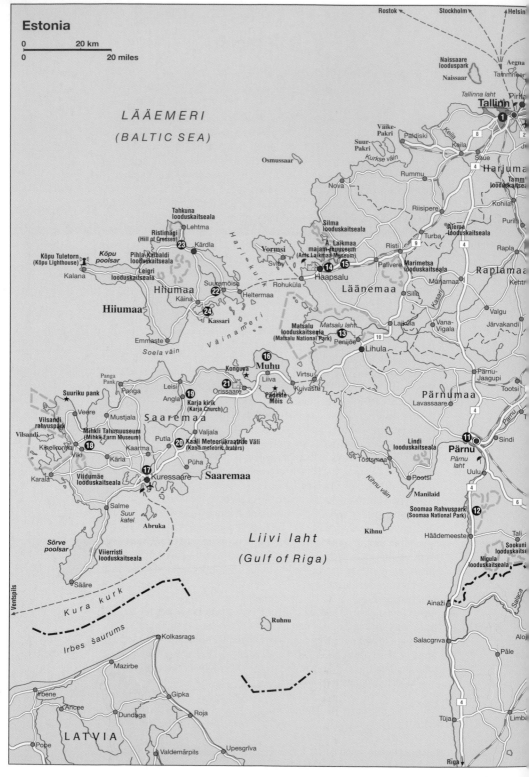

Estonia

0   20 km
0   20 miles

LÄÄEMERI
(BALTIC SEA)

Rostok ◣   Stockholm ◥   ◥ Helsin

Naissaare
loouspark
Naissaar   Aegna
                            Tammneer

Tallinna laht   Pirita
Tallinn ①   ②

Väike-
Pakri   Paldiski   Keila
Suur-   ⑧
Pakri   Kurkse väin   Keila   Ji
                                Saue
Osmussaar   ④ Harjuma

Rummu   Tamm
                              loouskaitsea
Nova   Riisipere   Kohila

Silma   Purila
loouskaitseala   ④lema
A. Laikmaa   Turba loouskaitsea
majam-muuseum Risti   Rapla
Vormsi (Arts Laikmaa Museum) ⑨   ④
Tahkuna   ⑭ ⑮ Palivere   Raplamaa
loouskaitseala   Marimetsa
Lehtma   Sviby   Haapsalu loouskaitseala   Kehtr
Ristimägi   Mänamaa
(Hill of Crosses) ㉓ Kärdla   Rohuküla Läänemaa Sild Valgu
Kõpu Tuletorn Kõpu Pihla-Kaibaldi   Siila Vana-   Järvakandi
(Kõpu Lighthouse) poolsar loouskaitseala Laikula Vigala
            Leigri Suuremõisa Heltermaa   ⑩
Kalana   loouskaitseala ㉒ Matsalu laht
            Hiiumaa   Matsalu   Lihula
        Käina   loouskaitseala ⑬
Hiiumaa   ㉔   (Matsalu National Park) Penijõe
        Kassari   Väinameri   Pärnu-
Emmaste   Jaagupi
    Soela väin   Muhu   Tootsi
                    Konguva ⑯   Virtsu   Pärnumaa
Panga   Leisi   Liiva Kuivastu Lavassaare
Pank Panga Angla ⑲ Orissaare ㉑   Pädeste ④
Suuriku pank   Karja kirik Mõis
        Veere Mustjala (Karja Church)   Lindi Pärnu ⑪
Vilsandi   Saaremaa Valjala   loouskaitseala Sindi
rahvuspark Mihkli Talumuuseum Putla   Pärnu ⑪
Vilsandi   (Mihkli Farm Museum) ⑳ Kaali Meteorikraatrite Väli Pärnu
Kihelkonna ⑱   Kaarma (Kaali meteoric craters) Tõstamaa laht
    Viki Kärla Püha   Pootsi Uulu
Karala   ㉗ Kuressaare Saaremaa   Manilaid
        Viidumäe   Saaremaa   ④
        loouskaitseala   ⑥
    Salme   Kuressaare   Soomaa Rahvuspark
Sõrve Suur   (Soomaa National Park) ⑫
poolsar katel Abruka   Tali
        Viierristi   Häädemeeste Sookuni
        loouskaitseala   loouskaitse
                                Nigula
    Sääre   loouskaitseala
        Kura kurk   Liivi laht
                    (Gulf of Riga)   Ainaži
    Irbes šaurums
                    Ruhnu   Salacgriva Aloj
Ventspils   Pāle
        Kolkasrags
    Mazirbe   ④
Irbene   Tūja Limba
    Ancee
        Dundaga Roja   Riga
LATVIA
    Pope Valdemārpils Upesgrīva

THE MAKING OF ESTONIA

Estonians' origins were "not of Europe", according to an early
traveller. Nobody could have such a thought today

In the days when visitors to Estonia often arrived by sea, the first glimpse of Tallinn, the capital, made a lasting impression. Its ancient ruins and quaint houses with steeply peaked roofs, more Mediterranean than Baltic, captivated many visitors. In summer, it might have been the South of France, with early 19th-century Russians making an annual summer pilgrimage from St Petersburg. "I have seen delicate creatures," wrote an English visitor in 1841, "who at first were lifted from the carriage to the bathing-house, restored day by day, and in a fortnight's time bathing with a zest that seemed to renew all their energies."

In the evenings, "a band of military music plays, and restaurants offer ices, chocolate, etc., and you parade about and your friends join you, and you sit down and the gnats sting you; and if you don't like this, you may adjourn to the *salle de danse* close by, where the limbs so late floating listlessly on the waves now twirl round in the hurrying waltz."

Estonia had been a Russian province since 1721, and while the lot of the Estonian peasant had been pathetic for many years (and most ethnic Estonians were peasants) tsarist rule became increasingly repressive. By the late 19th century there were no more foreign tourists, Russians excepted, and as far as most foreigners were concerned, Estonia ceased to exist.

A curious race

A declaration of Estonian independence after World War I caught the world by surprise. Russia, torn apart by revolution, was unable to do much to counter the move. Authors of travel guides rushed in to appraise the reincarnated nation. "The broad visage of the Estonian," wrote one, as if reporting on a newly arrived specimen at a zoo, "has slanting eyes, low forehead, high cheekbones and projecting lower jaw." His conclusion was that Estonian origins were "not of Europe".

Estonian independence lasted only until World War II. It then disappeared under the even heavier hand of communist Russia and was presumed lost for all time. Rather suddenly in 1988, extraordinary reports were received in the West of a "Singing Revolution". Tens of thousands apparently spent that summer giving throaty voice to all the old Estonian songs and defiantly waving the long-hidden national flag. Within two years, although not without moments of nail-biting uncertainty, Estonia was independent again.

For all the ravages of a Soviet economic policy that had aimed at turning Estonia into an annexe of heavy industry, much of the character that delighted visitors of 150 years ago had survived. Russians were still visiting in droves, but for the "Old European" atmosphere and the food rather than the beaches and swimming, which were prime casualties of environmental vandalism. As for the newly independent Estonians, they seemed to have borne the

---

LEFT: Saaremaa islanders, around 1920.
RIGHT: fishing village in the early 20th century.

burden of the previous half-century with fortitude. The "non-European" physical features of
the ethnic Estonians are a reflection of Finno-
Ugric ancestry. Because of the similarities
between the Estonian and Finnish languages,
Estonians had been able to follow Finnish television during the Soviet era. Its terms of reference did not flatter the Soviet system.

Estonia's frontiers have been chopped and
changed over the centuries. Their present con-
figuration makes Estonia a country of some
44,000 sq. km (17,000 sq. miles), small enough
to be covered by a day's driving in any direction, with a population of less than 1.4 million

of whom about 68 percent are ethnic Estonians. The remaining 32 percent are predominantly Russians, most of them relatively recent
arrivals sent in to man the industries which represented Estonia's role in the Soviet economic
scheme. A few people living in the eastern part
of the country are the descendants of 17th-
century Old Believers, a sect that fled from
Russia to escape, among other things, the tax
that Peter the Great imposed on the beards they
traditionally wore. An additional group are the
diluted remnants of Estonia's most influential
settlers, the Germans. The latter came in two
guises: the first were 13th-century Teutonic
knights who arrived ostensibly as bearers of

Christianity but also as migrants with an urgent
need to find somewhere to live, having recently
fallen on hard times in the Holy Land; these
people were followed by German craftsmen
and merchants who formed the burgher class
that ultimately monopolised the towns and
cities. To an unusual degree, Estonians have
taken a back seat while others have written their
history. These 13th-century Germans were not
the first to arrive, and there were others who
followed after them.

Hardy beginnings

The future Finns and Estonians were among
the first tribes to drift across Europe from Asia.
Leaving the lower slopes of the Urals, they followed the river courses, subsisting mainly on
fish and clothing themselves in animal skins.
They had already reached the Baltic coast when
mentioned by Tacitus in the 1st century AD.
"Strangely beast-like and squalidly poor, neither arms nor homes have they. Their food is
herbs, their clothing skin, their bed the earth.
They trust wholly to their arrows, which, for
want of iron, are pointed with bone… Heedless of men, heedless of gods, they have
attained that hardest of results, the not needing
so much as a wish."

There seems to have been some pushing and
shoving among new arrivals on the Baltic
shores, especially when large numbers of
Slavs turned up, but eventually the future
Finns, Estonians, Latvians and Lithuanians
took up positions in more or less the pattern
that persists today.

The first conquerors were the Danes under
Valdemar II, who arrived with what should
have been an invincible armada of 1,000 ships.
The Estonians resisted the invasion so fiercely
that the Danes were in danger of being routed.
They were rescued, so the story goes, by a red
banner with a white cross floating down from
heaven – the image that was to inspire the
future Danish flag. Their spirits up, they took
possession of Tallinn.

Some years earlier, in 1200, around 500
heavily armed German knights had landed further south in the Gulf of Rīga with a commis-
sion to spread the word of God. They did so
more efficiently than the Danes, who were
themselves recent converts.

In the end, the Danes asked the Teutonic
knights to lend a hand against the Estonian

pagans. The knights tackled the task with customary efficiency and declared, in 1227, that, finally, the job had been accomplished. The knights transformed an economy, which had previously rested on primitive agriculture and products of the forest, into one of the best centres of farming and commerce of the Middle Ages. They constructed castles and founded towns everywhere, filling them with craftsmen and merchants recruited from Germany. Their social system was simple: Germans occupied the positions of noble,

mans that they sought the protection of Sweden. Under Gustavus Adolphus, Sweden was energetically bent on expanding their Baltic holdings, but there was no desire to tamper unnecessarily with a German infrastructure which worked so profitably. Later Swedish kings, particularly Charles XI, did interfere by taking over German-owned estates and either giving them to Swedes or, increasingly, keeping them for themselves. The dispossessed and disgruntled who had previously turned to Sweden for protection

burgher and merchant; the Estonians were serfs. This system survived political and religious change for seven centuries. In the year 1347, the Danish monarchy was desperate for cash. Tallinn, or Reval as it came to be known, was sold off to the efficient and prosperous knights.

A large part of the commercial success of Reval and Narva, Estonia's two ports, was due to a virtual monopoly on trade to and from Russia. When Ivan III seized Narva and made it a Russian port it so alarmed the Baltic Ger-

LEFT: 15th-century Danish soldier in Tallin.
ABOVE: Alexander Nevski defeats German Crusaders in the "Battle of the Ice" on Lake Peipsi in 1242.

against Russia, decided they now needed protection from Sweden. With perfect impartiality, they turned to Russia. Peter the Great readily agreed to help.

The battle for Narva

The outcome was the titanic struggle between Peter and the equally legendary Charles XII of Sweden. A Russian force 35,000 strong made for Narva, held by a much smaller Swedish garrison in the castle. Charles, who was not yet 20, hurried to its aid. He arrived with 8,000 men and, in the middle of a snow storm, plunged straight into battle. The Russians were cut to pieces, losing every piece of artillery

Peter possessed. Charles's advisers urged him to press on to Moscow, but the young leader had other ideas. "There is no glory in winning victories over the Muscovites," he said breezily, "they can be beaten at any time."

While Charles went off in pursuit of other enemies, Peter laid the foundations of Petersburg and planned a second attack on Narva. He entrusted the command to a Scot named Ogilvie who not only succeeded in overwhelming the garrison but decided, apparently independently, to take no prisoners, military or civilian. A terrible massacre was finally stopped by the arrival of Peter the Great in the country.

pounded by plague. With the Peace of Nystad in 1721, Sweden finally ceded its Baltic possessions and Estonia, for one, prepared for its first taste of Russian rule.

Like the Swedes, Peter was not inclined to upset the way the German hierarchy ran Estonia, and the Estonians continued, according to one commentator, "to live and die like beasts, happy if they could subsist on dusky bread and water". Nothing much had changed by the middle of the 19th century. Lady Eastlake, who moved in privileged circles during her stay, kept her eyes open and provides a wonderful insight into conditions. The ruling Tsar

He is said to have stopped the proceedings by cutting down some of the crazed attackers with his own sword. Moreover, he said, there was a perfectly good use for able-bodied Swedish prisoners: the conditions at the Petersburg building site were so bad that the workforce was dropping like flies.

With Narva under his belt, Peter turned to Reval and its Swedish garrison. The defenders put up a great fight but ultimately they succumbed to thirst and an outbreak of plague. The Great Northern War between Peter and Charles was far from over, however, and in the course of fighting that swept across Europe the Baltic states were utterly devastated, the horror com-

VIEW OF THE ESTONIAN PEASANT

Early travellers were from the upper crust, and could not be expected to have much empathy with the working man. Lady Eastlake reported of the Estonian peasant, "Beyond his strict adherence to his church, we can find but little interesting in his character; nor indeed is it fair to look for any, excepting perhaps that of a servile obedience or cunning evasion, among a people so long oppressed… Provided he can have a pipe in his mouth, and lie sleeping at the bottom of his cart, while his patient wife drives the willing little rough horse… Offer him wages for his labour, and he will tell you, with the dullest bumpkin look, that if he works more he must eat more."

Nicholas I was so paranoid about revolutionaries – the insurrections of 1848 were just around the corner – that police surveillance everywhere was oppressive. If nothing else, though, it kept crime figures low. Over a whole year, Lady Eastlake reported, there had been only 87 misdemeanours among Reval's 300,000 population, "and five of these consist merely in travelling without a passport".

Most illuminating of all, perhaps, are Lady Eastlake's observations about the cloud that hung over young men in the form of military service in the Russian Army. The conscripts were chosen by ballot, No. 1 being the unlucky

to seek his daily bread by his own exertions for the remainder of his life, or to be chargeable to his parish, who by this time have forgotten that he ever existed, and certainly wish he had never returned."

Impossible choices

The last years of the 19th century saw the emergence of the Young Estonians, a sign of awakening nationalism. The social order as they saw it was still dominated by the German hierarchy, but being anti-German did not make them pro-Russian. They were simply against the status quo, and for people in that mood Marxism was

number. "From the moment that the peasant of the Baltic provinces draws the fatal lot No. 1, he knows that he is a Russian, and, worse than that, a Russian soldier, and not only himself, but every son from that hour born to him; for, like the executioner's office in Germany, a soldier's life is hereditary… If wars and climate and sickness and hardship spare him, he returns after four-and-twenty years of service – his language scarce remembered, his religion changed, and with not a rouble in his pocket –

LEFT: *Reval [Tallinn], South Entrance to the Gulf of Finland*, 1856. ABOVE: Fat Margaret tower on fire during fighting between nationalists and Bolsheviks in 1917.

a very reasonable answer. The savage oppression of the St Petersburg uprising in 1905 destroyed any sympathy for the tsar. For most Estonians, World War I presented an impossible choice between Germany and Russia when, in truth, they would rather have been fighting against both. Nevertheless, tens of thousands found themselves in tsarist uniform, their plea to form their own units under their own officers falling on deaf ears.

The Russian Revolution in 1917 simplified the choice, the more so when it was announced that an Estonian national army was to be formed. About 170,000 volunteers immediately joined up, while many Estonians preferred to join the supposedly internationalist ranks of the Bolsheviks. From their various places of exile, members of a provisional Estonian government sent up a cry for independence.

Numerous fierce battles were fought over Tallinn between local Bolsheviks, who were backed by Red Guards, and the nationalist irregulars, who included schoolboys and the Tallinn fire brigade. The tide at first went in favour of the Bolsheviks and by the end of 1918 they held Narva and Tartu, and Russian comrades had advanced to within 20 miles of Tallinn. The struggle amounted to civil war and this was fought with all the savagery

Communists elsewhere in Estonia were not inclined to accept the new government. There was an attempted putsch in 1924 which resulted in street fighting in Tallinn. Numerous other disturbances were countered by increasingly authoritarian measures. In the end these amounted to dictatorship and the sad conclusion among Estonia's allies was that the country was not quite ripe for parliamentary democracy.

Prior to the war, more than half of Estonia had belonged to 200 German-Balt families. An Agrarian Reform Law passed after independence took over all baronial and feudal estates,

associated with such a terrible event.

The tide eventually turned, although not without considerable clandestine help given to the nationalists by the British Navy. The details are veiled to this day, but it seems to have involved using captured Russian destroyers and a series of raids by torpedo boats that penetrated the naval defences with which Peter the Great had ringed the Russian Baltic ports. The final battle was at Narva, and resulted in the nationalist coalition driving some 18,000 Bolsheviks across the Russian border. One year later, with the Bolsheviks still engaged in heavy fighting elsewhere, Russia renounced sovereignty over Estonia "voluntarily and for ever".

together with those belonging to the church and the former Russian Crown lands. The land was redistributed and 30,000 new farms created. The lot of the previously hapless peasant was further improved by the establishment of the right to engage in trade.

Estonia was still struggling to find its feet when any gains were put in jeopardy by the secret protocol of the 1939 Nazi-Soviet Pact. Stalin and Hitler agreed that the Soviet Union would annexe Estonia, Finland and Latvia, and Germany could claim Lithuania, although this was later amended to give Lithuania to Russia as well. A blatantly rigged election set the stage for an outright annexation on 6 August 1940, and almost immediately 60,000 Estonians went missing. They had been forcibly conscripted into the Soviet Army, deported to labour camps or executed.

The collapse of the Nazi-Soviet Pact naturally changed everything. German forces invaded in July 1941, meeting determined resistance in Estonia where large numbers of Soviet troops were cut off. Estonia had only about 1,000 Jewish families, nothing like the numbers of Latvia and Lithuania, but even so 90 percent of these were murdered as Germany set about incorporating the country in the Third Reich.

By the end of the war, however, some 70,000 Estonians had fled to the West, so one way or another the population dropped from its pre-war level of more than 1 million to no more than 850,000. The educated classes did not wait to find out what would happen when the German forces in Tallinn surrendered to the Red Army on 22 September 1944.

Russian invasion

Tens of thousands of those who did not flee were consigned to Soviet labour camps. The vacuum was filled by the arrival of comparable numbers of Russians with the dual purpose of manning heavy industry and completing the Russification programme begun by the tsars. There was little Estonians could do except to turn their television aerials towards Finland to see how their Finno-Ugric cousins were getting along.

At home, Soviet policies continued unabated so that during the 1980s the proportion of Russians and other Soviet implants living in the country rose to 40 percent. With virtually the whole of the country's industry under Moscow's remote control, no thought was given to the ecological impact of belching industrial works which in some instances were erected in established residential areas.

With their stars firmly attached to Moscow's wagon, Estonia's loyal Communist Party members were totally opposed to any sign of a nationalist revival in Estonia. The long-term implications of *Glasnost* and *Per-*

LEFT: a 1930s advertisement for pork products.
RIGHT: Soviet tanks thwart a German invasion of Estonia, from *La Domenica del Corriere*, August 1941.

SINGING REVOLUTION

In 1988 nearly a quarter of the population of Estonia gathered in Tallinn in a mass singing demonstration against the USSR.

estroika were, however, not lost on them, and they took no comfort at all from the 2,000 demonstrators who summoned up enough nerve to mourn the anniversary of the Nazi-Soviet Pact in Tallinn's Hirvepark in August 1987. In this respect, the party hard-liners and the large Russian minority were as one.

While members of the Estonian Heritage Society went about discreetly restoring national monuments, the radical-chic banner of environmental concern brought the independence movement to life. The first scent

of this potential awakening came with the cancellation of plans for increased open-pit phosphorus mining in the northeast of the country. This was followed by demands for economic self-management and then, most extraordinarily, came the "Singing Revolution".

The extent to which the Estonian establishment fell into line with the new mood was revealed when the Estonian Supreme Soviet defied the USSR Supreme Soviet by endorsing the legitimacy of a declaration of sovereignty. When the independence movement properly got under way, there were tense moments as the world waited to see whether there would be a repetition of the events in

Czechoslovakia in 1968. In the event, the dissolution of the Soviet Union happened so rapidly and on so many fronts that Estonia moved very gratefully to the sidelines.

The Baltic Tiger awakes

The Russian connection, which had begun with Peter the Great's victory over Charles XII of Sweden, was ended when Estonia was offered – and politely declined – membership of the Commonwealth of Independent States, the hastily contrived successor to the USSR. Their long-awaited dream of regaining independence now realised, Estonians were faced with the

daunting realities of post-Soviet existence: decaying factories, triple-digit inflation and a colossal environmental clean-up bill, to say nothing of a largely unstable and often sabre-rattling neighbour to the east.

It was the swift and daring economic reforms carried out during these crucial days that laid the foundation for the country's "Baltic Tiger" economic growth in the mid-1990s. Aid and advice poured in from Western governments, while so-called "foreign Estonians" – those whose families had fled the 1944 invasion and settled abroad – flocked in from Sweden, North America and Australia bringing their expertise and investment dollars. Most notably, in June

1992, the Bank of Estonia ignored IMF warnings and launched the Eesti kroon. It became the first stable currency of the former USSR, thanks in a large part to the country's pre-World War II gold supply, which, as fortune would have it, was still kept by the Bank of England and the US Federal Reserve.

Fuelling the cautious optimism of these heady and hectic times was the prospect of ridding the Estonian territory once and for all of its many remaining Soviet – now Russian – military forces, a job that was finally accomplished on 31 August 1994. The joy of bidding farewell to Russia's troops was dampened three weeks later by the *Estonia* ferry disaster, which claimed 852 lives and left a lasting scar on the psyche of the young nation.

Along with fast-paced economic development, and the inevitable parliamentary scandals and corruption charges that came with it, the remainder of the decade was a time of reconnection with the West. One by one, European countries dropped their visa requirements for Estonians, and Estonia, in turn, made visa-free travel available to most Westerners, opening up the way for increased tourism and investment.

On the international political level, an unpredictable and outspoken President Lennart Meri, who served as head of state from 1992 to 2000, supplied world leaders with enough wry commentary on East-West relations to ensure that Estonia was never far from the minds of the major power players.

It was toward the end of the decade that the "little nation that could" hit the first serious pothole on its road to recovery. An economic slowdown in 1998, brought on by a monetary crisis in Russia, proved to any remaining doubters that, although Estonia could still fulfil its age-old role as a trade link between Russia and Europe, it was far wiser to keep its gaze firmly fixed westward. It came as no surprise then when, in the September 2003 referendum, 67 percent of Estonians voted to join the European Union. Indeed, when the nation subsequently joined the EU – and NATO – the following year, many saw it as the final step in restoring Estonia's proper place in the family of Western European nations. ❑

LEFT: the Russian border crossing at Narva, 1992.
RIGHT: independence demonstration, Tallinn, 1990.

TALLINN

*Estonia's fairytale port city has an enchanting, historic Old Town
with a cosmopolitan outlook and a village feel.
Tradition goes hand-in-hand with vibrant galleries and bars*

Map
on page
112

Tallinn

Estonia's capital is an exceptionally harmonious mix of the old and the new. Its historic Old Town, far from being a medieval museum piece, abounds in wireless internet zones and enjoys a cutting-edge club scene, while in the "new" downtown area, ancient wooden churches vie for space with gleaming glass high-rises. Its population is four times that of its next largest rival, Tartu, and though it has a cosmopolitan atmosphere, with only 400,000 inhabitants and a small city centre, Tallinn often feels like a village.

Stretched along the rim of Tallinn Bay, just across the Gulf of Finland from Helsinki and midway between St Petersburg and Stockholm, the city holds a blessed maritime position that has made it a little bit too interesting over the centuries to other nations. The resulting layers of cross-cultural history have given the city its unique flavour.

The Old Town

The first place to visit is the **Old Town** (Vanalinn), perched on a low hill by the shore. Set apart from the rest of the city by old fortification walls, this is one of the purest medieval old towns in all northern Europe. Upper town, or Toompea, site of the original Estonian fortification, crowns the hill at 48 metres (157 ft) above sea level. **Lower Town** (All-linn) spills out over an inclined horseshoe below. As they developed, each acquired distinct personalities: the ecclesiastical and feudal powers lived above, the merchants and guild members below.

The only practicable way to explore the winding, rough cobbled streets is by foot. Local women can occasionally be seen in high heels, but visitors should strap on their sturdiest walking shoes and head for the spires of the medieval district. There are several ways to arrive at the Old Town. Passing though the picturesque, 16th-century **Viru Gates** (Viru väravad) in the east and heading up the highly commercial Viru Street is the most travelled path into Old Town. As with routes from most other directions, it quickly leads to **Town Hall Square Ⓐ** (Raekoja plats).

A more appropriate place to start your tour, however, is just a bit further up, on **Toompea**, the birthplace of Tallinn.

Upper Town

One of Estonia's most famous legends holds that Toompea hill in the Upper Town (Toompea) is the burial mound of Kalev, the giant who founded Tallinn. When Kalev died, his widow Linda, in her immense grief, carried stone after stone to cover his grave until this massive hill was formed. It's no surprise that this spot is associated with the origin of the town – it was

PRECEDING PAGES:
city spires.
LEFT:
Town Hall Square.
BELOW:
flower sellers.

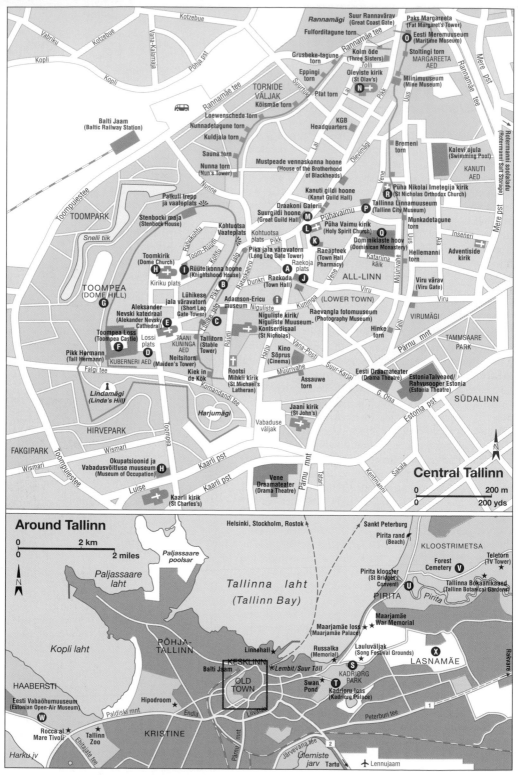

Kotzebue

Rannamägi

Suur Rannavärav
(Great Coast Gate)

Paks Margareeta
(Fat Margaret's Tower)

Fulforditagune torn

Vabriku

Kotzebue

Vana-Kalamaja

Kopli

Põhja pst

Rannamäe tee

O Eesti Meremuuseum
(Maritime Museum)

Grusbeke-tagune
torn

Kolm õde
(Three Sisters)

Stoltingi torn

MARGAREETA
AED

Rannamäe tee

Kopli

Tolli

Eppingi
torn

Oleviste kirik
(St Olav's)

Mere pst

Plat torn

Lai

Miinimuuseum
(Mine Museum)

Uus

N

TORNIDE
VÄLJAK

Köismäe torn

Pikk

Balti Jaam
(Baltic Railway Station)

Loewenschede torn

KGB
Headquarters

Bremeni
torn

Kalevi ujula
(Swimming Pool)

Suurtüki

Nunnadetagune torn

Rotermanni soolaladu
(Rotermann Salt Storage)

Kuldjala torn

Olevimägi

KANUTI
AED

Sauna torn

Mustpeade vennaskonna hoone
(House of the Brotherhood
of Blackheads)

Vene

Munkadetagune
torn

Inseneri

Nunna torn
(Nun's Tower)

Pühavaimu

Pühavaimu

Püha Nikolai Imetegija kirik
(St Nicholas Orthodox Church)

Patkuli trepp
ja vaateplats

Kanuti gildi hoone
(Kanut Guild Hall)

R

Adventiste
kirik

TOOMPARK

Stenbocki maja
(Stenbock House)

Köhtuotsa
Vaateplats

Draakoni Galerii

Suurgildi hoone
(Great Guild Hall)

M

Tallinna Linnamuuseum
(Tallinn City Museum)

P

Hellemanni
torn

Snelli tiik

Kohtuotsa
plats

Püha Vaimu kirik
(Holy Spirit Church)

Dominiklaste hoov
(Dominican Monastery)

Q

Katariina
käik

Ala

Toom-Rüütli

L

Raavukohtu

Toomkirik
(Dome Church)

Pika jala väravatorn
(Long Leg Gate Tower)

Raeapteek
(Town Hall
Pharmacy)

Viru värav
(Viru Gate)

TOOMPEA
(DOME HILL)

H

Rüütelkonna hoone
(Knighthood House)

I

A

Raekoja
plats

ALL-LINN

Viru

Kiriku plats

B

Raekoda
(Town Hall)

J

(LOWER TOWN)

Viru

Pikk

Aleksander
Nevski katedraal
(Alekander Nevsky
Cathedral)

E

Lühikese
jala väravatorn
(Short Leg
Gate Tower)

Adamson-Ericu
museum

Nigulste

Raevangla fotomuuseum
(Photography Museum)

VIRUMÄGI

Valli

G

D

C

Niguliste kirik/
Niguliste Muuseum-
Kontserdisaal
(St Nicholas)

i

Kuninga

Hinke
torn

TAMMSAARE
PARK

Toompea Loss
(Toompea Castle)

F

Lossi
plats

TAANI
KUNINGA
AED

Tallitorn
(Stable
Tower)

Kino
Sõprus
(Cinema)

Eesti Draamateater
(Drama Theatre)

Estonia Talveaed/
Rahvusooper Estonia
(Estonia Theatre)

Pikk Hermann
(Tall Hermann)

KUBERNERI AED

Neitsitorn
(Maiden's Tower)

Kiek in
de Kök

Rootsi
Mihkli kirik
(St Michael's
Latheran)

Assauwe
torn

G. Otsa

SÜDALINN

Falgi tee

Komandandi tee

Harju

Müürivahe

Estonia pst

Lindamägi
(Linda's Hill)

Harjumägi

Jaani kirik
(St John's)

Pärnu mnt

HIRVEPARK

Toompea

Vabaduse
väljak

Central Tallinn

FAKGIPARK

Wismari

Kaarli pst

Vene
Draamateater
(Drama Theatre)

Kentmanni

Sakala

N

Wismari

Okupatsioonid ja
Vabadusvõitluse muuseum
(Museum of Occupation)

H

Kaarli pst

Pärnu mnt

Tatari

0 _____ 200 m
0 _____ 200 yds

Luise

Toompuiestee

Kaarli kirik
(St Charles's)

Around Tallinn

0 _____ 2 km
0 _____ 2 miles

N

Helsinki, Stockholm, Rostok

Sankt Peterburg

Pirita rand
(Beach)

KLOOSTRIMETSA

Teletorn
(TV Tower)

Paljassaare
poolsar

Pirita klooster
(St Bridget's
Convent)

U

Forest
Cemetery

V

Paljassaare
laht

Tallinna laht
(Tallinn Bay)

Pirita

PIRITA

Tallinna Bokaanikaaed
(Tallinn Botanical Gardens)

Kopli laht

PÕHJA-
TALLINN

Linnahall

Maarjamäe loss
(Maarjamäe Palace)

Maarjamäe
War Memorial

Rakvere

Balti Jaam

Lembit/Suur Töll

Russalka
(Memorial)

Laululväljak
(Song Festival Grounds)

LASNAMÄE

X

KESKLINN

OLD
TOWN

Swan
Pond

T

KADRIORG
PARK

HAABERSTI

Eesti Vabaõhumuuseum
(Estonian Open-Air Museum)

W

Hipodroom

S

Kadrioru loss
(Kadriorg Palace)

Peterburi tee

1

Paldiski mnt

Endla

Lijivälac

Rocca al
Mare Tivoli

Tallinn
Zoo

KRISTINE

Pärnu mnt

Järvevana tee

2

Harku jv

Ülemiste
järv

Tartu

Lennujaam

here during pre-Christian times that the first permanent settlement in Tallinn was built. The foreign empires that ruled the northern Estonian lands all used Toompea as their power base, stationing their respective political representatives in Toompea Castle, now home to the nation's government.

Passage to Toompea from the Lower Town is provided by two scenic streets: **Pikk jalg** (Long leg) and **Lühike jalg** (Short leg), whose curious names have given rise to a tired joke, perpetuated by generations of tour guides, that Tallinn "walks with a limp." The long, sloping Pikk jalg is thought to be the oldest street in Tallinn, dating back to Viking times. It begins under the archway of the four-sided **Long Leg Gate Tower** (Pika jala väravatorn), built in 1380, and continues a straight, steady climb upward to **Lossi plats** (Castle Square). The extravagant mansions high up along the cliff to the right are a good indication of the wealth and power of Toompea's gentry, while the fortified defensive wall to the left is a testament to the political tensions and ill-will between the residents of Toompea and the Hanseatic Lower Town.

Lühike jalg, a narrow, winding lane with a staircase, was historically the main pedestrian passage into Toompea. Today it's flanked on both sides by some of Tallinn's more intriguing art shops. At its top stands the **Short Leg Gate Tower** (Lühikese jala väravatorn) built in 1456. The sturdy, wooden door you pass here is original and dates from the 17th century.

Around Castle Square

Reaching Lossi plats at the top of these streets yields the dramatic sight of the grand, onion-domed **Alexander Nevsky Cathedral** (Aleksander Nevski katedraal; open daily 8am–7pm). Built from 1894 to 1900, the impressive structure now serves as the most important place of worship for Tallinn's Russian Orthodox faithful, and its interior has been beautifully restored with a massive iconostasis and several icons. Originally, however, the church had a sinister political function. In the late 19th century, imperial Russia was carrying out an intense campaign of Russification in its outer provinces. As part of its drive to assert cultural dominance over the mainly Lutheran Germans and Estonians, the Tsarist government built this towering Orthodox cathedral directly in front of the castle, in the heart of what had been one of the city's best-loved squares. The name of the church is itself very telling – Prince Alexander Nevsky was the Russian military leader whose forces famously defeated the Baltic-based German crusaders in the "Battle on Ice" on Lake Peipsi in 1242, the climax of Sergei Eisenstein's classic 1938 film *Alexander Nevsky*.

During the construction of the cathedral, a rumour circulated that builders working on the foundation had stumbled upon an iron door bearing the inscription, "Cursed be anyone who dares disturb my peace." The story, with its obvious political undertones, was taken by superstitious locals to be a sign that old Kalev's grave had been discovered, and that he was not at all pleased with the building project. The notion soon gained further support when cracks began to appear around the building's base. The cathedral, however,

Map on page 112

TIP

Street finder:
tänav means street,
väljak/plats is square,
puiestee is avenue,
mantee (mnt) is road.

BELOW: Alexander Nevsky Cathedral.

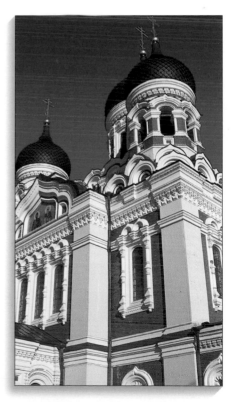

somehow managed to escape Kalev's wrath and, more miraculously, even survived the changing political winds of the early 20th century: after Estonia became independent in 1918, there was talk of removing the offensive structure. Reflecting popular sentiment, the writer Tuglas Friedeberg declared, "It looks like a samovar and should be blown up." Plans were put on hold indefinitely because the new state lacked the necessary funds for demolition.

Next to the cathedral stands **Toompea Castle** ❻ (Toompea loss), historic seat of power in Estonia and home to the *Riigikogu*, Estonia's parliament. As a permanent structure, the castle dates from 1229 when the Knights of the Sword built a square fortress surrounded by a circular, stone wall. In the 14th century this was rebuilt into a convent-style fortress with an inner courtyard, 20-metre (65-ft) high walls, and four corner towers, three of which are still standing. The baroque palace in front of you was built from 1767–73 on the order of Russian Empress Catherine the Great, and served as the administration building for the Russian provincial government in Estonia in tsarist times. The three-storeyed **Parliament Building** in the courtyard was built in 1922 on the foundations of the convent.

Around the castle's left side is the peaceful **Governor's Garden** (Kuberneri aed). This is the best place to view another Tallinn landmark, the 45.6-metre (150-ft) **Tall Hermann** (Pikk Hermann) tower dating from 1371. Tradition dictates that whichever nation flies its flag on Tall Hermann rules Estonia.

To see the castle's most medieval-looking side, you can take a quick detour down Falgi Street, which passes to the left of Pikk Hermann. Only when you reach the bottom of the hill and look back do you begin to understand just how daunting Toompea's defences were. On the way down, paths on the left lead to

Interior of Alexander Nevski cathedral.

BELOW:
Toompea Castle.

the small Lindamägi (Linda's Hill), topped by a small statue of the mythical Linda, grieving widow of Kalev. Tallinn residents adopted it during Soviet times as a kind of unsanctioned memorial to the thousands of loved ones who were deported to Siberia and never returned. Since there would be no gravesite for these victims, relatives would lay flowers here, at considerable risk to themselves if they were caught.

The beautiful **Toompark** starts just to the north of this spot, and circles around the entire northwest side of **Toompea** ⑥. With its forested pathways and moat, this is one of the town's most relaxing places for a summertime stroll, and yields unforgettable views of the town's medieval walls and towers.

Heading straight back up Falgi Street, however, gives the opportunity for a different kind of detour. A right turn on Toompea Street leads to the awkwardly named **Museum of Occupation and of Fight for Freedom** (Okupatsiooni ja Vabadusvõitluse muuseum) at Toompea 8 (open Tues–Sun 11am–6pm; admission fee), a high-tech and dramatic introduction to the 1940–91 period, when Estonia was occupied first by the Soviet Union, then briefly by Nazi Germany, then for another 45 years by the Soviets.

A return to the hill by the same route brings you firmly back into the medieval era. The sturdy-looking round tower on your right is **Kiek in de Kök** (1475–76). Its name, which in Low German literally means "peek into the kitchen", refers to the tower's 36-metre (118-ft) height. Soldiers stationed here joked that they could see right down the chimneys and into the kitchens of the houses below. During the Livonian War (1558–83), Ivan the Terrible's forces blew a massive hole in its top floor. As a memorial to the battle, six stone cannon balls were set into the tower's outer wall and are still visible today. Now the tower operates as

Map on page 112

LEFT:
Kiek in de Kök.
BELOW:
the symbolic
Linda monument.

a museum (open Mar–Oct Tues–Sun 10.30am–5.30pm; Nov–Feb Tues–Sun 11am–5pm; admission fee) displaying the development of the town and its defences from the 13th to the 18th century.

Another historic battleground is just steps away, along the wall that leads back towards Lossi plats. Crossing through a rectangular passage in the wall brings you to the **Danish King's Garden** (Taani kuninga aed) where, according to legend, King Waldemar II camped when his forces were first trying to conquer Toompea in 1219. It was here that a red flag with a white cross, which became the Danes' national symbol, supposedly floated downward from the heavens, spurring them on to victory. In reality, the battle was decided by a group of Slavic mercenaries who began attacking the Estonians from the opposite slope. The two towers here, the small, round **Stable Tower** (Talitorn) and the larger, square **Maiden's Tower** (Neitsitorn), both date from the 14th century. The name "Maiden's Tower" is ironic – the tower was a prison for prostitutes. For years, it operated as a café, and employees claimed to have heard ghostly noises.

The Danish King's Garden

The principal church

Both Toom-Kooli Street and Piiskopi Street lead from Lossi plats to Kiriku plats (Church Square) and the majestic **Dome Church** ❽ (Toomkirik; open Tues–Sun 9am–5pm), the prime Lutheran church of Estonia, established just after the Danes arrived in Toompea in 1219. When you step into the church, you will probably find yourself standing on the burial slab of Otto Johann Thuve, also known as "Tallinn's Don Juan". The hopeless playboy asked to be buried in this spot so that people entering the church would step on him, and by doing so wash away his sins. The church's baroque interior is dominated by a huge

BELOW:
Dome church.

STAGGERING BRITS

The first budget airline into the Baltics from the UK was Ryanair, and Rīga was its chosen destination, not just because it was the centre of the three states but, said CEO Michael O'Leary, because the Latvian government had been so willing to co-operate. Estonia had not been in a rush to see planeloads of Britons arriving, and some actively opposed it, seeing the effect that budget airlines' "low expectation" travel had on destinations such as Amsterdam and Prague. Besides, it already had its share of booze-tripping Finns, who in summer arrive on more than 40 ferries a day. But Tallinn could not hold out against the additional income budget airlines would bring, and by the end of 2004 some 25,000 passengers a month were pouring in to the new capital of stag weekends.

On offer in a city more suited to a honeymoon romance than blurry booze-ups were go-karting, paintballing, boar hunting and Kalashnikov shooting by day, and strip shows and all the alcohol you could drink by night. Tallinn is not a large town, and some bars are easily taken over by boisterous groups, but they are not difficult to avoid. Some hotels actively discriminate against stag tours, but while bad behaviour is controlled, it is not going away. Britons have become Tallinn's new Finns.

collection of coats of arms. These traditionally accompanied the casket during funeral processions, and were later kept in the church as a memorial. Along the northern wall, opposite the entrance, are the lavish tombs of some eminent historic personages, including Pontus de la Gardie, French-born head of Swedish forces during the Livonian war; A.J. von Krusenstern, a Baltic German explorer who in 1886 became the first mariner to circumnavigate the globe under the Russian flag; and Admiral Sir Samuel Greig of Fife, Scotland (1735–88), commander of Russia's Baltic Fleet and reputed lover of Catherine the Great.

Just outside the church is the green, two-storeyed, neo-Renaissance **Knighthood House ❶** (Rüütelkonna hoone), a grand structure with a distinguished history. Built in the late 1840s, it originally served as a meeting hall for the Knighthood, a guild-like organisation that united Toompea's noble families. Its more recent role as Art Museum of Estonia's main building ended in 2006 when that institution moved out to its new facility in Kadriorg Park.

Kohtu Street to the right of Knighthood House leads down past some impressive houses once owned by Toompea's noble elite. The street soon ends at the **Kohtu Street viewing platform** (Kohtuotsa vaateplatvorm) from where there is a spectacular view of the red-tiled roofs of the medieval Lower Town, as well as the modern city and port beyond the town walls. The nearby **Patkuli viewing platform** (Patkuli vaateplatvorm) can be reached by turning right on Toom-Rüütli, then left at the end of that street onto a nearly hidden passage. This platform looks over the northern section of the Lower Town and gives an excellent view of St Olav's Church *(see page 121)*, the town wall and several of its towers. From the Patkuli viewing platform you can head straight down Rahukohtu Street to continue touring Toompea, or make your way down the Patkuli Steps and into the Lower Town.

TIP

Kumu, a huge new art museum in Kadriorg Park *(see page 124),* has been designed by Pekka Vapaavuori to house the Art Museum of Estonia's collection of almost 60,000 works. It's a good reason to visit this interesting area east of the city.

BELOW: Patkuli viewing platform.

The Lower Town and Hanseatic City

In medieval times, the area now called the Lower Town (All-linn) was the Hanseatic city of Tallinn (or Reval, as it was then known), a busy trading city of international stature. In 1248 it was granted autonomous status and from then on had its own government, local laws, social institutions and defence forces. More importantly, it was the domain of merchants and artisans, labourers and servants, all of whom would have contributed to the general bustle of commerce as they went about their daily routines.

For at least seven centuries, the social and cultural heart of Tallinn has been **Town Hall Square** (Raekoja plats), the attractive open area at the centre of the Old Town. Even now the square acts as the chief gathering place for the city's residents. In spring and summer it's invariably covered in café tables, and in winter there is a Christmas Market. Presiding over the square is the **Town Hall ❶** (Raekoda; open July–Aug Mon–Sat 10am–4pm; admission fee). Historic records indicate that another town hall occupied this spot as early as 1322, but the present late-Gothic structure was completed in 1404. **Old Thomas** (Vana Toomas), the soldier-shaped weather vane on the spire, has been watching over the city since 1530 and has become a symbol of the town. The baroque spire and the fanciful, dragon-shaped drainpipes are from 1627. Visitors in July and August should not pass up an opportunity to see the interior, with its vaulted ceilings and wood-carved benches. Summer visitors can also climb the 64-metre (210-ft) Town Hall Tower (Raekoja torn; open 15 May–30 Aug daily 11am–6pm; admission fee) for spectacular views of the Old Town.

Tucked behind the Town Hall is the 15th-century **Town Hall Prison** (Raevangla) where those arrested were kept before trial. It now houses an interest-

Carving inside the Town Hall.

BELOW: the medieval spirit in Town Hall Square.

ing museum of photography (open Mar–Oct Thur–Tues 10am–6pm; Nov–Feb Thur–Mon 10am–5pm; admission fee) chronicling 150 years of Tallinn's photographic pursuits and displaying numerous antique cameras.

Across the square from the Town Hall stands the **Town Hall Pharmacy** Ⓚ (Raeapteek), one of the oldest, continuously running pharmacies in Europe. Records first mention it in 1422, but it may have been established decades earlier. From 1580 to 1911 it was managed by 10 generations of the same family. Some of the useful preparations sold here in centuries past included minced bat, burnt bees, snakeskin and powdered unicorn horn. These days the same cures are sold here as in any modern pharmacy, but in homage to its history the location maintains a small exhibition room (open Mon–Fri 9am–7pm, Sat 9am–5pm; free) displaying antique equipment and archaic medicines.

Just few paces from the square through the Saiakang (white bread) passage stands the **Holy Spirit Church** Ⓛ (Püha Vaimu kirik; open May–Sept Mon–Sat 10am–4pm; Oct–Apr Mon–Fri 10am–3pm; admission fee). In the 13th century it operated an almshouse tending to the city's sick, elderly and poor. Unlike other churches, the Holy Spirit Church's congregation was made up of Tallinn's lower class and included ethnic Estonians. It was here that the first sermons in the Estonian language were given after the Reformation, and in 1535 the church's pastor, Johann Koell, translated and published what's thought to be the first book in Estonian. The building was completed in the 1360s but its spire has been replaced numerous times following devastating fires, the last one in 2002.

The most eye-catching addition to the church is the large, blue-and-gold clock near the main doorway. Created by well-known Tallinn woodcarver Christian Ackermann in the late 17th-century, it is Tallinn's oldest – and by far most

Map on page 112

Tallinn's oldest clock, on the Holy Spirit Church.

LEFT: the Town Hall Pharmacy.
BELOW: Citizens' Hall in the Town Hall.

Doorway of the House of the Brotherhood of Blackheads.

LEFT:
St Olav's Church.
RIGHT: House of the
Brotherhood of
Blackheads.

captivating – public timepiece. The church's interior is every bit as awe-inspiring, particularly the altar, commissioned from renowned Lübeck sculptor and painter, Bernt Notke, in 1483. Figures of the Virgin Mary with child, apostles and saints, all painted in bright, clear blue, red and gold, stand at the centre of the cupboard-type altarpiece.

The church is on the corner of Pikk (Long) Street, which leads to the northern edge of the Old Town. This once-busy artery connected the port to the town's main marketplace. The grand-looking building at Pikk 17, opposite the Holy Spirit Church, is the **Great Guild Hall ⓜ** (Suurgildi hoone), which served as a meeting place for Tallinn's Great Guild, a wealthy association of merchants that wielded considerable influence over town affairs. The hall is now used by a branch of the **Estonian History Museum** (Eesti Ajaloomuuseum; open daily 11am–6pm; admission fee), which chronicles the nation's developments from prehistoric times up to the 18th century.

Architectural oddities along Pikk Street include the eccentric, Art Nouveau facade of the **Dragon Gallery** (Draakoni Galerii) at No. 18, with seahorse-tailed serpents and Egyptian slaves. Next to it is the Tudor-style **Kanut Guild Hall** (Kanuti gildi hoone), with statues representing St Canute (Canute IV of Denmark, martyred in 1086) and the founder of Protestantism, Martin Luther. High up, across the street from the Kanut Guild Hall, a man wearing a monocle gazes down. Popular legend says that a jealous wife installed it to break her husband's habit of spying on young women as they practised ballet in the upper floors of the Guild Hall.

At Pikk 26 is the eye-catching **House of the Brotherhood of Blackheads** (Mustpeade maja; open daily 10am–7pm; free). The exquisite Renaissance

Map on page 112

facade is from 1597, and its beautiful, carved wood door, one of the most recognised architectural elements in Tallinn, was installed in 1640.

A careful observer will notice something eerie about the building at Pikk 59. Its cellar windows are completely bricked over – this was the **KGB Headquarters** during the Soviet period. The placard on the front of the building reads "This building housed the headquarters of the organ of repression of the Soviet occupational power. Here began the road to suffering for thousands of Estonians."

Just a few paces further along is Tallinn's largest medieval structure, the enormous **St Olav's Church** (Oleviste Kirik). The church was first mentioned in historic records in 1267, and originally served a Scandinavian merchants' camp that occupied this end of Pikk Street. An absurdly tall, 159-metre (522-ft) Gothic-style pavilion steeple was built on the top of the tower in 1500, making St Olav's the tallest building in the world at the time. Numerous bolts of lightning hit the steeple through the centuries, however, and twice, once in 1625 and again in 1820, the church was burned to the ground.

The steeple you now see was installed after the first fire, and is 124 metres (407 ft) tall, 25 metres (82 ft) shorter than the original. In an odd, 20th-century twist, the spire was later used as a radio tower by the KGB *apparatchiki* stationed next door. In spring and summer, able-bodied visitors can make the rigorous climb to the top of the tower (open Apr–Oct daily 10am–6pm; admission fee) for spectacular views.

Humbler in size than the church but just as awe-inspiring are **The Three Sisters** (Kolm ode) at Pikk 71. This magnificently restored ensemble of three brightly painted, 15th-century terraced houses are a favourite for photographers

Smilšu, The Sand Road leading from the cathedral out across marshes and through the forests to St Petersburg, was at one time the only proper road from the city.

BELOW:
the Three Sisters.

and now serve as the premises for a luxury hotel. Their less spectacular counterparts, **The Three Brothers**, are located around the corner on Lai Street.

Pikk Street ends at the **Great Coast Gate** (Suur Rannavärav) and its famous 16th-century **Fat Margaret's Tower** (Paks Margareeta). With a diameter of 25 metres (82 ft) and walls up to 5.1 metres (17 ft) thick, the cannon tower was a formidable part of the town's defences. It's now occupied by the **Estonian Maritime Museum** ⓞ (Eesti Meremuuseum; open Wed–Sun 10am–6pm; admission fee). Four floors present an extensive look at the nation's seafaring history from Neolithic times to the present.

Heading back to the square via nearby Vene Street brings you past a well-restored medieval house at No. 17, which contains the **Tallinn City Museum** ⓟ (Tallinna Linnamuuseum; open Mar–Oct Wed–Mon 10am–6pm; Nov–Feb Wed–Mon 10am–5pm; admission fee). This is by far the city's most modern and engaging history museum, chronicling Tallinn's development from its founding until today.

Further up Vene Street is the area that came to be called the "Latin Quarter". In medieval times it was the domain of the powerful **Dominican Monastery** ⓠ (Dominiiklaste Klooster; open 15 May–30 Sept daily 9.30am–6pm; museum at Müürivahe 33 open 15 May –30 Sept daily 10am–5pm; admission fee). Known as **St Catherine's Monastery**, it was founded here in 1246 by the Dominican Order, and played a key role in the town's religious affairs. The Reformation movement in 1525 closed it down, and in 1531 the abandoned complex was ravaged by fire. Though not all of the building remains, the monastery's beautiful courtyard and ancient corridors still give an impression of monastic life in medieval times. The corridors display a collection of medieval stonemasonry salvaged from elsewhere in the Old Town.

A separate museum, round the corner at Müürivahe 33, gives access to the monastery's inner chambers, which exhibit additional stone carvings as well as archaeological finds from the monastery grounds.

Just south of the monastery, the narrow **St Catherine's Passage** (Katariina käik) that connects Vene and Müürivahe streets is absolutely not to be missed. One side of the picturesque passage displays some intriguing – if somewhat eerie – stone burial slabs that were removed from the former St Catherine's Church, directly behind them, during renovation. The lane leads to Tallinn's famous **Knit Market**, a section of the town wall where old ladies sell traditional woollen creations. From here, the **Viru Gates** are just a few steps away.

A walk down Harju Street, a few metres from Town Hall Square, reveals a very different aspect of the city's history: the devastation of World War II. Peeking out from a park area about halfway down the street are remnants of walls and cellars where several buildings, including a hotel and a cinema, once stood. On 9 March 1944, with Nazi Germany still occupying Estonia, the Soviet Air Force bombed Tallinn, destroying entire neighbourhoods and leaving 20,000 homeless. In 1988, independence-minded Estonians ended decades of Soviet cover-up by excavating and displaying the ruins, and in 2006 the site was converted into a public green. The **Church of St Nicholas** ⓡ (Niguliste kirik)

Dining out in St Catherine's Passage.

BELOW: performance in the Dominican Monastery.

Map on page 112

that lords over Harju Street was also destroyed in the raid, but it was reconstructed from 1956 to 1984. Dedicated to the patron saint of merchants and artisans, it was founded by a group of German settlers who had set up a trading yard here in the early 13th century. This was the only church in Lower Town that wasn't ransacked during the Reformation fervour of 1524, thanks to its head of congregation who kept the mobs out by pouring molten lead into the door locks.

The church now serves a purely secular function, operating as the **Niguliste Museum and Concert Hall** (open Wed–Sun 10am–5pm; admission fee), which showcases religious art from Estonia and abroad. It has the distinction of housing Estonia's most famous work of art, 15th-century artist Bernt Notke's mural *Dance of Death (see page 42)*, a macabre masterpiece depicting people from various walks of life dancing with skeletons. Other treasures in the museum include awe-inspiring altars from the 16th and 17th centuries, a collection of Renaissance and baroque chandeliers, and several curious 14th–17th-century tombstones.

Nearly 200 cruise liners steam in to Tallinn every year depositing around 125,000 visitors, who stay for just a few hours.

Around Tallinn Bay

The Old Town is the tourists' favourite part of Tallinn, but on weekends the locals wander in the parks on the east side of Tallinn Bay. The best-loved of these is **Kadriorg ❺**, a name synonymous with affluence, nature and, most of all, tranquillity. Kadriorg Park was laid out between 1718 and 1725 by the Italian architect Niccolo Michetti under the orders of Peter the Great, who named it in honour of his wife, Catherine. Most of it remains a wooded, informal park, planted with lime, oak, ash, birch and chestnut trees and punctuated by open fields. Among the more developed exceptions is the large rectangular Swan Pond with fountains and a beautiful, white gazebo provide a fittingly romantic

BELOW:
Tallinn Harbour.

Kadriorg Palace's impressive main hall.

BELOW: Kadriorg Palace and Art Museum.

introduction to the park. The jewel in the Kadriorg's crown is without a doubt the lavish, baroque **Kadriorg Palace** ❶ (Kadrioru Loss) that Peter had built in 1718. The palace is a stunning monument to imperial extravagance. In particular its two-storey main hall, decorated in rich stucco work and grandiose ceiling paintings, is considered one of the best examples of baroque design in all of Northern Europe. Equally impressive is the manicured, 18th-century-style flower garden, with erupting fountains, behind the building.

As the building is itself a masterpiece, it's somehow appropriate that it houses one of the nation's top art museums. The **Kadriorg Art Museum** (open May– Sept Tues–Sun 10am–5pm; Oct–Apr Wed–Sun 10am–5pm; admission fee) is the main home for the Art Museum of Estonia's foreign collection. While here, those interested in art should also visit the **Mikkel Museum** (open Wed–Sun 11am–6pm; admission fee), just across the street in what used to be the palace's kitchen house. Exquisite works include Flemish and Dutch paintings, Italian engravings, Chinese porcelain and etchings by Rembrandt.

A quick walk up the hill from the museums will take you to the **Presidential Palace** (1938) with ceremonial guards, and then to a small cottage, now a museum, where Peter stayed during visits while the palace was under construction. The road ends at Estonia's largest and most complete art museum, the **Kumu** (open May–Sept Tues–Wed, Fri–Sun 11am–6pm, Thur 11am–9pm; Oct–Apr Wed–Sun 11am–6pm; admission fee). Opened in 2006, this sprawling, modern complex serves as the main building of the Art Museum of Estonia. Works produced by the nation's artistic heroes of the 19th and 20th centuries make up the permanent collection, while temporary exhibitions focus primarily on contemporary art. The facility itself, designed by Finnish architect Pekka Vapaavuori, is a fascinating,

multi-functional maze of copper, limestone and glass that deserves exploration.

The path from Kadriorg Palace to the sea leads to the angel-like **Russalka memorial**, built to commemorate 177 men lost when the Russian warship, *Russalka* (Mermaid), sank en route from Tallinn to Helsinki in 1893. The dramatic monument is now a popular spot for Russian wedding couples to visit and fulfil their tradition of laying flowers. The wreck, incidentally, was discovered by Estonian researchers in 2003.

Opposite the monument, slightly further down the coast is the entrance to the **Song Festival Grounds** (Lauluväljak), scene of Estonia's "Singing Revolution". The Song Festival Arena, with a distinctive, curving roof, was built in 1960 and is Tallinn's largest outdoor stage.

Further along the coast to the north, beside the coast road, is the Maarjamäe Palace (Maarjamäe Loss), a grand, pseudo-Gothic manor built by Count Orlov-Davidov in 1874. First used as a summer home, the "palace" changed hands several times, serving as a Dutch consul's residence, a prestigious hotel, an aviation school and a Soviet army barracks. It now houses the branch of the **Estonian History Museum** (open Mar–Oct Wed–Sun 11am–6pm; Nov–Feb Wed–Sun 10am–5pm; admission fee) that chronicles the 19th and 20th centuries.

Just beyond is the site of the sprawling Maarjamäe War Memorial, an overbearing, cement-filled park that could have only been born of the Soviet 1960s and '70s. It is divided into five sections: an obelisk dedicated to the 1917 revolution; two human-sized palms with a (no longer) eternal flame; a "wounded seagulls" archway representing the resilience of the revolution; a headstone for the Tallinn divisions of the Great Patriotic War of 1944–45; and a grave to a World War II sailor named Yvgeny Nikolov, martyred at the hands of the Nazis.

Map on page 112

Memorial to the victims of the Estonia ferry disaster.

BELOW: The Estonian Art Museum

Map on page 112

Pirita district

Pirita Tee, a pleasant place to stroll beside the sea, leads on to the Pirita district, home to the city's most popular beach. It is also the site of the Olympic Yachting Centre, which was built for the sailing events of the 1980 Olympic Games in Moscow and is still used by locals.

Pirita Convent ⓤ (Pirita klooster; open June–Aug daily 9am–7pm; Apr–May & Sept daily 10am–6pm; Oct–Mar daily noon–4pm; admission fee) lies over the Pirita river and across the road. It was built in 1407–36 for the Swedish-based St Bridget's order of nuns and in its time was one of the two largest buildings in Tallinn (the Dominican monastery was the other). The convent was destroyed in 1577 during the Livonian War but the 35-metre (115-ft) high western facade with an arched portal of flagstones is still quite beautiful and the shell of the rest of the main church is intact. Peasants continued to live on the site for a considerable time after its destruction and their gravestones are visible in its front yard.

The Balts are fond of their cemeteries and some say that the **Forest Cemetery ⓥ**, situated at Kloostrimetsa, down the road from Pirita, is the most beautiful place in all of Tallinn. It looks almost like a national park, with graves running up and down small hills under a deep forest of fir trees. In 1933, the writer Eduard Vilde was the first to be buried here and most of Estonia's stars have since followed suit, including the singer Georg Ots 1920–75, the poet Lydia Koidula (1843–86) and Konstantin Päts, President of Estonia from 1992 to 2001. Rising just to the right of the main gates is the so-called "hill of celebrities".

Just to the east the space-age **Teletorn** (TV Tower; open daily 10am–1am; admission fee) dominates the skyline. At 314 metres (1,030 ft), this is by far the tallest structure in town. Unforgettable views of the city and surrounding ports unfold from its observation deck and restaurant at the 170-metre (558-ft) level. A few metres from the tower's base is the **Tallinn Botanical Garden** (Tallinna Botaanikaaed; open Tues–Sun 11am–7pm; admission fee) covering 123 hectares (304 acres) of the Pirita Valley with its beautiful gardens and nature trails.

On the western side of Tallinn and within easy reach of the city is an **open-air Museum ⓦ** (Vabaõhu-muuseum). Situated at Rocca al Mare on the Kakumäe Peninsula, overlooking the sea near some of the most exclusive property in town, the museum was opened in 1964 and contains more than 60 buildings, brought here from all over the country, showing how life has typically been lived in rural Estonia.

Suburban reality

To understand Tallinn fully, you must venture off into one of the residential neighbourhoods. Not far from the Forest Cemetery is **Lasnamäe ⓧ**, an enormous concrete sea of nearly identical buildings with virtually no landscaping, which was the source of great controversy during the Soviet years. Begun in the late 1970s, it was nicknamed the "suburb of Leningrad" because the housing authorities repeatedly installed new immigrants from Russia in them, no matter how long locals had been on the waiting list. It is now more than 70 percent Russian. ❑

At Pirita harbour you can take a boat to the nearest islands of Aegna (40 min) and Naissaar (1hr) where there's a nature reserve and small railway.

BELOW: tradition survives in the open-air Museum.

E-stonia

One of the first things visitors notice on arrival in Estonia is the overwhelming presence of all things high-tech. Everybody, from small children to grandmothers, is talking on – or typing into – a mobile phone. And in cafés and bars, locals are hunched over laptops, surfing the Internet via a wireless connection.

These outward signs are just the tip of a technological iceberg. Over the past few years, Estonia has become enamoured – some would say obsessed – with the idea of remodelling itself into an information society. The result is that new technologies, particularly those involving Internet and mobile phones, have worked their way into every aspect of life, from farming to dating to buying soda at vending machines.

Estonia has a high-tech history. In Soviet times this was where advanced software programming was developed, for espionage and space programmes, and Tallinn was a major centre for developing artificial intelligence. After independence, a "Tiger Leap" programme was introduced, to push the nation ahead by using computer technology in every field, and connecting every school to the Internet. In February 2000, Estonia declared Internet access a "constitutional right", and six months later, the government became the first in the world to convert cabinet meetings to paperless sessions, saving €200,000 a year in photocopying costs. A more recent programme has trained more than 100,000 adults, mostly retired people and blue-collar workers, in how to use the Internet.

A decade after independence, around 90 percent of the Estonian population are mobile-phone subscribers. Nearly all customers paying for parking in central Tallinn are doing so by SMS text message, and other text-message systems are being widely used for everything from buying bus tickets to checking bank balances to getting weather reports. Most Estonians are regular Internet users, and nearly all connections are broadband. There are over 800 WiFi (wireless Internet) "hot-spots" around the country, allowing laptop users high-speed net access in cafés, pubs, hotels, city squares, beaches and even petrol stations.

Wireless connections are spreading broadband into rural areas where ADSL and cable connections don't reach. Farmers have been using the Internet to track cow herds, and if rural dwellers don't have computers, they can look for official blue road signs with the "@" symbol pointing to a nearby place to log on.

A smart ID card, which can serve as a passport within the EU, is doing away with both money and paperwork. It can be used on public transport and for filing taxes. Estonia is continually innovating, and a responsive public means that the country is often used by foreign companies as a test market for new technologies.

Linnar Viik, the Tallinn-born guru behind Tiger Leap, recently told *Forbes* magazine: "People like to say, don't touch things that work. But Estonians like to look behind the thing and wonder whether there's anything we can change about it. In Estonia you might say, if it works, you can break it." ❑

RIGHT: member of the highly mobile society.

TARTU AND THE SOUTH

The brains of the country are nurtured in Tartu, the university town in the "real" Estonia of the south, where there are lakes, historic sights and the country's "winter capital", Otepää

Maps
96–7
Tartu 132

People often call southern Estonia the "real" Estonia. This is where ties to the land go back countless generations, the dialect is deep Finno-Ugric, and the locals have kept up a tradition of hospitality and generosity. The region is split roughly between the undulating Sakala, Otepää and Haanja highlands. Each has its own "metropolitan" focus – Viljandi, Otepää , and Võru – but these cities have a predominately rural feel. For the most part, industrial activity is secondary or subordinate to agriculture.

Tartu, the intellectual capital

The largest city in the southern half of Estonia, with around 101,000 residents, is **Tartu ➋**, 187 km (116 miles) southeast of Tallinn. Just as many say the south is the real Estonia, many call Tartu its real capital. At the very least, Tartu is the intellectual capital. Roughly a quarter of its population is made up of students, attending one of the city's 16 institutions of higher learning.

Chief among these is Tartu University, founded in 1632, which was a powerhouse for Estonian (as well as Latvian) intellectuals during their National Awakening. It has endured as the main seat of higher education in the humanities and currently has around 18,000 students.

Tartu was first recorded in 1030 as a stronghold built by Grand Duke Yaroslav of Kiev. The city has been razed on several occasions since – by Estonians in 1061, Germans in 1224, the Northern War in 1708 and by fire in 1775 – and most buildings in Old Town date from the 18th century.

The city has developed in a north-south fashion along the River Emajõgi, with most of the main university buildings sprinkled on the northern end where Old Town lies. This district is immediately distinguishable by the wide cobbled Raekoja plats (Town Hall Square) in its centre, anchored by a pinkish neoclassical **Town Hall ➊** (Raekoda) at its head, from 1798. The grey clock-tower rising from the middle of its roof was added in the 19th century to help the students be on time for classes.

In front of the Town Hall stands a fountain with a kissing couple under an umbrella. The statue, a symbol of Tartu's student population, was designed by the Estonian artist Mati Karmin in 1999 and quickly became a meeting point. Running along the northern side of the square is an unbroken row of pastel-coloured buildings greatly responsible for Tartu's reputation as the neoclassical prima donna of Estonia.

The most noticeable of them is the "**Leaning House**" (1793) at No. 18. Erected on the old city wall and partly on marshland that later dried up, it leans noticeably to the left. Inside is the **Kivisilla Art**

PREVIOUS PAGES:
Oscar Wilde and
Eduard Wilde.
LEFT: the Town Hall.
BELOW: statue of
the kissing students.

Gallery (Kivisilla Pildigalerii; open Wed–Sun 11am–6pm; admission fee), with a collection that centres on the Pallas Higher Art School that ran in Tartu from 1919 to 1940. At the foot of the square is the **Arched Bridge** (Kaarsild), which replaced the 18th-century Stone Bridge destroyed in 1994. Taking a daring walk over the bridge's top rail has become a time-honoured student tradition.

Tartu Ülikooli Peahoone, the university's main building, lies just a couple of blocks away from the Town Hall, at 18 Ulikooli Street, a stately oasis in the cramped and crumbling side streets of Old Town. Pale yellow with six white columns, the University Building is the most impressive neoclassical structure in Estonia. Completed in 1809, it was designed by the architect Johann Krause. Visiting its **Art Museum** (Kunstimuuseum; open Mon–Fri 11am–5pm; admission fee) will allow you to take a peek at its impressive concert hall, collection of classical statuary replicas, and a Student Lock-up, where students were incarcerated for such infractions of conduct as duelling or insulting cloakroom attendants.

Further down Jaani Street is the 14th-century brick Gothic **St John's Church** (Janni Kirik). The renovation of the interior, which lasted for many years, was completed in 2005. On the exterior you can admire hundreds of tiny terracotta sculptures. The 15 faces above its pointed portal represent the Last Judgement.

The neoclassical rule is further broken on the south side of Town Hall Square. First along Vabaduse Street is the grim brown **Market Hall** (1937). The renovated bus station stands on the next block, and then the **Outdoor Market**, which is devoted half to foodstuffs and half to dry goods. The river bank is dominated by the modern glass Emajõgi Business Centre office tower, known locally as "the flask". A short walk down the road is the **Aura Keskus**, a recreation centre

Statuary in Tartu's Art Museum.

BELOW:
the Town Hall.

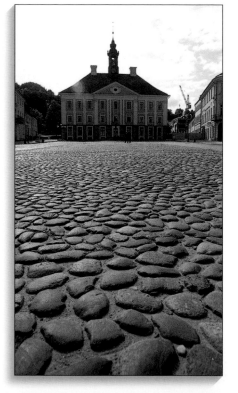

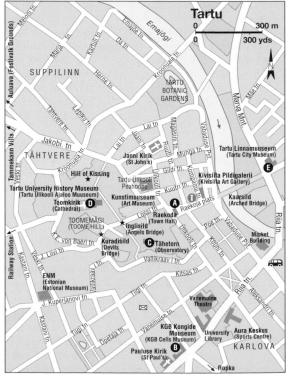

with indoor swimming pools and waterslides. Across the road on Riia Street is another set of modern buildings comprising the Tartu Department Store and the Hansakeskus (Hansa Centre) with the Pallas Hotel on its fourth floor.

A short walk uphill from here, at Riia 15b, brings you to the **KGB Cells Museum** ❸ (KGB Kongide Muuseum; open Tues–Sat 11am–4pm; admission fee). Built into what was the local NKVD/KGB in the 1940s and '50s, the museum covers themes of repression and the Estonian resistance movement.

The **Vanemuine Theatre** (1977), at Vanemuise 6, and adjacent **University Library** (1980), at W. Struve Street 1, are the final modern touches. Both are white and functional, but the library is distinguished by the students perpetually gathered on its wide fountain-clad plaza for a quick smoke.

Two streets to the north is the **Estonian National Museum** (ENM; Kuperjanovi 9; open Wed–Sat 11am–6pm) with the country's most important permanent folklore collection.

Toome Hill and Toome Hill Park

It is a short, pleasant walk from here to **Toome Hill** (Toomemägi), the hilly park that dominates Old Town. In the southern side of the park stands the early 19th-century **Observatory** ❻ (Tähetorn), which once had the world's largest refracting telescope. From the west entrance on Vällikraavi Street turn up under the grey Kuradisild (1913) or **Devil's Bridge**. This is named after a Professor Mannteuffel from Germany who, in the late 19th century, introduced Estonia to the use of rubber gloves in surgical operations, but whose name resembles the German "man-devil." You will find yourself between the University Internal Hospital (1808) and the University Maternity Hospital (1838). Straight ahead is the ochre **Angel's Bridge** (Inglisild), also named as a result of a linguistic confusion: **Toomemägi Park** was laid out in English style and the locals confused the words "English" and "angel".

Toomemägi is strewn with statues of people connected with Tartu University. In spring biology students traditionally wash the pensive head of Karl Ernst von Baer – a professor linked to Darwin – with champagne. The monument to the writer Kristjan Jaak Peterson – the first Estonian national to enter the university – is shown erect with a stick in his hand because he is said to have walked the 155 miles (250 km) from Rīga to Tartu. The "Romantic Corner" of the park lies to the left from the statue of Baer. It consists of a stone mound called the Hill of Kissing to the top of which bridegrooms must carry their new wives, a low Bridge of Sighing with a well-worn cement bench, and a Sacrificial Stone where the lovelorn can leave a prayer to the ancient gods.

Sacred stones are found all over Estonia; people used to gather round them on a Thursday full moon, and leave (non-bloody) sacrifices. Tartu students have continued this ritual by ceremonially burning their notebooks here at midnight on the Thursday before their exams.

The monumental ruins of the **Toom Cathedral** ❶ (Toomkirik), which gives the hill its name, loom above this part of the park. Begun in the 13th century, this

Town Hall detail.

BELOW: street bookstall.

was once the largest brick Gothic church in the Baltic countries, but the majority of it was destroyed in the Livonian War (1558–83). The broken wings of 10 flying buttresses give an idea of its former grandeur. While the project to shore up the ruins continues, summer visitors can pay to climb its two renovated towers. The huge choir on the church's eastern end was completely restored in the early 1800s under the direction of Krause. For a time it served as the university library, but it now contains the **Tartu University History Museum** Tartu Ülikooli Ajaloo Muuseum, open Wed–Sun 11am–5pm; admission fee). On each floor are exhibitions of the history of the university, from its opening in 1632 in honour of the Swedish King Gustavus Adolphus to the present day. A lovely white baroque hall on the second floor is a public concert room with walls lined by cases of antique biological species. Downhill, on the southeast edge of the park is the **Gunpowder Cellar** or Pussirohukelder Restoran (1778), now a restaurant and nightclub built into the side of Toome Hill.

A trip across the Arched Bridge leads to **Tartu City Museum E** (Tartu Linnamuuseum; open Tues–Sun 11am–6pm; admission fee) at Narva mnt 23. Housed in a late 18th-century mansion, this new museum covers the entire history of the town.

Tartu's districts

Tartu is divided into different districts, each with its own name. Lai Street divides Old Town from **Suppilinn**, or Soup Town, so called because its streets are called after soup ingredients such as Bean and Potato. The industrial area south of Old Town is the **Ropka District**, and the attractive **Karlova District** has cut-corner wooden houses built during the Estonian Republic as boarding

BELOW: Tartu's ruined cathedral.

houses. The area of stately homes behind Toomemägi Park – and very popular with university professors – is the **Tähtvere District**, where some of the architecture was inspired by the Bauhaus movement. Just beyond here are the Song Festival Grounds (laulava) where the first Baltic gathering was held in 1869. Today the stadium, with a canopy built in 1994, can hold 10,000 singers.

Some of the most curious buildings in Tartu are ordinary houses. The weathered house at 65 Marta Street, beside the wooded park in which the dilapidated **Karlova Manor** stands, for example, is a marvel of wood and stone edging work. At Riia 27, **St Paul's Church** (Pauluse kirik, 1919) was designed by the Finnish architect Eliel Saarinen. Created in red brick with a square tower, it looks a bit like a fire station. Another architectural curiosity is the constructivist Tammekann Villa, built by Finnish architect Alvar Aalto in 1932 on Kreutzwaldi 6.

West of Tartu

The small city of **Viljandi** ❸, 77 km (48 miles) west on main road 92, clings to the slopes of a primeval valley plumbed by Lake Viljandi. Now the capital of the Sakala upland, with about 21,000 inhabitants, the site has been settled since AD 1000, but the Old Town is tiny; one small grid between Tallinna and Tartu streets and the **Castle Park** (Lossipark). Its appeal depends on its lovely lakeside setting and the ruined castle perched on a series of hills above the water, but it is perhaps better known among Estonians for the Viljandi Folk Music Festival, held each summer.

A good place to start a tour of the town is the Museum of Viljandi (Viljandi Muuseum; open Wed–Sun 10am–5pm; admission fee) at Kindral Laidoneri Square 10, in the Old Town. This square used to be the marketplace, and its cen-

Maps
96–7
Tartu 132

TIP

Country words.
rand (beach), *järv*
(lake), *mets* (forest),
jõe (river), *puu* (tree),
põld (field).

BELOW:
dancers in Viljandi.

tral fountain covers the town well. The museum is downstairs in Viljandi's third-oldest building, originally a pharmacist's shop (1779–80), and contains a model of the former castle. It also houses many painstakingly decorated old objects of daily use, such as tankards and horse yokes, as well as exhibitions covering Viljandi county's late 19th-century history and the period of Estonia's first independence (1918–40).

Two houses down, at No. 8, is the Culture Academy. Viljandi has contributed substantially to Estonia's cultural history, and the town now has three well-known choirs: the Koit Merited Mixed Choir, the Sakala Male Choir and the Eha Female Choir. A professional drama company is housed in one of the town's few contemporary buildings, the Ugala Theatre (1981), beside the Valuoja river.

Initially a grand hotel, the Culture Academy building was occupied during World War II by the Nazis, who called it "the hospital". It is presumed to have been a site of human experimentation. The 18th-century Town Hall (Raekoda) stands one block away from here on Linnu Street. The neighbouring Old Water Tower (Vana Veetorn; open May–Sept daily 11am–6pm; admission fee), dates from 1911 and has been refurbished.

The entrance to the Lossipark is just down Lossi Street, over a long wooden footbridge. Begun in 1223, the Order Fortress of Viljandi (Viljandi Ordulinnus) is presumed to have been the largest fortress in the Baltics, designed to stretch over three adjacent hills, with its only entrance on the first hill, occupied by servants. The second fold, once split between servants and horses, is now a field edged with bits of old wall. If you climb (carefully) up on the stone by the edge, you will get a great view over a long and narrow lake. The third

BELOW:
cycle marathon
in Otepää.

hill supported the castle, the church and the prison. This final section has more ruins than the other two and they stand out starkly against the sky.

A bright red-and-white suspension bridge (Rippsild) leads from this end of the castle grounds into the rest of the park. Built in 1879, the 50-metre (164-ft) bridge was brought to the town from Rīga in 1931 by a German count whose favourite daughter, the story goes, had persisted in using it for racing her horse across.

The 15th-century church of the former Franciscan monastery, St John's Church (Janni kirik), has its own wooden footbridge, at the head of Lossipark just off Pikk Street. It is used primarily for concerts. The town's main Lutheran church, St Paul's (Pauluse kirik, 1863–66), lies outside the park across Vaksali Road. Red brick with stone inlay, it has an industrial-age Gothic veneer.

By the lake's shore Viljandi has a different feel – it is considerably sportier, happier and younger. At one end are tennis courts and a town stadium, and there is also an athletes' hotel. Boats and pedalos can be rented from the pier beside the restaurant. Viljandi Lake is supposedly not polluted, but it is advisable to row out to the centre if you want to jump in because the bottom of the lake is so muddy.

Estonia's "Winter Capital"

Estonia's entire southern region is dotted with pretty lakes, many of which are swimmable (though it is always best to check with a local). The largest, at 270 sq. km (105 sq. miles), is **Võrtsjärv**. It is, however, only 6 metres (20 ft) at its deepest. The lakes of **Otepää** in the **Otepää Highlands** help make this cosy town not just one of Estonia's most popular winter resorts but also a gracious rest spot during the summer months.

Otepää ❹ is a short drive southwest from Tartu, but in its tranquillity it could be a million miles away from the city. Its population of around 4,500 doubles in winter. Tourism has become a mainstay of the economy in Estonia's "Winter Capital" since independence. Resort facilities include a ski jump, cross-country ski paths, three downhill skiing centres, a public beach and a few hotels. The town's biggest events are the World Cup Cross-Country Skiing Championship, which attracts around 10,000 participants each January, the 60-km (37-mile) Tartu Marathon that involves 2–3,000 skiers in February, and an ice-fishing competition.

The town and its surroundings have been designated a "protected area". Building above three storeys is forbidden, salt cannot be used against ice on the roads, and motorboating on Otepää's lakes and hunting and camping in its woods are restricted, though "bloodless" hunting – with a camera – is always allowed.

The town clusters up against these woods, and the centre has a pleasantly closed-in feeling, accentuated by a narrow triangular central park. The Tourist Information Centre is based here, at Lipuväljak 13. The oldest building in town is Otepää church. Opened in 1608, it was built by Estonian peasants so

Map on pages 96–7

 TIP

Otepää's two gentle downhill slopes lie south of the town, at Väike Munamägi and Kuutsemäe, where equipment can be rented.

BELOW: Otepää skiers.

that they wouldn't have to attend the church of the German population. The folklorist Jakob Hurt was its first Estonian pastor, from 1872 to 1880. The current steeple was added in 1860 and is 52 metres (168 ft) high.

When the Estonian Students Co-operative was forbidden from consecrating their flag in Tartu in 1884, they defiantly brought it to the Otepää church. Their trek is honoured in the tiny Estonian Flag Museum (Eesti Lipu Muuseum; open in summer) in the nearby rectory. Stone reliefs on the church's front doors that depicted this momentous nationalistic event were destroyed by the Soviets, but the locals replaced them with bronze casts in 1990. The "Monument to the 54" in front of the church, dedicated to the soldiers from Otepää who died in the War of Independence, was also blown up by the Soviets – once in the 1950s, and again in the early 1980s – but each time it was replaced by the people of Otepää.

Linnamägi, former site of a 10–11th-century wooden stronghold and a bishop's 13th-century stone castle, is a small tree-covered hill a short walk south from the church past a municipal garden. The first level of the hill is marked with a large stone monument dated 1116, the year when Otepää first appears in the records. Locals use this spot for their midsummer celebrations. The excavated ruins of the castle stand on the shelf above. The expansive vista from here makes it easy to imagine why ancient warriors fought for the site.

Magic oak

In ancient times Estonians gathered under oaks whenever they had to make important decisions. The most famous oak – the one chosen to decorate the 2 kroon bank note – is a couple of kilometres outside the centre of Otepää.

Every summer Pühajärv hosts a lakeside "beach party", a festival of non-traditional music that attracts muscians from far and wide.

BELOW: the magic Pühajärv Oak.

Standing wide and noble between a cow pasture, vegetable patch and Pühajärv lake, the **Pühajärv Oak** is 20 metres (65 ft) tall. Five people linking arms can reach around it and it is believed to be the biggest and oldest tree in the country. Its popular name is the War Tree (Sõjatamm), because of its part in independence history. In 1841, a local German landlord tried to force the Estonian peasants on his land to use heavier equipment than they felt their horses could draw. They refused, which resulted in a battle beneath the oak. The peasants lost, but their act became a legend of Estonian solidarity.

Neitsijärv, or Virgin's Lake, which you pass on the way from the town to the War Tree, derives its name from the Middle Ages when the *droit du seigneur* meant that brides had to spend their first married night in the bed of the Pühajärv landlord. One young girl left her wedding for the manor and never appeared. In the morning, they found her bridal dress beside this lake, where she had drowned herself.

Pühajärv, the largest of the lakes in the area, literally means "Holy Lake". The public beach here is a well-maintained "Blue-Flag"-quality beach where there is a lifeguard on duty all summer, and boats can be rented out. Soviet dissidents Andrei Sakarov and Alexander Solzhenitsyn both used to spend quiet weeks by Lake Püha and, if you ask, locals will show you where the prime minister of Estonia during the Soviet era kept his holiday home. He alone was allowed to use a motorboat here. His house is now a guest house owned by Tartu University.

The southern border

About 20 km (13 miles) south from here is **Sangaste Loss** ❺ (Sangaste Castle; open May–Aug daily 10am–6pm; Sept–Apr daily 10am–4pm; admission fee)

Map on pages 96–7

BELOW: ice fishing on Lake Pühajärv.

built in 1874–81 for Count Friedrich Georg Magnus von Berg as a small-scale copy of Windsor Castle in England. It is a particularly incongruous-looking orange-brick mansion set back amid acres of agricultural plains. The manor was seized in the 1930s and most of the family fled to Finland. Sangaste has passed through many hands since, even housing hay and a tractor in its octagonal, multi-vaulted ballroom after World War II. In the 1970s, it was used as a Young Pioneers' Camp. These days it is a hotel and a conference centre, and is open for tours.

Wide pastureland separates Sangaste from **Valga** ❻, the southernmost city in Estonia, whose main claim to fame is that it straddles the border with Latvia where it becomes Valka. When both countries became independent in 1918, the new border divided streets and in some cases, even houses. After a brief respite during Soviet times, border posts went up again in the early 1990s, and are expected to remain until both countries adopt the Schengen accords. Many non-Estonians live here, and unlike other southern towns it is not in the hills and it is industrially developed.

If you edge down along the border for about 45 km (30 miles), you will reach one of Estonia's largest forests. The **Mõniste Open-Air Museum** ❼ (Mõniste Vabaõhumuuseum; open May–Sept daily 10am–5pm; Oct–Apr Mon–Fri 10am–2pm; admission fee) here contains a reconstruction a 19th-century southern Estonian farmhouse. Between Mõniste and Võru is the peaceful hamlet of **Rõuge** ❽. A picture of southern harmony, Rõuge curls in around seven clear lakes. One, called Rõuge Suurjärv, or Rõuge's Big Lake, is the deepest in Estonia (38 metres/125 ft). The Rõuge church (1730), with a white exterior and red-roofed bell-tower, is delightful. Its organ was built by the local Kriisa Brother

TIP

Rõuge makes a good base for exploring southern Estonia. Ask at the tourist office in Haanja mnt 1 (tel: 785 9245) for farm and rural accommodation.

BELOW: view from Big Egg Hill near Võru.

organ makers. Behind the church lies the Valley of Nightingales, which attracts hundreds of these birds in spring.

Map on pages 96–7

The Hannja Highland

To the east lies the **Haanja Highland**. Haanja is slightly higher than the Otepää and Sakala uplands and its forests are deeper, but it has also been widely tamed by potato fields and pastureland. Its summit is **Suur-Munamägi**, or Big Egg Hill due east of Rõuge. The highest peak in Estonia, reaching 318 metres (1,044 ft) above sea level, it has a 35-metre (115-ft) observation tower on its summit, and the result is a view that is truly heavenly. On the clearest days, you can see all the way to Russia and Latvia.

It may also be possible to glimpse the ruins of **Vastseliina Castle**. To reach it, head east towards the "new" Vastseliina village, whose cultural centre is in an 18th-century manor house. The "old" village, called Vahtseliina, was built in the 14th century around the castle, but not much is left of either. The red and beige brick castle has been reduced to two towers and one section of wall, lost in an overgrown section of field. The 19th-century Vahtseliina coach stop, where a tsar once stayed, has been turned into a restaurant.

The folds of Haanja were created during the Ice Age, and the landscape is smooth and unending. Gentle pastures are edged by lone farmhouses and tiny lakes that appear then fade. The most popular place for fishing is **Verijärv**, or Blood Lake, a bit closer to Võru and filled with perch and pike. Large and picturesque, at the base of another steep forested valley, it got its name because a servant supposedly once drove a cruel lord of the manor into its waters.

BELOW:
Vastseliina Castle.

Võru **9**, the urban centre for the Haanja Highland, sprawls around the biggest lake in the town, Tamula järv. Along with agriculture, Võru depends on forestry, furniture-making and dairy production. The population is about 16,000 and the local dialect, Võru-Seto, which is spoken by the southern Estonians from Võrumaa and Setuma, was recently declared a separate language.

The town was officially established in 1784, and both the small yellow Orthodox church and St Catherine's Church (Katariina kirik) were built soon after. The most famous 18th-century structure in Võru is the Friedrich Reinhold Kreutzwald Memorial Museum (F.R. Kreutzwaldi memoriaalmuuseum; open Wed–Sun 11am–6pm) on Kreutzwald Street 31. This is where the Estonian writer and doctor lived for most of his life. Kreutzwald was born in the Rakvere region in 1803 and studied in Tartu from 1826 to 1833. However, he spent the next 44 years practising medicine in Võru where he compiled *Kalevipoeg*, the Estonian national epic.

The museum is divided between three houses. The first is where the small home of Kreutzwald's Estonian mother stood; she could not bear to live in the same house as Kreutzwald's wife, Maria, who was from a wealthy German family in Tartu. This house has an exhibition of his life and many publications. His own home has been kept as much as possible as it was when he lived there and it includes portraits of the family, who, ironically, spoke only German at home. Maria could not understand why her husband bothered with Estonian. On the walls of the low building at the back of the yard are interpretations of *Kalevipoeg* from a panorama of artists, including some of Estonia's best-known, such as Erik Haamer, Juri Arrak and Kristjan Raud.

Kreutzwald Park runs towards the lake down Katariina Street to a statue of

The home of doctor and writer Freidrich Reinhold Kreutzwald.

BELOW: the Estonian Agriculture Museum.

Kreutzwald. The Võru County Museum (Võrumaa Muuseum; open Wed–Sun 11am–6pm; admission fee) stands at the start of the park. Exhibits range from the area's 5,000-year-old settlement to life in the 20th century. Art and handicraft displays change every month.

Map on pages 96–7

Return route to Tartu

The drive from Võru back up to Tartu gradually becomes less hilly but the forests remain. Main road No. 2 is the most direct route, but the 64, an older road, is a more leisurely option. Tucked into a forest that has been protected by the state as a "gene bank", just beyond **Põlva** ❿ on the right, is the impressive **Kiidjärve Mill**. Constructed in 1914 and trimmed with orange brick, it is the largest functioning watermill in Europe. The **Põlva Peasant Culture Museum** (Põlva Talurahvamuuseum; open May–mid-Oct daily 9am–6pm; admission fee) lies on the other side of the Tartu road, in the village of Karilatsi just beyond **Kiidjärve**. One section displays farm equipment in sheds that look very well-worn. The other section is home to an old schoolhouse that is still set for lessons, a windmill that you can enter and a garden that was designed to be a map of the region.

Setu has traditional "song mothers", women who have kept local songs alive and can recite many hours of verse.

Just outside Tartu, 7 km (5 miles) from the city centre on the Võru road, is a better maintained outdoor museum of agricultural history, the **Estonian Agricultural Museum** (Eesti Põllumajandusmuuseum; open 15 May–15 Sept daily 9am–5pm; 16 Sept–14 May daily 10am–4pm; admission fee). Fittingly, the surrounding landscape is anchored by far-flung farms, many of which have been renovated. It is a sign that the south is ploughing on, refusing to be shaken by the north's vagaries. ❑

BELOW: cat on the road back to Tartu.

THE WEST COAST

Estonia's west coast is famous for its spa resorts of Pärnu and Haapsalu, its ghostly castles and the abundant flowers and birdlife in the Sooma and Matsalu National Parks

T he spas of Estonia's western shore used to be favoured by Russian tsars, and even under Soviet rule Russians flocked here for their summer holidays. Today they attract Western – and in particular Finnish – visitors. Estonia's prime spa resort, **Pärnu** ⑪, is one of the few places outside Tallinn where people traditionally know how to deal with a tourist. Known as Estonia's "Summer Capital", the town of 44,000 inhabitants is 130 km (80 miles) due south of Tallinn on the E67. Its recent revival began in the 1990s when the majestic Rannahotel (1937) overlooking the beach was refurbished, and the Art-Nouveau gem, the Ammende Villa, reopened, both restoring touches of pre-war elegance to the city's beach area. More recently, the Hotell St Peterburg has added some 18th-century class to the mix, and the modern Tervise Paradiis health resort has made a loud splash with its gigantic, indoor water park.

The long beachfront and numerous parks are restorative places to stroll, and the Old Town is ripe with structural curiosities. Younger Estonians particularly like Pärnu; all summer the bars and cafés are hopping, and the cultural calendar is packed with concerts and festivals.

The city proper, first noted in 1251, is divided by the River Pärnu. Rather confusingly, the Old Town lies on the south bank within what the locals refer to as the "new" city. The "old" city, north of the river, is where the majority of newer buildings are located. The reason for this is linked to Pärnu's complex history. During the 14th century, the area where the Old Town stands was occupied by a castle and fortification. But when the Swedes took power in 1617, they began to build across the river instead. The castle fell into decay and was finally destroyed during the Great Northern War (1700–21). This made the section on the north bank the oldest part of the city when, in subsequent centuries, development began to spill back over to the former castle area. This "old city" was, however, flattened during World War II, putting the area with the oldest buildings, or the "old town", back on the south side of the river.

LEFT: kite flying on the beach at Pärnu.
BELOW: Pärnu's Tallinn Gate.

Pärnu Old Town

Touring Pärnu's Old Town is far less complicated. For one thing, it isn't very large. Visiting would take only a couple of hours, if so many of the most eye-catching buildings didn't also contain enticing bars and cafés. Its main street, the pedestrianised Rüütli Street, runs nearly the entire length of the Old Town, and is by far the city's most active. Smaller cross streets, however, provide some of the town's more interesting architectural finds.

Pühavaimu Street, running through the Old Town's centre, is one example. First on the block is a deli-

TIP

The David Oistrakh
Festival is a highlight
of the summer season
in Parnü. It takes place
in the town's new
five-storey concert
hall every July.
Masterclasses by
Estonian conductor
Neeme Järvi are part
of the festival.

BELOW: Pärnu Town
Hall and, in the
distance, the spires of
St Catherine's Church.

cate yellow building (1670), fronted by an imposing balcony that bears four small lions' heads. Squeezed in next to it is an odd red- and mustard-coloured house (1877) that mixes everything from Corinthian columns to a flowery grey trim. It in turn merges into a green baroque structure (1674) trimmed with courtly white and crowned with an old street lamp. The nearby Seegimaja (Almshouse), at Hospidali 1, dates from the 1600s. The grand, peaked edifice was built in 1658, and now operates as a restaurant.

Generally, however, the Old Town isn't so old; most buildings date from the 19th century. But it does have two intact 18th-century churches, which are perhaps most remarkable for their physical proximity but absolute disparity. St Catherine's Church (Ekateriina kirik, 1765–68) is a weird Orthodox conglomeration of knobs and ledges, with green roofing and unevenly soaring spires. The interior is almost lunatic in its iconography; silver shield-like icons crowd the white walls. Meanwhile, the red-and-white Lutheran church, St Elisabeth's Church (Eliisabeti kirik, 1747) at Nikolai 22 a few blocks away, is austere by comparison, but nonetheless impressive. Its charming interior and acoustics have made it a much-used venue for classical music performances.

There are also two remnants of the original 14th-century fortifications. One is the Punane Torn (Red Tower), saved during the Swedish era to house prisoners. Tucked down a small alley off Hommiku Street, it is easy to miss, particularly since, contrary to its name, it is coloured a gleaming white.

The other piece left of the ancient walls is the Tallinna Väravad (Tallinn Gate). Grey and white with tall green doors, it doubles as a bar; Baar Tallinna Väravad has been carved into the earthworks above it.

Passing through the gate, you find yourself on a lovely, long, tree-lined

walk beside a finger of the River Pärnu curled inwards to create a duck-filled pond. This is the beginning of the lush parks that surround the sanatoriums in a rather awesome silence.

Mud treatment

The sanatoriums offer a wide variety of treatments, from aromatic massages to the more traditional mud baths for muscle and joint aches. Though no longer considered a cure-all, mud has been a mainstay of Pärnu's resort industry since the 19th century. The most striking symbol of this activity is the Pärnu Mudaravila (Pärnu Mud Baths), housed in a neoclassical building (1926) at the end of Supeluse Street. Now used primarily as a cultural centre, it no longer provides treatment, having long since handed over the task to more modern equivalents nearby. The elaborate, mint-coloured Pärnu Kuursaal (Beach Salon), next door at Mere Avenue 22, functions as a gigantic tavern, as well as a cultural centre with a bandstand behind it. Its front pavilion, facing the beach, has a picturesque fountain and a row of ornamental wicker arches, festooned with vines each summer.

These two buildings stand by the northwest edge of Pärnu Beach, beginning with the Women's Beach where only women and small children are allowed so that they can sunbathe nude in peace. You can walk for miles from here along the tree-lined promenade that parallels the beach; continuing north brings you past a summer Tivoli and through a collection of modern sculptures and finally fields of dank, waving reed, while a turn south leads to the more crowded sections of waterfront, ad-hoc cafés, the functionalist-style Rannahoone (Beach House), and mini-golf course.

The elegant Scandic Rannahotell in Pärnu was designed by the Estonian functionalist architects Olev Siinmaa and Anton Soans. Have a drink on its roof terrace and check out its style.

BELOW:
mud house and sanatorium, Pärnu.

Haabja are the traditional boats, hollowed out of single tree trunks, on Soomaa National Park's waterways. They are available for hire, as are kayaks and canoes.

The Old Town has its own walks, the most famous of which is the triangular Lydia Koidula Park. The poet Koidula (1843–86) was born in a village outside Pärnu but she lived in the city from the age of seven until, at 20, she moved with her family to Tartu. Many consider Koidula's collection of verse, *The Nightingale of Emajõgi*, to be the foremost work of Estonia's period of National Awakening, and the pen-name Koidula, given to her by a fellow artist, means literally "singer of the dawn". Her real maiden name was Jannsen, and the modest wooden schoolhouse where her family lived is on Jannseni 37. The house itself is now the Lydia Koidula Museum (open Wed–Sun 10am–6pm), but for those who don't speak Estonian it is a bit dull since the contents are mostly cases of her poetry, books and writings.

The Pärnu Museum, on the other hand, is surprisingly rewarding. Located in a dim, Soviet-style building, its outward appearance is dreary but the artefacts within are worth a look. Archaeological finds date from as early as 8000 BC. A 13th-century woman's costume, a 16th-century Gothic chalice and embossed-leather Bible, and 19th-century furniture are also on display.

National Parks

From Pärnu, a side-trip to the **Soomaa National Park** ⑫ (Soomaa rahvuspark) provides a look at a landscape that's little seen elsewhere in Europe. At the end of route 59 through **Tori** and **Jõesuu**, signs direct drivers into the heart of the 371 sq. km (143 sq. mile) nature reserve. *Soomaa* literally means "land of bogs", and while the area is known for its floodplains and fauna, its most unique feature is its mysterious and often misty high bogs – clear areas with peaty land, low trees and small ponds – a scene that doesn't look like it belongs on our planet. They can only be reached by carefully walking over specially

BELOW:
Tori farmyard.

built plank pathways. Soomaa's Visitors' Centre (open 1 May–15 Sept daily 10am–3pm; 16 Sept–30 Apr Wed–Sat 10am–3pm) will provide trail maps. Early June, when flowers are in bloom, is the best time to visit. In late June–August, mosquito repellent is a must.

Route 60 northwest from Pärnu leads to the small town of **Lihula** which has a huge, Soviet-built cultural centre, a plaster-and-stone Orthodox church and a point-spired Lutheran church. Just 3 km (2 miles) north from Lihula, the village of **Penijõe** is the gateway to the **Matsalu National Park** ⓭ (Matsalu Rahvuspark). Matsalu Bay has a range of habitats including reed beds, water meadows, hay meadows and coastal pastures. It was already noted for its birdlife back in 1870. Among the species found here today are avocet, sandwich tern, mute swan, greylag goose and bittern. There are also some white-tailed eagles. The reserve was formed from 39,700 hectares (98,000 acres) of the bay area in 1957. It can be visited by car or, since water covers some 26,300 hectares (65,000 acres) of this same area, by boat. Boat excursions of the rivers and the bay can be arranged though the Visitors' Centre in Penijõe (open 15 Apr–15 Sept daily 8am–noon & 1–5pm; 16 Sept–14 Apr Mon–Fri 8am–noon & 1–5pm), located in a restored 17th-century manor house.

Haapsalu and Matsalu Bay

Matsalu Bay (Matsula laht) lies in the southern part of the coastal district of Läänemaa. One of the flattest sections of the already rather flat Estonia, it is also low in arable land but the overall impression is certainly pastoral. The main town is **Haapsalu** ⓮, which has close to 12,000 inhabitants. A large military base and fishery were established here under the Soviets and although the entire

Map on pages 96–7

BELOW: local stables.

district has been under either Russian or Soviet control since 1710 (except for the 20 years of the republic), many locals identify strictly with the Swedes, who ruled over them from 1581 to 1710. It was under the Russians, however, that Haapsalu became a spa of great repute and it was to satisfy Russian demands that many of its fanciest buildings were constructed.

The town originally centred around the Haapsalu Episcopal Castle (Haapsalu Piiskopilinnus, which dates from 1279. Little of the castle remains, but its courtyard has become a favourite spot for picnics and concerts, and technological additions mean that visitors hear sound effects emanating from various corners. In summer, the castle doubles as a museum (open Tues–Sun 10am–6pm; admission fee) chronicling the town's history, and its watchtower is open to the public.

The best-preserved part of the castle is the Romano-Gothic cathedral, one of only three functioning cathedrals in Estonia. Single-naved and towerless, it was built to double-up as a fortress, and its immense facade looks stubbornly impenetrable. Inside, the tall white walls and high-vaulted ceiling are almost bare. In a side chapel is a baptismal font from 1634, with Adam, Eve and the serpent etched into its bowl; a vivid reminder of original sin to be washed away. Against its wall leans a sad wooden sculpture of a woman holding a child; a memorial to the people from Läänemaa deported to Siberia. The box beneath it, marked "1949–1989", contains Siberian soil. Directly above it is the window of the White Lady, focus of Haapsalu's favourite local legend (*see box below*).

Directly in front of the castle entrance is the large square that used to house the town market and just to the left (or west) is the space that served as the Swedish Market (Roosti Turu). It now encloses a very pleasant café, open in summer. On the square's east side is the Läänemaa County Museum (open

Haapsalu wooden houses.

RIGHT:
Haapsalu Castle.

THE WHITE LADY

The "white lady" is Haapsalu's favourite local legend. As the story goes, a monk from the cloister of the castle fell in love with a sweet village girl and brought her into the castle disguised as a boy. When she began to sing in the choir, their treachery was discovered. As punishment, she was built into the walls and he was thrown into the cellar.

Every August, at the time of the full moon, the poor girl is reputed to return, and there are few villagers who do not claim to have seen her white reflection in the window of the cathedral above the memorial to those deported to Siberia. She is not timid; she will appear before even a large crowd, and during this time, in fact, Haapsalu holds a "White Lady Festival" of cultural events that climaxes with the audience walking en masse to the southwest side of the cathedral where this window stands, with someone enacting the white lady's role.

16 May–14 Sept Wed–Sun 11am–4pm; 16 Sept–14 May Wed–Sun 10am–6pm; admission fee), within what used to be the Town Hall. Many of the artefacts inside come from the castle and there are exhibitions about the region's old farms and Haapsalu's days as a summer resort.

Across the street from the Läänemaa Museum is a new museum that shows off the works of one of Haapsalu's most famous residents, Ilon Wikland, illustrator of the Pippi Longstocking books. She was born in Haapsalu and, although she fled with her family to Sweden at the age of 14, she has depicted the town and the small house on Rüütli Street beside the Adventist church where her father was minister in many drawings.

The town has also been rich in handicraft artists, and the "Haapsalu Shawl", created of such fine wool that it can be drawn through a ring, is known throughout Estonia. A couple of shops specialise in local crafts, and one particular shop/museum near the Swedish Market allows visitors to try their own hand at craftmaking.

Promenade and Africa Beach

Just a couple of streets to the north is to the seaside Promenaadi (promenade). Here you can see the ghosts of Haapsalu's spa days by walking down to the "African Beach", so called because locals sunning themselves here, covered with the town's famous curative mud, were said to resemble dark-skinned Africans. Additionally, in the early 20th century there used to be, along with little bathing houses, statues of wild animals set in the water. Although the water isn't safe for swimming any more, locals are still fond of strolling the path alongside it. The restored Haapsalu Kuursaal (Resort Hall), built in the 1900s,

Map on pages 96–7

TIP

Haapsalu's best beach is Paralepa, 1km west of the railway station.

BELOW: Haapsalu.

is an historic delight with green-painted timber, lacy cut-out porticos, and surrounding rose garden. For generations, concerts have been held in the bandstand beside it. Of interest here are a sundial and a set of steps by the artist R. Haavamägi, who was born in Haapsalu, and the Tchaikovsky Bench. The Russian composer used to favour Haapsalu for his holidays and even used a motif from a traditional Estonian song in his 6th Symphony. The bench is decorated with the composer's likeness and, at the press of a button, it plays some notes from the 6th. This is the spot where he came every evening to watch the sun set. The Tchaikovsky festival is one of a number of music festivals held here during the summer.

The Estonian Railway Museum

Continuing further down Sadama Road from this point will bring you to the Estonian-Swedish Museum (Rannarootsi muuseum; open May–Aug Wed–Sun 10am–6pm; Sept–Apr Wed–Sun 10am–4pm; admission fee), where the history of the local seafaring Swedish community comes to light. Swedes settled along Estonia's coasts and islands as early as Viking times, and maintained a culture separate from the Estonians. Nearby, the Haapsalu Yacht Club continues to thrive, but has been upstaged by a Grand Holm Marina, which has been built to cater for the summer Baltic yacht crowd, a few metres away.

Town activity has moved away from the castle and beach down the lengthy Posti Street. However, if you wander the quaint back streets or the curious and creepy overgrown Old Town Graveyard – which lies on Posti Street opposite the very comfortable Haapsalu Hotel – you will find it easy to understand the appeal that Haapsalu has held for artists.

BELOW: Haapsalu railway museum.

From here, Jaama Street leads off to the right. At its end is the splendid railway station, built in 1905 to receive Tsar Nicholas II on his summer holiday.

Map on pages 96–7

After years of neglect, it was spruced up for the town's 725th anniversary celebrations in 2004. A number of antique locomotives are on display on the tracks, and the station's Emperor's Salon houses a small branch of the Eesti Raudteemuuseum (Estonian Railway Museum; open Wed–Sun 10am–6pm; admission fee). Further on, paths lead through a park, ending at the reedy, calm Paralepa Beach.

Eccentric side trip

Heading out of town back towards Tallinn will take you past the home of Ants Laikmaa, an influential early 20th-century Estonian painter. Laikmaa was an eccentric, and the home he designed for himself, which has been turned into the **Ants Laikmaa Museum** ⑮ (open 16 May–14 Sept Wed–Sun 11am–4pm; 16 Sept–14 May Wed–Sun 10am–6pm; admission fee) is a peculiar blend of red-and-white piping with a steep moss-covered roof that has to be seen to be believed. A small sign points towards a bumpy road leading through the woods. The house at its end, in a large yard, was begun in 1923 and was changed in design so many times that it was never finished during Laikmaa's lifetime. Laikmaa was immensely popular in Haapsalu.. He was known for known for his handsome moustaches, for using carriages long after the advent of the car, and for appearing in costume when the mood struck him. He was also the host of many unusual house parties.

From here Tallinn is about an hour's drive northeast. If you feel that you have not yet truly experienced the sea, head west. At **Rohuküla**, 8 km (5 miles) away, you can catch a ferry to the islands of **Vormsi** or **Hiiumaa** *(see page 161)* where the water is clean and tourists are few and far between.   ❏

BELOW:
quiet waters.

THE ISLANDS

*Saaremaa and Hiiumaa, the two largest islands off the west coast,
are idyllic rural retreats of windmills, fishing boats
and farmhouse bed-and-breakfasts*

Map
on pages
96–7

Most of the 1,500 or so islands off the coast of Estonia are mere hiccups, but two are so sizeable that island acreage ultimately accounts for some 10 percent of Estonia's total land territory. These larger islands, Saaremaa and Hiiumaa, are perhaps the most unspoilt and attractive corners of the country. Their pristine condition is due partly to the Soviet occupation. Clustered off the western shore, these islands were, rightly, considered likely points of escape to the West as well as strategic security posts. They were therefore kept for the most part incommunicado from the rest of the Soviet Union. At the same time, since they clearly were impractical for any industrial projects, they were spared the scars of heavy development. A few scattered military installations – now eerily abandoned – are the only reminder of the area's former status as a high-security zone.

The Soviets were by no means the first of Estonia's neighbours to have territorial designs on Saaremaa and Hiiumaa. In the 13th century the islands were divided between the Oesel-Wiek (Saare-Lääne) bishopric and the Livonian Order. Three centuries later, Saaremaa (Oesel) reverted to Denmark while Sweden took Hiiumaa. In 1645, Saaremaa also was assigned to the Swedes and from then on they were destined to share Estonia's fate. Somehow, the islanders stubbornly retained a distinct way of life. They also began to stockpile impressive monuments left behind by the parade of conquering egos. The 13th-century churches and 18th-century manor houses that decorate their shores have now been mostly repaired, and have become mainstays of the islands' budding tourism industry. There are some delightful farm bed-and-breakfasts to chose from, too.

LEFT: perfect boating waters.
BELOW: Saaremaa windmill keeper.

Across the sea

To reach Saaremaa, the largest of all the Estonian islands, it is necessary first to cross **Muhu** ⑯, where the ferry from **Virtsu** on the mainland docks. Estonia's third-largest island, Muhu is only 201 sq. km (78 sq. miles) and, along with about 500 smaller islands, belongs to the greater Saaremaa County. Muhu does not hold nearly the number of attractions as its larger neighbour, but it does have sights worth stopping to see.

The most commercial of these is unquestionably **Pädeste Mõis** (Pädeste Manor). The estate, which dates from the 16th century, was once the home of the Baltic-German Buxhoveden family. Its Tudor-style main building (1875) is now being restored, but the beautifully decorated outbuildings have been turned into a luxury guesthouse and exclusive gourmet restaurant – reputed to be one of the best in the Baltics. More down-to-earth sightseeing can be found in the village of **Koguva**, where the outdoor Muhu Museum (open 16 May–31 Aug daily 10am–7pm; 1 Sept–15 May Wed–Sun 10am–5pm; admission fee) is located. The area nearby is thought to have been settled in the late Iron Age, but this still-inhabited fishing village was first documented in 1532. Of the 105 buildings that remain, parts of three date from the early and mid-18th century, making it the oldest preserved conglomerate of peasant architecture on the islands. A stroll through the village, with its thatched roofs, moss-covered rock walls and windmill, evokes images of a much quieter age.

Koguva is not far from the causeway that leads to Saaremaa. It is a beautiful road, and terribly romantic. The water on either side is filled by a beckoning green carpet of swaying reeds. In spring, it changes to white as thousands of swans come here to mate.

Saaremaa island

Saaremaa is, at some 2,668 sq. km (1,030 sq. miles), a spacious, quiet and unassuming place. Much of its land has been cultivated, and the simple island roads are laced with field after field of livestock and wheat, interrupted only by patches of thick forest. Industry is at a minimum and, with the exception of those involved in tourism, those inhabitants who aren't at work on the land tend to be connected to the sea.

There is only one town of real consequence, **Kuressaare** ⑰, on the south side of the island, where 16,000 of Saaremaa County's 38,000 inhabitants live. Kuressaare is said to have been particularly popular with party officials during the Soviet regime and it certainly is extremely handsome.

Most of the buildings in the centre are gems of late 18th- and early 19th-

TIP

Try to avoid visiting Saaremaa on a summer weekend. It is a favourite with Estonians, and queues for the ferry can be long.

BELOW: Koguva farm village, Muhu.

century neoclassicism, with pretty wooden houses and gardens mixed in beside them. Side streets reveal an ancient hand-pump for water or a freshly painted home with a paint-can tied proudly to its wooden gate. On Kaevu Street, an old windmill has been transformed into the unabashedly touristy Veski bar and restaurant.

Activity focuses around the triangular plaza where Tallinna Street turns into Lossi Street. At this junction are the market, the administrative halls and, after 9pm, the main spot for local youths to see and be seen. The yellow Town Hall, (Raekoja, 1654–70) lies along the hypotenuse of this triangle, its entrance protected by stone lions. A peek inside is a good idea, as the building houses art exhibitions as well as the town's Tourist Information Centre.

To the left of the Town Hall stands an 18th-century fire station of burnt-brown wood. Opposite it is the Weigh House (Vaekoda), with a stepped gable. Dating from 1663, the Weigh House is now a popular café and pub, and encloses one side of the tiny Market Square. Here, in addition to jars of gooseberries in season you will find a range of distinctively patterned, hand-made woollen sweaters and mittens for sale, and items carved from the island's famous, fragrant juniper wood. Sometimes there will also be a table or two piled high with slippery black mounds of the expensive Saaremaa speciality, eel.

A second, smaller square lies a few steps down Lossi Street. This has the County Seat and a monument for the fallen in the War of Liberation. This is actually the third such monument erected here; twice the Soviets tore it down only for the locals to re-erect it.

Continuing down Lossi will take you past the Apostolic Orthodox St Nicholas Church (Nikolai kirik, 1790). Its fancy front gate tied with large silver-painted bows is unmistakable and its white exterior is topped with rounded green spires. The interior echoes this colour scheme, and treads between neoclassical and Byzantine styles.

Kuressaare's main tourist attraction and its *raison d'être* is at the end of the street. The Kuressaare Episcopal Castle (Kuressaare Piiskopiliinus) was built as the bishop of Oesel-Wiek's foothold on Saaremaa, and first recorded in 1384. It is the only entirely preserved medieval stone castle in all of the Baltic nations. Ringed by a large and beautiful public park, a moat and imposing bastions erected during the mid-17th century, the castle is in the unyielding, geometric, late-Gothic style, made of white-grey dolomite quarried in Saaremaa. Each corner is crowned by a tower with an orange turret and at the heart of the castle is a tiny, symmetrical courtyard. From the courtyard, stone steps lead down to basement rooms and up to a narrow, vaulted cloister. The former refectory lies on the west, and to the north are the austere former living quarters of the bishop.

Ten elaborate wooden epitaphs from the 17th century represent coats of arms of noblemen in Saaremaa and their individual occupations. One has oars, another tools, a third stags and arrows. Climbing the towers is worthwhile but requires fortitude; the watchtower in the southeast corner of the convent building is connected by a drawbridge suspended 9 metres (30 ft)

BELOW:
Kuressaare castle.

TIP

The Vilsandi National
Park Visitors' Centre is
in Loona Manor (Loona
Mõis) 3 km (2 miles)
south of Kihelkonna.
It has rooms to rent,
tel: 454 6510.

above the ground, and the defence tower is honeycombed with stone stairways. Some of the castle's upper rooms house the Saaremaa Museum (open May–Aug daily 10am–6pm; Sept–Apr Wed–Sun 11am–6pm; admission fee). This rich collection traces the inhabitants of Saaremaa from the 4th millennium BC and has a number of fascinating wood carvings, including its pride and joy, the late 16th-century *Coronation of St Mary* attributed to Lübeck artist Henning van der Heide, and the oldest preserved wooden sculpture in Estonia: *Seated Madonna with the Infant* (1280–90). Other sections of the museum encompass the late-Tsarist and pre-World War II period, as well as the island's natural history.

From the castle, it is a pleasant walk down to the small, newly built yacht harbour. Nearby is Kuressaare's popular public beach. More secluded bathing can be found just a few minutes south of the town at the Mandjala-Järve beach.

Other spots to visit in Kuressaare include the restored Kuursaal (Resort Club), a grand, ornate, wooden recreation hall built for tourists in 1861. It stands not far from the castle. At Vallimaa 7 is the Aaviks' Memorial Museum (Aavikute Maja-muuseum; open Wed–Sun 11am–6pm; admission fee), a tiny, old-fashioned house that was once home to a renowned linguist, Johannes Aavik (1880–1973), and his cousin Joosep Aavik (1899–1989), a musician and composer.

Saaremaa Island road trip

Travelling to **Kihelkonna** ⑱ in the west, and following the coast up to Leisi in the north, then back south to Kuressaare will take you into **Vilsandi National Park** (Vilsandi rahvuspark), which encompasses Vilsandi and 150 other offshore islets. Many of Saaremaa's interesting sites will be passed on the way. First stop is the Mihkli Farm Museum (Mihkli Talumuuseum; open 15–30 Apr &

BELOW:
island fishermen.

Map on pages 96-7

Sept Wed–Sun 10am–6pm; May–Aug daily 10am–6pm; admission fee) near the town of Viki. Although small, this open-air museum shows exactly what a typical farm in western Saaremaa is like. The main dwelling house (1834) stands with most of the other buildings in a circle enclosing a yard and a quaint little flower garden. Most of the roofs are covered with reed, and the walls are of dolomite or wood. Original objects from the farmstead include household equipment with the Mihkli family emblem.

Turning at Kihelkonna north towards **Mustjala**, you will first catch a glimpse of the pointed red bell-tower of the medieval Kihelkonna church and then the ancient, weathered-grey Pidula watermill. From here it is a short drive to the **Panga Pank** (Panga Scarp). This steep limestone outcrop is one of the highest points on the island and one of the loveliest. The water below is almost olive green but so clear you can easily make out the thousands of pebbles that line the sea floor. In the distance, the horizon stretches blue and endlessly, except for the tiny shadow of Hiiumaa Island. In summer the sound of crickets fills the air.

Unsurprisingly, this very magical place has played a central role in island superstitions. In pre-Christian times, locals would throw one baby boy, born the winter before, off the cliff into the water every spring; this was an offering to the sea god with the prayer that he send back a lot of fish. In later times, they threw a ram instead, and even up to the 1930s, there are records of barrels of the island's famous beer being poured over the cliff's edge to ensure a good catch. Island brides have continued the long-established tradition of "scarp pitching" to this day: on the eve of their wedding they often write their maiden name on a piece of paper, put it into a bottle and throw it off the cliff.

Turning east takes you to **Leisi**, an attractive rural town, from where the road

BELOW: Saaremaa family home.

TIP

Bicycles are the best way to get around Saaremaa, which has a poor transport system but some delightful rural bed-and-breakfasts.

heads south and in a few miles reaches the **Angla Windmills** (Angla Tuulikud). In the mid-19th century, there were about 800 windmills on Saaremaa, and the windmill has become the most recognised symbol of the island. Only a small proportion of the original windmills have survived, but at Angla there are five left, sticking up suddenly on a slight swell amid windswept wheat fields.

Nestled behind a moss-covered stone wall on a sloping lawn across from fields of cattle 2 km (1 mile) from here is one of Saaremaa's greatest treasures: the 14th-century **Karja church** ⑲. Saaremaa is packed with some of the earliest churches in the Baltics but no other has such marvellous stone sculptures still intact. These sculptures tell a thousand tales (*see box below*). Like all medieval churches on the islands, Karja church keeps its doors open for visitors during the summer months. Otherwise, in most cases, a caretaker can be found nearby who will unlock the doors with a large iron key and let you in.

If you head south again, turning right at the Liiva-Putla fork, you will reach the tiny hamlet of **Kaarma**, site of another medieval church. Work began on Kaarma church in the latter half of the 13th century but it was rearranged over subsequent centuries and is strikingly large. Its artefacts are more varied than those of Karja. The christening stone, for example, dates from the 13th century, the wooden "Joseph" supporting the pulpit is from around 1450, and the elaborate Renaissance pulpit was finished in 1645. Current restoration work has exposed fragments of early mural painting.

Other 13th- and 14th-century churches in the area worth visiting include Valjala church and Püha church situated east of Kuressaare. The latter most clearly shows how these churches were built not just to be religious centres but also to serve as defensive strongholds.

BELOW: Kaarma church sculptures.

STORIES ON THE CHURCH WALLS

A relief on the first left buttress upon entering Karja kirik (Karja church) depicts village life. A woman listens to another with a pig on her back, symbolising gossip, while the man beside her has a rose behind his ear, representing silence. This is on the northern and thus colder side of the church, the side where the women sat because they were considered to be stronger. St Katherine of Alexandria, to whom the church is dedicated, is carved into the northern arch before the altar. This 14th-century beauty, the legend goes, was wooed by King Maxentius of Egypt who was already married. She refused him and, enraged, he had her arrested and torn to pieces. The sculpture shows her with Maxentius's wife on her left, clinging to her skirt, St Peter on her right and the evil king crushed beneath her feet. Directly opposite is St Nicholas, the protector of seamen and on his left are three village girls who were too poor to marry until he became their benefactor. Painted on to the ceiling above the altar is a table of Christian and pagan marks: the Star of Bethlehem and the symbol of Unity, both drawn with endless lines; the three-legged symbol of the sun; the "leg" devil; and two pentagons, symbols of gloom, which locals point out were also symbols of the Soviet Union.

Map on pages 96–7

If you turn left at the Liiva-Putla fork, you reach a much older landmark, the **Kaali meteoric craters** ❷⓿ (Kaali meteoriidikraatrite väli). These are not particularly beautiful – the largest one is referred to as Lake Kaali and it looks like a big opaque green puddle – but it is remarkable to think that the bowl surrounding it was carved out by part of a 1,000-ton meteor that hit the earth here nearly 3,000 years ago. Eight smaller craters, made from other chips of the meteor, dot the woods surrounding it. There is a large visitors' centre and a guesthouse.

Finally, before leaving Saaremaa, a stop at the **Maasi Order castle ruins** ❷❶ (Maasi Ordulinnuse Varemed) 4 km (2 miles) north of **Orissaare** on the Orissaare–Leisi road rounds out the story of the island's medieval struggles. The Maasi fortress was in many senses Kuressaare Castle's less-fortunate sister. Established by the Livonian Order in the 14th century, it was meant to defend the island's eastern side. Denmark took possession when it purchased this part of Saaremaa in the 1560s, but more than once the fortress was taken over by attacking Swedes and used against the Danes. To prevent a repeat of this tactic, King Frederik of Denmark ordered it destroyed in 1576. Today, some exterior walls are still visible, and the newly excavated vaults have been restored to make it possible for visitors to enter.

Wilder Hiiumaa

For natural beauty, **Hiiumaa Island** is perhaps more rewarding than Saaremaa. At 989 sq. km (382 sq. miles), it is Estonia's second-largest island but has only 11,000 inhabitants, 4,000 of them in the capital of Kärdla on the north coast. There is virtually no settlement in its heart where there is a peat moor (peat

BELOW: Angla windmills.

bogs growing directly on sand) and swamp – and almost all agriculture focuses on the southern and western edge. Some yet to be cultivated areas in the south contain another natural oddity, "wooded meadows", and the rest of the island is overwhelmed by pines and junipers. A road rings the island, conveniently passing its most interesting sights, but there are so few cars on it that inhabitants typically drive on either the left or right according to whim.

Fishing is the most important industry, although until the late 1980s barbed-wire was wrapped along the shore from Kärdla in the north to Emmaste in the far south. The coast is also notoriously treacherous to approach because of the shallow waters of endless shoals and rocks. This means that you have to walk out quite a way over pebbles simply to get your stomach wet, but don't let this deter you from taking a swim in the clean, peaceful waters.

The eastern harbour of **Heltermaa** has been slightly dug out, and it is to here that the ferry from the mainland, at **Rohuküla** by Haapsalu, arrives. Just inland is the historical hamlet of **Suuremõisa ㉒**. Hiiumaa once had around 25 stately manor houses, but most have either been destroyed or have irreparably deteriorated. The Suuremõisa manor is one exception. Built by a Swedish family called Stenbock in 1772, then bought by O.R.L. von Ungern-Sternberg – for decades Hiiumaa's richest and most powerful landowner – this manor still has its main building, stable-master's home and stables, several outbuildings and cellars, and expansive front and back lawns. Under the trees at the back there are gravestones for the family's much-feared guard dogs. Inside the main building are 64 rooms, some with original painted ceilings and ceramic fireplaces. The ground floor currently houses a primary school and the top floor an agricultural school, but in summer the building is open to tourists.

Just down the road is the attractive **Pühalepa Church**. Built of timber in the mid-13th century, then replaced with stone in 1770, its tall white bell-tower, topped by a hexagonal brown roof, has been extended three times since then. Turned into a cellar by the Soviets, the church resumed services on Christmas Eve 1990.

On its south side stands a rather squat white chapel containing the tomb of Ebba Margarethe Gräfin Stenbock, Suuremõisa manor's first owner. On its north side, strewn amid alders, are a tumble of other old graves. Around the northeast corner is a log inset in the church wall; this is the spot through which the priest used to hand out bread to the poor and needy.

A few feet down the gravel road to the north, away from the main road, brings you to the **Contract Stones**, otherwise known as "Hiiumaa's Stonehenge". The origin of this large pile of boulders, which were evidently brought here by hand, is unclear. One popular theory is that before going out to sea local sailors would bring one heavy stone to this spot, and by doing so make an agreement with God to ensure a good voyage and a safe return.

Back up the coast in the main town of **Kärdla**, the Rannapaargu Café, in front of the grassy Kärdla Beach, has been named after this same special type of kitchen. To reach the café, you must walk down Lubjaahju Street past yet another Hiiumaa peculiar-

In winter, when the sea is frozen, a 25-km (15-mile) ice road links Hiiumaa to the mainland, though ferries continue to operate in the path they have kept clear.

BELOW:
crab fisherman.

Map on pages 96–7

ity, the giant swing. Found in villages all over the island, the swings are particularly busy on Midsummer's Eve. A new holiday centre is another place for summer activity in Kärdla, offering horse riding, and a spot where visitors can catch trout and have them prepared on the spot. The Hiiumaa Museum (open Mon–Fri 10am–5pm, Sat 11am–2pm; admission fee) is housed in Kärdla's 19th-century Pikk Maja (Long House).

Swedish memorial

Outside town, 5 km (3 miles) west on the road to the **Kõpu peninsula**, is a more sombre attraction, the **Hill of Crosses ㉓** (Ristimägi). Like many Estonian coastal areas, Hiiumaa was populated for centuries by a large group of Swedes, who, by a time-honoured arrangement with the Swedish crown, were given a special status as freemen. In 1781, however, Stenbock, with the help of Russian Empress Catherine the Great, arranged for around 1,000 of Hiiumaa's Swedes from the village of Reigi to be stripped of their land and rights, and forcibly resettled in Ukraine. Their last church service, a tearful farewell, was held on this hill. According to legend, a local farmer marked the spot with a small, wooden cross. Later, a tradition was established that each new visitor would add his own cross made from sticks found on the ground. The site is now eerily covered with thousands of crosses.

Some of Hiiumaa's most interesting structures are the lighthouses that twinkle along the shore. The most remarkable is the **Kõpu Lighthouse ㉔** (Kõpu Tuletorn; open 1 May–15 Sept daily 9am–10pm; admission fee), halfway out along the thickly forested Kõpu peninsula, on the windswept western wing of the island. This soaring four-cornered and red-crested white lighthouse looks like

BELOW: Tahkuna lighthouse.

Map
on pages
96–7

a cross between a space rocket and a pyramid. First lit in 1531, it is considered to be the third-oldest continuously operating lighthouse in the world. There is a wonderful view from the top; the world below spreads into a sea of dark-green pine and endless water.

Kassari island: an artists' retreat

Understandably, many of Estonia's best-known artists and writers keep summer retreats on Hiiumaa; conductor Eri Klas, for example, has his on Kõpu. But the most popular spot for summer cottages is **Kassari** ㉔, just southwest of Heltermaa. Kassari is one of between 200 and 400 islands (depending on the water level) that cling to the coast of Hiiumaa. It curves in so close to the shore by the town of Käina that it has been incorporated into the larger island with two short bridges. The bay between them, Käinu Bay, is rich in sea mud that attracts birds, including golden eagles and other rare species. You may even see an eagle or two flying over the road. These birds, in turn – along with the island breezes and the sea – are responsible for the richness of flora all over Hiiumaa.

In fact, the island has about 975 different species of plant, some of them, such as the orchids, also quite rare. Kassari, however, is richest in junipers, whose berries and bark might be called the island staple. Its uses include the wood for butter knives that keep butter from turning rancid; the branches for sauna switches to perk up the kidneys; the berries for a vodka spice, a source of vitamin C; and for medicinal purposes. This scraggy dark bush has even been fashioned into furniture. Junipers crowd the pebbly projection of Saaretirp with special determination. This mile-long promontory is a favourite place to picnic or ponder for Kassari residents. The island's sheltered position makes the water warm, and beside it the apples crop early. The last owner of the former Kassari manor house, Baron Edvard Stackelberg, had an especially large orchard, though neither it nor his home still remains. But the small servants' house directly opposite where it stood is in good shape and houses a branch of the Hiiumaa Museum. The exhibition contains a huge light reflector from the 19th-century Tahkuna lighthouse, maps of island history and traditional fishing tools.

Down one more pebble-laden lane is the Kassari chapel, the only stone chapel surviving in Estonia with a roof of thatched reed. Carefully restored in 1990, it has been kept without electricity and is illuminated by a simple central candelabra and candles burned into the end of each old blue-coloured pew. The walls are decorated only with ancient oak-leaf wreaths, taken from funerals in the surrounding graveyard. The graveyard spills out around the church, darkened by shivering trees. Baron Stackelberg's grave is where he wanted it, next to a swineherd's, to show that in front of God all people are equal.

One final church to note back on Hiiumaa island just inland from Kassari is the **Käina church** (Käina kirik), built between 1492 and 1515. Although it was heavily bombed during World War II, it is still a very moving spot. The wind rushes through the limestone shell and over the old tombs that are set directly into its floor. ❏

At the end of the Saaretirp headland nothing remains but a needle point and a large heap of stones: if you find a pebble with a hole in it, make a wish and place it on the pile, and your wish should come true.

BELOW: island cottage.
RIGHT: Saaretirp, at the end of Hiiumaa.

EAST OF TALLINN

Two of Estonia's important wildlife regions are Lahemaa National
Park and Lake Peipsi, the fifth largest in Europe.
Beyond them lies industrial Narva

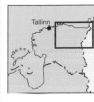

East from Tallinn on the E20, the Narva Highway, the capital's industrial
sprawl gives way to a scene more typical of the country – vast, flat
stretches of road flanked on both sides by forests and ponds. About an
hour's drive from the capital, this road becomes the southern border of **Lahemaa National Park** (Lahemaa Rahvuspark), a truly peaceful and intriguing
area of the country close enough to Tallinn to make it a practical day trip. More
than 75 percent of the 72,500-hectare (180,000-acre) park is woodland and the
population is fewer than 20 per square kilometre. There are remains of ancient
settlements, freshwater lakes, wetlands, a few farms, fishing villages and four
manor houses. Sheltered bays dip between craggy promontories that jut into
the Gulf of Finland. It is an important wildlife area with deer, elk and bear, and
during the migration season, for special species such as the black stork. Plant life
abounds and among the 850 documented varieties is the rare arctic bramble.

    Loksa ㉕ and **Võsu** ㉖ are the park's two main towns. They are the best
stopping points for food shops and cash machines, though neither are of intrin-
sic interest. Loksa is much the larger, with a cargo port, and a mainly Russian
population. It is easy to make trips around the park from either town, but one can
just as easily use the E20 itself as a starting point.

LEFT: Lahemaa
National Park.
BELOW:
Palmse Manor.

Palmse Manor

The turn-off at **Viitna** leads north, to Lahemaa's most
famous landmark, the striking **Palmse Manor** ㉗
(Palmse Mõis; open May–Aug daily 9am–7pm; Sept
daily 9am–5pm; Oct–Apr Mon–Fri 10am–5pm;
admission fee). The beautiful house and grounds are
a testament to the luxuries of 18th-century aristocracy, but this land's history goes back much further. In
1286, a group of nuns from the Cistercian Order of St
Michael in Tallinn were given the land by the King of
Denmark. The pond they built here for their fish farm
is still in use. In 1673, the Von der Pahlen family,
Baltic-German nobles, bought the estate, and in 1730
built the manor house. It was rebuilt in 1782, and was
their home until Estonia's first independence in 1918
when the property was nationalised.

    After World War II, the manor served as a Soviet
Pioneer camp and fell into disrepair. Renovation lasted
between 1972 and 1985, and today the estate is a perfect period piece, filled with Empire furniture. Visitors
are welcome to stroll the grounds where they'll find a
peaceful swan pond, landscaped gardens and a café.

    During the warmer months (May–Oct), one of the
outbuildings flanking the manor's front courtyard
displays an altogether different kind of history – it
houses a coach and car museum exhibiting antique
bicycles and buggies, early 20th-century European

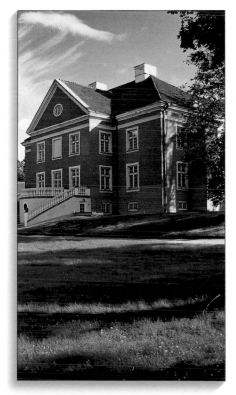

Map on pages 96–7

roadsters and an enormous Zil-111 limousine used by Nikita Khruschev. Across the courtyard is the **Lahemaa Visitor Centre** (open May–Aug daily 9am–7pm; Sept daily 9am–5pm; Oct–Apr Mon–Fri 9am–5pm). Here you'll find information in English on the park's sights and nature walks, and more importantly, detailed maps – a necessity in this area of small, confusingly marked roads.

The nearby church of **Illumäe**, northwest of Palmse, was built by and contains the grave of the most illustrious member of the Von der Pahlen family, Carl Magnus. He fought against Napoleon Bonaparte, allowed the peasants who worked the farm to use his last name, and in 1823 opened the first school for local children. In front of the church is a memorial to those killed during the 20th-century's wars and those who perished in the Gulag.

A turn from Palmse to the northwest leads to another impressive German estate, **Sagadi Manor** (open May–Sept daily 10am–6pm; admission fee). It was built in 1749 and renovated at the end of that century in a classical style. Like Palmse Manor, it has been decorated to reflect 18th-century elegance. One of the renovated outbuildings is a hotel and restaurant, another is a museum of forestry. A stroll behind the main house leads to a pond and swathes of lawn where interesting and often bizarre modern wooden sculptures are on display.

Seaside hamlets

Most of Lahemaa's other attractions can be found to the north in the form of several tiny seaside hamlets that dot the area's four rocky peninsulas. One of these gems is **Altja ㉘**, a wonderful example of a timeless Estonian fishing village. The old, thatched-roofed wooden buildings here were restored in the 1970s, and the village has since become a popular local tourist spot. Here you'll find

Viinistu Art Museum, founded by the former manager of pop-group Abba.

BELOW: "Old Jüri" boulder, Käsmu.

a 19th-century inn, a traditional village swing and several paths along the coast. The nearby headland is dotted with attractive sheds for storing fishing gear.

Another coastal village, **Käsmu** ㉙, is much less typical. This is called "captains' village" because of the the lavish houses that sea captains built here, giving it a decidedly affluent look. A drive through the village reveals some of the most unusual and beautiful residential property in Estonia. There is a slightly dark side to all this beauty, however. The village's original economic prosperity is linked to its residents' salt-smuggling activities in the 19th century. In the 1920s, when Finland imposed the prohibition of alcohol, the economic focus here shifted to alcohol smuggling. Käsmu is now also known for its Maritime Museum (free), housed in what was a school of navigation in the late 19th and early 20th centuries. The musty and somewhat jumbled museum displays a collection of sailing artefacts, as well as works by local artists and a few Saku beer bottles from a century ago.

Like Käsmu, the tiny village of **Viinistu** ㉚, north of Loksa, also made a good share of money from smuggling alcohol, but what puts it on the map nowadays is something else entirely – art. This village of just 150 is home to the Viinistu Art Museum (Viinistu Kunstimuuseum; open daily 11am–6pm; admission fee), which has the largest private art collection in the country, with between 200 and 300 19th- and 20th-century Estonian paintings on display, easily rivalling the state-owned museums in Tallinn. The reason the collection is here is that former resident Jaan Manitski fled as a child with his family to Sweden during World War II. After making his fortune as financial adviser to the famous pop group ABBA, he returned to Viinistu, eventually converting the town's Soviet-era fish collective into this art and cultural centre. Next to the main complex, a pair of

Map on pages 96–7

Most villages in Estonia once had wooden swings like the one in Altja. They were social gathering places for young people.

BELOW: Altja, one of the prettiest villages in Estonia.

water towers have been refitted for temporary exhibition space. Beyond them lies an amphitheatre where local plays are staged. The village has a modern guesthouse and restaurant, as well as a respectable, old-fashioned tavern. The road that leads through the village ends in a small trail that follows its rocky coastline. Offshore, **Mohni Island**, an uninhabited nature reserve, is visible.

On the western side of the park another manor, **Kolga Mõis** ㉛, remains unrestored; plans for its makeover have been indefinitely postponed due to a lack of funds. The graceful 18th-century building is a cliché of a crumbling pile with falling plaster, peeling wallpaper and a cracked exterior. One floor of the interior, however, has been turned into a restaurant, and one of the old stable blocks is a small hotel.

Rejoining the E20, one can either head back west to the modernity of Tallinn, or turn east, towards the Russian border and what was Estonia's heavy industrial zone during Soviet times.

Industrial Estonia

If Estonia were a jigsaw puzzle, the northeast corner would be the one piece that didn't fit. Ida-Viru County, which straddles the main transport routes leading to Narva at the Russian border, is the heavily industrialised region of Estonia. It is rich in energy-producing oil shale and supplies more than 90 percent of the nation's electricity. During the Soviet period, thousands of ethnic Russians were settled in the region to work its plants and mines, and small villages suddenly became factory towns filled with rows and rows of apartment blocks. When Soviet industry collapsed, following *perestroika*, this area was hardest hit. Most jobs here disappeared, leaving decaying buildings, environmental hazards and

Mohni Island is a popular spot for wreck diving, though visibility can be low in the Baltic Sea. A number of vessels have come to grief on the islands.

BELOW: open-air theatre, Käsmu.

Map on pages 96–7

a population of mainly ethnic Russians whose role in the newly independent Estonia was far from clear.

So many years later, the situation has been slow to improve. The area's economy still lags far behind that of the rest of the nation, and the eyesores of the last century – dilapidated buildings and enormous hills of mining waste – line the roads. For this reason, Estonians from other areas have written off the northeast as not worth visiting. But it is for this same reason that many foreigners find it fascinating. It offers the chance to see a side of Estonia ignored by most guidebooks, and to glimpse the Soviet past without a Russian visa. It also has its own medieval castles, natural beauty and some sights that aren't found anywhere else in Estonia.

The E20 leads into the area from the direction of Tallinn. Before reaching the heart of Ida-Viru County, it passes some points worth mentioning. One of these is **Rakvere** ㉜, the country's seventh-largest city, located at the midpoint between Tallinn and Narva. For Estonians, the name Rakvere is always associated with the town's meat-processing plant, but its main attraction for tourists is Rakvere Castle (Rakvere linnus; open May–Sept daily 11am–7pm; admission fee). The castle was built in 1253 on the site of a wooden one that was destroyed during the Livonian War. For better or for worse, it is the most commercially developed of Estonia's castles. It not only has the obligatory historical displays in its interior, but also features such crowd-pleasing amenities as a tavern, wine cellar and a medieval torture and horror chamber. In summer, its front courtyard has a number of smithies, a petting zoo, archery range and other activities. Other sights in Rakvere include the ruins of a Franciscan monastery dating from 1515 and several charming streets of late 19th-century buildings.

The much smaller castle at **Purtse** ㉝ (open May–Sept daily 10am–6pm) is another medieval sight worth seeing. It is easily missed, as it stands several hundred metres away from the highway in the middle of several other buildings. The red-roofed edifice dates from 1533, the Swedish period, when Purtse was a free port. Although the castle was partially destroyed during the Great Northern War (1700–21), it was inhabited until 1938, and fell into disrepair. Now restored, it serves as a concert hall and exhibition centre.

Kohtla-Järve ㉞, the heart of Estonia's mining region, is further east. Though by population it is Estonia's fourth-largest city, it has a decidedly sleepy, residential feel, and other than a large monument to miners, it has virtually no points of interest.

The area's real gem, by far one of Estonia's most fascinating museums, lies instead 10 km (6 miles) south of here in the village of **Kohtla-Nõmme**. The short drive past forlorn, abandoned houses and emaciated cockerels leads to the Kohtla Mine Park Museum (Kohtla Kaevanduspark-muuseum; open Mon–Fri 10am–5pm, Sat & Sun 10am–3pm, admission fee). Opened in 1937, the Kohtla mine was one of a dozen shale mines that operated in Ida-Viru County during Soviet times, and grew to encompass around 60 km (37 miles) of tunnels. After it closed in 2001, about 1.5 km (1 mile) of it was turned into this hands-on "underground museum". Visitors are given hard

BELOW:
Rakvere Castle.

Moose alert.

hats, electric lamps and overalls before descending into the tunnels. The tour guides, all former mine workers, demonstrate the gigantic digging and clearing machines, give children rides on the tiny train that once carried miners to their stations, and let guests put a few holes in the rock with a large mining drill. The museum has become a popular attraction, so pre-registration by phone is required (tel: 3 324 017).

Hub and spokes

The road reconnects with the E20 at **Jõhvi** ③⑤, the administrative centre of Ida-Viru County. Many Estonians wryly refer to this town of 12,000 as "the real border of Estonia", since it is the last where the majority are Estonian speakers, and all towns to the east of it have a decidedly more Russian feel. Apart from Narva, Jõhvi certainly has more commercial activity than anywhere else in the county, but it also has its historic sites, such as the charming green-topped Orthodox Church of the Epiphany (Issanda Ristimise kirik). It was built in 1895, and Alexy II, Patriarch of Moscow and all of Russia, was the rector here in the 1950s.

Jõhvi's more impressive church, however, is St Michael's (Mihkli kirik) in the centre of town. Built in 1364, it served as a church and fortress until it was destroyed in the Livonian War in the 16th century. Its present form comes from a 1728–32 reconstruction. Inside is the Jõhvi Fortified Church Museum (Jõhvi Kindluskiriku muuseum; open Tues–Sat 11am–4pm; admission fee), which outlines the church's history and displays archeological finds from the location. The 30-minute CD tour is available in English.

BELOW:
Valaste waterfall.

More than anything, Jõhvi is a regional hub. From here, roads lead in several directions and into very different types of territory. To the north lies some truly

Map
on pages
96–7

spectacular scenery. The coastline from **Toila** to **Ontika** and **Saka** is made up of dramatic high cliffs, rising up to 56 metres (184 ft) out of the sea. This natural monument is a symbol of Estonia, and is referred to as the **North Estonian Klint**. It is the edge of the vast, limestone plateau on which this region sits. The waterfall in **Valaste** is Estonia's highest at 26 metres (85 ft), but is somewhat artificial in that it was created by diverted water.

Toila is home to the picturesque Oru Park. The large, regional park contains more than 200 different plants, nature walks and a pebble beach. The land is on the former property of a German baron who had a manor house built here in 1899. Estonia's first president used the house as a holiday retreat but it was destroyed in 1943. The park remains, and many of the paths pass through manicured gardens and statuary.

East from Jõhvi is **Sillamäe** ❸, an intriguing, Soviet-era relic that should not be passed up. The entire town is a perfect museum piece of Stalinist-style architecture. Though there was a village here as far back as 1502, Sillamäe really came into being during the Soviet period, when it was a centre for mining and processing uranium. The town, which retains its look of a grandiose, planned city from the early 1950s, was a secret military area, populated exclusively by Russians and not marked on local maps.

Its main street, Kesk, cuts through the small town centre, where nicely trimmed gardens, a town hall and a community centre are accented with an unmistakably socialist-realist statue of a bare-chested man holding an atom aloft. A grand formation of steps leads to the park-like Mere Avenue, and then towards the seaside promenades. A block west, at Majakovski 18a, is the Sillamäe Museum (open May–Sept Mon–Fri 10am–6pm; Oct–Apr Tues–Sat 10am–6pm; admission fee) where, among the various minerals and Soviet banners on display, is a re-created apartment from the 1950s.

On the Border

The E20 reaches the Russian border at **Narva** ❸. With just under 68,000 inhabitants, it is Estonia's third-largest city, and its least Estonian. Nearly 96 percent of its inhabitants are Russian speakers. Here more than anywhere in Estonia, questions of citizenship and of the role of minorities in the Estonian republic become acute. Many residents feel that they are neither part of Estonia nor Russia, living in a kind of no-man's land.

Indeed, the border itself is the city's most striking feature. Ivangorod Castle and Narva Castle stand facing one another across the Narva river like sentries guarding their respective lands. The "Friendship Bridge" stretches across the river between them, with EU flags on one side and Russian flags on the other. Ignoring geopolitical concerns, locals casually stroll across to the Russian side for cheaper grocery shopping. Western visitors wishing to follow them will need a Russian visa, something that takes several days and considerable expense to procure.

The city was first mentioned in 1240 when it was listed in census records compiled by the Danes, who built Fort Narva. They sold the castle, along with the

BELOW:
Narva Castle.

rest of northern Estonia, to the Teutonic Order in 1347. In 1492, the year the Russians finally repelled the Mongols, Tsar Ivan III built a fort at Ivangorod on "his" side of the river.

One of Narva's largest companies is the Kreenholm textile mill. In 1872 its 5,000 workers went on a famous strike that has become part of labour history.

Narva flourished in the Swedish period, taking over Tallinn's position as the primary trading port between Russia and the rest of Europe. It continued to flourish under tsarist rule as well. By the late 19th century Narva was an industrial giant and a major seaport. Its largest company, Kreenholm Textile Manufacturing, employed more than 10,000 people in its factories: Estonia's first strike was organised here in 1872.

During the first republic Narva remained part of Estonia. The city was affected by economic depression during the 1920s and 1930s, and suffered terribly during World War II. On 17 August 1941 the Germans entered Narva and when, in July 1944, they were finally driven out, 98 percent of the city had been destroyed. After the war, the Russians set about rebuilding the town. Two electric plants that were subsequently constructed now produce most of Estonia's energy.

Almost nothing remains of Narva's Old Town, which is filled with block apartments. The Town Hall, built by the Swedes, was one of the few buildings that survived the war, but is now in a serious state of neglect. Narva Castle, to the right of the bridge, is the city's only real tourist attraction. Narva's statue of Lenin stands in the grounds of the castle; it is hidden on the left-hand side of the compound, symbolically facing east across the river towards Russia. The walls around the fort are walkable and photographers should note that in the late afternoon the southwest corner bastion offers superb views of both forts. Or you may want to walk along the river's edge to the beach and

BELOW: Swedish Town Hall, Narva.

then up the headland for pictures of both forts separated by the river. Inside its multi-storey tower, the Narva Museum (open Wed–Sun 10am–6pm; admission fee) displays artefacts from the town's history, as well as exhibitions on Estonian history and modern art. Of particular interest are the photos of Narva's Old Town taken before the war.

The 15-km (9-mile) drive north along the river leads to **Narva-Jõesuu**, a popular beach resort town in the 19th century. It is trying, with very limited success, to recapture some its past glory, despite intrusive factory smokestacks and other post-Soviet debris. The town is still filled with early 20th-century gingerbread houses, and one of the most colourful is just off Ranna Street. The Orthodox Church, created from rough-hewn logs, is a gem. Two spa resorts operate here during the summer.

South to Tartu

Backtracking to Jõhvi, the final spoke of the Ida-Viru County hub leads south, through an area where nature and spirituality replace the noise of human development. Highway 3 provides the quickest access to Tartu 132 km (82 miles) away, but a small detour on Highway 33 leads to **Kuremäe ㊳**, home of the striking Orthodox **Convent of Pühtitsa**, the only Eastern Orthodox nunnery in the Baltic states.

Orthodox priest, Kuremäe

Approaching Kuremäe, the green domes of the Pühtitsa Cathedral beckon through a forest of oak and pine. The convent's official name is Kuremäe Jumalaema Uinumise nunnaklooster (Pühtitsa Dormition Convent). Pühtitsa is Estonian for "holy place", and indeed the convent is built on a site that has been sacred since the 16th century when a peasant saw a vision of the Virgin

BELOW: outside the communal dining hall, Kuremäe nunnery.

Map
on pages
96–7

*Sudak (pikeperch)
on the menu in local
restaurants is one of
the main catches of
Lake Peipsi.*

Mary on the top of a hill. An icon was found beneath an ancient oak tree near the same spot, and the icon of the Assumption of the Mother of God is still the convent's most prized possession, surrounded by precious gems and mounted on a pillar to the right of the cathedral altar.

The first nun was sent to Pühtitsa in 1888 to establish the convent, and the complex of buildings, circled by a high granite wall, was designed by Mikail Preobrazhensky, a professor at the St Petersburg Academy of Arts. The five-domed, three-aisle Cathedral of the Assumption, which can accommodate up to 1,200 worshippers, was finished in 1910. There are five other churches in the complex, including a small one just outside the main walls, which is used for funeral services. Today there are more than 100 nuns in residence. Some 24 hectares (60 acres) of the 75-hectare (187-acre) property is farmed. Cash is raised from the sale of icons and other religious items made by the nuns, who also give tours from 9am to 4pm daily for a fee. At other times, visitors are welcome to explore on their own.

From Kuremäe either take a road that links up with Highway 3 at **Jõuga** to continue south, or extend the detour to historic **Vasknarva** ❸, at the Russian border. The town was founded at the beginning of the 12th century as a way-station on the trade route linking the principalities of Novorod and Pskov with Tartu and Tallinn. All that remains of its Livonian fort is two broken walls.

Lake Peipsi

BELOW: gathering
shells on the shore.
RIGHT: Lake Peipsi.

Either route leads to the shore of **Lake Peipsi**, (Peipsi järv) where there are forests of tall conifers and beside white beaches of bleached oyster shells. There are occasional fishing villages strung along the water's edge, their attractive clapboard houses painted a variety of colours, each fronted by banks of vibrant flowers and backed by greenhouses which are used to extend the short growing season.

Mustvee ❹, 65 km (40 miles) north of Tartu, is Lake Peipsi's largest town, and the centre of Estonia's community of Old Believers. These are Russians who fled to Estonia in the 17th century to avoid religious persecution *(see page 44)*, and they have since developed their own distinct culture and traditions. There are approximately 15,000 Old Believers in Estonia today, most of them living here along the shore of lake.

The town itself has two churches and several incongruous modern apartment blocks. Just south of Mustvee, the 7-km (4-mile) village street that connects **Kükita**, **Raja**, **Tiheda** and **Kasepää** is perhaps more indicative of the Old Believer culture. It is lined with two-storey houses, most with small towers or balconies. Every one of these houses should traditionally have an icon inside and a spade in the yard. The Old Believers Museum in **Kolkja** will provide more insight into the history and practices of this group, but visits must be pre-arranged by someone who speaks Russian or Estonian (tel: 53 922 444).

From Raja, the highway to Tartu leads away from the lake and the realm of Russian village life, and back into 21st-century Estonia. ❑

LATVIA

*The middle of the three countries has the largest capital city,
the longest river and a great recreational national park*

The main highway of the Baltics is the 1,030-km (640-mile) River Daugava, which starts in Russia near the source of the Volga and arrives, via Belarus, in the south near Daugavpils. "Its banks are silver and its bed is gold," said Ivan the Terrible, who failed to get his hands on it. Others were more successful, starting with the German crusaders who arrived in Rīga, near the river's estuary, which they made their base for the conquest of the Baltic peoples and the expansion of Hansa trade.

Today, Rīga is the most exciting city in the Baltics. It is rich with the architecture of the merchants, who built and funded gabled homes and storehouses dating back to the 15th century. In the expanded late 19th- and early 20th-century city there are exquisite Art Nouveau buildings, many designed by Mikhail Eisenstein, father of the film-maker Sergei Eisenstein, who was born here. Rīga also has the most exciting market in the Baltics and one of the most popular seaside resorts at nearby Jūrmala.

Nearly a million of the country's 2.3 million population live in Rīga, and there is no other city in the country approaching its size, though Ventspils and Liepāja are busy ports and popular resorts. Along the coast, around Rīga Bay and into the Baltic Sea, are small villages that house the last of the Livs, an almost mythic race.

Second to the Daugava is the River Gauja, which is the centre of a fine national park. To the east are the more remote blue lakelands of Latgale, a Catholic stronghold and place of pilgrimage where you can find excellent local pottery. To the west is Kurzeme, the former domaine of the Lutheran Duchy of Courland, where tall pines became masts in Duke Jacob's shipyards at Ventspils. Too grand for a duke, but lacking the power of a king, he built an empire with toeholds in the Caribbean and in Africa.

One building belonging to a Courland duke that has survived is Rundāle Palace, the most spectacular piece of civic architecture in the Baltics. It was built by Bartolomeo Rastrelli, architect of the Winter Palace in St Petersburg, for Ernst Johann Biron, a lover of the Empress Anna Ivanovna and briefly Regent of Russia.

The soul of Latvia and the Latvians is not in buildings but in the countryside among its magic oaks and ancient hill forts. People are happiest spending a weekend on the family farmstead tending vegetable gardens, singing songs and drinking beer by a bonfire or just relaxing in a steamy sauna. In a country with countless rivers and lakes and more than 500 km (300 miles) of pristine beaches, it is not difficult to imagine why Latvians prefer nature to urban living. ❑

PRECEDING PAGES: the River Gauja; Rīga from the rooftop bar at the Reval Hotel.
LEFT: folk dancers in the Old Town.

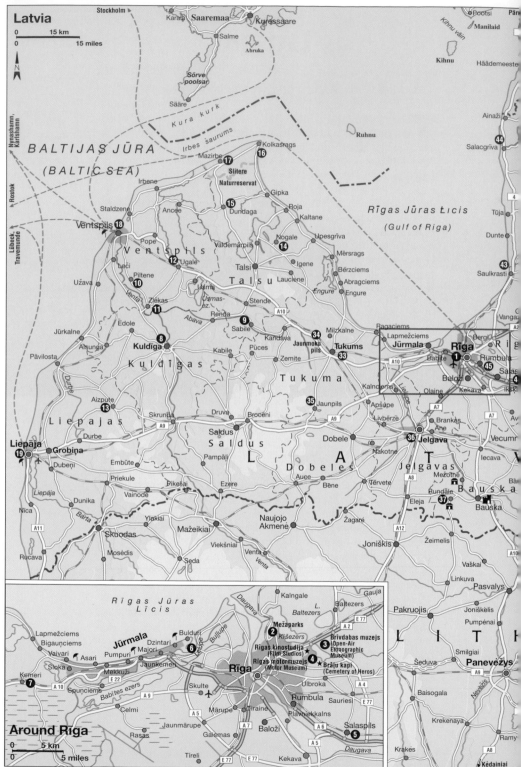

THE MAKING OF LATVIA

The Baltic states' first woman president was elected in a country
shaped by Hansa traders and Russian maritime ambition

When Latvian independence was self-proclaimed in 1918, the country had to be assembled like a jigsaw puzzle out of territory inhabited by Lettish-speakers. This amounted to the southern half of what had previously been Livonia together with Latgale and the Duchy of Courland.

To complicate matters, the city of Rīga, Latvia's capital, had hitherto been for all practical purposes an independent city-state with an overwhelmingly foreign population. It was a German city from the day the crusaders landed, and it had remained a predominantly German city of Hanse merchants through all the vagaries of Polish, Swedish and Russian rule. The Latvians managed to restore themselves to a majority of something like 75 percent over the country as a whole between the world wars, but independence was then snuffed out by Soviet annexation. The combined effect of mass deportations and Russian immigration inexorably reversed the trend, so that by 1989 the Latvians were reduced to the barest majority of 52 percent.

Against the backdrop of massive impending change in Eastern Europe and the Soviet Union, Latvians knew they were in a private race against time. It had been the Kremlin's intention all along to obliterate the 1918 frontiers so that Latvia, like Estonia and Lithuania, was in effect an unbroken extension of Russia itself. The struggle which ensued was a replay of events leading up to World War I, the reincarnation of the land of the Latvians.

Crusaders' arrival

Curious events had led to the arrival of the German crusaders in 1200. Almost 1,000 years after Christianity had been adopted as the official religion in Armenia and then Rome, it had still not reached the eastern shores of the Baltic,

---

LEFT: Rīga port by an unknown artist, from the second half of the 17th century.
RIGHT: figure from the banner of the first all-Latvian song festival, held in 1873.

and there was rather a rush among the Pope and various Christian princes to make up for lost time.

To this end, a number of missionary monks were despatched. Meinhard of Bremen established a colony at Ikšķile roughly 25 km (15 miles) upstream from present-day Rīga in 1180

and persuaded Latvians to be baptised in the river in such satisfactory numbers that he was made a bishop. The real test came when he informed his converts that the price of salvation was the payment of a tithe. They not only abandoned the faith en masse but put the good bishop in fear of his life. He implored Pope Clement III to send help, but died before any was forthcoming. His successor, Bishop Bertold, called for nothing short of a holy crusade in the Baltics, but met his end soon after on the tip of a pagan spear.

The Pope had other problems. The crusade in the Holy Land had gone disastrously wrong and large numbers of crusaders, expelled from their strongholds, were homeless. Led by Bishop Albert (Albrecht von Buxhoevden), they were dispatched to the Daugava where they went about their business with Teutonic efficiency. "All the places and roads were red with blood," wrote a chronicler of the Knights of the Sword.

Almost at once, Rīga had a defensive wall, a fortress and at least one church. By 1211, Bishop Albert was ready to start building a cathedral. Word was sent to the Pope that the Daugava mission had been accomplished and

> **SAVAGE BLOW**
>
> The Swedish–Polish War was followed by the bitter winter of 1601 in which 40,000 Latvian peasants died from cold and hunger.

that a contingent of knights was being sent north – to Estonia – where the Danes were experiencing similar difficulties with truculent pagans.

The Knights of the Sword were in due course amalgamated with other orders; these came to be known collectively as the Teutonic Order. Having discharged their divine duties, they tackled the secular task of creating a city-state for themselves with immense zeal. They imported fellow Germans not merely to build the city and port but also to organise the region's agriculture. The Latvians were excluded from the process except as labourers.

Looking to Lithuania

The military power of the Teutonic Order was eclipsed in the 15th century, but by then the German economic and land-owning oligarchy was thoroughly entrenched in Latvia. It was safe as long as Russia was kept out of contention by the Mongol Empire. With the demise of the latter, however, an alarming threat materialised in the person of Ivan the Terrible. The only recourse was to seek the protection of Poland-Lithuania, and then there was a price to be paid. Lutheranism had made inroads in Latvia under the German influence and Poland was uncompromisingly Catholic. The Jesuits were to be given a licence to bring Latvians back into the fold.

The way the Jesuits went about their task revived memories of the Teutonic Order, and this was coupled with a rigid Polish feudal order that was harder on the peasants than anything previously experienced. The country was sharply divided on the desirability of Polish protection. Rīga profited enormously by being elevated to the role of Poland's principal port, so the merchants had no reason to complain.

The landed gentry and the peasants, however, were paying the price and they became increasingly desperate for protection against the protectors. Protestant Sweden seemed the most likely candidate. The resulting Swedish–Polish war saw the Swedes repulsed but Latvia was left a wreck from which they took a long time to recover.

Gustavus Adolphus tried to topple the ruling order again 20 years later and this time a Poland

> ### THE HANSA CONNECTION
>
> Rīga's wealth in the late Middle Ages was in part due to its joining, in 1282, the Hanseatic League, Europe's first free-trade organisation. The league was started by German merchants societies *(Hanse)* to protect the herring trade in Lübeck and its vital salt suppliers in Hamburg. The alliance soon developed into a powerful one of more than 150 port-cities that came to control the shipping of fish, flax, fur, grain, honey and timber from Russia and the Baltics, and cloth and other goods manufactured by Flemish and English guilds. Rīga had exclusive rights to transport goods along the Daugava and Livonia had its own Hanseatic diet or parliament.

much weakened by events elsewhere succumbed. The Swedes rebuilt Riga castle, added barracks outside the Swedish Gate and built castles on the River Daugava. Poland remained in charge of Latgale in the east and, in the south and west, the Duchy of Courland.

In 1561 this small slice of Latvia had been awarded to Gotthard Kettler, the last Grand Master of the Teutonic Order, who, fearful of Russian incursions on his land in the north, had submitted to Poland, and had been granted a degree of independence. Its importance grew under Duke Jacob, who became a prince of the Holy Roman Empire.

the south of the country. In the north there had been few tears when the Jesuits were sent packing by the Swedes. Historians consider this period of Scandinavian rule, which brought with it unprecedented construction of schools and hospitals, the implementation of a code of laws and the translation and publication of the Bible in Latvian, a golden age. The barons, however, were horrified when their estates were expropriated and given to the Swedish aristocracy. Hoping to be third time lucky, they looked again for a more sympathetic protector: their choice this time was Russia. Latvia then produced someone who

RIGA

A duke's empire

Though Protestant, the Kettlers had been friends of the English Stuart kings and Jacob (James) had been named after his godfather, James I. He had been a great shipbuilder, and at Ventspils he built an impressive navy, turning out 24 men-of-war for France and 62 for Britain. With unbounded ambition he acquired territory for the duchy in the Gambia and Tobago and he devoted much of his long rule to attempting to colonise them.

The duchy brought a degree of stability to

proposed to take matters into his own hands: Johan Reinhold von Patkul.

Patkul, a German landowner, sent word to Charles XII that the Teutonic Knights had conquered Latvia and converted it to Christianity long before he or his ancestors came on the scene. Therefore, the descendants of those knights, among whom he numbered himself, had an inexpungable right to rule. Charles's reply to this tirade was to sentence Patkul to death. With this sentence hanging over him, Patkul approached Augustus II, the odious Elector of Saxony, who prevailed upon him to include Russia in his scheme in return for a promise that there would be none of the "usual

LEFT: a knight of the Livonian Order.
ABOVE: copperplate engraving of Rīga, 1638.

barbarities" in the event of an invasion of Latvia. Peter had got wind of Patkul's proposal and thought it was excellent, but he wanted to modify the division of the spoils. Russia would take Estonia, Augustus could have the rest of Livonia, and Denmark could help itself to what was left, including Sweden itself.

The Great Northern War

The Great Northern War of Sweden versus Russia, which began in 1699, was a titanic struggle that swept across the entire breadth of Europe. In and around Latvia, the Swedish crown sought to finance the war by taking 80 percent

Sweden was not destined to hold on to Latvia or its neighbours for much longer. Peter the Great's ultimate victory in his duel with Charles XII opened the way to realising his dream of Russian control of the eastern Baltic. By then he had another, purely personal, interest in the region. Some years earlier, he had been struck by a woman called Martha who had arrived at court on the arm of first one and then another of his ministers, the second being Prince Menshikov. She was a servant, the daughter of a Lithuanian peasant, who had been employed by a Protestant pastor in Latvia before marrying a Swedish army officer. The marriage had

of the estates, dispossessing both the Swedish barons, who had only just been given them, as well as the remaining Germans. These lands were squeezed for all they were worth and reached the point where they were providing the Swedish crown with more revenue than all other sources put together.

Augustus launched an invasion of Livonia in 1700 that got as far as Rīga before it was halted. Peter the Great was called on for help, but his forces were tied down at Narva in Estonia. In the event, the Russians suffered a shock defeat at Narva and the victorious Charles turned his attention on Augustus. The Elector of Saxony was in no position to resist, and he surrendered.

failed and Martha was pursuing other interests among the Russian nobility.

Menshikov loyally relinquished the lovely Martha and she became Peter's mistress. On embracing the Orthodox faith, she changed her name to Catherine and after eight years of companionship he married her. Peter changed the law to allow him personally to crown her Empress in 1724.

On Peter's death, Catherine was proclaimed empress in her own right. The accession to the Russian throne of a Latvian peasant was all the more extraordinary because there was practically no social or economic mobility in Latvia: ethnic Latvians weren't even allowed to own property in their own capital. Martha's change of name and religion is an indication of the way in which ambitious Latvians had to leave behind the indigenous culture in order to break out of a rigidly tiered system. The result was that the Latvian language and everything that went with it was pushed further and further into rural backwaters. As these conditions applied for seven centuries, it is amazing that there was anything left in 1918.

Balts at the Russian court

Catherine I died after a reign of only two years, but the Latvian connection with the Russian

was her chamberlain and lover, Ernst Johann Biron, who has left the greatest mark. An opportunist and a scoundrel, he became the Duke of Courland after Anna's husband died and was a power behind the throne. He managed to find enough money to bring in architect Bartolomeo Rastrelli, who would later build St Petersburg's Winter Palace, to construct the sumptuous palace at Rundāle. He was also responsible for sending some 20,000 to Siberia. When Anna died he became Regent of Russia, but was eventually himself sent to Siberia for a brief term of banishment.

The German Balts in Russia's courts used

crown was renewed when Peter's niece Anna acceded to the throne. While Catherine was undoubtedly fast, Anna was downright debauched. More to the point, she was the dowager Duchess of Courland, and she brought German Balts from Jelgava, Rīga and elsewhere to the Russian court en masse. Jelgava, then called Mitau, was the capital of Courland. Anna's father-in-law was Duke Jacob's son, and he had introduced French opera and ballet into its social milieu. Anna granted the first Russian constitution in Jelgava in 1731, but it

their influence to restore the port of Rīga after the depredations of the Russo-Swedish wars. This care did not extend to other parts of the country. They ignored a countryside that was devastated and stricken by plague. It was said that, Rīga apart, Latvia was ruled by wolves for a century afterwards.

Neglect and ghastly conditions led, in 1802, to a peasant uprising led by "Poor Conrad" who, reflecting the revolutionary mood in France, was called "the Lettish Bonaparte". The revolt was put down ruthlessly and Poor Conrad died an excruciating death. There was a repetition in 1840, with the peasants directing their fury at the Lutheran church.

LEFT: Town Hall Square, Rīga, by K.T. Fechhelm, 1819.
ABOVE: festivities on midsummer's eve, 1842.

Four centuries after the demise of the Teutonic Order, the Latvian establishment was still dominated by German aristocrats and burghers. The country had subsequently been ruled by Poland, Sweden and Russia, but the old German system had somehow endured in spite of the efforts, particularly by Sweden, to dislodge it. To rebellious 19th-century peasants, the Lutheran church was a symbol of German domination. The Russian Orthodox church hastened to exploit anti-Lutheran feelings. The Orthodox catechism was translated into Latvian and given away free in large numbers. German landowners retaliated by refusing to make any

more land available for Orthodox churches. German-Russian rivalry took on a life of its own, and the role of the German Balts sparked a furious row between Tsar Alexander III and Bismarck. Lutheran pastors were locked up or sent to Siberia, and as many as 30,000 of their flock were formally advised that they were henceforth Orthodox.

The Latvian peasant derived some benefits as the region was drawn into the Russian economic sphere to counteract German influence. The Russian railways were extended to the Baltic coast, and Rīga handled a large share of Russia's trade. At the same time there was a remarkable sprouting of literary activity in Latvian.

Rich Germans held on to their positions, but the lower rungs had to make room for Latvians. All of this increased Latvian political awareness, but satisfaction at overcoming the old German obstacles did not necessarily make organisations like the New Latvians pro-Russian. Political sympathies on the workshop floor in Rīga were more inclined towards Karl Marx.

The Baltic Revolution

The Baltic Revolution of 1905, which coincided with the St Petersburg uprising, was aimed with equal venom at everything German and Russian. Order was restored in Rīga only by the intervention of the Imperial Guard. The tsar had no qualms about letting the outraged German barons take their revenge, and when they had done so he rewarded them with concessions, such as granting permission to reopen five German schools. One way or another, the German element clung on and at the onset of World War I, the population of Rīga was still at least 50 percent Baltic-German.

The wounds of the rebellion had not yet healed when World War I broke out. The country was at first occupied by a defensive Russian Army. In 1915, and not without Russian misgivings, the Latvians were permitted to raise a national army.

When the Russians withdrew in confusion after the Bolshevik revolution, the Latvians put up a spirited defence of Rīga against the advancing Germans at the cost of some 32,000 casualties. When the Germans took Rīga, it was not the prize that they were hoping for. The port was inactive, the machinery having been stripped and shipped to Russia.

A secret national organisation bent on Latvian independence was formed within the first months of German occupation and was in contact with refugees in Russia and exiles who had fled after the 1905 rebellion. The Allied victory in November 1918 simplified matters. A state council simply proclaimed independence and offered citizenship to all residents apart from Bolsheviks and German Unionists. The fly in the ointment was that 45,000 German troops still occupied Rīga and there were as many again scattered about the rest of the country. When they withdrew, the Bolsheviks arrived and there was no organised force to stop them. They declared Latvia a Soviet republic. The situation was rescued by Estonia which drove the

Bolsheviks off its soil and then crossed the border to help the Latvians do likewise.

Independent Latvia was in a sorry state. The population was a third below pre-war levels, industrial output was virtually nil, and many children had never been to school. A land-reform programme expropriated the German baronial estates and redistributed them in parcels to Latvian peasants.

The Bolsheviks professed an end to tsarist imperialism, but in reality they were as determined as Peter the Great had ever been to hold on to the Baltic coast. Hanging by a thread, independent Latvia nevertheless went ahead. Agrarian reform was supplemented by a takeover of industry and commerce, or what was left of them. The Latvian language was of course given official status, and there was a general revival of Latvian culture. Perhaps the most significant statistics were the changing population ratios. By 1939, Latvians enjoyed one of the highest standards of living in Europe and were once again in a commanding majority in the country, as high as 75 percent.

The Nazi-Soviet pact

Progress came to a jarring halt in 1940. The Bolshevik undertaking to respect the independence of the Baltic states "voluntarily and for ever" vanished with the Nazi-Soviet Pact of 1939. A Soviet invasion was followed by annexation, although not one that was ever recognised by the Western powers. The Nazi-Soviet Pact was short-lived, and in June 1941 the German Army drove out the Soviet forces. Latvia, together with Estonia and Lithuania, was made part of Hitler's Ostland. The consequences for Latvia's 100,000 Jews were horrific: 90 percent were murdered.

Rīga was reconquered by the Soviet Army on 8 August 1944, and with that the NKVD set about restoring order in its customary manner. An estimated 320,000 people out of a population of just 2 million were deported to the east; most never returned. Tens of thousands more fled westward only to be forced to work in Ger-

man factories under daily bombardment by the Allies. Active guerrilla resistance to the Soviet regime continued until as late as 1951, but little news of it leaked out to the West.

More executions and deportations followed in the purge of so-called bourgeoisie nationalists in 1949–53, and all the time Russians were surging in ostensibly to man the industrial machinery of the Five-Year Plans. Khrushchev purged 2,000 influential locals who raised their voices in protest, replacing them either with Russians or so-called

Latovichi, Russians who purported to be Latvians on the strength of a few years' residence in the country. Notorious *Latovichi* such as Arvīds Pelše and Augusts Voss enforced Russification policies with a severity that at least matched anything attempted by the tsars. Even folk singing was driven underground. Signs of a revival surfaced in the 1980s. It began with the unobtrusive restoration of derelict churches and the odd historical monument. Poets and folk groups also performed discreetly.

The principal catalyst that brought protest out into the open was the green movement. Environmental concern served as cover for the formation of nationalist pressure groups, and

LEFT: traditional "Lettish" costume, 1920s.
RIGHT: Krišjānis Valdemārs *(second left)* and other key figures of Latvia's National Awakening.

before very long the underground press was addressing such taboo subjects as the activities of the secret police and human-rights violations. The breakthrough occurred in 1986, when public protest managed to stop the construction of a hydro-electric scheme on the River Daugava.

With this victory in hand, and a softer line on public protest coming from Moscow, the resistance movement grew. The National Independence Movement of Latvia (NIML), founded in June 1988, maintained that the illegal annexation of 1940 invalidated the Soviet regime. A census taken in 1989 revealed that Latvians were on the brink of becoming a minority in their own country – they represented a mere 52 percent of the total population, around 30 percent in Rīga – and this lent an air of urgency to the campaign. The Russian minority rallied in opposition, forming an organisation called Interfront.

Return of the republic

The Soviet Union eventually collapsed so quickly and so passively that it is all too easy to forget how bravely Latvians demanded "total political and economic independence" and, specifically, a free market economy and a multi-party political system. Nor will Latvia forget the five killed by Soviets at the Ministry of the Interior in January 1991, nor the freezing cold nights on makeshift barricades against Soviet tanks in Old Rīga. Elections gave the nationalists a two-thirds majority, and the country was renamed the "Republic of Latvia".

The regaining of independence in 1991 was the first step in a sequence of events that would reunite Latvia with the rest of Europe. In 1994 Latvians celebrated the final withdrawal of Russian troops with the demolition of a Cold War radar station in Skrunda. Cultural life returned to the sovereign nation, and a free market economy struggled with bank crises and privatisation scandals, often involving politicians and prominent members of society, but eventually experienced unparalleled, and necessary growth. The question of citizenship for Russian residents has largely been resolved, but not without acrimony. Parliament also experienced growing pains, with the collapse of 11 governments in nearly as many years. But in June 1999, Vaira Vīķe-Freiberga was elected president by the *saeima*, the first woman head of state in the post-Communist world *(see box)*. She was in place in time to steer the country through negotiations to join both NATO and the European Union in 2004.

Having re-taken its place among nations, Latvia continues to wrestle with an antiquated healthcare system, corruption, money laundering and the proper use and distribution of EU funds, while endeavouring to promote democracy in its authoritarian neighbours to the east. ❏

THE FIRST WOMAN PRESIDENT

Born in Rīga in 1937, Vaira Vīķe-Freiberga fled the country with her family ahead of the invading Soviet Army, arriving in Germany where she spent much of her childhood in a displaced-persons' camp. The family emigrated to Canada where she gained her bachelors and masters degrees in psychology and a PhD in experimental psychology. In 1998, repatriated to Latvia, she became director of the Latvian Institute and a year later was elected Latvia's president. Intelligent and erudite, Freiberga speaks five languages fluently and is the author of several books and scholarly articles. In 2006, nearing the end of her term of office, she applied for the job of United Nations General Secretary.

LEFT: Latvian president Vaira Vīķe-Freiberga.
RIGHT: empty streets in a Soviet-built suburb of Rīga as independence dawned in 1991; 53 percent of the city's population was then Russian-speaking.

RĪGA

The Baltic states' largest city is the most diverse. Set beside the wide River Daugava, it has a Unesco-status Old Town with stunning Art Nouveau buildings and an enormous Central Market

With a population of nearly a million, **Rīga ❶** is the largest and most cosmopolitan city in the Baltic states. It almost seems too big for the country it occupies: roughly a third of the nation lives in the Latvian capital. Spread either side of the River Daugava, the city lies some 8 km (5 miles) from the great sagging dip of Rīga Bay and for some 3,000 years these warm waters have provided both a gateway and an outlet for the continental heartlands.Like Tallinn in Estonia, its skyline is an impressive collection of towers and spires. Expertly manicured parks, a meandering canal that once served as a moat and tree-lined boulevards separate the old town from the sprawling "new" city. Rīga's status as a Unesco World Heritage Site is more than evident in its medieval churches, guildhalls and winding cobblestone streets as well as in its ornately decorated Art Nouveau buildings, many of which have been lovingly restored to their original 19th- and early 20th-century grandeur.

A final blessing for Rīga's citizens and an ever-growing number of foreign visitors is Jūrmala, the lovely sandy beach just a half hour's drive from the city centre *(see page 215)*. This collection of seaside residential towns spread out over 20 km (12 miles) has been favoured by generations of holidaymakers from its beginnings as a 19th-century spa to its heyday as a fashionable haunt in the 1930s and later the premier destination for rest and relaxation in the Soviet Union.

PREVIOUS PAGES: House of Blackheads. **LEFT:** Old Town spires. **BELOW:** Freedom Monument.

The Old Town

Rīga is not a difficult town to get around and nearly everything of merit or note can be reached on foot. The dead-straight Brīvības iela (Freedom Street), is the main artery of the city and leads directly to the **Freedom Monument ❹** (Brīvības piemineklis, *see page 209*): the perfect place to begin a tour of Old Rīga, known locally as Vecrīga.

Walk down Kaļķu iela (Lime Street) to **Līvu Square ❺** (Līvu lakums), named after the now nearly extinct Finno-Ugric people who founded a fishing village here long before Germans or even Latvians arrived on the scene. Today the square is the city's liveliest, populated by buskers and souvenir touts and hundreds of locals and tourists taking advantage of the fantastic views provided from a large concentration of summer beer gardens.

On the opposite side of the square is the yellow **Cat House** or Kaķu māja, whose two felines perched on top of its towers caused quite a stir nearly a hundred years ago. Local lore has it that the owner of the building was engaged in a dispute with the powerful Great Guild across the street. To show what he thought of them, he turned the cats around so that their backsides faced his foes. The dispute was later settled and the

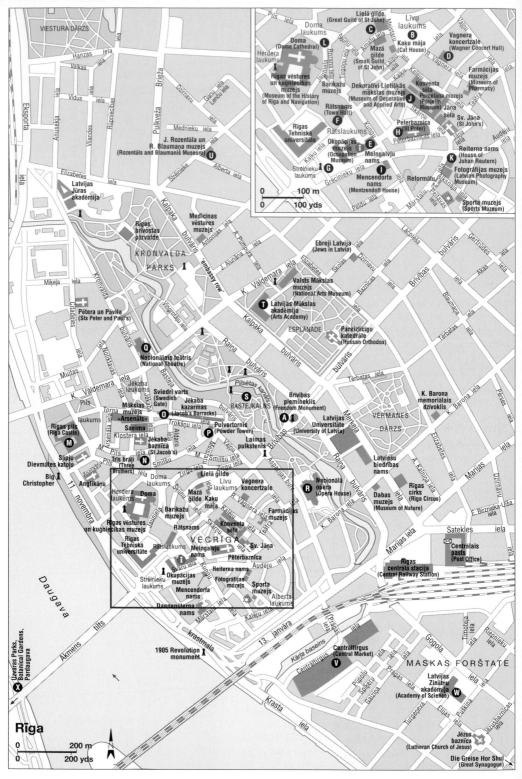

Inset map (Vecrīga)

Pils iela
Doma laukums
Lielā ģilde (Great Guild of St John) **C**
Līvu laukums
Herdera laukums
Doma (Dome Cathedral) **L**
Mazā ģilde (Small Guild of St John)
Kaķu māja (Cat House) **B**
Vagnera koncertzale (Wagner Concert Hall) **D**
Rīgas vēstures un kuģniecības muzejs (Museum of the History of Riga and Navigation)
Barikāžu muzejs
Dekoratīvi Lietišķās mākslas muzejs (Museum of Decorative and Applied Arts)
Konventa sēta
Porcelāna muzejs (Porcelin Museum)
Farmācijas muzejs (Museum of Pharmacy)
Sv. Jāna (St John's)
Rātsnams (Town Hall) **F**
Rīgas Tehniskā universitāte
Rātslaukums
Pēterbaznīca (St Peter) **H**
Reiterna nams (House of Johan Reutern) **K**
Okupācijas muzejs (Occupation Museum) **E**
Meļngalvju nams **E**
Strēlnieku laukums **G**
Mencendorfa nams (Mentzendoff House)
Reformātu
Fotogrāfijas muzejs (Latvian Photography Museum)
Sporta muzejs (Sports Muzeum)

0 ___ 100 m
0 ___ 100 yds

Main map (Rīga)

VIESTURA DĀRZS
Hanzas iela
Lenču iela
Ganu iela
Brieža iela
Dzirnavu iela
Vidus iela
Valkas iela
Rūpniecības iela
Mednieku iela
J. Rozentāla un R. Blaumaņa muzejs (Rozentāls and Blaumanis Museum) **U**
Elizabetes iela
Latvijas Jūras akadēmija
Strēlnieku iela
Alberta iela
Rīgas brīvostas pārvalde
Medicīnas vēstures muzejs
Ebreji Latvijā (Jews in Latvia)
KRONVALDA PARKS
Valsts Mākslas muzejs (National Arts Museum)
Pētera un Pāvila (Sts Peter and Paul's)
Latvijas Mākslas akadēmija (Arts Academy) **T**
ESPLANADE
Pareizticīgo katedrāle (Russian Orthodox)
Nacionālais teātris (National Theatre) **Q**
Svēdri varts (Swedish Gate) **S**
Jēkaba kazarmas (Jacob's Barracks)
Pilsētas kanāls
BASTEJKALNS
Brīvības piemineklis (Freedom Monument) **A**
K. Barona memoriālais dzīvoklis
Mākslas muzejs «Arsenāls» **O**
Saeima
Jēkaba baznīca (St Jacob's)
Pulvertornis (Powder Tower) **P**
Laimas pulkstenis
Latvijas Universitāte (University of Latvia)
VĒRMANES DĀRZS
Rīgas pils (Riga Castle) **M**
Trīs brāļi (Three Brothers) **N**
Lielā ģilde
Vagnera koncertzale
Nacionālā opera (Opera House) **R**
Latviešu biedrības nams
Sāpju Dievmātes katoļu
Big Christopher
Angļikāņu
Doma laukums
Herdera laukums
Doma
Mazā ģilde
Kaķu māja
Līvu laukums
Farmācijas muzejs
Dabas muzejs (Museum of Nature)
Rīgas cirks (Riga Circus)
Rīgas vēstures un kuģniecības muzejs
Barikāžu muzejs
Rīgas Tehniskā universitāte
Rātsnams
Konventa sēta
VECRĪGA
Sv. Jāna
Meļngalvju nams
Rātslaukums
Pēterbaznīca
Okupācijas muzejs
Reiterna nams
Fotogrāfijas muzejs
Sporta muzejs
Strēlnieku laukums
Mencendorfa nams
Dannenšterna nams
Rīgas centrālā stacija (Central Railway Station)
Centrālais pasts (Post Office)
Satekles iela
Marijas iela
Daugava
1905 Revolution monument
Krastmala
13. Janvāra
Centrāltirgus (Central Market) **V**
MASKAS FORŠTATE
Latvijas Zinātņu akadēmija (Academy of Science) **W**
Uzvaras Parks, Botanical Gardens, Pardaugava **X**
Akmens tilts
Krasta iela
Jēzus baznīca (Lutheran Church of Jesus)
Die Greise Hor Shul (Great Synagogue)

Rīga

0 ___ 200 m
0 ___ 200 yds

cats were returned to their original positions where they remain to this day. The city's two guild halls are on the west side of the square. Traditionally only Germans were allowed to belong to the **Great Guild of St John's** ⓒ (Lielā Ģilde), a merchants' guild founded in 1384. The building was last redesigned in 1866 by the city architect J.D. Felsko and today it is the home of the Philharmonic Orchestra. The **Small Guild of St Mary's** (Mazā Ģilde) was for artisans and was started in the mid-14th century. Both functioned until the 1860s but they were not finally dissolved until the 1930s.

To the left of the guild halls, on Richard Wagner Street is the **Wagner Concert Hall** ⓓ (4 Vāgnera koncertzāle), the concert hall named after the illustrious German composer who conducted in the building for two years before he fled to avoid his creditors. The clandestine journey on the stormy, unforgiving Baltic Sea would inspire him to write the *Flying Dutchman*. Beyond the courtyard at No. 13 is the **Museum of Pharmacy** (Farmācijas muzejs; open Tues–Sat 10am–4pm; admission fee) that displays old bottles, many of which still contain their original ingredients. Of equal significance is the building's rococo doorway, one of the few examples of the style in Rīga.

Statue of the Latvian Riflemen.

Town Hall Square

Continue walking up Kaļķu iela until you reach the next square. Rātslaukums encapsulates all of Latvia's history and in its centre stands the **House of Blackheads** ⓔ (Melngalvju nams; open Tues–Sun 10am–5pm; admission fee). This historic gem was heavily damaged during World War II. The remains were destroyed by the Soviets after the war, but the Dutch renaissance guild house was rebuilt with private donations and opened in time for the city's 800th anniversary in 2001. The building also houses a **Tourist Information Centre**. Founded in the 13th century, the brotherhood organised the city's social life and the house became a meeting place for bachelor merchants arriving from abroad. One of the community's patron saints was Saint Mauritius, who was black and gave the brotherhood its name. The historic **Town Hall** ⓕ (Rātsnams) opposite, also recently rebuilt, is the seat of local government. A third floor was added to the original architectural plan as well as a modern wing behind the building.

BELOW: statue of Roland outside the House of Blackheads.

Adjoining the Blackhead Brotherhood house is an ugly black building, the former Museum of the Latvian Red Riflemen, home to the excellent and chilling **Occupation Museum** (Okupācijas muzejs; open 10am–5pm, closed Mon in winter; admission free). The museum retraces Latvia's plight under the Nazi and Soviet occupations from 1940 to 1991, with explanations in English, German and Russian. The moving exhibit depicts the life of Latvians deported to Siberia and those who fought the Soviets in the forests. The museum is important for anybody interested in recent Latvian history.

In front of the Occupation Museum, facing Akmens Bridge is **Latvian Riflemen Square** ⓖ (Strēlnieku laukums) with a red granite Monument to the Latvian Riflemen in its centre. This controversial landmark was once dedicated to the riflemen who joined the

Bolsheviks after the revolution. In a time of dramatically changing fortunes, the Latvian Riflemen split, some remaining true to the tsar, others joining the Latvian freedom fighters and still others swearing allegiance to the Reds. Some of the latter gained respect as the bodyguards of Lenin and infamy as the executioners of the Romanov family in 1918.

Churches with a view

Facing the rebuilt Blackheads' house is the elegant steeple of the **Church of St Peter** ⓗ (Pēterbaznīca; open Tues–Sun 10am–5pm; admission fee). A lift glides heavenwards to a viewing platform 72 metres (236 ft) up in the 122-metre (380-ft) steeple. The first church here, made of wood, was built by the city's craftsmen in 1209. Two centuries later it was rebuilt in stone. In 1709, 15 years after the steeple was completed, the city fell to the Russians and Peter the Great took a special delight in climbing to the top of the tower, then the tallest wooden structure in Europe. When it was struck by lightning in 1721, he personally helped to put out the fire.

Young performers outside St Peter's.

In the corner of the square, at Grēcinieku Street 18, is the half-timbered **Mentzendorff House** ⓘ (Mencendorfa nams; open Wed–Sun 10am–5pm; admission fee), which offers a good idea of what life was like in a prosperous German's home in the 17–18th century, though the building itself dates back to the 16th century. Among its former owners was Andreas Helm, head of the Small Guild, and Rheinhold Schlevgt, master of the Order of the Blackheads who established a pharmacist's on the premises. Its restored interior has *trompe l'oeil* wall decoration and painted ceilings inspired by Jean-Antoine Watteau. The rooms have been furnished with period pieces from

BELOW: the soaring nave of St Peter's.

the Museum of the History of Rīga and Navigation. Facing St Peter's on the north side are two other important churches. **St George's** now houses the **Museum of Decorative Art and Design ❶** (Dekoratīvās mākslas un dizaina muzejs; open Tues–Sun 11am–5pm; admission fee) and it should be visited if only to see the building's interior. This was the original church in the city, founded by the crusading Bishop Albert of Bremen in 1204 as a chapel for the Sword-Bearer's Order. It stood beside the castle complex which launched the first crusades against the Baltic people. Rebuilt after a rebellion in 1297, it was the first stone building in the city and it remains one of the few examples of Romanesque. It has not been used as a church since the Reformation when it was turned into a storehouse.

Next to St George's is **Jāņa Sēta**, a small square abutting part of the old red-brick city wall, on the other side of which is the red-bricked **St John's** (Jāņa baznīca; open daily 11am–6pm; free), which is distinguished by a steeply stepped Gothic pediment. The church started life in 1234 as the chapel of a Dominican abbey. In 1330 it was enlarged and its buttresses became the dividing walls of the new side altars. It was taken from the Dominicans during the Reformation and in 1582 a divine service in Latvian was held here for the first time. On the south wall, facing St Peter's, is a grille covering a cross-shaped window behind which two monks were cemented up during the building of the church and for the rest of their short lives they were fed through the small gap.

Opposite the entrance to the courtyard is the **Statue of the Bremen Town Musicians** from the Grimm fairytale. It was a recent gift from the city of Bremen, home of Bishop Albert, founder of Rīga. Sandwiched between the two churches is Ecke's Convent that once belonged to the mayor of Rīga. In 1596,

Map on page 200

TIP

Street finder:
iela means street,
laukums is square,
bulvāris/prospekts is avenue, *ceļš* is road.

LEFT: St John's Courtyard.
RIGHT: the Mentzendorff House.

after allegations of embezzlement circulated around town, Ecke was forgiven after donating his lavish home to an order of nuns that cared for widows who could no longer support themselves. It currently houses a teashop.

Behind the building is a futher courtyard, **Konventa Sēta**, which is now home to an upmarket hotel, dozens of shops and cafés as well as the **Rīga Porcelain Museum** (Rīgas porcelāna muzejs; open Tues–Sun 11am–6pm; admission fee). Its medieval architecture has been lovingly restored making it difficult to imagine that this complex of houses once supported a convent that looked after the city's poor.

Head southeast to the corner of Audēju iela (Weavers' Street) and Mārstaļu iela and look out for the **House of Johan Reutern ⓚ** (Reiterna nams) where exhibitions are often held. It was built by this rich German merchant in 1685, during the Swedish occupation, and beneath the roof is a frieze showing the Swedish lion devouring the Russian bear. At No. 21 is another baroque mansion, which was built in 1696 for Reutern's son-in-law, a burgher named Dannenstern. Both have fine doorways by the local stonemason Hans Schmiesel, who was responsible for the handsome if rather out of place portal on St Peter's Church.

Next door is the **Latvian Photography Museum** (Latvijas fotogrāfijas muzejs; open Wed–Thur noon–7pm; Tues, Fri & Sat 10am–5pm; admission fee) that has a collection of late 19th-century photographs of rural landscapes as well as some impressive pictures from World War I. A highlight of the museum is the Minox spy camera produced in Latvia just prior to the war and later manufactured by the famous German firm Leica.

Just past the museum on the left is Peitavas Street where a **Jewish synagogue** has been beautifully restored. The only Jewish place of worship in Rīga

Chimneysweeps claim to have the oldest guild in Rīga, and you may still see them, wearing top hats and white gloves. Rub their brass buttons for good luck.

BELOW: Dome church with St Peter's.

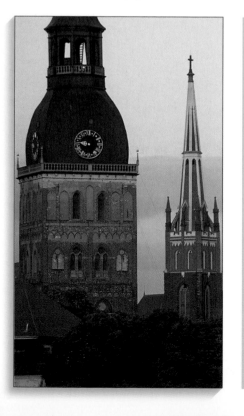

THE BURNING OF RĪGA

For nearly 100 years before Peter I's arrival, the city had been under the control of the Swedes, who had rebuilt its castle, the flag-topped citadel to the north just by Vanšu Bridge. Rīga had been the largest city in their empire, bigger even than Stockholm. But after they had been driven out in a nine-month siege by Peter's Russian Army, the city was in no great shape, and two-thirds of the population had died. Among them were many Latvians who were barred from living within the city walls. Since the arrival of the German crusaders and the construction of the city in stone, they had been relegated to the lands beyond the city walls, and to Pārdaugava on the river's far bank, where they lived in buildings that had to be built out of wood. Each time the city was threatened, as it had been by the Russians, they had to burn their property and accept the protection of the city walls. The eighth and last time this happened was in 1812 when an eagle-eyed watchman on St Peter's belfry spotted a distant cloud of dust heralding the French invasion. Four churches, 705 houses, 35 public buildings and hundreds of acres of vegetable plots were torched before it became clear the dust was caused by a herd of cows. Napoleon crossed Latvia via a different route.

that survived the Nazi occupation of Latvia, it was spared for fear that a blaze might spread to other nearby buildings. It is open to visitors, and services are held here every Saturday.

Cathedral and castle

All streets in the old town lead to **Dome Square** (Doma laukums), the cobbled focal point of the old city, where tourists pose for photos in front of the largest church in the Baltics and then spend far too much money for a drink at a beer garden with a view. **Dome Cathedral** (Doma baznīca; open Sat–Tues, Thur 9am–6pm, Wed, Fri 9am–5pm; admission fee), or St Mary's, is a magnificent red-brick structure, with a gable like a Hanseatic merchant's house and a bulbous dome of northern Gothic solemnity. Steps lead down to the north door because the city's constant rebuilding has meant the ground level has actually risen over the years.

The cathedral was begun by Bishop Albert just after St George's, in 1211, and he is buried in the crypt. The plaques, tombs and headstones decorating the interior show just how German the city remained, no matter who owned it. Especially notable is the 6,768-pipe organ, which was, at the time of its completion in 1884, one of the world's largest. It was such a grand project that the tsar himself donated money to the cause and Franz Liszt composed music for its inauguration. Sadly, the cathedral is in poor repair and is in desperate need of renovation. Its massive columns have been reinforced with steel, but some areas are still off limits to the public due to safety concerns.

The cloister gardens are surrounded by a 118-metre (387-ft) vaulted gallery (open daily May–Sept 10am–5pm; admission fee), one of the most outstanding

Map on page 200

TIP

Visit Emīla Gustava Šokolāde's chocolate cafe in Berga Bazārs, Marijas iela 13, where you can see chocolate being made by hand and can sample the final product.

LEFT:
al-fresco dining in Dome Square.

examples of north European medieval construction work, which also houses hundreds of pieces of local history including tombstones, the original Dome cockerel and a huge stone head thought to be an ancient pagan idol. Enter to the left of the **Museum of the History of Rīga and Navigation** (Rīgas vēstures un kuģniecības muzejs; open Tues–Sun 11am–6pm; admission fee) at Palasta Street 4. This is an eclectic collection of historical items and memorabilia, and does not have too much to do with the sea. Its scope is very wide and it is one of the best museums in the city, reflecting the wealth of its merchants. It was the first public museum in the Baltics when it opened in 1773 and it was based on the collection of Nicolaus von Himsel, a medical practitioner who died nine years earlier at the age of 35.

The beautiful decorative arts in the Museum of the History of Rīga and Navigation give an insight into the rich and cultured life of merchants in the city.

Pils iela (Castle Street) leads off Dome Square in front of an elegant, green 19th-century Venetian Renaissance building with ruched curtains that give it something of the air of a boudoir. This is now the city's stock exchange.

In the corner of Anglikāņu Street off Castle Street is a smart brown Renaissance-style building, which belongs to the **Danish Embassy**. It was built as the British Club for expatriates, merchants and sundry travellers (Napoleon called Rīga "a suburb of London"), and every brick and detail of the Anglican church behind it was brought from Britain, including a shipload of earth to provide the foundations. Women were allowed in the club once a year.

Pils Street arrives at **Rīga castle**  (Rīgas pils), which the Swedes redesigned in 1652. The first castle was built here in 1330 by the Livonian Order, who later decamped to Cēsis. In 1481, in one of many internecine wars within the city, it was razed by the townspeople, but the Livonian Order returned to besiege the town 34 years later, eventually prevailing and forcing the locals to rebuild it. Today it houses two museums of interest: **History of Latvia** (Latvijas vēs-

BELOW:
the Three Brothers.

tures muzejs; open Wed–Sun 11am–5pm; admission fee) and **Foreign Art** (Ārzemju mākslas muzejs; open Tues–Sun 11am–5pm; admission fee).

Opposite the castle, Mazā Pils Street dives into the narrow lanes of the Old Town again. The most attractive group of buildings here are the three buildings known as **The Three Brothers** (Trīs brāļi). These are the oldest residences in the city, merchants' homes of almost doll's-house proportions dating from the 15th century. They have been colourfully restored, and they show how the families would live on the lower floors while leaving the upper areas for storage. One of them is home to the city's small **Museum of Architecture** (Arhitektūras muzejs; open Mon–Fri 10am–6pm; free).

Nearby is the red-brick **St Jacob's** (Jēkaba baznīca; open Sun–Fri 9am–7pm; free), the principal Catholic church. Its 73-metre (240-ft) thin green spire, topped by a gold cockerel, is one of the three sky pricking steeples that shape the city's skyline. In 1522 it became the first church in Latvia to hold a Lutheran service, but 60 years later, when the Polish King Stephen Bathory took the city for a brief spell, it was handed to the Catholics who have kept faith here ever since. In front of it is the peach-coloured residence of the archbishop and on the north side is the parliament building on Jēkaba Street which was blockaded against Soviet attack in 1991. One of the original cement barricades erected to protect the building is displayed in front of the church.

Turn right along Trokšņu Street, leading directly to the charming **Swedish Gate** (Zviedru vārti). Built in 1698, this is the only gate left in the city walls and through it the condemned were led to their fate. The executioner lived in the apartment next to the gate; he would place a red rose on his window ledge on any morning he had to perform. The street on the far side of the gate is lined by

Map on page 200

LEFT: Swedish Gate. **BELOW:** the Powder Tower.

Art Nouveau

A rt Nouveau, the architectural style that brings such an unexpectedly decadent air to Rīga's streets, celebrated the triumph of the bourgeoisie at the end of the 19th and beginning of the 20th century. In highly developed Rīga more than in any Russian city, the new urban middle classes found prosperity.

A new wave of architects jumped at the task of designing residential blocks, academies, schools, department stores, libraries, banks, restaurants and factories. The result is that nearly one in three buildings in Rīga – some 40 percent of the boulevard city that grew up in the 1900s – is in Art Nouveau or Jugendstil.

Rīga hosted a mixture of new, often decorative approaches to building. The residential houses in Alberta Street, built by civil engineer Mikhail Osipovich Eisenstein, father of the great Russian film maker, are saturated in finishing details. Inside the entrance hall to 2A Alberta Street the exterior decoration evolves into a turquoise hall of columns, embroidered with leaves and curves.

Eisenstein's "decoratively eclectic Art Nouveau", a staggering synthesis of rationality and ornament, is shared by other contemporary Rīga architects including the Baltic Germans Friedrich Scheffel, Heinrich Scheel and Reinhold Schmaeling. All studied in St Petersburg, where Art Nouveau flourished. The entrance hall to Scheel and Sheffel's residential block with shops at 8 Smilšu Street shows a characteristic affinity with the Arts and Crafts Movement.

That thread takes the curious visitor back to one of Rīga's most important architects, the Baltic German Wilhelm Bockslaff. Bockslaff built the graceful turreted brick Stock Exchange (1905), on Kalpaka Boulevard. Since 1919 the building has housed the Latvian Art Academy. Its pastel-coloured celing is embroidered after the style of William Morris, is a treasury of stained glass and the whole building is a fine monument to the eclecticism of Art Nouveau.

Houses, shops and banks on Brīvības Street and nearby Ģertrūdes and A. Čaka streets employ the perpendicular to express the solidity and the excitement of town life. Architects of this so-called "rational" Art Nouveau from the mid-1900s include Latvians Jānis Alksnis, Eižens Laube, Paul Mandelstamm and Konstantīns Pēkšēns.

Laube, Mandelstamm, Pēkšēns and Aleksandrs Vanags all graduated from Rīga Polytechnical Institute, which encouraged them to develop a specific Latvian style. A general heaviness, in some cases as if the building had been poured out of a mould, in others as if it were a test-run for many different building materials, including stucco, wood, stone, brick and plaster, characterises this national romanticism.

It incorporated stylised ethnographic ornaments and the natural materials used in an urban setting, together with tapered window recesses and steep roofs, suggested a continued link with rural life.

The individual features of scores of these buildings, testaments to high-spirited urban living, make a walk around Rīga a joy. ❏
www.artnouveauriga.lv

LEFT: dramatic figures in Elizabetes Street.

the yellow **Jacob's Barracks** (Jēkaba kazarmas), erected for the occupying Swedes. Turn right up Torņa Street past the old houses built against the red-brick city wall that has been partially restored. At the end of the street is Pulvertornis, the **Powder Tower** , the last of 18 city towers. Its round red-brick walls and concave, conical roof, topping 26 metres (85 ft), are reminiscent of Lübeck, Queen of the Hansa cities. The **Latvian Museum of War** (Kara muzejs; open Wed–Sun 10am–6pm; free) is housed inside.

Parks and art

To say that the old city is an island is rather fanciful, but it is entirely surrounded by water. The old moat that encircles it on the landward side is now a small canal running through a series of attractive parks from the ferry terminal in the north on the far side of the castle, to the railway station and market in the south. To the north, on Kr Valdemāra Street, is the **National Theatre** **Q** (Nacionalais teātris). To the south, between Brīvības and Kr Barona Street, is the fine 19th-century **Opera House** **R** (Nacionālā opera), formerly known as the German Theatre, which has been lovingly renovated with private donations.

The National Art Museum.

In the park just to the north of Brīvības is **Bastejkalns** **S**, the high spot of the city and not much more than a hiccup with little waterfalls and pleasant summer terraces by the canal. Five inscribed stones nearby commemorate the film cameramen and policemen killed here during the Soviet attack in January 1991.

The rallying point for the nation is the **Freedom Monument** **A** (Brīvības piemineklis) on Brīvības, the elegant lady designed by K. Zāle in 1935. Locally known as Milda, she holds aloft three golden stars representing the three regions of Latvia: Kurzeme, Vidzeme and Latgale. An honour guard keeps watch over Milda while Latvians lay flowers at her feet, an act

BELOW: pedallos on the canal.

that once held the prospect of a one-way ticket to Siberia. The sentries are ceremoniously replaced on the hour from 9am to 6pm.

Beyond the monument on the left is the **Russian Orthodox Church** (Pareizticīgo katedrāle), which was gutted by the Soviets for use as a planetarium. The Esplanade park behind it leads to the 19th-century **Arts Academy** **T** (Latvijas Mākslas akadēmija) and the **National Art Museum** (Valsts mākslas muzejs; open Wed–Mon 11am–5pm; admission fee). It has a permanent exhibition of paintings by 18th-century Baltic Germans and the Latvian masters Rozentāls, Annuss, Valters, Padegs and Liberts, and frescos by the nation's most revered artist Vilhelms Purvītis. Outside is a statue of Janis Rozentāls (*see next page*).

Just off the park on Skolas is **Jews in Latvia** (Ebreji Latvijā; open Sun–Thur noon–5pm; admission fee), a museum dedicated to the achievements and history of the Latvian Jewish community.

Art Nouveau

Elizabetes iela at the top of the park should be followed for a while to appreciate its Art Nouveau and National Romanticism buildings (*see left*). Nos 10a, 10b and 33 were designed by Mikhail Eisenstein, father of Rīga's most famous film maker, Sergei Eisenstein, director of the 1925 epic *Battleship Potemkin*.

But most of his work can be seen in Alberta Street (second right and first left after Kr Valdemāra) where he was responsible for nearly all of the houses on the right side plus No. 13 opposite. After years of neglect during the Soviet era most of the buildings have been renovated with a few glaring exceptions. At the end of the street is Strēlnieku Street, with another Eisenstein masterpiece at 4a, which has his typical bright blue touch. On the corner of the two streets was the house the Latvian architect Konstantīns Pēkšēns built for himself. Two other famous people lived there: the artist Janis Rozentāls (1866–1916) and the writer Rūdolfs Blaumanis (1863–1908). The **Rozentāls and Blaumanis Museum**  (Jaņa Rozentāla un Rūdolfa Blaumaņa muzejs; open Wed–Sun 11am–6pm; admission fee) on the top floors contains their respective study and studio. It's worth a look at the building's fantastic interior and decorated spiral staircase. Rozentāls' work can also be seen on the facade of the former Latvian Society building near the university by the corner of Kr Barona and Merķeļa streets. His most famous painting, *Leaving the Cemetery* is in the National Art Museum.

Janis Rozentāls, self-portrait, 1900.

Across the intersection is the **Rīga Circus** (Rīgas cirks), which has been in operation more or less since 1889. On the opposite side of Merķeļa is the **Museum of Nature** (Dabas muzejs; open Wed–Sat 10am–5pm, Sun 10am–4pm; admission fee), which displays all manner of objects from rare fossils to freaks of nature preserved in glass jars.

The Central Market and Moscow District

BELOW: Academy of Science in the Moscow District.

Beyond the railway station are the five 35-metre (39-ft) high zeppelin hangars, built by the Germans in Vainode, south-western Latvia, in World War I and brought here in the 1920s to house the **Central Market**  (Centrāltirgus) – one of the real wonders of Rīga. The city's market had for three and a half centuries been sited beside the Daugava and even then it was one of the largest in the Baltic region. It must still be a contender for the title of Europe's largest market with more than 1,200 vendors. It is built over a large underground storage system, and each hangar has its speciality: meat, dairy products, vegetables. Cream is sold in plastic bags, there are barrels of sauerkraut, fancy cakes, pickled garlic, dried herbs and mushrooms, smoked fish and whole stalls selling nothing but tins of sardines. Down by the waterfront the old flea market spreads across acres of pavement. Open every day, it is at its busiest on Friday and Saturday.

The market is at the edge of the **Moscow District** (Maskavas Forštate), known locally as "Little Moscow", where for centuries, ethnic Russians have lived. Among the oldest of its communities are the Old Believers who setted here after fleeing from the late 17th-century religious persecution in Russia. The area was also a vibrant centre for Jewish life in Rīga, extinguished under the Nazis. Unlike the orderly German-influenced streets and manicured parks of the city centre, the Moscow District always had a wild streak and character of its own. Its 19th-century wooden houses and Art Nouveau buildings have yet to benefit from the city's economic boom.

In the middle of it is the squat, brown, Empire-State

Map on page 200

replica belonging to the **Academy of Science** Ⓦ (Zinātņu akadēmija) and just beyond, in Jēzusbaznīcas Street, is a fascinating octagonal wooden **Lutheran Church of Jesus** (Jēzus baznīca), built in 1822 from solid, wide boards. At the end of the street are the ruins of the **Great Synagogue** (Die Greise Hor Shul) that was burned to the ground on 4 July 1941 with dozens of Jews inside.

The Moscow District is typified by dilapidated 19th-century wooden buildings, Soviet concrete monstrosities and post-independence prosperity that has run amok in the form of shiny glass car dealerships and shopping malls. But some things never change and among them is the only gold dome in the city peeking out from the skyline in a clump of lime trees. Named after its principal benefactor, a businessman named Alexei Grebenschikov,

Grebenščikova baznīca is the place of worship for the Old Believers. The church now has the largest parish of the faith in the world, with a congregation of approximately 25,000. It has a unique collection of 17th and 18th-century icons, and a rich and contemplative atmosphere that is broken only by the rather incongruous chimes of a grandfather clock. Services are held at 8am and 5pm in Church Slavonic, the liturgical language of the Russian Orthodox church.

Vegetable seller in the Central Market.

The left bank

On the opposite bank across Stone Bridge (Akmens tilts) is the attractive suburb of **Pārdaugava**, which has many wood-built houses. From here there is a good view of the Old City skyline. Victory Park (**Uzvaras Park**), has a Soviet victory monument and is popular with Russians. Near the park are a railway and a theatre museum and about a mile from the bridge is the **Botanical Gardens**, with palm house. ❑

BELOW: Zeppelin hangars of the Central Market.

AROUND RĪGA

*Just a short bus or train ride from the centre of Rīga are
a number of places to have fun, from the Open-Air Ethnographic
Museum to the city's seaside playground at Jūrmala*

While high society in London and Berlin was thinking only about green spaces to live in, Rīga's wealthy elite were already designing **Mežaparks ②** (Forest Park), one of Europe's first garden cities. Tired of overcrowding and the squalor of the city proper, prosperous Germans created this place, known then as Kaiser Park, beside **Lake Ķīšezers**, where only summer cottages and entertainment facilities were permitted. Neglected during the Soviet era, many of the impressive Art Nouveau properties have been renovated and the park is once again inhabited by the cream of local society, its property commanding some of the highest prices in the country.

The park is also home to **Rīga Zoo** (Zooloģiskais dārzs; open 10am–6pm; admission fee), which has brown and polar bears, and is well worth a visit, and the expansive **Song Festival Stadium** (Lielā estrāde), which can accommodate 10,000 singers and 25,000 spectators. They gather every five years for a major festival as they have done since 1873.

A small beach on the lake is also a popular destination for swimmers and sunbathers. **Aktīvās Atpūtas Centrs** (Pāvu iela, tel: 29 55 41 55) on Lake Kisezers is an activity centre where you can hire bicycles and ice skates, and go boating, jet-skiing, windsurfing, water-skiing and parasailing. "Ice boating"

BELOW:
Lake Ķīšezers

was first held on Lake Kīšezers in 1926 and it was here that the Rīga Yacht Club devised the rules for the sport.

Open-Air Museum

Perhaps of greatest general appeal is the **Open-Air Ethnographic Museum ❸** (Brīvdabas muzejs; open daily 10am–5pm; admission fee), 10 km (6 miles) northeast along Brīvības Street. More than 100 buildings are set out in 100 hectares (250 acres) of woodland beside Lake Jugla. The idea for the museum arose in the wake of the desolation of the countryside after World War I, and work began on it in 1924.

The most impressive building is the 18th-century Lutheran church (Usmas baznīca) just to the left of the entrance. The whole building, including its figurative woodcarvings, was made with axes. There is a special highly-decorated seat beside the altar for the local German landlord, and the front pews were reserved for imported German workers. Attending church was obligatory for all workers at that time and those caught skiving were put in the stocks or the pillory exhibited outside. Before the 19th-century organ was installed, the only music would have been an accompanying drum.

The museum display is divided into Latvia's ancient regions and it shows the contrasts between the rich Kurzeme farmers and those of poorer Latgale. By and large the farmsteads were built solely for the family unit, which usually meant three generations. In the museum, costumed figures populate the village and a blacksmith, potter and spoonmaker often perform. There are occasional folk gatherings here and a major crafts fare is held on the first weekend in June – it's very entertaining and should not be missed.

Map on pages 184–5

TIP

For both the zoo and for Lake Kīšezers, take tram No. 11 from Barona iela *to Zooloģiskais dārzs.

BELOW: Open-Air Ethnographic Museum.

*Film maker Juris
Podnieks (1950–92),
a watchful eye in a
changing world.*

Film and motor museums

In the same direction is the Motor Museum about 5 km (3 miles) from the centre of town along Brīvības iela. Šmerļa Street leads down to it from Brīvības, passing by the city's large **Film Studios 4** (Rīgas kinostudija), which operate an open-door policy. Since 1940 it has produced mainly documentary films and its proteges included Juri Podnieks. His 1989 film about the Soviet Union, *Hello, Do You Hear Us?*, which won the Prix d'Italia, included extraordinary footage of the Chernobyl disaater. There is a museum on the premises with changing exhibitions.

Just beyond the film studios, the street forks right into Sergeja Eizenšteina Street where the glistening facade of the **Motor Museum** (Rīgas motormuzejs; open Tues–Sun 10am–6pm, Mon 10am–3pm; admission fee) stands out like a brand new Rolls-Royce radiator grille. Rīga has been a key player in motor manufacturing in Eastern Europe: its Russo-Balt factory, for example, presented Russia with its first car and tank. However, the fruits of its labours are rather poorly represented in this museum. The high spots are waxwork figures of the famous with their vehicles: Stalin in his 7.3-tonne bullet-proof car which had hydraulic glass windows 8 cm (3 inches) thick; the writer Maxim Gorky with his 1934 Lincoln; Foreign Minister Molotov's Rolls-Royce raith; USSR President Leonid Brezhnev at the moment of impact when he crashed his 1966 Rolls-Royce, together with the subsequent press cuttings saying that his non-appearance was due to a "sudden bad cold".

Just to the south are the three great cemeteries of the city, which are highly regarded by Latvians who use them almost like parks: the **Cemetery of Heroes** (Brāļu kapi) for the casualties of World War I and the War of Independence

BELOW:
Jūrmala villa.

Map on pages 184–5

(1915–20); **Raiņa Cemetery** (Raiņa kapi) for the great and the good of Latvian literati; and the old **Forest Cemetery** (Meža kapi), final resting place of heads of state as well as common folk.

Salaspils

The A6 follows the right bank of the River Daugava for 16 km (10 miles) to **Salaspils ❺**, where the Livonian Order built its first palace, in the 14th century, and in 1412 signed an important agreement with the Bishop of Rīga, establishing shared rule over the capital. On this site in 1605 the Swedes suffered a crushing defeat by the Poles. But Salaspils is destined to go down in the history books primarily as the site of a nightmarish World War II concentration camp where 53,000 died.

A 40-hectare (100-acre) memorial park was opened in 1967, centred on a long, sloping concrete building inscribed: "The earth moans beyond this gate." On the far side are half a dozen monumental statues and a lengthy, low black box where wreaths are placed. It emits a continuous and eerie ticking noise, supposed to represent a beating heart. The sites of the former barracks are marked and an inscribed stone marks the place of the gallows. There were 7,000 children killed among the Latvians, Belarussians, Poles, Czechs, Austrians, Dutch and Germans who died here. On the opposite side of the highway is a memorial to 47,000 Soviet prisoners of war who perished under the Nazis.

The seaside

The word *jurmala* in Latvian simply means seaside, and this is the name given to the Baltics' most famous resort, exending west from **Lielupe ❻**. **Jūrmala** has long been the playground of Rīga, from its 19th-century spa days to its heyday in the 1930s. Peggie Benton, an English diplomat's wife, was in Rīga at the outbreak of World War II and like many people from the city rented a villa at Jūrmala for the summer. "The Latvians kept up the delightful Russian custom of bathing naked," she wrote in *Baltic Countdown*. "One soon learned not to worry and got used to strolling up to a policeman, tightly buttoned into his uniform, to ask how much longer until the red flag went up and we had to put our clothes on again." During the Soviet era Jūrmala became *the* destination for holidaymakers from across the USSR and ugly concrete hotels began to overshadow the quaint European atmosphere which attracted so many people here.

Today, Jūrmala is still a favourite for Russian tourists, and although many of the buildings have been restored or renovated, a slightly Soviet atmosphere, and mentality, remains. This frustrates locals and fascinates tourists.

Not actually a proper city, rather a collection of small seaside towns, Jūrmala stretches along a narrow strip of land, pressed against the beach by the River Lielupe, which follows the coast for about 8 km (5 miles) before emptying itself into Rīga Bay just west of the mouth of the Daugava. The main beaches at Majori and Dubulti have both been awarded blue flags guaranteeing water purity and a

BELOW: the beach at Jūrmala.

At the start of the 19th century a local forester named Ķemeris discovered the health-giving properties of the sulphur springs, peat and mud found in the area and built simple baths and huts to encourage people to visit what is today the resort that bears his name.

BELOW AND RIGHT:
the sea at Jūrmala.

variety of services such as changing stations, toilets, fresh water for rinsing off and emergency medical support, not to mention seaside bars and cafés. On a typical summer day you can expect the beaches to be packed and to see football and volleyball games as well as the occasional woman in nothing more than a bikini and high heels using the beach as her personal catwalk. Topless sunbathing is fairly common, but nude beaches are rare. The various spas around town are yet another reason to visit.

A casual stroll down the main pedestrian street of Jomas iela in **Majori** will afford every visitor with countless opportunities to eat, drink and shop. At the end of the street is the **Antique Automobile Exhibit** (Seno spēkratu izstāde; open 11am–6pm; free), which displays classic vehicles from the early to mid 20th century. The cultural high point of Majori is the **Rainis and Aspazija Summer Cottage** (Raiņa un Aspazijas memoriālā vasarnīca; open Wed–Sun 11am–6pm; admission fee), an attractive wooden house once lived in by the poet, playwright and journalist Jānis Rainis in a street called J. Pliekšāna iela, which was Rainis' real name. He lived here during his last three years, from 1926 to 1929, and a museum preserves his effects, which include more than 7,000 books in 11 languages. In fact, he usually rented out the large house to holidaymakers opting to live and work in the smaller house next door where he used to complain about the noise from his tenants' gramophone. His wife, the poet and writer Aspazija, is also commemorated at the house.

There is an abundance of seaside entertainment to enjoy all along this coast, but just strolling round brings rewarding sights such as the renovated Lutheran church in **Dubulti** (Dubultu luterāņu baznīca), whose towering steeple can be seen from a great distance, and the bright blue wooden Orthodox church nearby.

Jūrmala is also home to dozens of spa hotels that offer mud baths and scores of other health treatments often used by German and Finnish pensioners who can't afford such luxurious lifestyles in their own countries. The urban centres provide top-notch restaurants and nightlife as well as excellent examples of wooden Art Nouveau buildings.

To the east, in Bulduri, is the **Līvu Water Park** – with water slides and pool – not to mention bars and an upmarket restaurant.

Getting to the beach

Anyone driving to Jūrmala, or even through it, needs to buy a permit for the day from the roadside offices on its outskirts. A ferry service runs every summer from Rīga to Majori on weekends, but most people just take the frequent trains which leave the Rīga station roughly every 20 minutes.

There are a dozen train stops to choose from between Lielupe and **Ķemeri ❼**, a spa town set back from the sea. In its heyday the grand Ķemeri Hotel had a cosmopolitan air, hosting international chess championships and social events, and it is scheduled to reopen in 2007 as part of the salubrious Kempinski chain. Majori is the central stop, and the main pedestrian road, Jomas Street, has numerous cafés, restaurants, souvenir shops and an outdoor concert hall, all within easy reach of the railway station. ❑

KURZEME: THE WEST COAST

*To the west of Jūrmala lies a rural area of blue cows
and amber-washed beaches that was once owned
by the powerful Duke of Courland*

Map on pages 184–5

Kurzeme is the westernmost region of Latvia, a healthy agricultural area half surrounded by sea. It was once known as Courland (Kurland in German), named after the Kurši, the amber-rich seafaring people who dominated the coast before the arrival of the German crusaders. Not unlike their contemporaries, the Vikings, the Kurši often supplemented their incomes by sailing across the sea to Sweden, and even as far as Denmark, to wreak havoc on local populations, stealing everything that was worth taking. Several of their exploits are mentioned in Scandinavian sagas. In 1561, after the break-up of Livonia, Courland came into its own. It became a duchy under the sovereignty of Poland, and included the region of Zemgale (formerly Semigallia) to the south of Rīga, plus a small corner of modern Lithuania.

Its dukes enjoyed a degree of independence, building castles for themselves and Lutheran churches for the people. Many became rich and powerful, notably Jacob Kettler (1642–82), who went empire-building and collected a couple of outposts, one in Gambia, West Africa, the other the Caribbean island of Tobago.

Kettler amassed his fortune largely from the pines that grow exceptionally tall and straight. The most impressive forests are in the Slītere Nature Reserve (Slīteres Nacionālais parks; *see page 226*) and along the sandy coastal region, which was once below the sea. Trees grow to around 35 metres (110 ft) and some of them are up to 500 years old.

Kurzeme's thriving shipbuilding and trading activities were conducted at the two important ice-free ports of Ventspils and Liepāja, which have once again become major trading hubs, rivalling even Rīga.

The coast around Kurzeme is a continuous white sandy beach, from just north of the major Lithuanian resort of Palanga up to the Kolka peninsula and down to the fishing village of Mērsrags and Lake Engure in the Bay of Rīga. Beyond this is Jūrmala, Latvia's riviera *(see previous chapter)*, and Zemgale *(see page 237)*. For 45 years, until 1991, most of this coast was used by the military and was therefore inaccessible: today, even in the heat of summer, much of it remains completely deserted save the occasional kite-flyer or windsurfer. Between the coastal lowland in the west and Rīga Bay in the northeast, towns, villages, churches and estates are tucked in the valleys and wooded corners of a landscape that rolls between rivers and hills. Kuldīga and Talsi are the principal inland provincial towns.

PREVIOUS PAGES:
Nogale manor.
LEFT: Courland countryside.
BELOW: Kuldīga.

Starting point

The town of **Kuldīga ❽** is 160 km (100 miles) west of Rīga, and is a good centre for exploring the region. A castle was first built here in 1242, and in 1561 the

The bad woman in Zlēku church.

town, known then as Goldingen, was made the capital of Courland by the first duke, Gotthard Kettler. The castle was built beside the River Venta, which was navigable all the way to Ventspils and the sea.

The city declined after the Great Northern War (1700–21) and the castle was reduced to little more than a ruin: only a park and an engraved stone marking its location remain. The churches are worth exploring: St Anne's (Sv Annas baznīca) has an impressive neo-Gothic spire, St Catherine's Lutheran Church (Sv Katrīnas luterāņu baznīca) has a fine wooden altar and pulpit from 1660, and there is a grand view over the town from the top of its 25-metre (85-ft) tower. The altar of the Holy Trinity Catholic Church (Sv Trīsvienības katoļu baznīca) in Raiņa Street also has an impressive altar, which was donated by Tsar Alexander I in 1820.

Part of the town's charm is derived from the Alekšupīte, a tributary to the River Venta, which runs by a mill and between wooden houses that date from the 17th century. Most of the old red tile-roofed buildings are centred around the square overlooked by the 19th-century town hall, but the main pedestrian street today is Liepājas, which runs back from Raiņa Street a few streets back. With a wooden building that looks as if it might be a Wild West saloon, this street leads to the main modern square dominated by two Soviet-style buildings housing a hotel and supermarket – practically the only eyesores in an otherwise charming medieval town.

At the old 19th-century brick bridge over the Venta you can see the Ventas rumba, Europe's widest waterfall that runs the 110-metre (360-ft) width of the river. In the park overlooking the river is the Kuldīga Museum (Kuldīgas novada muzejs; open daily 11am–5pm; admission fee), whose building is more inter-

esting than its exhibits. It served as part of the Russian pavilion at the 1900 World's Fair in Paris and was bought by a wealthy businessman who had it shipped to Kuldīga as a gift to his fiancée.

Roma villages and vineyards

A pleasant drive leads northeast of Kuldīga, to Sabile and Kandava, towards Tukums. These villages are known for their Roma population. Vīna kalns, Wine Hill, in **Sabile** ❾ is in the *Guinness Book of Records* as the most northern place in Europe where vines are grown and the town has one of the region's few surviving synagogues, which is now an arts centre. On the other side of the river is the Pedvāle Outdoor Art Museum, created in 1992 on a former baronial estate (Pedvāles brīvdabas mākslas muzejs; open daily May–Oct 9am–10pm; admission fee). Visitors can explore 150 hectares (370 acres) of rolling hills covered in sculptures and modern art on a grand scale and can even book a room at the museum's guesthouse.

Kandava has a pleasant old town, but only a fortification wall and powder tower remain of its original castle. It does, however, boast the oldest fieldstone bridge in Latvia. Due south of Kandava at **Zante** you'll find the Kurzeme Fortress Museum (Kurzemes cietokšņa muzejs; open Wed–Sun 10am–5pm; admission fee) where you can explore restored trenches, bunkers and military machinery, including a Soviet tank and airplane, from the two world wars.

Between Kuldīga and Ventspils is the small town of **Piltene** ❿, the seat of a bishopric that retained its independence from 1234 to 1583. The remains of its castle of the Livonian Order lie behind the church, built in 1792.

TIP

Country words:
beach is *pludmale*,
castle is *pils*,
field is *lauks*,
forest is *mežs*,
lake is *ezers*,
river is *upe*,
tree is *koks*.

BELOW: the pulpit in Ugāle church.

Ancient churches

Danish craftsmen were imported via Piltene and art historians detect their hand on the robust folk carvings of the altars and pulpits of local churches. But the principal carvings at Piltene, which have not survived, were by the 18th-century master carvers from Ventspils, Nicolas Soeffren the older and younger, ship carvers who turned their skills to church work.

Among other local churches with fine carving is **Zlēkas** ⓫, between Piltene and Kuldīga. This is the largest church in Courland and it has a fine black and gold baroque pulpit and altar which were carved by local craftsmen. Its confessional dating to the late 16th century is the oldest in Latvia. At Ēdole on the opposite side of the main Ventspils road and about 20 km (12 miles) northwest of Kuldīga, there is a church that dates from the 17th century. It also has a restored 13th-century castle (Ēdoles pils).

One of the most interesting churches is at **Ugāle** ⓬, directly north of Kuldīga on the road between Tukums and Ventspils. Built in 1694, its organ was installed four years later, making it the oldest in the Baltic. Is has 28 stops, including the only surviving baroque register. It was built by Cornelius Rhaneus from Kuldīga.

The beautiful, unpainted lime-wood carvings by Michael Markwart from Ventspils include stars that once revolved and angels' wings designed to flap. The

neighbouring village of Usma is the origin of the 18th-century Lutheran church in Rīga's Open-Air Ethnographic Museum and its location on the shore of Lake Usma makes it an excellent destination for water sports including fishing and sailing.

After Courland's incorporation into Russia in 1795, the small town of **Aizpute** ⑬ to the south earned the nickname "Klein Danzig" because nearly two thirds of the population were Jews. The town makes a pleasant stop and has a church dating back to 1254 and castle ruins from the same period. A more recent castle built entirely from stacked firewood is its latest tourist attraction.

Around Talsi

A native Curland "Blue" cow.

The region northeast of Kuldīga is **Talsi** ⑭, centred on the market town of the same name. Like a painting on a chocolate box, it is a pretty, tranquil idyll tucked under hills beside a large pond. Not surprisingly, it has long been an artists' haunt. In its cobbled streets is a small local museum and a Lutheran church, whose pastor, Karl Amenda, was an accomplished musician and a friend of Beethoven.

The oldest wooden church in Latvia is 16 km (10 miles) northeast of Talsi at **Iģene**. It has been a working church since 1555, though most of it dates from 1757. The altar, however, is original. It was moved here from a nearby plague-stricken village. Approach it from Vandzene along a gravel road, taking the first left after the village pond.

BELOW:
smalltown Kuldīga.

North of Talsi is a series of former large country-house estates. The palace at **Nogale** (Nogales pils) is a particularly good example. It was built in 1880 for Baron von Firks as a summer residence and hunting lodge, and from 1920 to

1980 it was a school. It has now been restored and is once again privately owned. The two-storey neoclassical building overlooks a lake and 70 hectares (170 acres) of parkland.

The neighbouring village to the west is **Valdemārpils**, where the main estate is now a school. It takes its name from Krišjānis Valdemārs, one of the leading lights of the National Awakening, who was born in nearby **Cīruļi** in 1825. He became enchanted by the sea near here at Roja and went on to found Latvia's first seamen's school at Ainaži, right up by the Estonian border. Outside his country manor in Valdemārpils is one of the oldest elm trees in the country and the biggest in the Baltics, a huge and crippled beast that once served as a pagan holy site for worship and sacrifice. Lake Sasmaka is nearby and the village has a church dating from 1646 that still has its original altar and pulpit.

The largest estate in the whole of the Baltics was **Dundaga** ⓰, the north-ernmost village of any size on this cape. In the 18th century the castle's lands stretched for 700 sq. km (270 sq. miles), and today some attempts are being made to restore some of its former glory. The crozier and sword, symbols of the Church and the Sword Bearers, are inscribed on its entranceway and the main door inside the courtyard is guarded by a statue of a bishop and a crusader. The estate belonged to the bishops of Courland, the last of whom was Herzog of Holstein, brother of Germany's Frederich II.

There are seven coats-of-arms on the castle, belonging to owners going back to 1245 including those of the von Bülows and the Osten-Sachens, subsequent inheritors of the estate. Today the building houses two schools and a tourist information centre and is used as a venue for local events and concerts.

The local church (Dundagas baznīca), which is dated 1766, has wood carvings

Map on pages 184–5

BELOW: café and chat, Aizpute.

by Soeffren and an altar painting by Latvia's great 20th-century artist, Janis Rozentāls. Memorials to several members of the Osten-Sachens family are scattered in the church grounds but the most notable memorial (Krokodils), located due north, is dedicated to local boy Arvīds Blūmentāls who emigrated to Australia and, after hunting 10,000 crocodiles, served as the prototype for the character "Crocodile Dundee".

The radio-telescope at Irbene, between Kolka and Ventspils, with a 32-metre (105-ft) dish, is sometimes open to the public.

Secret coast of the Livs

On the Rīga Bay side of the cape, the road from Jūrmala continues through pine trees of extraordinary stature, which have provided masts for many ships throughout the ages. Dozens of sleepy fishing villages, which were completely isolated during the Soviet era, dot the coast. Even today, one has the feeling that not much has changed here save a rejuvenation of traditional summer sea festivals. All around this peninsula, which encircles the carefully controlled **Slītere Nature Reserve** (Slīteres Nacionālais parks), there is scarcely any sign of life. The reserve is an important wildlife area caring for a number endangered plants, and supporting the busiest birdlife in the region; in April some 60,000 congregate here. The reserve is divided into four areas. A Landscape Protection Zone has been organized to conserve the forest landscape and biological diversity along the sea coast, while allowing visitors to enjoy the area. **Kolka ⑯** is the main centre for information about the park.

At the top of the peninsula, just beyond Kolka, is a point where the waters of Rīga Bay meet the Baltic Sea. The marked line where the seas meet runs out past the half washed-away lighthouse to the horizon, and when the wind blows, the waters are whipped up into a great crashing wall. Kolka is also home to the

BELOW: Kolka peninsula, where Rīga Bay meets the Baltic sea.

THE LAST OF THE LIVS

At the Liv Centre in Kolka you can learn about the region's indigenous people who were the first settlers of Rīga and gave their name to the province of Livonia. This proud race, who are regarded by many Latvians with some reverence because they are apparently racially pure, have all but been assimilated into the population. By the late 19th century, when their culture and language were for the first time academically assessed, there were barely 2,000 Liv speakers. Their numbers continued to decline, especially during the Soviet years when the military curtailed coastal ways of life, and many left for the cities.

Today, they are on the verge of extinction and while there are about 250 members of the Union of Livs, only a handful of Liv speakers remain. Finno-Ugric by origin, their language is more like Estonian than Latvian, and Finns and Estonians have contributed funds and helped in a programme to try to keep the language alive.

Songs, as well as the language, are taught at the Liv House in Mazirbe, which also organises a Liv festival every August, when their ancient green, white and blue flag is in evidence. Examples of their ancient farmsteads can also be seen at the Open-Air Ethnographic Museums in Rīga and Ventspils.

Liv Centre, which is part Liv history museum, part information centre (Kolkas līvu centrs; open Tues–Sat 9am–5pm; free), where you can learn about the proud people that once populated the coastline *(see box below)*.

Continuing down the western, Baltic side of the coast are a further series of former fishing communities. Typical is **Mazirbe** ⑰, where farmlands stretch back from the dunes of the bleached sand, which is strewn with small cockle and mussel shells. If you're lucky you might even find a chunk of amber. A white wooden hall built with help from neighbouring Estonia serves as a meeting-place for the last of the Liv community.

Duke Jacob's port

The heyday for **Ventspils** ⑱ was under Duke Jacob, who launched his ships for the Caribbean and West Africa from here. But, after his death, Ventspils went into decline and after the plague of 1710 was reduced to just seven families. It enjoyed a cultural renaissance during the years of independence, however, and after World War II the Soviet Union built it up as an industrial centre. Of late, Russian petrodollars have made the tiny town the wealthiest in Latvia and its manicured parks, tidy streets and renovated buildings are a testament to this prosperity. The pipeline has, however, dried up in the wake of worsening relations between the two countries putting its future in jeopardy.

Liepāja beach.

Ventspils' charming historical centre is tiny and can easily be explored on foot. The town's most striking attraction is the restored Livonian Order castle (Ventspils pils) dating back to 1290, which also houses the Ventspils Museum (Ventspils muzejs; open daily 10am–5pm; admission fee) and a medieval restaurant. Behind the castle is the promenade on the bank of the River Venta where visitors can watch ships passing by or, in the summer, take a short cruise from the east end. The 18th-century baroque town hall is also worth a visit, as well as St Nicholas Church, built in 1835 on the opposite side of the square. Sunbathers can take advantage of the city's Blue Flag beach, and a few hours can be whiled away at the Seaside Outdoor Ethnographic Museum (Piejūras brīvdabas muzejs; open daily May–Oct 10am–6pm, Nov–Apr 11am–5pm; admission fee), where the main attraction is a working narrow-gauge railway. Nineteenth-century houses and fishing boats hundreds of years old are also on display. A camping site and an aqua theme park are nearby.

BELOW: Ventspils.

The other significant port on this coast is **Liepāja** ⑲, 130 km (80 miles) south of Ventspils with almost twice its population (86,400). Liepāja is a centre of metal smelting and was a major Soviet military base with submarine pens. Although smaller than Daugavpils, Liepāja is Latvia's second city and its inhabitants, Liepājnieki, are fiercely proud of their home. Known throughout the nation as the city where the wind is born, Liepāja was Latvia's Gdansk, where the first organised grass-roots opposition to Soviet rule began in the 1980s. The city is also a major cultural centre claiming some of the nation's best musicians and artists as its own. While it's often hard to find a live act in Rīga, rock bands perform every night at "Latvia's 1st Rock Café", in the city centre. There's

Map on pages 184–5

Awaiting sentence at Liepāja Old Prison.

BELOW: Liepāja.
RIGHT: view over the Trinity Lutheran Church.

plenty to see and do in Liepāja. Start in the old town at the 18th-century Trinity Lutheran Church (Sv Trīsvienības luterāņu baznīca), built in 1758, with an unusual baroque facade and elaborate rococo interior. Its most impressive asset is its organ dating from the same period which, until 1912, was one of the world's largest with 7,000 pipes and 131 registers. Head down Lielā iela or The Big Street to Rožu laukums, the main square, designed in 1911 with more than 500 rose bushes, giving it its name. Walk down Zivju (Fish) Street for a look at 17th-century warehouses and wooden homes with red-tiled roofs. To the left on the corner of Kungu and Bāriņu streets is the old Liepāja Hotel where Peter the Great once slept. Ironically, across the street is another historic home where the Russian tsar's adversary, Charles XII, King of Sweden, supposedly spent the night. At the end of Zivju Street is St Anne's Lutheran Church (Sv Annas luterāņu baznīca), Liepāja's oldest place of worship dating to the early 16th century, with a beautiful altar carved by Nicolas Soeffren.

The Liepāja Museum (Liepājas muzejs; open Wed–Sun 10am–6pm; admission fee), located in a fine 19th-century house on Kūrmājas prospkets, is also worth a visit. The street ends at the "Blue Flag" beach, one of only three in Latvia, where a monument to mariners lost at sea was erected in 1977. Just south of the bronze statue are the main beach, seaside park and concert hall.

North of the canal separating the old from the new city is the fascinating Karosta or military naval base built in 1893 by Tsar Alexander III. It was a city unto itself with its own housing, schools and churches but now is little more than a collection of empty administrative and apartment buildings and military barracks. The only building that seems to have withstood the test of time is the colourful St Nicholas Orthodox Church (Sv Nikolāja pareiztcīgo katedrāle). The old prison (Karostas cietums) is now a museum and the years of suffering have supposedly left their mark on the building as it is purported to be haunted. Daring visitors and sceptics of the supernatural can participate in "Behind Bars", a theatrical performance where tourists are locked up in cells overnight. This can be arranged at the tourist information centre. Just north of the city, ruined fortifications slowly recede into the sea creating an eerily beautiful landscape.

Breeding ground

To the south of Liepāja, the immaculate beach continues its drift towards distant Lithuania, passing eroded sandbanks and dunes on the coast before crossing the border and arriving at the large resort of Palanga *(see page 321)*.

Birdwatchers and nature lovers who might have enjoyed the Slītere Nature Reserve should also stop at the **Pape Nature Park** (Papes dabas parks) at **Rucava**. With money from the World Wildlife Fund, the pristine seaside breeding ground for birds and other animals has been preserved. Wild cattle and horses that have been reintroduced in this thriving ecosystem also inhabit Lake Pape and its surrounding swamps. A bird-watching tower has been erected and several miles of hiking trails have been created to make the park accessible. Accommodation can also be arranged at the Rucava tourist information centre. ❑

LATGALE

Ceramics, glassware and local produce are the rewards for exploring this land of myriad lakes, gentle uplands, Old Believers and deep Catholic faith

Rīga

L atvia's easternmost region is "The Land of the Blue Lakes". A mass of deciduous trees makes it not just bluer, but greener, too. It is the poorest and the most remote of the regions. Its people, who speak a dialect some regard as a separate language, have larger families and are more gregarious. They sometimes like to think of themselves as the Irish of Latvia. If there is any festival or gathering here it is bound to be lively. Traditionally, the people of Latgale had homesteads adjoining each other, rather than isolated country homes as in the rest of Latvia. They continue their established crafts, especially ceramics, making big, chunky jugs and candelabra which are thickly glazed and seen everywhere in the country.

Rubbing up against Russia, Belarus and Lithuania, Latgale's geography has given it a different history, too. While Kurzeme and Zemgale were being recruited to the Lutheran cause by the dukes of Courland, the Swedes in Rīga and Vidzeme were banishing practising Catholics, and many of them came to Latgale, where Catholic Poland held sway. They left their mark in the baroque Jesuit style of their grand churches: St Peter's in Daugavpils, St Ludwig in Krāslava, the Holy Cross of Pasiene and the huge, white, country church at Aglona, where Catholics from all over Europe gather in their thousands on the Feast of the Assumption.

LEFT: Assumption Day procession in Aglona.
BELOW: bee keeper.

But among these slightly distant lands is Daugavpils, Latvia's second-largest city, tucked in the far southeast 224 km (140 miles) from Rīga, and the best part of a day's train ride away.

River road

The town of **Pļaviņas** ⓴ is the last on the A6 from Rīga before Latgale. Here the River Daugava spreads out like a vast mirror in the summer and in winter is the place to see the collision of huge ice sheets in the winter. Just beyond Pļaviņas the road follows the Daugava upriver to **Jēkabpils** ㉑, named after the Courland duke. Beside the road on this north bank is **Krustpils castle** (Krustpils pils), built in 1237 and added onto over the years. Once a fortress of the Livonian Order it came into the possession of the Korf family in the 16th century and remained their property until it was seized by the Latvian Government in 1921 as part of the land reforms and used as a military base. It is now home to the Jēkabpils Museum (Jēkabpils muzejs; open Mon–Fri 9am–5pm, Sat & Sun 10am–3pm; admission fee).

The town of Jēkabpils, marked by the dome of a Russian Orthodox church (Sv Gara pareizticīgo baznīca) of 1887, lies on the far bank of the river. It was a main river staging post for logging and fur trade and had a settlement of Old Believers. It is famous as

the birthplace of Jānis Rainis (1865–1929), the most important literary figure of the National Awakening. His father was an estate overseer and he built Tadenava, the house where Jānis was born. The building is now the **Rainis Museum** (Raiņa muzejs; open May–Oct Tues–Fri 10am–5pm; admission fee) containing the family's household items. Of all local attractions, the **Open-Air Ethnographic Museum** (Sēļu sēta; open Mon–Fri 9am–5pm, Sat & Sun 10am–3pm; admission fee) displaying old farm buildings and antiquated agricultural contraptions is the most interesting.

Līvāni ㉒, the next town upstream, is known for its excellent blown-glass art, some of which was used as decoration in the Olympic village in Athens, produced at the Līvānu stiklu fabrika. Call ahead for a demonstration and tour (tel: 530 71 62).

Russified town

Daugavpils ㉓, near the Lithuanian and Belarus borders, is at a crossroads on between the Baltic and Black Sea routes, and the road and railway from Warsaw to Moscow. This former capital of the Duchy of Pārdaugava, known as "Polish Livonia", has a sprinkling of 18–19th-century mansions and the odd bright splash of Art Nouveau. Around the town, doors, shutters and whole wooden houses painted bright blue are signs of Russians in residence. In its streets and in its markets, Latvian is rarely heard. The city has been attracting "foreigners" for many centuries, from the Old Believers, the sect exiled from Moscow in the 18th century, to others just coming to this relatively prosperous town to find work. Many left, too, including Markus Rothkowitz, who went to the USA in 1903 at the age of 10 to become the painter Mark Rothko. It is an

Jēkabpils is one of the three sugar manufacturing towns in Latvia. "Three spoons of sugar in your coffee," people used to urge: "one for Liepāja, one for Jelgava and one for Jēkabpils."

BELOW: "Land of the Blue Lakes".

Map on pages 184–5

industrial town and Russification under the Soviets was intense. Prior to World War II one-third of the 40,000 population was Russian or Polish. Now there are 117,500 inhabitants, only 16 percent of whom are Latvian. The industries that the Soviets built up – textiles, bicycle manufacture and locomotive repair sheds – have suffered a depressing slump, but its importance as a service and transportation hub has grown substantially.

The stunning white Catholic church of St Peter's (Sv Pētera katoļu baznīca) is perhaps the most striking attraction in the centre apart from a series of bars and cafés on the city's busy pedestrian street of restored 19th-century apartment blocks named after the Latvian capital. This mid-18th century former monastery building is an example of a fortress church and its twin-towered facade is a mark of the Jesuit baroque which was brought in from Lithuania. It is a basilica with three naves, the middle one rising to an impressive tunnel vault. At the end of the street by the river is the **Daugavpils Museum** (Daugavpils novadpētniecības un mākslas muzejs; open Tues–Sat 11am–6pm; admission fee), which is worth a quick stop.

The three most impressive structures in the city, however, are located outside of the centre. Follow the main street next to the river across the train tracks to see two beautiful churches located a stone's throw from one another. The 10 onion domes of the Orthodox Sts Boris and Gleb Church (Sv Borisa un Gļeba pareizticīgo katedrāle), built in 1904, are only outdone by the blue pastel colour of its facade and the Catholic church (Dievmātes katoļu baznīca) across the street looks like a smaller copy of the basilica at Aglona. Daugavpils' pride and joy is the huge red-brick fortress (Daugavpils cietoksnis; open Mon–Fri 9am–5pm; admission fee) which is the only example of this type of architecture to have survived in the Baltics. Completed in 1810, it was destroyed two years later by Napoleon's troops only to be rebuilt again. It later served as a tsarist prison and notorious prisoner-of-war camp during World War II. There is also a working synagogue serving the town's population of some 400 Jews.

Some 45 km (30 miles) east of Daugavpils is the town of **Krāslava** ㉔, and in its centre is Krāslavas pilsmuiža, one of the finest examples of an 18th-century Polish manor house, which has suffered much over the years and is currently closed to the public. It also has a distinguished church in St Ludwig's (Sv Ludviķa baznīca), built between 1755 and 1767 in baroque style.

The stretch of river between the two towns is particularly enchanting, and it was here that the Soviets wanted to install a hydroelectric power station, causing protests that helped to fuel calls for independence in the late 1980s. Belarus has since announced plans to build more dams across the border, ignoring requests from Latvia to provide environmental-impact reports and further details about the project, and it remains a contentious issue.

Lakeland

Rolling lands of rivers and lakes spread north from Krāslava, towards Rēzekne, Latgale's capital. Just above Krāslava, lying next to the Hill of the Sun,

BELOW: agriculture remains important.

(Sauleskalns), is **Drīdzis ㉕**, probably the most beautiful and certainly the deepest of Latvia's lakes at 65 metres (213 ft). **Ežezers ㉖** (hedgehog) lake, full of little islands, is to the northeast and nearby is Velnezers (the devil's lake) whose crystal-clear blue waters are so unusual that for centuries locals have claimed that it has mysterious properties, thus earning its dubious name.

Rāzna ㉗, just south of Rēzekne, is the country's second-largest lake at 56 sq. km (21 sq. miles), and there are plenty of local houses to rent as well as some camp sites. Northwest of Rēzekne is Latvia's largest lake, **Lubāns ㉘**, but much of its 82 sq. km (32 sq. miles) is hardly more than marshland making Rāzna a much more impressive body of water.

The traditional wooden architecture in this part of the region is particularly attractive, with splashes of colour and embellishments on doors and window shutters. Small sauna sheds are stuck out in all the gardens, which are planted with fruit trees and bushes and beds of bright flowers.

Prepared for a cold winter.

Pilgrims' progress

Northeast of Daugavpils, down stony tracks on the east side of the road to Rēzekne, is the village of **Aglona ㉙**, which is much too small for its grand baroque church (Aglonas bazilika) to which thousands of pilgrims make their way on the Feast of the Assumption (15 August) each year, on foot, by gypsy cart, car and charabanc.

The object of their veneration is a picture of the Virgin Mary, kept behind the altar, which is said to have healing powers. The picture is reported to have been presented by Manuel Palaeologus to Lithuania's Vytautas, who gained favour with the Byzantine emperor when he brought Benedictine monks to the county.

BELOW: hot shots.

In 1700 the picture was copied and either the copy or the original, depending on which camp you follow, remained in Lithuania while the other came here to Aglona the year that the church was founded. Money came from Jeta-Justine Sastodicka, a local Polish aristocrat, whose portrait hangs on the present basilica's west wall. The church was built to accommodate Dominicans from Lithuania whom Sastodicka invited to teach, heal and convert.

This is the second church on the site. The first one was made of wood and built just to the north of the current church's site. In 1787 it burnt down and the present shining white, two-towered Italianate creation rose up around the original organ, which was saved. A monastery and cloister are attached to the church; Dominicans lived here for 150 years until the tsar forbade people from becoming involved in the church.

In 1992, when a visit by the Pope to Aglona was announced, five Lithuanian-trained Latvian novices took up residence, while the grounds in front of the church were completely levelled to pave the way, literally, for the hullabaloo of a papal visit. Directly east of the church near the shore of Lake Aglona is a spring also said to having healing powers.

Although modern and rather unprepossessing, **Rēzekne** ㉚, 60 km (38 miles) north of Daugavpils, is a relaxed place and a good centre for exploration. Its population of 38,000 is about one-third that of Daugavpils, but Rēzekne is the capital of Latgale. The Regional Museum (Latgales Kultūrvēstures muzejs; open Tues–Fri 10am–5pm, Sat 10am–4pm; admission fee) is just up from the trio of churches in the main street, and has a nostlgic look at the town as it used to be before it was largely destroyed in World War II. The statue in the middle of the road, Latgales Māra, which symbolises the liberation of Latgale from the Bolsheviks in 1920, was destroyed twice by the Soviets in 1940 and 1950, but was erected for the third time on this spot in 1992. Rēzekne is one of many ceramics centres in the region, and typical pottery makes an attractive souvenir from shops and work shops in and around the town.

On a steep hill overlooking the city you'll find a lonely stone arch, practically all that remains of an ancient castle (Rēzeknes pilsdrupas).

Some 25 km (15 miles) southeast of Rēzekne is **Ludza** ㉛, one of the most attractive towns in the country and home to one of the most picturesque castle ruins (Ludzas pilsdrupas). Perched upon a hill overlooking two lakes, a three-storey brick wall marks the place where the largest fortress in Latgale protected Teutonic crusaders since the 14th century. A museum has local ceramics and finds from the 10th century onwards.

From Ludza the road goes east to Russia at Zilupe. To the south is the fourth of Latgale's great Catholic church at **Pasiene Church** ㉜ (Pasienes katoļu baznīca). An echo of the church at Daugavpils, a twin-towered wedding cake built in 1761, 67 years after a Dominican mission was founded. From here there is a magnificent view across the plains of Russia.

To the north is the region of Abrene, which was incorporated by Russia after World War II and to which Latvia no longer lays a claim. ❑

TIP

The Paulāns and the Ušpelis are two familes that have been working for eight generations in the pottery capital of Rēzekne. Call ahead (tel: 29 46 63 72) to see Aivars Ušpelis demonstrate his craft.

BELOW: the Virgin Mary in Aglona's church.

ZEMGALE

Latvia's smallest region stretches from Rīga Bay south through fertile plains that have produced a number of glittering palaces, most notably Rastrelli's Rundāle

The region of Zemgale was for a time linked with Courland, and from Lithuania in the south to Lake Engure halfway up the west side of Rīga Bay it borders the modern region of Kurzeme. Skirting Rīga, it then slips below the River Daugava and slides along the length of the Lithuanian border tailing away to the far southeast. Apart from the northerly area around Tukums, most of Zemgale is characterised by a dead flat, fertile plain, part of the central lowlands that in places actually sink below sea level. This is considered to be the breadbasket of Latvia.

There are comparatively few lakes, and the main river is the Lielupe, which flows through the ancient towns of Bauska and Jelgava, Zemgale's capital, which the dukes of Courland and Semigallia made their home. There are a number of large 18th- and 19th-century estates in the region, but this was the front line in World War I, and many were burned by the retreating Russian Army. One exception is the palace at Rundāle near Bauska, which has been magnificently restored and is now the finest in the Baltics. All of these places are within easy striking distance of Rīga.

A step west

The region of Tukums lies to the west of Rīga and Jūrmala, and is a stepping-stone into Kurzeme and the Baltic coast. Heading west from the capital, the A10/E22 passes through scenes of World War I conflict, notably at Ložmetējkalns, site of "the Christmas battles," heroic attacks by the Latvian Riflemen on a strong German position in late 1916/early 1917.

Tukums ㉝ is the first town of any size on this road. It has a castle mound and was originally a Liv settlement. It has a pleasant old centre, and a tradition of weaving, which is carried on in an artisan's workshop on Smilšu iela (open Tues 3–6pm, Wed 11am–3pm; free). In Harmonijas Street is the art museum which has a collection of works by the most important 20th-century Latvian artists, including Rozentāls. The Lutheran church dates from 1670.

To the south of the town is the 17th-century **Durbe Castle** (Durbes pils; open Tues–Sat 10am–5pm, Sun 11am–4pm; entrance fee), set in a park with a collection of textiles and agricultural implements. Another manor house, to the north of Tukums, is **Milzkalne**, on the highest spot in the region with a view over Rīga Bay, and is home to Šlokenbeka Castle. It was built as an estate in the 15th century, and its buildings were erected in a square formation and surrounded by walls to serve as a fortress. It is the only example of this type of medieval architecture left in the Baltics. An odd museum dedicated to road building in Latvia with

LEFT AND BELOW:
Rundāle Palace.

exhibits of antique machinery is located inside (open May–Oct Wed–Sun 10am–5pm, Nov–Apr Mon–Fri 10am–5pm; admission fee).

A few miles past Tukums on the Ventspils road is **Jauņmoku pils ③**, a renovated hunting lodge. It was built in 1901 by Wilhelm Bockslaff, who designed the Art Academy building in Rīga for George Armitstead, one-time mayor of the capital. Its most striking features are its ceramic stoves, built by the firm of Celms & Bēms, especially one imprinted with old postcards of Rīga from the city's 700th anniversary celebrations in 1901. On the first floor is the Museum of Hunting and Forestry (open daily 10am–5pm; admission fee), which includes a collection of around 40 different animal horns from all over the world. The lodge provides facilities for hunters' holidays in the area.

Coastal communities

From **Lapmežciems** to **Bērzciems**, most of the communities on the coast have names ending with -ciems, meaning village. Their attractive farm buildings stand near the sea and lurk in the wood. The **Engure Lake and Nature Reserve** lies beyond the thatched church tower roof at the little port of Engure. This beautiful body of water stretches along the coastline separated from the sea only by a narrow strip of land. Some 50,000 birds visit this extensive (18-km/12-mile), shallow lake every year and nearly 170 different species inhabit the reserve.

South of Tukums, on the road to Dobele, is **Jaunpils ③**, a village with a lakeside manorial castle and church dating back to the 16th century. This was the estate of one Baron Reke, whose coat of arms is hung over the church altar. Visitors can also spend the night at the castle for a pittance and dine at the medieval tavern where all dishes are made in accordance with an 18th-century

Accompanied by guides, ecotourists to Lake Engure can camp overnight, use the small boat marinas and ride on horseback through the reserve. Further information from the tourist information office in Tukums (tel: 312 4451) or Talsi (tel: 322 4165).

BELOW: Jaunmoku pils hunting lodge.

recipe book loosely translated as *How to Cook for Nobility*. Dobele's chief claim to fame is a ruined castle of the Livonian Order.

Dukes' domain

South of Rīga, the only town of any size is **Jelgava** ㊱. Though you would not know it to look at it, Jelgava is an historic town, formerly called Mitau, that once rivalled Rīga. The history of the town, and of the 11 dukes of Courland and Semigallia, who were friends of the Russian Romanovs and influential at court in St Petersburg, is laid out in the History and Art Museum (open Wed–Sun 10am–5pm; admission fee). This is housed in the Academia Petrina, built for Duke Peter von Biron in 1775 and once an important educational and scientific centre. It lies just behind the landmark tower of the ruined Holy Trinity Church, which is due to be restored, more than half a century after its destruction. Exhibits include gold and silver ducats minted here and a waxwork of Duke Jacob. Also in the old part of town is St Ann's Church, from 1619, which has an altar painting by Janis Rozentāls.

The wide, slow Lielupe, which slips north into Rīga Bay, has always carried river traffic. Past the bridge on the right is **Rastrelli Palace**, a large and solid Italianate building on the site of the town's original castle (1265). Since 1957 this three-storey, brick-red and cream building set around a square has housed an agricultural college. It is an impersonal resting place for the dukes of Courland and Semigallia, but their tombs are worth a look (open Mon–Fri 10am–4pm, admission fee).

Frederick-Wilhelm, the penultimate of the Kettler dynasty of dukes, altered the family's fortunes when he married Ivan V's daughter Anna Ivanova, in St

Map on pages 184–5

BELOW: re-enacting the past at Jaunpils.

*James Kettler, 1st
Duke of Courland
(1660–81) was
godson of James I of
England, and during
the English civil war
supplied Charles I
with six men-of-war.*

Petersburg in 1710. The 17-year-old newlyweds had just started back to the young duke's palace in Jelgava when he became ill and died. Reluctantly, Anna was obliged to continue her life in Jelgava. Bored and confined in what to her must have seemed something of a backwater of wooden homes and flat farmlands, she began an affair with Ernst Johann Biron, an ambitious Courlander on the palace staff.

In 1727 Anna became Empress Anne of Russia, peopling her court with German Balts and making Biron a count. Within nine years he was wealthy enough to employ Bartholomeo Rastrelli (1700–71), the architect who later built St Petersburg's Hermitage or Winter Palace, to design a manor for himself at Rundāle, to the south of Jelgava, which he at first called *Ruhetal*, meaning Peaceful Valley in German.

Rundāle Palace ❸ (open daily 10am–5pm; admission fee) is an imposing, well-restored palace of 138 rooms, approached through a grand drive flanked by twin semi-circular stables. At the height of its construction between 1736 and 1768 it employed 1,500 labourers and artisans. Work on the building and grounds, which still have to be restored, was interrupted first in 1738, after Biron had achieved his ambition of becoming Duke of Courland and diverted Rastrelli into turning Jelgava Castle into Rastrelli Palace. The second interruption was more serious when, after becoming regent of Russia for a year following the empress's death, Biron was banished to Siberia for 23 years.

In the 19th century it was used by the tsarist governors, and the new government took it over in 1920, restoring its war damage. Rundāle has been under reconstruction since 1972. Its stairways, galleries, landings, rooms and halls are gracious and well decorated. The wall paintings are by the Italians Francesco

BELOW:
Rundāle Palace.

Martini and Carlo Zucchi and the exquisite decorative moulding is by Michael Graff from Berlin. His oval Porcelain Study is particularly striking. On the ground floor there is a collection of period furniture and ornaments. The finest rooms are upstairs, where some interesting Dutch, Flemish and Spanish paintings from the 17th and 18th centuries are hung. The dukes' throne stood in the Gold Hall, which is matched in magnificence by the White Hall or ballroom where the intricate stucco work includes a delicate heron's nest on the ceiling.

At the entrance to the palace is an exhibition of Ventspils church wood carvings by Nicolas Soeffren, whom Peter the Great invited to work on his ships. The pieces are all carved from ships' timbers.

Rundāle was the apogee of the fusion of German and Russian society which came together and flourished in the region in the 18th and 19th centuries. A number of important manors were built in this accessible area. The one at **Mežotne**, on the River Lielupe a few kilometres northeast of Rundāle, which was given by Tsar Paul I to his children's governess, Charlotte von Lieven, in 1797, has been restored and is now an elegant hotel and conference centre. One of the grandest houses otherwise was at Eleja, due south of Jelgava on the main road to Vilnius, but it is now just a forlorn ruin.

Mežotne manor's grand interior.

Semigallian roots

The flatlands of Zemgale were originally inhabited by the Semigallians, who in the 13th century produced one of the greatest Latvian leaders, Viesturs. The centre of his domains was to the west of Rundāle in **Tērvete**, but the tribe was pushed south by the German crusaders who built a castle on the site of their stronghold, some of which still remains. Nearby is the Meža Ainavu Park which has a museum dedicated to one of Latvia's most respected writers, Anna Brigadere, who lived here from 1922 to 1933 (open May–Nov Tues–Sun 10am–5pm; admission fee).

BELOW: Bauska's old castle.

Her most famous creation was Sprīdītis, an impish chartacter who overcomes great obstacles to gain the heart of the woman he loves. The park has a vast selection of foreign and domestic trees, wooden sculptures of characters from many of Brigadere's literary works and castle ruins. A number of walking trails begin in the town.

To the east of Rundāle is **Bauska**. On arrival there is a car park just beyond the bridge over the River Mūsa. The river shortly converges with the Mēmele, helping to form half a moat for the Livonian Order's castle, which was not rebuilt after its destruction in the Great Northern War. The huge red brick ruins at the confluence of the two rivers are among Latvia's largest and most picturesque. Climb the tower for a good view from the top.

Every September the castle puts on an arts festival with a medieval theme. There is a small museum in the castle, and another in the town, where there is also a synagogue.

From Bauska the road leads directly north back to Rīga, past Iecava, which is best known for its large egg factory, fine Lutheran church from 1641 and neighbouring cemetery. ❑

VIDZEME

The River Gauja runs through the rural heartlands of eastern Latvia to make Gauja National Park the country's great outdoor leisure area, centred on Sigulda and Cēsis

Map on pages 184–5

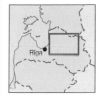

Lying to the east of Rīga, Vidzeme is the largest of the country's four regions. In the north it stretches from the Bay of Rīga all along the Estonian border, and in the south it lies beside the right bank of the Daugava from the capital to the eastern region of Latgale. Beside the river's banks, there are castles and remains of ancient settlements, pointers to a powerful past.

At the heart of the region is another river route which, though less exalted, is just as ancient and rather more beguiling. This is the River Gauja, which runs through a deep gorge at the centre of the **Gauja National Park** (Gaujas Nacionālais parks). It is Latvia's showcase rural attraction, rich in wildlife, full of prehistoric hill forts and containing one of the most important archaeological sites. They call it "Little Switzerland", and have installed a bobsled run, but "little" is the key word. The Baltics' second highest point is in Vidzeme: it is just 312 metres (1,025 ft).

Excursions in Gauja National Park

Gauja National Park begins at **Sigulda ㊳**, 50 km (30 miles) northeast of Rīga and is an easy day trip from the capital by the A2 or by public transport. From Sigulda the park extends north through Cēsis to Valmiera. Sigulda and Cēsis are the main centres for information about activities and excursions such as walking, biking and boating, particularly canoeing on the River Gauja, which is a popular way to appreciate the park. The park covers around 900 sq. km (350 sq. miles) along more than 100 km (60 miles) of river, and is divided into sections with varying degrees of access. All boating activity is popular on the river, and organised parties embark in inflatables for overnight camps, taking three days to travel from Valmiera to Sigulda. Logging on the river was ended when the area was designated a national park in 1973.

There is something rather sedate about Sigulda. It is a pristine and airy little town which hides its affluent past beneath a film of cleanliness. It became popular during the National Awakening as a place where Latvians from Rīga could discover their rural roots. It has more recently become a winter sports centre, with a bobsleigh run and ski slopes on the far side of the railway crossing.

The castle (Siguldas pilsdrupas) is through the town on the left. Deeply moated and once incoroprating a convent, it was built by the Crusaders' Order of Sword Bearers who came here as soon as they arrived in Latvia in 1207. They used large boulders and stuck them together with mortar mixed with eggs and honey. Today, it is a crumbled ruin with an open-air concert hall in its midst. The large and not particularly attrac-

LEFT: cable car over Sigulda.
BELOW: Sigulda castle.

*Sigulda
bobsleigh run.*

tive country house beside it is the modern "castle" (Siguldas pils), built in 1878. It now houses the city council and an upmarket restaurant. Artists and writers of the Awakening used to come for inspiration, and Rozentāls and other painters used to like to hike up to Gleznotāju kalns, Painters' Hill, just to the east, which has one of the best views over the Gauja (walk from the car park on the far side of the old castle). Kronvaldu Atis (1837–75), a teacher of Latvian, is remembered by a statue outside the new castle, and some of the stained glass produced during his lifetime is still in situ in what is now a sanatorium.

One of the best places to see wildlife and natural scenery, with possibilities of sighting at least a deer, is just beyond Sigulda in **Līgatne**. There are also some rare plants here, such as Lady's Slipper orchids, Linnaea borealis and woodland tulips, and in spring it is carpeted with lily-of-the-valley. Turn left to Līgatne through **Augšlīgatne** on the Sigulda to Cēsis main road, turning left again just before the river, where there are two parking spots and day tickets to the parks can be bought. Nature trails are mapped out, and a ferry takes cars over the river. From Sigulda there are two ways across the Gauja. The road goes over a bridge, and every 30 minutes a cable car swings alongside it, 40 metres (135 ft) above the river, taking 3½ minutes to cover the 1 km (½ mile) distance. On the far side, the road falls away to the right to reach the side of the river where day tickets to the park can be bought in the car park.

Castles and caves

BELOW: picnic overlooking the River Gauja.

The banks of the Gauja are characterised by red sandstone cliffs and caves, the deepest of which is **Gūtmanis' Cave** ❸❾ (Gūtmaṇa ala), found opposite the car park. Scratched by graffiti more than 300 years old, it is 19 metres (62 ft) deep

and the fresh spring water that wore it away still bubbles up into it, tasting strongly of iron. The cave is named after a healer called Gūtmanis who first used the water as a cure.

Some 10 minutes' walk further up the road is **Turaida Castle** (Turaidas pils; open 10am–6pm, until 5pm in winter; entrance fee), a fort of red bricks and a single round tower, which breaks up through the forest heights. This is all that remained after lightning ignited the castle's gunpowder store in the 17th century.

In the language of the ancient Livs who first settled this valley, Turaida means "the Garden of the Gods". Inside the castle there is a gallery and a small museum charting its history. On the path to the castle is a wooden Lutheran church (1750), the oldest in Vidzeme, and a few yards away, beneath a large elm tree, a black marble slab marks the grave of Maija, the Turaida Rose (Turaidas Roze), murdered in 1620. This 19-year-old local girl was in love with a castle gardener, and, when a Polish officer approached her and asked for her hand in marriage, she refused. Angry and spiteful, he lured her to the Gūtmanis Cave where he attempted to force himself on her. She devised a scheme to be killed rather than submit to a fate worse than death. She told him she had a magic scarf, which he could have if he promised to leave her alone: to prove the scarf's effectiveness, she put it around her neck and told him to try to cut off her head. Which he did.

From Turaida the road continues to **Inciems** where it meets up with the road to Valmiera. Time allowing, a pleasant detour on the P9 to **Bīriņi** is also recommended. The 19th-century neo-Gothic manor house at Bīriņi (Bīriņu pils) is surrounded by a beautiful park with a lake and a charming tavern – a perfect place for lunch.

Map on pages 184–5

BELOW:
Turaida Castle.

Horse-drawn transport in Cēsis.

Back on the A3 the next small town along this road is **Straupe**, where there is something familiar about the old castle (Lielstraupes pils), dating from 1263. The square tower, which rises in a dark dome and lantern, and the scrolled and stepped gable of the building below, are reminiscent of the cathedral in Rīga. The castle is in a pleasant setting beside a large pond near the Brasla River, and today it is used as a clinic for rehabilitating substance abusers. There is not much to see in the castle itself, except for some wood panelling and several grand ceramic stoves. Parties may be shown up the main tower. Call ahead for a tour (tel: 29 42 67 05).

In the grounds is a bell tower and a Lutheran church that has some interesting 17th-century painted panels. Tombstones and tablets mark the passing of generations of the von Rosen family, owners of the castle and fierce protectors of the German Baltic way of life. The present generation is scattered, though some have helped in its restoration. It has an organ made in Rīga in 1856 by the firm of Martin, and the acoustics make it a good recital venue.

Another German monument is nearby at **Ungurmuiža** (open Tues–Sun 10am–6pm; admission fee), on the way to Cēsis. This belonged to the von Campenhausens who had it built in 1751. It is the only existing wooden baroque building of this period left in Latvia and although it has been pillaged many times over the years, its fantastic 18th-century wall paintings on the second floor have been restored to their former glory. A park surrounds the building and many ancient trees can be seen here.

Between Ungurmuiža and Cēsis is **Raiskums** ㊵, beside a lake of the same name, where there is threshing barn, school house and a curious wood and stone chapel from the 19th century.

Below: opening concert of Cēsis festival.

Excursion centre

Surrounded by nature trails, **Cēsis** ㊶ is a major centre of leisure activities in both summer and winter. A pleasant, wide-open town, it was a popular cultural centre during both the National Awakening and first independence. Its attractive yellow-and-white, two- and three-storey buildings date back several centuries, and a Lutheran church, St John's (Sv Jāņa baznīca), was started in 1281. There are several hotels and good places to eat, but don't leave without tasting the local Cēsu beer from Northern Europe's oldest brewery (Cēsu alus darītava), which has been in operation since 1590. Once produced in the castle, brewing operations are now in the red-brick building next door where you can buy mugs and souvenirs.

Cēsis was a walled town and a member of the Hanseatic League and its history is well documented in The Cesis Museum of History and Art (Cēsu pilsdrupas; open Tues–Sun 10am–5pm; admission fee), which occupies the Medieval Castle, Cesis Manor, the New Castle and Coach House. The castle is a chalky-white fortified convent that served as a power base for the Livonian Order. Cēsis also has the distinction of being the birthplace of the Latvian flag. At the end of the 13th century, an ancient chieftain was killed in battle and was laid out on a white sheet. His blood stained the sides leaving a white stripe in the middle. The locality

Map on pages 184–5

was inhabited by Baltic Finns until the Letgallians moved in around the 6th century, and it has provided much archaeological information. But the most impressive digs have been in **Āraiši** 7 km (4 miles) to the south of the city. It was here that the Letgallians built a large lakeside fortress in the 9th century, and its excavation has been one of the most important finds of this kind in northern Europe. Burial barrows have been uncovered as well as graves and today you can visit the reconstructed fortified town of tiny wooden buildings on the lake (Āraišu ezerpils; open May–Oct daily 10am–6pm; admission fee). A stone castle built by the Livonian Order has also been excavated, and guides wear clothes from the Viking era.

Beyond Cēsis, reached by a popular cycle path, is **Valmiera** ❷, which also has an ancient castle and was once a member of the Hanseatic League. An observation tower gives a good view of the valley. North of the town up towards **Strenči** is one of the most picturesque stretches of the River Gauja. To the northwest is **Mazsalaca**, an attractive, out-of-the-way town on the River Salaca.

Coastal route

The Gauja was strategically important as the main route to Tallinn and St Petersburg. Today, the most pleasant way to drive to Tallinn is up the scenic coast, around the eastern edge of Rīga Bay, which allows views of the Baltic Sea through the pines. Unlike the rest of Latvia's coast, its sandy beaches are scattered with boulders and stones. From Rīga the A2/E67 goes past summer villas up to the resort town of **Saulkrasti** ❸ or "sunny shores", beyond which lie small communities, such as **Dunte** where the infamous tall tale-teller Baron von Münchhausen (1720–97) lived from 1743 to 1750. Although the roadside tavern and museum where he once drank burned down, it was

TIP

In a workshop in Cēsis Castle you can discover the meaning of ancient Latvian decorated jewellery.

BELOW: folk dancers at Cēsis.

rebuilt in 2005 and the charming Liepupe Church (Liepupes baznīca) where he married is open to the public.

Salacgrīva ㊹ provides a convenient stopping point, and between here and **Ainaži**, the coast takes on a different aspect as meadows push out into the sea. Ainaži is right up by the border, and was out on the map as the port Krišjānis Valdemārs chose to base Latvia's Maritime Academy in 1864. Ainaži flourished for a while as a port and shipbuilding centre, but now it has returned to being a backwater, with a small museum charting its moment of seafaring glory (Ainažu jūrskolas muzejs; open Tues–Sat 10am–4pm; admission fee).

Epic region along the Daugava

To the southeast of Rīga the A6/E22 follows the north bank of the Daugava, leaving Rīga through the Moscow District with its Old Believers and traditional Russian community. Just beyond it is **Rumbula** ㊺, where the big weekend market draws people from miles around; mostly a car mart, its reputation is a touch below spotless and tourists are not encouraged to browse.

The road continues towards the big textile town of **Ogre**, past **Ikšķile** ㊻, which in the Liv language was called Üxküll. The first settlement is on an island on the Daugava, accessible to the passing traveller only by boat in the summer and on foot in the winter when the river is frozen over. It bears the remains of the oldest stone church in Latvia (Ikšķiles baznīcas drupas), built in 1186.

At **Ķegums** ㊼, the country's first hydroelectric scheme, built between the world wars, has pushed back the river's banks and created a long lake. The change of landscape is a source of regret to the historians and traditionalists who converge at its centre, around **Lielvārde** ㊽. Staburags, a natural wonder

Teiči Bog in the Teiči Reserve 25 km (15 miles) north of Madona is the largest moss bog in the Baltic states, with a range of wildlife from golden eagles to brown bears. On the bog island of Sīksala is an observation tower – and a community of Old Believers.

BELOW: cottage for rent, Cēsis.

Map on pages 184–5

mentioned in the *Lāčplēsis* epic and a source of national pride, is now completely submerged in the River Daugava.

Lielvārde is the home of this Latvian legend, recorded in a 19th-century epic written by Andrejs Pumpurs *(see page 60)*. Its protagonist and namesake, Lāčplēsis, was brought up by a bear until found by Lielvārdis who adopted the young boy. On one occasion he saved his father from a rogue bear by tearing him apart with his bare hands and giving him the name "bear-slayer". He was last seen in a fatal struggle with the Black Knight, symbolic of the Teutonic crusaders, but he will return, it is said, to throw the enemy into the sea and make the land free again.

As you approach Lielvārde you'll notice a reconstructed wooden fortress (Uldevena pils; open Apr–Nov 10am–7pm; admission fee) on the right side of the road. Inside you can see how ancient Latvian tribes once lived and it's also a great place for a picnic by the river. Just outside of the city centre you can visit the Andrejs Pumpurs Museum where the writer once lived (Andreja Pumpura muzejs; open Wed–Sun 10am–5pm; admission fee). You can also visit an old church and the ruins of a 13th-century castle located in the same park overlooking the river.

Before the A6/E22 turns north to Madona, away from the Daugava River, it is worth noting the 13th-century crusader castle at **Koknese** ㊾, which was once perched high on a hill above the river, but is now at the water's edge. Following the river downstream past a white Lutheran church set on a wide sweep in the river, the road comes to the ruins of the two-storey castle (Kokneses pilsdrupas) where the Pērse meets the Daugava, a point appreciated by teenagers who dive in to the green waters off the old walls. A Swedish grave and some cannon from the Great Northern War lie in the surrounding woods.

Madona ㊿ is the next town of any size, a quiet spot with a renovated inn from the 16th-century Swedish days. Just north of Madona is **Cesvaine** (51). Its impressive late 19th-century "castle" (Cesvaines pils), a mix of neo-Gothic with an Art Nouveau interior, was the hunting lodge of Baron Adolf von Wolf, who had no fewer than 99 estates in the Baltics. The castle was badly damaged in a fire in 2004 but plans were soon afterwards set in motion to restore it. The estate has a 25-hectare (60-acre) park which supposedly sustains 200 animal species. A squat tower to the left of a summer house is all that remains of the 14th-century bishop's palace.

West of Madona is **Gaiziņkalns**, the highest hill in Latvia, a stunningly low 312 metres (1,025 ft). In case you might miss it, a 15-storey red-brick lookout tower of graphic ugliness has been built on top of it, but will soon be replaced by a new tower which promises to be part functional viewing platform, part work of art. Its summit provides a 360-degree view of the lakes, pastureland and acres of deep green forest. There is a resort at **Mežezers**, a lakeside complex of boating and camping facilities with A-frame cabins in the woods, which is sorely in need of holidaymakers.

North of Cesvaines is **Gulbene** (52), where a manor house with a fine portico lies in ruins: bullet holes

BELOW: the train from Gulbene to Alūksne.

Map
on pages
184–5

still pepper its facade. In 1944 the Germans blew up the church tower before the advancing Russians to deprive them of a viewing platform: it fell on the church, destroying the roof. Beside it is the only statue of Martin Luther in the Baltics.

From Gulbene a narrow-gauge railway runs up to the attractive town of **Alūksne ⑤**, which is centred on a ruined 14th-century Livonian castle (Livonijas ordeņa pils) on a lake. It sits on an island reached across a small wooden bridge and is devoted today to sports activities. A granite rotunda was built on top of the site of an ancient Letgallian fort on the southwestern shore of the lake by the Nietinghoff family to honour the dead of the Great Northern War. One of the town's main claims to fame is that its pastor, Ernst Glück, adopted Martha Skavronska, the daughter of a Lithuanian grave-digger. She went on to marry Peter the Great and become Catherine I of Russia.

Glück also produced the first Latvian translation of the Bible, in 1689, and a copy of it, one of only a dozen left in the world, is kept along with many others in the Bible Museum (Ernsta Glika Bībeles muzejs; Pils 25a). The earliest Latvian religious tract, *God's Word* dates from 1654 and a copy is also in the museum. When Glück first arrived in Alūksne, he lived in the castle, but he later moved to a single-storey wood manse behind the Lutheran church, and his plantation of oaks is still standing.

Literary trail

BELOW: the Lutheran church at Alūksne in winter. **RIGHT:** Straupe in summer.

Between these eastern towns and the Gauja National Park, a number of Latvian literary figures, who play such an important part in the country's nationhood, are remembered in a pastoral setting that can have changed little since they knew it more than 100 years ago. Beneath shady trees are several wood barns, cottage gardens full of flowers and small platforms for the delivery vehicles to collect and return the milk churns.

Beside **Lake Alauksta ⑤** is the Skalbe Museum (Kārļa Skalbes memoriālais muzejs; open May–Oct daily 10am–5pm; admission fee), which contains local painted furniture. Kārlis Skalbe (1879–1945), a writer of fairy tales, died in Sweden where he had emigrated. His remains were returned in 1992 and buried beneath a stone overlooking the lake.

The museum (Brāļu Kaudzīšu memoriālais muzejs; open May–Oct daily 10am–5pm; admission fee) at the nearby village of **Vecpiebalga ⑤** celebrates the Kaudzītes brothers, Reinis and Matīss, who jointly wrote Latvia's first major novel, *The Time of the Land Surveyors* (1879). Much of the house, Kalna Kaibēni, was designed by the brothers and the lathe used by Rainis is one of the earliest surviving in the country. A granary and sauna are part of the well preserved home. Not far away is a museum dedicated to the composer Emīls Dārziņš, with an exhibition of writers and composers who have emigrated (Emīla Dārziņa muzejs; open May–Oct Tues–Sun 10am–5pm; admission fee).

At **Ērgļi ⑤** there is a museum (Rūdolfa Blaumaņa memoriālais muzejs; open May–Oct daily 10am–5pm; admission fee) where the playwright Rūdolfs Blaumanis was born. **Indrāni** nearby is the setting of one of his most famous plays. ❑

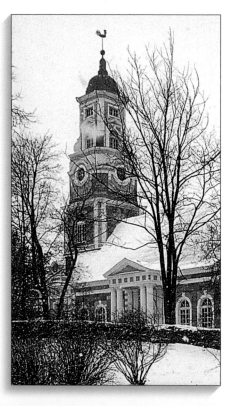

LITHUANIA

The southernmost Baltic state, bordering Poland and Belarus,
has a baroque capital and a fabulous sandy coast

The people of the largest of the three countries are predominantly Catholic, a fact that is impossible to miss. Vilnius, the capital, owes its splendid baroque flavour to the Jesuits who built its fine university as well as many of its churches, throughout the country are roadside wooden shrines; and the ever-growing Hill of Crosses just north of Šiauliai is an extraordinary symbol of a nation of believers.

These shrines are part of a folk tradition of wood carving, which can be seen everywhere, from the Witches' Park on the Neringa Spit to the monuments to the victims of World War II's genocide. Sometimes the 20th century's wars do not seem far away. Some will always think of Vilnius as the "Jerusalem of Lithuania", a vibrant Jewish community and centre of Yiddish publishing that did not survive World War II.

In spite of their deep Catholicism, Lithuanians were the last nation in Europe to convert to Christianity. At the height of their glorious history their Grand Duchy stretched from the Baltic to the Black Sea. Such grandeur can be glimpsed at the dukes' principal residence, the restored red-brick castle of Trakai set in the natural moat of Lake Galvė, west of Vilnius. For some time the Grand Duchy's southern border was along the River Nemunas, where many castles were built.

Vilnius today is a lively city with a nightlife to rival Estonia's but it lies rather inconveniently in the far southeast of the country, near the border with Belarus. More central is the country's second city, Kaunas, which was a temporary capital between the world wars. This is where to find the country's best museums including one devoted to Lithuania's towering artistic figure, M.K. Čiurlionis.

The River Neris, which connects Vilnius with Kaunas, runs down to a lagoon a couple of hundred kilometres away where it is kept from the Baltic Sea by the Neringa or Curonian Spit. This exceptional sand bar of small fishing villages stretches down into Lithuania Minor, formerly Königsberg, where the kings of Prussia were crowned. It is now the Russian enclave of Kaliningrad.

Though the coast is shorter than those of its Baltic neighbours, it is extremely popular. All kinds of accommodation is on offer, from quaint bed and breakfasts to large sanatoriums as well as dozens of restaurants and nightlife spots. Klaipėda is the centre of coastal activity, and from there it's a brief ferry crossing to the slender Curonian Spit, made a World Heritage Site in 2000. The spit awes most visitors with its fragile network of trees and dunes, and the village of Nida is its prime resort.   ❑

PRECEDING PAGES: Maritime Museum in a fisherman's cottage, Nida; Trakai castle.
LEFT: a good day's catch.

Lithuania

0   30 km

0   30 miles

THE MAKING OF LITHUANIA

One of Europe's most devout Catholic countries,
Lithuania did not at first take willingly to the baptismal font

The story of modern Lithuania could easily begin in 1385 with the unhappy tale of the 11-year-old Princess Jadwiga of Poland, who was due to marry young Wilhelm von Habsburg, whom she had known and been betrothed to since infancy. The wedding was to take place in Krakow, then capital of Poland, and the prisoners were released from the city dungeons as part of the celebrations welcoming Wilhelm's arrival at the castle to claim his bride. The festivities were in full swing when, unexpectedly, a delegation of Lithuanian nobles arrived and went into urgent conference with their Polish counterparts. The outcome was that the archbishop headed for the castle with unsettling news for little Jadwiga. The wedding was called off and she was going to marry another man instead.

For the Polish nobility, if not for Jadwiga, the proposal just put forward by the Lithuanian delegation made more sense than her marrying a Habsburg. A conjugal union between Poland and Lithuania with its huge, albeit rather ramshackle, empire would create a force capable of seeing off the Teutonic knights, who were grabbing ever more of the Baltic lands.

Jadwiga must have seen things differently; at least the Habsburgs were Christians. The Lithuanian Grand Prince she was now supposed to marry was an outright pagan. The Lithuanians had resisted every attempt to convert them to Christianity. Moreover, Prince Jogaila was three times her age and it was known that he had already murdered a number of close relatives. Little Jadwiga watched helplessly as the castellan of Krakow entered the castle, seized the downcast von Habsburg and banished him from the kingdom.

For his part, Jogaila had no more love for the Poles than he did for their religion. The Lithuanians were proud to be pagans. Their warrior elite claimed direct descent from Perkūnas, the god of thunder. Jogaila had distinguished antecedents including Mindaugas, the first to unite the peoples of Lithuania in 1230. He joined with the neighbouring Letts in attacks on the German crusaders. In 1251 Mindaugas was baptised into Christianity and on 6 July 1253 he was crowned King of Lithuania. Both

Christianity and the idea of the king didn't really take; Mindaugas is the only King of Lithuania and, though baptised, his adherence to Christianity was minimal at best. Most of the country remained pagan.

Founder of Vilnius

The next strong leader to emerge was Gediminas (1316–41), the founder of the Gediminaičiai, or as it was later called the Jogaiłłian (Jogailaičiai) dynasty that ruled Lithuania and Poland for the next 250 years. He founded Vilnius, where he built his hill-top castle overlooking the Neris and Vilnia rivers. Though he remained pagan he brought in Dominican and

LEFT: logging on the River Nemunas in the mid-20th century.
RIGHT: Grand Duke Vytautas.

Franciscan teachers and he also encouraged the immigration of artists and craftsmen. By the time he died, Gediminas had so successfully fought against the Tatars of the east that the Lithuanian Empire reached down as far as Kiev and the Black Sea. In the west, the coast around Klaipėda (Memel in German) had been seized by knights of the Livonian Order in 1225. Before the orders merged, however, they also had to fight the Teutonic knights of the southern lands that

GONG FOR A GONG

The Order of the Lithuanian Grand Duke Gediminas, re-instituted after independence, has been awarded to Olympic boss Antonio Samaranch, philanthropist George Soros and musician Mstislav Rostripovich.

some territorial concessions to Poland and release all Polish prisoners and slaves.

On 15 February 1386, Jogaila bowed his head for a splash of baptismal water, assumed the Christian name Ladislaus (the Poles afterwards called him Władysław-Jagiełło), and three days later he married a still confused and unhappy Jadwiga. The following month they assumed the crowns of both Poland and Lithuania. The marriage, alas, did not have a fairy-tale ending. Jadwiga hated her

became Prussia, as well as Lithuania's dukes. One of Gediminas's grandsons was Jogaila. He had become embroiled in a bloody family feud and was as vulnerable to the acquisitive Teutonic knights as Poland itself was. The Lithuanian nobles had calculated the strength of a dynastic union with Poland, hence the delegation's trip to Krakow to seek out young and eligible Jadwiga.

Poland was very much Rome's champion and the marriage was not agreed without conditions. First Jogaila would have to become a Christian. Second, he would have to convert his whole empire to Christianity. The terms of the marriage also required Lithuania to make

husband from beginning to end and sought consolation in burying herself in good works for the poor. She died leaving her fortune to the educational establishment in Kracow, which later became the Jagiełłonian University.

King Ladislaus V – Jogaila's full title – fulfilled one of his contractual obligations by going straight to Vilnius and smashing Perkūnas's statue. What followed was the usual fusion of old pagan beliefs and new-fangled Christianity. Perkūnas's mother was transformed into the Lithuanian Madonna. A bishop was appointed and mass baptisms were organised at which converts were presented with a white smock and given a Christian name.

Last of the great rulers

The new king's previous position as Grand Prince of Lithuania per se was given to his cousin Vytautas, another grandson of Gediminas, who was the last of the great Lithuanian rulers. He built the impressive red-brick island castle at Trakai after the nearby castle of his father, Kæstutis, had been attacked once too often by the German crusaders. He drove back the Turks and mustered a bodyguard of Turkic Karaites whose descendants live by the castle today. In 1410 he and Jogaila decisively defeated the German crusaders at Grünwald/Tannenberg (Žalgiris) and under Vytautas's rule

again went to different individuals, but the union was solidified by two sets of "Lithuanian Statutes" and finally written down in constitutional form agreed in 1569 at the Union of Lublin. The two countries were to share a king and a two-tiered government, but Lithuania kept a separate administration and its name.

Although Lithuania was territorially the larger of the two partners, Poland exerted the greater cultural influence. The Lithuanian nobility were Polonised and spoke Latin at court and Polish at other times. For the other social strata, the effects of the union were more painfully felt. The Polish social order was rig-

the Grand Duchy became one of the largest states in Europe, occupying Belarus and the Ukraine. Even with shared privileges, the rivalry between the Polish and Lithuanian nobilities see-sawed for many years. The union, which came perilously close to falling apart, was considerably strengthened by Jogaila's son Casimir (by a later wife), who held the position of both King of Poland and Grand Duke of Lithuania. There were times when the titles

orously imposed throughout the joint empire. Unlike the nobility, the Lithuanian bourgeoisie did not assume the status of their Polish counterparts. They were summarily demoted, disenfranchised and lost the right to own land.

The Lithuanian peasant had even more reason to rue the Polish take over. "Common cruelty was an established feature of social life," argues the distinguished historian Norman Davies. "Faced with the congenital idleness, drunkenness and pilfering of the peasantry, the nobleman frequently replied with ferocious impositions and punishments. The lash and the knout were the accepted symbols of noble authority. The serfs were beaten for leaving the

LEFT: *The Battle of Tannenberg* when the Teutonic knights were vanquished, 1410. **ABOVE:** *The Union of Lublin* confirms the Polish-Lithuanian pact in 1569. Both paintings are by Jan Matejko (1838–93).

estate without permission, for brawls and mis-demeanours, and for non-observance of religious practices. A dungeon, together with chains, shackles, stocks, hooks and instruments of torture, were part of the regular inventory."

Shared history with Poland

The history of Lithuania right up to the partition of the union by Prussia, Russia and Austria at the end of the 18th century is therefore tied to Poland's. Lithuania's separate identity had grown progressively weaker, and the partitions made matters worse. "Little Lithuania" or "Lithuania Minor", which included Kaliningrad

and the coast, was detached and given to Prussia; Russia took the rest. Tsar Alexander I toyed with the idea of reconstituting the Grand Duchy – with himself as Grand Duke – but was prevented from pursuing his idea by Napoleon's invasion. Welcomed as a liberator, Bonaparte was given the keys of Vilnius on his march with his 500,000-strong Grand Armée towards his 1812 defeat in Moscow.

To begin with, it was the Lithuanian nobility and educated classes who fretted under the Russian yoke. They joined the Polish uprising of 1831, and paid dearly. Next time round, about 30 years later, it was a stirring among the

NAPOLEON'S GRAND FROZEN ARMY

The Žirmūnai suburb of Vilnius was the focal point of historical fanfare in early 2001 when workers from a housing development stumbled on a mass grave. At first, the remains were thought to be victims of the Soviet regime. A second trench with nearly 20,000 skeletons was unearthed a few months later revealing coins and army uniform fragments that made it clear these were soldiers from Napoleon's Grand Army. In June 1812 they had marched through Vilnius on their way to Moscow. Welcomed as liberators from the Russian occupation, they were embraced by the city's residents. However, on their defeated trail back to Paris from Moscow five months later,

the remaining half-starved and sickly soldiers arrived when the city's temperature was –30°C (–22°F). The army of nearly half a million – the largest ever raised in Europe – had been reduced to 40,000. That winter in the freezing city a further 30,000 died. As the corpses littered the streets, residents did not know how to dispose of them. When Russian forces re-occupied the city, the corpses were placed in the thawed ground of trenches the French had dug on their advance to Moscow, hoping for the first major confrontation with the Russians. They had dug their own graves. The bones were placed in the sanctuary of Antakalnis Cemetery and commemorated with a statue.

peasants, which the Russian Government quelled with reforms giving peasants the right to hold up to 120 acres of land each. This satisfied some of them, but others were firmly under the thumb of the Roman Catholic clergy and could not accept with good grace anything on offer from Orthodox Russia. The Russian administration responded by decreeing that only Orthodox subjects were to be employed by the state, even in the most menial capacity.

Russification

From 1864 onwards, the tsars did their utmost to Russify their Lithuanian holdings, and it was the declared policy of Muraviev, the Russian Governor, to eradicate the traces of ancient Lithuania once and for all. That generally took the form of imposing Russian Orthodoxy. Non-Orthodox nobles were not allowed to buy property. They were permitted to rent it, but only for 12 years. Peasants could not buy land without a "certificate of patriotism", for which one of the qualifications was that they were Orthodox. An otherwise qualified landowner could lose his privileges simply by taking a non-Orthodox wife. Land for Jews was completely out of the question.

The programme of Russification reached its extreme in education. The university was closed down and only Russians were admitted to schools above elementary level. The use of the Lithuanian language was banned for all official purposes, and the Latin alphabet, in which Lithuanian was customarily written, was also prohibited. It became a punishable offence to be in possession of a prayer book that was written in Latin characters.

The Russian Revolution of 1905 gave the Lithuanians a chance to reclaim some of their dignity, if not their independence. Resolutions were passed demanding the creation of an autonomous state with a "Seimas", or National Assembly, with Vilnius as the capital. Threatened with a campaign of passive resistance, concessions were made such as the reintroduction of the Lithuanian language in schools. National literature sprouted with amazing rapidity, but the great symbolic victory was that

Vilnius, effectively part of Poland for five centuries, was restored as the Lithuanian capital. Just as it seemed that the country might be freed of its shackles, World War I broke out.

Driven out of East Prussia, the Russian Army rampaged through Lithuania, burning, plundering and taking away all Lithuanian men of military age. The German troops in pursuit were received almost as liberators, but it was quickly apparent that Germany also considered Lithuania a source of cheap labour. Any remaining hopes of independence were dashed when it emerged that longer-term German policy was to reintegrate Lithuania into occupied

Poland. The cruellest blow fell in September 1915 when, having occupied Vilnius, the German Military Governor announced that the city would be returned to Poland. He called it "the Pearl of the Polish Kingdom". Germany's subsequent defeat meant all its plans for Lithuania were shelved, and the question of the country's future was transferred to the Paris Conference.

The various claims submitted to the conference by a Lithuanian delegation were made to look irrelevant as the Russian revolutionary war, not to mention the activities of a renegade German force under General Bermondt, overflowed into Lithuania. A combined force of Estonians, Poles and Lithuanians managed to

---

LEFT: Napoleon's Grand Army crosses the Nemunas at Kaunas in 1815 at the start of his Russian campaign.
RIGHT: 1920s illustration of wolves attacking a woman and child in Lithuania.

repel a Bolshevik invasion, but while they were thus engaged the Polish Army marched into Vilnius and was able to hold the capital. This take-over was in direct violation of the 1920 Suwałki Treaty signed by both Polish and Lithuanian governments. Polish forces held on to it even as the Bolsheviks swept towards Warsaw. In the end they surrendered it to the Bolsheviks rather than to Lithuania, and Kaunas became the interim capital. It was a small compensation when Lithuania reclaimed Klaipėda (Memel) and the coast from Germany in 1923.

The possession of Vilnius (Wilno in Polish) bedevilled relations between Poland and

Vilnius to Lithuania by the Red Army in 1940 was mourned in Poland as a national tragedy.

The Red Army occupied Lithuania in 1940 under the terms of the secret Nazi-Soviet Pact. "Whether you agree or not is irrelevant," Molotov told the Lithuanian Government, "because the Red Army is going in tomorrow anyway." The invading troops had an approved "government" trailing in their wake. The existing parties were dissolved, and those leaders who had not already fled were sent to Siberia.

The Soviet propaganda machine then went into action. The previous government, it said, was "indifferent to the real interests of the peo-

Lithuania. The city was undoubtedly the ancient capital of Lithuania, but over the course of 500 years it had become overwhelmingly Polish in every other respect, or so Poland claimed. In 1910 a Russian census, which has since been frequently contested, broke down the population as 97,800 Poles, 75,500 Jews and only 2,200 Lithuanians.

The argument centred on the issue of whether language determines nationality. After five centuries of Polonisation and Russification, the Lithuanian language tended to be spoken only in rural areas and among peasants. The national revival did not take off until the first quarter of the 20th century. In any case, the transfer of

ple, has led the country into an impasse in the fields of both domestic and foreign policy. The vital interests of the Lithuanian people have been sacrificed to the mercenary interests of a handful of exploiters and rich people. The only thing left to working people in the towns and in the country has been unemployment, insecurity, hunger, indigence and national oppression." Lithuanians steadfastly denounced the Soviet annexation as illegal.

The first Soviet deportations of Lithuanians began in June 1941. Soon after, Lithuania, together with Latvia and Estonia, was occupied by the Germans. The 150,000 Jews in Lithuania – Vilnius was then the Jewish capital of Eastern

Europe – all but vanished in Hitler's grim "final solution". In common with all the Baltic areas reoccupied by the Red Army in 1944, Lithuania lost another 200,000 people to Stalin's deportation orders. By 1950 Lithuania itself had all but vanished as an incorporated unit of the Soviet Union.

Soviet tanks roll in

When the three Baltic states moved almost in unison out of Soviet control in the late 1980s the lead in Lithuania was taken by the Sąjūdis, a breakaway movement drawn largely from the Institute of Philosophy of the Lithuanian Academy of Sciences. Its objective was full independence. There was no need to consult the Soviet Union, it said cheekily, because no one had ever recognised the 1940 annexation. This was too provocative even for the easygoing Soviet leader Mikhail Gorbachev and, on the day that the parliament voted for unilateral independence, Soviet tanks drew up outside. Despite the freezing temperatures, thousands found themselves on the streets. There were shootings at the TV tower in Vilnius where 14 were killed and 700 injured.

In July seven border guards were killed in Medininkai, in the south of the country, by Soviet special forces. But on 21 August 1991 Soviet troops began to leave the country and the statue of Lenin in Lukiškiū Square was torn down. By September all three Baltic countries had been re-admitted into the UN. Kaunas-born Vytautas Landsbergis, a doctor of music and author of a number of books on Lithuanian artists and musicians, served as de-facto head of state until 1992, when elections for the presidency took place.

Through the hardship of the 1990s, self-esteen began to return, Pope John Paul II paid a visit almost as soon as he could, in September 1993, clearly delighted once more to be united with such a faithul congregation who were busily looking for funds to restore their churches. In Vilnius hard work was rewarded in the granting of Unesco World Heritage to the Old Town.

The economy slowed at the end of the 1990s, following Russia's crisis, but recovered in the first decade of the 21st century. Lithuania's own crisis struck in 2003 when Rolandas Paksas, a populist president, was impeached for corruption involving the awarding of Lithuanian citizenship to a rich Russian financial backer and gaining him the distinction of being the first political leader in Europe to have been judicially removed from office. A former president, Kaunas-born Valdas Adamkus, who had had a

career with the Environmental Protection Agency in the US, was re-elected in time to preside over Lithuania's admission into the EU and Nato in 2004, a year that saw Olympic victories for the national basketball team. Relations with its neighbours were beginning to normalise, too, with agreements reached with Moscow about Russian citizens travelling across the country to reach the anomolous Russian outpost of Kaliningrad.

Lithuania is now well and tuly on the world map. And even though 70 percent of the population practises Roman Catholicism, nationalism has allowed a lingering pride in the country's pagan past. ❑

LEFT: the Jewish quarter of Vilnius before World War II.
RIGHT: President Valdas Adamkus casts his vote following the scandal that ousted his predecessor.

VILNIUS

A beautiful city, both ancient and modern, Lithuania's capital
is renowned for its baroque churches and an Old Town
that is both a delight and an education to explore

Map
on page
272

L ithuania's capital lies rather inconveniently in the far southeastern corner of the country only a couple of dozen kilometres from Belarus. **Vilnius ❶** grew up on a hill beside the River Neris, near the point where it is met by the smaller River Vilnia. It was a stronghold against first the German Teutonic knights and then the Crimean Tatars.

The Neris flows westwards towards Kaunas, Lithuania's capital during the period in the 20th century when Vilnius and the surrounding area was occupied by Poland. For 17 years the two countries were not on speaking terms. Poland and Lithuania had been joined by marriage in 1386. In 1795 Vilnius was swallowed into the Russian Empire and as Russification followed Polonisation many churches the Jesuits had built, evolving a local baroque style, were given over to the Russian Orthodox belief.

In spite of many decades of neglect, Vilnius has one of the largest old towns in Eastern Europe, bristling with the confident and robust baroque towers of churches that seem too large and too numerous for the half a million population. In 1994 the Old Town was designated a Unesco World Heritage Site. Ensuring that the maintenance and upkeep of these churches, along with the streets, is considered an important aspect of the city's budget.

About half the population is Lithuanian, while smaller percentages of Poles (18.7 percent), Russians (14 percent), Belorussians (4 percent) along with others comprise the majority of the city's various ethnic groups. Before the war Vilnius was one of the great Jewish cities of Europe, and the centre of Yiddish publishing. New streets and buildings in its centre mark the site of their ghetto: some 150,000 of its inhabitants were killed by the Nazis.

Besides the variety of churches the city's historical legacy can be viewed in a very hands-on and real way by visits to the 16th-century Gates of Dawn, with an icon believed to work miracles, to the former KGB building where ex-inmates work as tour guides. Most pleasure is to be had from inspecting the churches and simply walking the cobbled streets. These are brightened by antiques shops, restaurants, bars and cafés. There are several outstanding restaurants. The beer bars that in summer tend to bloom on the city's streets and the cavernous cellars that become the city's pulse in colder months are also an important aspect of Vilnius's charm.

Castle Hill starting point

The best place to start a tour of the city is from the top of the **Gediminas Tower ❹** (Gedimin bokštas) on **Castle Hill** (Gedimino kalnas) overlooking the red-tiled roofs and the church towers of the Old Town,

PRECEDING PAGES: rooftop view of the Old Town. **LEFT:** high rises in the Snipiskes area. **BELOW:** St Anne's and St Casimir's.

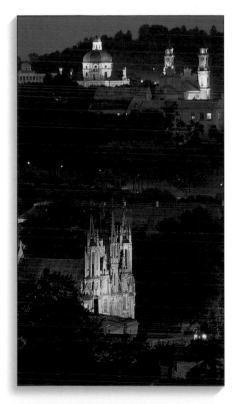

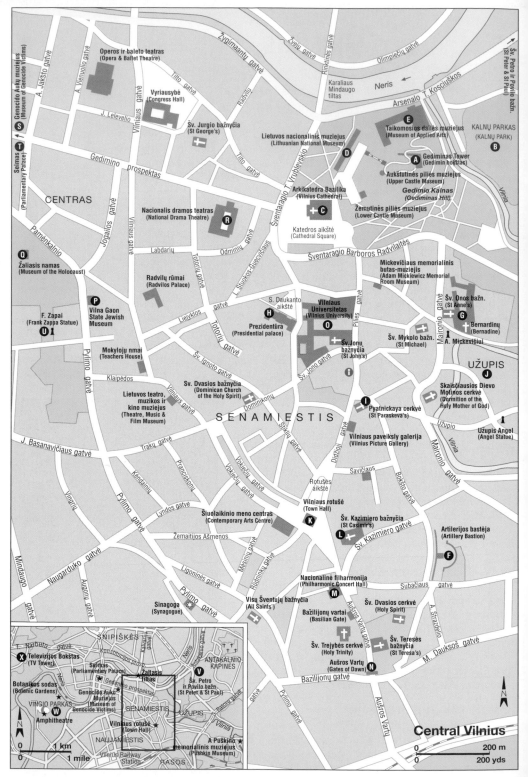

Central Vilnius

Žygimantų gatvė

Žvejų gatvė

Rinktinės gatvė

Olimpiečių gatvė

Karaliaus Mindaugo tiltas

Neris

Arsenalo T. Kosciuškos

Operos ir baleto teatras
(Opera & Ballet Theatre)

Tilto gatvė

Radvilų

Vyriausybė
(Congress Hall)

Genocido Aukų muziejus
(Museum of Genocide Victims)

A. Jakšto gatvė

A. Vienuolio gatvė

Šv. Jurgio bažnyčia
(St George's)

J. Lelevelio gatvė

Vilniaus gatvė

Ŝ

T

Gedimino prospektas

Seimas
(Parliamentary Palace)

Tilto gatvė

Lietuvos nacionalinis muziejus
(Lithuanian National Museum)

Šventaragio T. Vrublevskio

Taikomosios dailės muziejus
(Museum of Applied Arts)

E

D

Gediminas Tower
(Gedimin bokštas)

A

Aukštutinės pilies muziejus
(Upper Castle Museum)

KALNŲ PARKAS
(KALNŲ PARK)

B

Gedimino Kalnas
(Gediminas Hill)

Vilnia

CENTRAS

Jogailos gatvė

Pamenkalnio

Nacionalis dramos teatras
(National Drama Theatre)

R

Labdarių

Odminių

Arkikatedra Bazilika
(Vilnius Cathedral)

C

Katedros aikštė
(Cathedral Square)

Žemutinės pilies muziejus
(Lower Castle Museum)

Šventaragio Barboros Radvilaitės

Žaliasis namas
(Museum of the Holocaust)

Q

Radvilų rūmai
(Radvilos Palace)

Totorių gatvė

L. Stuokos-Gucevičiaus

S. Daukanto aikštė

Mickevičiaus memorialinis butas-muziejus
(Adam Mickiewicz Memorial Room Museum)

Vilna Gaon State Jewish Museum

P

F. Zapai
(Frank Zappa Statue)

U 1

Vilniaus Universitetas
(Vilnius University)

H

Prezidentūra
(Presidential palace)

O

Pilies gatvė

Šv. Onos bažn.
(St Anne's)

G

Bernardinų
(Bernadine)

A. Mickevičiui

Šv. Mykolo bažn.
(St Michael)

Maironio gatvė

UŽUPIS

Mokyklojų nmai
(Teachers House)

Klaipėdos

Pylimo gatvė

Vilniaus gatvė

Totorių gatvė

Šv. Ignoto gatvė

Šv. Jono bažnyčia
(St John's)

Šv. Jono gatvė

i

Skaisčiausios Dievo Motinos cerkvė
(Dormition of the Holy Mother of God)

Užupio

Užupis Angel
(Angel Statue)

Lietuvos teatro, muzikos ir kino muziejus
(Theatre, Music & Film Museum)

Vilniaus gatvė

Šv. Dvasios bažnyčia
(Dominican Church of the Holy Spirit)

Dominikonų

SENAMIESTIS

Šiklų gatvė

J

Pyatnickaya cerkvė
(St Paraskeva's)

Vilnia

Maironio gatvė

J. Basanavičiaus gatvė

Traku gatvė

Pranciškonų

Vokiečių gatvė

Vokiečių gatvė

Didžioji

Vilniaus paveikslų galerija
(Vilnius Picture Gallery)

Savičiaus

Bokšto gatvė

Kėdainių

Pylimo gatvė

Lyndos gatvė

Žemaitijos Ašmenos

Mėsinių gatvė

Rūdninkų gatvė

Šiuolaikinio meno centras
(Contemporary Arts Centre)

Rotušės aikštė

Vilniaus rotušė
(Town Hall)

K

Šv. Kazimiero bažnyčia
(St Casimir's)

Šv. Kazimiero gatvė

L

Artilerijos bastėja
(Artillery Bastion)

F

Mindaugo gatvė

Naugarduko gatvė

Algonų gatvė

Ligoninės gatvė

Nacionalinė filharmonija
(Philharmonic Concert Hall)

M

Subačiaus gatvė

A. Strazdelio

M. Daukšos gatvė

Sinagoga
(Synagogue)

Pylimo gatvė

Visų Šventųjų bažnyčia
(All Saints')

Bazilijonų vartai
(Basilian Gate)

Aušros Vartų gatvė

Šv. Dvasios cerkvė
(Holy Spirit)

Šv. Trejybės cerkvė
(Holy Trinity)

Šv. Teresės bažnyčia
(St Teresa's)

Aušros Vartai
(Gates of Dawn)

N

Bazilijonų gatvė

Aušros Vartų

N

0 _____ **200 m**

0 _____ **200 yds**

SNIPIŠKĖS

T. Narbuto gatvė

Konstitucijos prosp.

Televizijos Bokštas
(TV Tower)

X

Neris

ANTAKALNIO KAPINĖS

Seimas
(Parliamentary Palace)

Gedimino prospektas

Žaltasis tiltas

Botanikos sodas
(Botanic Gardens)

Genocido Aukų Muziejus
(Museum of Genocide Victims)

Šv. Petro ir Povilo bažn.
(St Peter & St Paul)

SENAMIESTIS

UŽUPIS

Vilnia

VINGIO PARKAS

Amphitheatre
(Vingio)

W

V

Vilniaus rotušė
(Town Hall)

NAUJAMIESTIS

A Puškino memorialinis muziejus
(Pushkin Museum)

RASOS

Vilnius Railway Station

0 _____ **1 km**

0 _____ **1 mile**

Šv. Petro ir Povilo bažn.
(St Peter & St Paul)

the cathedral, the administrative buildings along the main avenue, Gedimino prospektus and the modern business and shopping centres on the right bank of the Neris stretching to the television tower in the Lazdynai district and beyond.

The castle on Castle Hill, the oldest settlement of Vilnius, was built by Grand Duke Gediminas (1316–41) at the confluence of the Neris and Vilnia rivers. It was to this spot that he invited merchants, artisans and friars from various German towns. According to legend, Gediminas dreamt of a powerful iron wolf howling from a hill at the mouth of the Vilnia, a dream which signified that at this spot a magnificent fort and a town would arise.

All that remains are the ruins of the southern part and the western defence tower, Gediminas Tower, which houses the **Upper Castle Museum** (Aukštutinės pilies muziejus; open May–Sept daily 10am–7pm; Oct–Apr daily 10am–5pm; admission fee). The 14th-century, three-storey octagonal brick tower houses a small exhibit of archaeological findings and the history of the castle, which is one of the symbols of Lithuania's independence. The independence movement scored its first victory when the old Lithuanian yellow, green and red tricolour was raised on the observation platform on 7 October 1988. There is a newly constructed funicular railway should you not feel like hiking up the hill.

On the nearby **Hill of Three Crosses** Ⓑ (Trijų kryžių kalnas) are the symbols of Lithuanian mourning and hope which were rebuilt and unveiled on 14 June 1989. The first crosses were erected on the hill in the 17th century in memory of martyred Franciscan monks. During Stalin's time they were removed and buried. The crosses standing today are reproductions of the originals.

At the foot of Castle Hill lies the **Lower Castle** (Žemutinės pilies), which was constructed in the 16th century. The palace built in the reign of Žygimantas Augustas was levelled at the end of the 18th century to make way for a market, and only the drawings of Pranciškus Smuglevicius are left as a reminder of its beauty. Excavations at the Lower Castle, which later served as the city's law courts and a prison, are currently being undertaken. Plans to rebuild the castle are set for 2009.

Grand Duke Gedimius, founder of Vilnius.

BELOW:
Gediminas Tower.

The cathedral

The settlement's original church, which became the **Cathedral** Ⓒ (Arkikatedros bazilica) was built in the 13th century by the order of King Mindaugas. After his death the church reverted back to its original use as a pagan shrine until the structure was re-commissioned in 1387 by Grand Duke Jogaila (Jagieło). The structure then became a symbol of Lithuania's conversion to Catholicism. It occupied the northern part of the Lower Castle and it was rebuilt 11 times.

The present white neoclassical building by Laurynas Stuoka-Gucevičius dates back to 1777–1801 when it was given its dominating portico of six doric columns topped with the imposing renovated statues of Sts Helen, Stanislaus and Casimir. The facade has large baroque statues depicting Abraham, Moses and the four evangelists. The interior has three naves of equal height divided by two rows of massive pillars. The main altar is classical and there are several

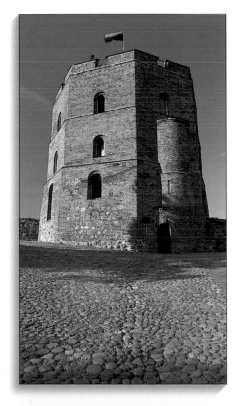

Buildings in the city are constantly under construction and areas can close with little to no warning. Travellers need to be bold, knock on closed doors, turn on the charm and say, *Galima*? (May I?), as Vilnius isn't always aware that, technically, it is open for business.

LEFT:
votive offerings
in the cathedral
RIGHT:
St Casimir's chapel.

interesting chapels on the right, especially the baroque chapel of St Casimir (1623–36), which now contains the mausoleum of kings Alexander and Ladislaus IV. As the patron saint of Lithuania, Casimir is believed to have had miracle-working powers, hence the ex-votos, the silver body parts left by the faithful as a prayer for the release from some particular ailment. Also of interest are the cathedral crypt, which serves as the final resting place for many of the country's leaders, noblemen and archbishops. In 1985 a fresco was found along the crypt's wall. It is believed to have been painted at the end of the 14th century, making it the country's oldest wall painting.

In the Soviet era the cathedral served as a picture gallery. As a symbol of national revival, it was the first church to be reconsecrated, on 5 February 1989. The 52-metre (170-ft) **Belfry** which stands to the front and to the right of the cathedral was originally part of the Lower Castle's defence walls. Although closed to visitors, it is a distinctive landmark and a good meeting point.

Walk away from the cathedral towards the Neris to find the **Lithuanian National Museum D** (Lietuvos Nacionalinis muziejus; open Wed–Sat 10am–6pm, Sun 10am–3pm; admission fee), the country's biggest museum. Founded in 1855, closed by the tsarist authorities and re-opened in 1968, the exhibits therein illustrate the history of the people of Lithuania from the Stone Age to 1945. There are costumes, farming and fishing equipment and re-created interiors of houses from different regions along with weapons and armour. In front of the museum sits the statue of King Mindaugas.

Further round the hill on the right at No. 2 Arsenalo is the **Museum of Applied Arts E** (Taikomosios Dailės muziejus; open Tues–Sat 11am–6pm, Sun 11am–4pm; admission fee). The museum hosts a number of changing exhi-

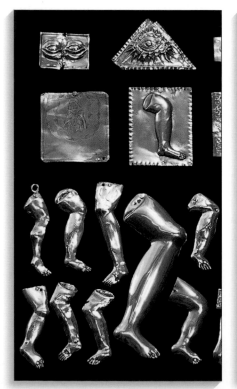

bitions. It has a permanent collection of paintings and folk pieces, for the most part focusing on wooden sculptures and other Christian art.

Map on page 272

The Old Town

Covering 269 hectares (665 acres), Vilnius's **Old Town** (Senamiestis) is one of the largest in Eastern Europe. The main artery running through the medieval city was Pilies gatvė (Castle Street), which begins at the southeast corner of Katedros aikštė (Cathedral Square) and runs into Didžioji gatvė (Big Street), past Town Hall Square to the Gates of Dawn, the only remaining gates of the town fortifications built against the Tatar invasions in the early 16th century. Only a few parts of the town wall remain in Bokšto, the street with the **Artillery Bastion ⑤** (Artilerijos Bastėja; Bokšto 20; open Tues–Sat 10am–5pm, Sun 10am–3pm; admission charge).

On the cobblestoned Pilies Street lie numerous historical buildings and from the balcony at No. 26, Lithuania's independence was declared in 1918. It is well worth venturing into the side streets and courtyards for a glimpse of the 19th-century city. There are a number of antique shops, cafés and cellar bars tucked away down these quiet lanes.

Bernardinų Street at the northern end of Pilies leads to **St Anne's church ⑥** (Šv Onos bažnyčia; Maironio 10), one of the best examples of Gothic architecture in Lithuania. Its western facade is patterned with 33 different varieties of bricks, making it amazingly graceful and harmonious. The original chapel was built in the 16th century during the reign of the Jagiełonian king Žygimantas Augustas (1520–72). The church has no foundations; it rests on alder logs. The original interior was destroyed by fires and is of little interest.

Legend has it that a dragon, the Vilnius Basilisk, lived in the Artillery bastion (above). He turned people to stone with his gaze until he saw his own reflection in a mirror.

BELOW: cathedral and belfry.

Napoleon Bonaparte is said to have been so enraptured by St Anne's that he exclaimed his desire to bring the church back to France in the palm of his hand and set it down next to Notre Dame.

Napoleon stayed in Vilnius on the way to Moscow in 1812, at the Bishop's Palace in Daukantas aikštė behind the university, which is now the **Presidential Palace** ⓗ. The French writer Stendhal was in charge of food and provisions and it was in Vilnius, he said, that he learned to drink like a Russian. The euphoria that greeted the French Army's arrival evaporated on their retreat when the city was plundered by the hungry troops. In early 2001, workers from a housing development stumbled on a mass grave of about 30,000 Napoleonic soldiers *(see page 264)*. Some of their bones now lie in white bags in the sanctuary at Antakalnis Cemetery.

Adam Mackiewicz.

The palace was built for merchants in the 16th century and redesigned at the end of the 18th century by Laurynas Stuoka-Gucevičius, whose monument stands nearby. In tsarist times it was the residence of the governor general, and under the Soviets it was the Palace of the Art Workers. Today it is the official residence of the President of Lithuania.

Next to St Anne's is the **Monastery of the Bernardines** (Bernadinų bašnyčia), who came here from Poland in 1469. It has a Gothic roof and a baroque belfry, and being built on the edge of the town it was fortified with gun ports. The nearby statue represents the Polish-Lithuanian writer Adam Mickiewicz (1798–1859), born in Lithuania and educated at Vilnius University, who wrote the brilliant epic *Pan Tadeusz* about Lithuanian society.

BELOW: Bernardine Monastery.

Facing St Anne's is **St Michael's Church** (Šv Mykolo bašnyčia), built between 1594 and 1625 in the style of the Lublin Renaissance as a family mausoleum for Leonas Sapiega, Chancellor of Lithuania. The interior, burnt and desecrated by Cossacks in 1655, is light and spacious. To the left of the altar is the funerary monument of Sapiega and his two wives, while in the catacombs are the mummified members of the Sapiega family.

The many churches in the Old Town are signs of Vilnius's geographical situation on the border of Catholicism and Orthodoxy. **The Orthodox Church of Paraskovila Piatnickaya** ❶ (Pyatnickaya cerkvė) on Didžioji Street was constructed for the first wife of Grand Duke Algirdas in the 14th century, and Peter the Great baptised Alexander Pushkin's great-grandfather here. Further up the street, in the former Slav quarter, the **Orthodox Church of the Holy Mother of God** belonged to Algirdas's second wife.

The breakaway republic

Opposite St Anne's on the far side of the small River Vilnia lies **Užupis** ❶, the first "suburb" outside the fortified city walls. This slightly scruffy but up-and-coming district, once dubbed the Montmartre of Vilnius because of its arty population, has designated itself as a "breakaway republic". On 1 April, the appropriate day of their declared independence, border patrols are set up and passports must be shown to their fake policemen. Their antics have been tolerated to such an extent that the Lithuanian Ministry of Foreign Affairs has opened up diplomatic relations with them. The area is as fun-loving as its residents. The tongue-in-cheek Užupis Constitution can be seen in Paupio Street and is translated into English.

Some places to explore are the main workshop and art gallery of the republic, the **Užupis Gallery** (Užupio galerija; Užupio 3; open Tues–Fri 11am–7pm, Sat 11am–5pm; closed Sun–Mon), the always pleasant Užupis Café (Užupio kavinė; open 10am–11pm) beside the river where pieces of sculpture are dotted around. The Angel statue at the intersection of Užupio and Malūnų streets is a symbol of the republic, and inside a courtyard across the street one can learn about the potter's ancient art of black ceramics at the **Black Ceramics Centre** (Juodosis keramikos centras; open Tues–Sat noon–6pm; closed Sun–Mon).

Constitution Wall, Užupis.

The hub of the town

Town Hall Square Ⓚ (Rotušė aikštė) was the political, cultural and economic centre of Vilnius. The original 15th-century **Town Hall** (rotušė) didn't survive, and the present one, which was designed by Stuoka-Gucevičius, the architect of the city's cathedral, was completed in 1799. In the 19th century it was frequently used for cultural events, and it became the first town theatre in 1845. Past the Town Hall square up Didžioji Street lies **St Casimir's** Ⓛ (Šv Kazimiero bažnyčia), the oldest baroque church in Vilnius, built in 1604–15 and named after the patron saint of Lithuania. The saint was the son of Casimir IV of Poland; the crown on the church roof represents his royal connections.

The church has long been an object of persecution. Under the tsars it was converted into the Orthodox Church of St Nicholas and the crown of St Casimir was replaced by an onion dome; during World War I the occupying Germans

BELOW:
Town Hall Square.

turned it into a Protestant church and the Soviets subsequently made it the Museum of Atheism and History of Religion. St Casimir's reopened for public worship in 1989.

Didžioji Street leads into Ausros Vartų Street. The **Philharmonic Concert Hall**  (Nacionalinė filharmonija), built in 1902, is at No. 5. This is the city's main music venue with both a concert hall and chamber music hall, where the national orchestra and choir regularly perform,

The Madonna of the Gates of Dawn.

The street rises to the only remaining city gate, the **Gates of Dawn** ⓝ (Aušros Vartai; Ostra Brama in Polish). In 1671 Carmelite nuns from neighbouring St Theresa's built a chapel above the gates to house a holy image of the Virgin Mary, said to have miraculous powers. Its artist is unknown and it has been encased in gold and silver by local goldsmiths, leaving only the head and hands uncovered. The chapel's interior was refurbished in the neoclassical style in 1829, and from the street below pilgrims can be seen singing and praying in front of the Virgin. Thousands of votive offerings decorate the walls and many pilgrims come to pray, queuing up on the stairs installed in the 18th century to connect the chapel to the adjacent **Church of St Theresa** (Šv Teresės bažnyčia). Mass is said in Polish and Lithuanian.

On the way up to the Gates of Dawn, in the courtyard of the only Russian monastery to operate during the Soviet era, stands Vilnius's most important Orthodox church, the **Church of the Holy Spirit** (Stačiatikių Šventosios Dvasios cerkvė). It was built in the 17th century to serve the Russian Orthodox community, and it bears similarities to Catholic architecture. Before the altar stands a glass case containing the well-preserved bodies of saints Anthony, Ivan and Eustachius, martyred in 1347 because of their faith, at the behest of Grand

BELOW:
the Gates of Dawn.
RIGHT: rector's room
at the university.

Duke Algirdas. The three saints are clothed in white during the Christmas period, black during Lent and red on all other occasions. However on 26 June the bodies, believed to have healing powers, are left naked.

Seat of learning

A tour of the Old Town should include a visit to **Vilnius University** (Vilniaus Universitetas), founded in 1570 by the Jesuits and one of the most important centres of the Counter-Reformation. For almost 200 years the Jesuits' college was the source of enlightenment, science and culture. It was closed under the tsarist regime in the 19th century. Today, some 21,000 students study at its 12 faculties. The four-storey building with an observatory tower dates back to 1569 and its windows are rococo. The library contains nearly 5 million volumes, making it the richest collection of Lithuanian books, as well as 180,000 manuscripts from the 13–16th century. Soon after it was founded, it became one of the best-known libraries in Eastern Europe.

At Universiteto No. 7 there is a map and on the north side of the building stands a small door where visitors are required to pay an admission fee. There are 13 courtyards on the grounds. The first is named after the poet and humanist Motiejus Kazimieras Sarbievijus (1595–1640). Directly across from the entrance is a 19th-century building which houses Littera, the university bookstore, with frescos painted in the late 1970s. The staircase adjacent to the bookshop entrance leads to a hall with a fresco depicting scenes from the life of Lithuanian peasantry. Take the passageway to the right of the bookstore and go up the stairs to reach the broad, open piazza and the impressive ring of arched galleries of the Grand or Skarga Courtyard. Here is Sts Johns' Church

Map on page 272

BELOW:
view from the university tower.

(Švs Jonų bažnyčia), named after St John the Baptist and St John the Evangelist. It was built in 1427, but its present baroque look is from restoration work from 1737. The adjacent 68-metre (223-ft) bell tower is the tallest structure in the Old Town. During the Soviet occupation, the church was used as a Museum of Scientific Thought. Today the working parish church has kept some flavour of its former incarnation as exhibits, including a 1613 map of the country along with some scientific books from the 14th century, can be found within its six chapels.

Opposite the church is another passageway leading to the Observatory Courtyard and the university's **Observatory**, founded in 1753, when it ranked third in importance in Europe after those at Greenwich, London and the Sorbonne, Paris. The top of the facade is crowned with the signs of the zodiac. Further on, in Daukanto Courtyard, the offices of the **Yiddish Studies Centre**, the first of its kind in post-Holocaust Eastern Europe, are helpful to walk-in visitors who need help investigating their Jewish past in Lithuania or surrounding countries.

The "Jerusalem of Lithuania"

An essential part of pre-war Vilnius was the Jewish ghetto and the Jewish population, which made up nearly half of the city. Today virtually nothing remains of the "Jerusalem of Lithuania", as Vilnius was once called. The Great Synagogue and the Schulhoyf, the traditional centre of Jewish culture around Vokiečių, Žydų and Antokolskio streets, suffered heavy damage during World War II. The ruins of the synagogue, which dated back to 1661, remained for some years before the Soviet authorities decided to blow up what was left to make way for a kindergarten and a basketball field, and dispite the small present-day congregation, there continue to be proposals to

"Courage illuminated the old world with light."

– VIRGIL, QUOTED IN THE OBSERVATORY

RIGHT: Pylimo Street Synagogue.

see it rebuilt The only remaining prayer house for the small surviving Jewish community is the **Synagogue** at Pylimo gatvė 63.

The **Vilna Goan Jewish State Museum** (Pylimo 4; open Mon–Thur 9am–5pm, Fri 9am–4pm; admission fee) is named after a rabbinical scholar, the Gaon of Vilnius, who lived in the latter half of the 18th century. Housed on the second floor of the Jewish Community Centre, it has an extensive library, though it is moving into the **Tolerance Centre**, with a larger collection, in Naugarduko gatvė nearby. A few yards to the northwest is the **Museum of the Holocaust Q**, also called the Green House (Žaliasis namas; Pamėnkalnio 12; open Mon–Thur 9am–5pm, Fri 9am–4pm; admission fee), which tells the harrowing details of Jews in Lithuania during World War II. In front of the museum stands a monument to Chiune Sugihara, Japanese Consul in Kaunas from 1939–40. He and his colleagues helped save 6,000 Jews by issuing them with papers to leave the country.

Around Pylimo Street

The western section of the Old Town is hemmed in by Pylimo gatvė, but dominated by Vokičių gatvė (German Street) especially in summer when it is lined with outdoor cafés. The street is one of the oldest in the city. Its name comes from the large numbers of German traders or "traders of German belief" living here. Most buildings on the east side have been rebuilt since being bombed in World War II. The wide pedestrian pavement flanked by narrow lanes of traffic going in opposite directions makes it a prime outdoor seating spot in the warmer months. At the southern end of Vokičių is the **Contemporary Arts Centre** (Šiuolaikinio meno centras; open Tues–Sun 11am–7pm; admission fee) with changing contemporary exhibits, except for the Fluxus room, where there

Monument to the wartime Japanese consul Chiune Sugihara who helped many Jews escape.

BELOW: the Great Synagogue in 1944.

JEWISH EXTINCTION

A centre of Jewish culture that produced the artist Chaim Soutine and violinist Jascha Heifitz, Vilnius once had 96 synagogues stretching from Gaono to Pylimo streets and Trakų to Rūdninkų streets, all of which were razed during World War II. In 1941 some 50,000 Jews were herded into two ghettos. The small ghetto around Stiklių Street lasted from 9 June to 29 October. Its 15,000 inhabitants were sent to labour and concentration camps. The bigger ghetto, established on 6 September around Žemaitijos and Rūdninkų streets, was liquidated two years later. Today, on Rūdninkų No. 18, a map showing the outlines of these two Jewish ghettos can be seen.

Most of the 50,000 Jews were killed in Paneriai, 10 km (6 miles) southeast of Vilnius off the A16 (E28) on Road 106. There is also a small museum, but working hours are erratic, especially in the cooler months, so it is best to arrange an appointment (tel: 260 2001).

The Yiddish Studies Centre in Vilnius University is the first of its kind in post-Holocaust Eastern Europe and it holds popular Yiddish language summer courses. The students and professors in the office welcome anybody who wants to find out more about their Jewish past in Lithuania or the surrounding countries.

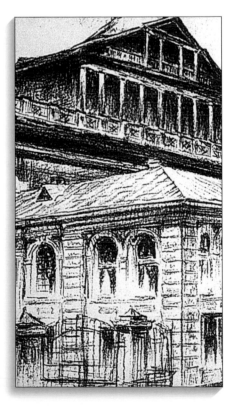

are numerous works by the 1960s Fluxus Movement, the best known being the late John Lennon's paramour, Yoko Ono.

Along Vilniaus Street stands the Radvilos family palace (known in Polish as the Radziwiłł), all that remains of the city estate of a noble Lithuanian family. Part of it functions as the **Radvilos Palace Museum** (Radvilų rūmai; open Tues–Sat noon–6pm, Sun noon–5pm; admission fee), where close to 200 of their family portraits are on display along with a small collection of foreign fine art. Further along the street is the **Theatre, Music and Film Museum** (Lietuvos teatro, muzikos ir kino muziejus; open Tues–Fri noon–6pm, Sat 11am–4pm; admission fee) with the emphasis on theatre and music. There are lovely music boxes from the early 1800s, pianolas and harmoniums, theatrical costumes and set designs, with a minimal nod to cinema.

Cells in the former KGB building.

Inside the **Teacher's House** (Mokytojų namai; Vilniaus 39) is what is considered the finest art gallery in the city, **Vartai** (open Tues–Fri noon–6pm, Sat noon–4pm). Founded in 1991, it never seems to have an empty foot of wall space. Expect thought-provoking pieces that centre around the schools of naive and surrealist art.

Commercial Street

New Vilnius unfolds along the central pedestrianised avenue **Gedimino prospektas**, opposite the cathedral. This is where most of the administrative buildings are situated, and it is the main shopping area. There are a number of striking new buildings as well as old ones in the street, including the Hotel Neringa, at No. 23, once a meeting place for the city's intellectuals and decorated with murals of the coast. **The National Drama Theatre ⓡ** (Nacionalinis

BELOW: the Green Bridge.

deamos teatras) at No. 4 has black-robed, gold-faced muses symbolising Drama, Tragedy and Comedy on its facade. Its repertoire is principally the classics.

The former KGB building on Lukiškių Square was transformed into the **Museum of Genocide Victims** ⑤ (Genocido Aukų muziejus; open Tues–Sat 10am–5pm, Sun 10am–3pm; admission fee), where tours are given in Russian or Lithuanian of the prison. The descriptions are very graphic. Pre-recorded English audio tours are also available. On the exterior of the building find the names of all who perished inside the prison. The stones in front of the building were gathered from throughout the country and signify the far-reaching effects of the Soviet system.

The 1.5-km (1-mile) long avenue ends at the modern **Parliament** ❶ (seimas) building, which was surrounded by barricades for years after the Soviets attempted to storm the building in 1991. The great concrete blocks, flowers and graffiti that regularly featured here were a constant reminder of the struggle for independence.

Vilnius has shed its Soviet symbols. The statues of Stalin, Lenin and Kapsukas, a local communist leader, are now sited with all other Lithuanian Soviet monuments in the tiny village of Grūtas near Druskininkai *(see page 315)*. However, in the middle of Gedimino near the **Green Bridge** (Žaliasis tiltas) over the River Neris, there are Soviet-era statues of sturdy peasants and factory workers.

Another statue to note is the bust of **Frank Zappa** ❶ (1940–93), at Kalinausko 1. Made in the mid-1990s, the bust is the work of the local sculptor Konstantinas Bogdanas, who is known for his many Soviet realist statues. The American rock musician had no connection whatsoever with Lithuania.

Frank Zappa memorial.

LEFT: shopping mall by the Green Bridge.
BELOW: figures outside the National Theatre.

Outside the Old Town

One church outside the Old Town but worth making the effort to reach is the **Church of Saints Peter and Paul**  (Šv Petro ir Povilo bažnyčia; Antakalnio 1). Commissioned in 1668 by Michael Casimir Pac, a Lithuanian army commander, it is the best example of baroque architecture in the city . Pac's tombstone, inscribed *Hic jacet peccator* ("Here lies a sinner"), is embedded in the wall to the right of the entrance. Despite a plain facade, the baroque interior is breathtaking with more than 2,000 undecorated stuccoed figures crowding the vaults, representing mythological, biblical and battle scenes. The boat-shaped chandelier is also spectacular.

The black granite tomb in Rasų Cemetery contains the heart of Polish hero Józef Piłsudski.

Beyond this church to the northeast of the city is the **Antakalnis Cemetery** (Antakalnio kapinės; Karių Kapų 11; open daily sunrise–sunset), which symbolises Vilnius's tormented history. In the Soldiers' Cemetery German, Polish, Russian and Lithuanian soldiers lie in the same soil. In a clearing at the back four giant Soviet granite soldiers stand next to a hall of fame where the dignitaries of Soviet Lithuania are buried, while 1,700 skeletons from Napoleons Grand Army are in a hilltop chapel. In the centre of the cemetery lie the graves of the seven border guards and the civilians killed beside the TV tower during the fight for independence by the same Soviet Army *(see page 286)*.

Some 5 km (3 miles) north of the centre over the Green Bridge and along Kalvarijų gatvė is **Verkiai Palace** (Verkių Rūmai; Žaliųjų Ežerų 49), a singular neoclassical manor house now used by the scientific community. The surrounding gardens and forest are a lovely place to relax.

BELOW: picnic with a view of the city.

The other major cemetery is to the southeast of the city. **Rasų Cemetery** (Rasų kapinės; intersection of Rasų and Sukilėlių; open daily sunrise–sunset),

Map on page 272

founded in 1801, is known as the "Pantheon of the Famous". Prominent politicians, academics (Joachim Lelewel), poets (Ludvik Kondratowicz) and painters (Prancšizek Smuglevicius (1745–1807) are among those buried here. Of particular interest are the graves of the artist and composer Mikalojus Konstantinas Čiurlionis (1875–1911), the writer Balys Sruoga (1886–1947) and author Jonas Basanavičius (1851–1927). The heart of Józef Piłsudski, the Polish military general, who ensured southern Lithuania was under Polish control from 1920–39 is also buried here. The rest of his remains are in Wawel Castle in Kracow, but as he always felt his heart was in Vilnius, his was buried along with his mother's body under a black granite slab.

Just out of town to the southeast, on the far side of the Markučiai district, is the **Pushkin Memorial Museum** (Puškino memorialinis muziejus; Subačiaus 124; open Wed–Sun 10am–5pm; admission fee) in the home of Alexander Pushkin's son, built in 1867. One room contains the poet's possessions, and you can also see the 19-hectare (47-acre) grounds where the anti-tsarist uprising of 1863 was hatched.

West of the Old Town

To the west of the city, inside a crook in the meandering River Neris is **Vingis Park W** (Vingio parkas), a popular place for cyclists and skaters. The park dates back to the 16th century when it was part of the aristocratic Radvila (Radziwiłł) estate. Tsar Alexander I was at a ball in Radvila Palace, then in Vingis, when he received the news of Napoleon's invasion in 1812 – the episode is detailed in Tolstoy's *War and Peace*. The first **National Song Festival** took place here in 1947 and a special stage was built in 1960 to absorb the 20,000

TIP

With half a dozen gambling casinos, Vilnius aspires to be Las Vegas. If you want to try your hand, visit the friendly Grand Casino at Vienuolio 4, tel: (8-700) 555 99.

BELOW:
Verkiai Palace.

Map on page 272

TIP

Don't leave Trakai without trying a *kininai*, a pastry filled with meat and onion that is a Karaite national dish.

BELOW AND RIGHT: boating around Trakai castle.

singers, dancers and musicians who still flock here every five years to take part in one of the country's great celebrations.

The new housing districts on the far side of the river are the work of Soviet-Lithuanian architects. In 1974 the designers of the new **Lazdynai District** received the Order of Lenin for their grey pre-fabricated ferro-concrete housing blocks. The **Karoliniškės District** to the west of the city on the right bank of the Neris is dominated by the **Television Tower ❿** (Televizijos bokštas), which has become infamous for the massacre in the night of 12–13 January 1991 when the Soviet tanks crushed and shot 14 unarmed civilians who were defending the building. The memory of the "defenders of freedom" is preserved in a small hall of fame at the foot of the tower (open daily 10am–10pm; admission fee) as well as in the Lithuanian State Museum. The 326-metre (1,070-ft) television tower is the tallest structure in Lithuania and has a restaurant halfway up, from where there is a breathtaking view of the capital.

The castle of Trakai

The former capital of the Grand Duchy of Lithuania, 27 km (18 miles) to the west of Vilnius, is a favourite place for a family outing. The resort village of **Trakai ❷** is surrounded by five lakes up to 48 metre (158 ft) deep. In summer people swim and sail in Lake Galvė, which acts as a kind of moat around Trakai Castle's peninsula. *Galvė* is the Lithuanian for "head" and the story is that the lake would not unfreeze in spring unless it had been fed the heads of the Grand Duke's enemies. Lithuania's most photographed castle was the heart of the Grand Duchy until 1323, when Grand Duke Gediminas moved the capital to Vilnius. The five-storey, red-brick fortifications were constructed by Vytautas and have been undergoing reconstruction since 1952.

Trakai Castle Museum (Trakų pilies muziejus; open Tues–Sun 10am–7pm, 5pm in winter; admission fee) in the rooms around the internal courtyard offers an exhibition on prehistoric discoveries and the splendour of Lithuania's Grand Duchy, which extended from the Baltic to the Black Sea. In the outer buildings are antiques from the feudal houses of later centuries. The ruins of the dukes' earlier castle can be seen in the town park.

In the 14th century Grand Duke Vytautas invited his bodyguard of Tatars from Crimea to come to Trakai, where they settled around the castle. Their descendants, the Karaites (a Turkish ethnic group, which practises a particular kind of Judaism) still give the royal town its distinctive touch. Numbering only 200, the Karaites are the smallest ethnic minority in Lithuania. Karaimų, the main street of town, is a good place to learn more about their culture. At No. 22, the **Karaite Ethnographic Museum** (Karaimų Etnografijos muziejus; open Wed–Sun 10am–6pm; admission fee) has traditional costumes, jewellery and photographs of the Karaite people alongside weaponry and cooking utensils. A Kinessa, or prayer house, of this fundamentalist Judaic sect – which, strangely, celebrates Easter – is at Karaimų 30.

There are a number of guest houses in the area and a music festival brings many visitors in August. ❑

KAUNAS

On the confluence of the Neris and Nemunas rivers, Lithuania's second city is in many ways the centre of the country, with the best museums and a thriving commercial life

Map on page 292

The third-largest city in the Baltic states, **Kaunas** ❸ is the heart of Lithuania. An hour or two from Vilniuis, it can be enjoyed on a day trip, though visitors may want to stay longer. There is no shortage of places to stay. More than any other city it has preserved its Lithuanian identity. It was relatively unscathed by World War II and large parts of the old city remain untouched. The country's second-largest city has a long-lasting rivalry with Vilnius, 106 km (60 miles) to the east, dating back to 1920 when it became the "provisional capital" after Vilnius became a part of Poland. A New Town of grand buildings was then built to befit its new status.

During its two decades as Lithuania's interim capital it developed rapidly from a Russian garrison town to a European city and many of the elegant buildings from that period remain. It is the major commercial centre of the country, manufacturing textiles and food products, and if Vilnius now provides the country with intellectuals, Kaunas provides it with traders and businessmen.

The two cities are connected by the River Neris. The point where it joins Lithuania's major river, the Nemunas, was chosen for the siting of the original castle. The Nemunas, once Lithuania's southern border, was on the German traders' route and Kaunas became a Hansa town. Today, the dam on the east side of the city has turned the river into a recreational area but pleasure boats are still able to make the journey from Kaunas to Klaipòda and the seaside.

PRECEDING PAGES:
Marionis Museum,
Town Hall Square
LEFT:
Kaunas Town Hall.
BELOW: café in
Laisvos aleja.

Around the cobbled square

The city was first mentioned in 1361 and its historical heart is by the castle in **Town Hall Square** ⓐ (Rotušės aikštė), surrounded by numerous 16th-century German merchant houses. In the middle of this cobblestoned open area is the **Town Hall** (Kauna rotusė), known as "The White Swan" for its elegance and 53-metre (175-ft) tower. Designed in late baroque and early classical style, it was begun in 1542 as a one-storey building. The second floor and the tower were added at the end of the 16th century. The Gothic vaulted cellar of the tower served as a prison and a warehouse, the ground floor was reserved for traders and prison guards, and the first floor housed the magistrate's office, treasury and town archives.

Part of the building was destroyed during the Swedish-Russian war (1655–60). After reconstruction in 1771 it housed the local government. In 1824, under the tsarist regime, it was transformed into an Orthodox church and later it became the warehouse of the artillery. It served as the provisional residence of the tsar (1837) and as a theatre (1865–69). Under the Soviet regime it was used by the engineering depart-

Post Office and Perkūnas House.

ment of Kaunas polytechnic (1951–60). Renovated between 1969 and 1973, it now serves as the "wedding palace", and happy couples and their entourages often line up for photographs in the square outside. The cellar of the Town Hall houses a small **Ceramics Museum** (open Tues–Sun 11am–5pm; admission fee) with to archaeological finds, 20th-century pottery and porcelaine from around the country, and contemporary exhibitions.

The Jesuits started to buy land and buildings in Kaunas in the early 17th century. The construction of **St Francis Xavier** (Šv Prancišlans Lsavero bažnyčia) and the Jesuit residence was finished in the middle of the 18th century. After 1812 it served as a hospital and in 1824 it became the residence of the bishop. In 1924 it was returned to the Jesuits who used it for a boys' school. The church, which has a basilica layout, fine marble altars and wood carvings, was built in 1666 and was frequently destroyed by fires. In 1825 it became the Alexander Nevski Orthodox church and under the Soviets it was transformed into a vocational school. In 1990 it was returned to the church.

The house at 10 Rotušės Street, which has a Renaissance facade, was once a hunters' inn and now houses a hunter's restaurant decorated with the taxidermist's art. A statue for the great Lithuanian poet and priest J. Mačiulis-Maironis has been erected in front of No. 13, where he lived from 1910 until his death in 1932. The baroque building from the late 16th century served as a military hospital in 1812. During the 1861 uprising against Russia its cellars were used as prisons. At Rotušės 19 there is a diminutive tribute to the country's various communications through the ages, most interestingly in the form of antique telephones and stamps at the **History of Communication Museum** (Ryšių istorijos muziejus; open Wed & Thur 10am–6pm, Sat & Sun 10am–5pm; admission fee).

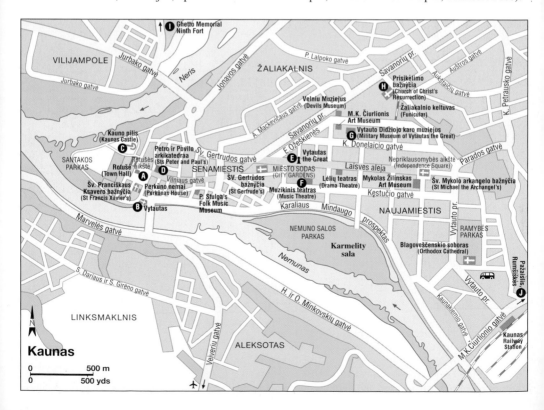

In the northwest corner of the square is the **Bernardine Monastery**. Renaissance with Gothic elements, it dates back to the late 16th century, when the first house was bought by nuns. Its church, Holy Trinity (1668), was rebuilt in baroque style. In the 19th century it possessed nine wooden altars but these were lost during World War I. In 1978 it was given back to the Catholic seminary. In 1933–34, the late-Renaissance belfry was incorporated into the seminary, which is located between the church and the belfry. The building was given back to the seminary in 1982.

The **Museum of Medicine and Pharmacy** (Medicinos ir farmacijos muziejus; Rotušės 15; open Tues–Sun 11am–5pm; admission fee) is a 17th-century building that used to house a pharmacy. On display are old instruments and a reconstructed interior of a Lithuanian pharmacy from the beginning of the 20th century.

To the river

From Town Hall Square walk down Aleksoto Street to the banks of the Nemunas. At Aleksoto Street 6 is **Perkūnas House** (Perkūno nemai). Historians cannot agree if the original purpose of this picturesque 15th-century Gothic brick building was a chapel or the Hansa office. The more romantically minded maintain it was the temple of Perkūnas, the god of thunder, since during renovation in 1818 workers found a 27-cm (11-inch) tableau of a town and temples with three fishes which came to symbolise the rivers Nemunas, Neris and the god Perkūnas. The statue has since been lost but the name remained.

Similar to St Anne's church in Vilnius, Perkūnas House is one of the most original examples of late Gothic in Lithuania and its rich architecture is a monument to the economic power of the Hansa and Germany. After reconstruction

Map on page 292

BELOW:
Town Hall Square.

in the early 19th century it served as a school and in 1844 the first Kaunas Drama Theatre was established here. After 1863 the house fell into ruins. Renovated at the end of the 19th century it served as a religious school, and returned to the Jesuits.

On the banks of the River Nemunas stands **Vytautas Church**  (Vytauto bažnyčia), built at the beginning of the 15th century for Franciscan monks. Here foreign merchants celebrated Mass. It was built in the Gothic style and a tower was added at the end of the same century. French troops used it to store their ammunition in 1812, and in 1915, when the German Army occupied Kaunas, it was used as a potato warehouse. In 1990 the church, with its sober white interior, was reopened for worship. The grave of priest and writer J. Tumas Vaižgantas (1869–1933), who organised the renovation of the church in 1920, is in the outer walls on the left.

A pathway leads to the confluence of the Neris and the Nemunas rivers. From the bank where they meet there is a good view of the Old Town spires, the Town Hall and the Jesuit and Vytautas churches. Midsummer Eve (St John's) on 23 June is celebrated every year on this piece of ground.

On the banks of the Neris lies **Kaunas Castle** ⊙ (Kauno pilis). First mentioned in the 13th century, it was the earliest stone castle in Lithuania. The surrounding walls, 2 metres (7 ft) wide and 13 metres (43 ft) high, could not fend off the crusaders who destroyed the castle in 1362 after a three-week siege. Six years later a stronger castle was built with walls 3.5 metres (12 ft) thick and four towers. Nevertheless, over the centuries it was washed away by the Neris and the northern walls with the towers collapsed. Today, only part of the castle remains.

From Napoleon Hill in Kaunas the French general watched his Grande Armée cross the Nemunas to start his Russian campaign. To commemorate the event, every July people in the city dress as Napoleonic soldiers and parade through the streets.

BELOW: Lieva ijela looking towards St Michael's.

Using Valančiaus Street, walk back to Town Hall Square and turn left into Vilniaus Street at the **Basilica of Sts Peter and Paul** Ⓓ (Petro ir Povilo arkikatedraa bazilika), which towers 42 metres (138 ft) above the corner. The first church was built here in the early 15th century but its original shape is unknown. The naves were added in the 15–16th century and the construction was completed in 1655. Of particular interest are the baroque high altar of 1775 and the neo-Gothic chapel to the right. It belonged to Augustine monks until 1895 when it became a cathedral. It was elevated to the rank of basilica in 1921. On the right intersecting Vilniaus Street, Zamenhofo Street leads to the **P. Stulga's Folk Music Museum** (Zamenhofo 12; open Wed–Sun 10am–5pm; admission fee). Inside, find a range of Lithuanian traditional instruments, including *kanklės*, usually a trapezoidal shaped piece of wood with string attached *(see page 63)*.

In Kaunas cathedral.

Little Champs-Elysées

Continue along Vilniaus Street to Birštono Street on the left. In a small yard is the **Prezidentūra**, the residence of the Lithuanian President during the inter-war period. The one-storey building has been renovated and is the president's base when he is in town.

Vilniaus Street leads into **Laisvės alėja** (Freedom Avenue), the main thoroughfare of the New Town often optimistically compared to the Champs-Elysées in Paris or Unter den Linden in Berlin. Kaunas residents love to stroll along the 1.6-km (1-mile) long pedestrian street, designed in the late 19th century. In 1982 it was closed to traffic and the central tree-lined pathway was dotted with numerous benches. Reposing and green in the summer, it can be quite grey and

BELOW: shopping for baskets in Lieva ijela.

depressing in winter. Between the wars a number of administrative buildings were put up along this classy avenue now lined with shops.

At the crossing of Sapiegos Street stands the **Monument to Vytautas the Great E**. The bronze statue of "the creator of Lithuanian power" stands proudly over four defeated soldiers: a Russian, a Pole, a Tatar and a German crusader holding a broken sword, symbolising the defeat of the Teutonic knights. A bronze plaque shows a map of medieval Lithuania extending from the Black Sea to the Baltic Sea.

In Miesto sodas, the city park facing the **Music Theatre F** (Muzikinis teatras) lies a granite monument where the name of Romas Kalanta is written into the pavement, marking the spot where the 19-year-old student immolated himself on 14 May 1972 in protest against the Soviet system.

The large pedestrian mall ends in **Independence Square** (Nepriklausomybės aikštė), which is dominated by the **Church of St Michael the Archangel** (Sv Mykolo arkangelo bažnyčia). The imposing blue neo-Byzantine building was built in 1893 by Russian architects as the Orthodox church for the army at Kaunas Castle. It was closed in 1960 and transformed into a permanent exhibition of stained glass and sculpture, but after independence it reopened to public worship. Inside are several interesting frescoes of the evangelists and Orthodox saints and the stained glass represents the Assumption. In autumn, which is the favourite time for weddings in Lithuania, couples queue up outside the church to be married.

On the right-hand side of the square is the modern building of the **Michael Žilinskas Art Gallery** (Mykolas Žilinskas dailės galerija; open Tues–Sun 11am–5pm; admission fee). The avant-garde glass-and-granite building houses 1,670 works of art donated by Lithuanian-born Žilinsko (1904–92). It has Chinese, German and Dutch porcelain, Italian paintings of the 16th and 18th centuries and an interesting collection of 20th-century art. In front of the museum stands a statue of a naked man created by Petras Mazūras and put up in 1991 despite some objections.

The best museums

Kaunas has the country's best museums. Parallel to Laisvės Street on Donelaičio Street lies Unity Square (Vienybės aikštė), where the symbols of Lithuanian statehood have been re-erected. A hall of fame with the portraits of famous Lithuanian politicians and writers leads from the Liberty monument to the eternal flame, flanked by traditional wooden crosses remembering those who died for Lithuania's independence.

The entrance to the **Military Museum of Vytautas the Great G** (Vytauto Didžiojo karo muziejus; open Wed–Sun 11am–6pm; admission fee) is on Unity Square. Lithuania is shown through the ages from prehistoric times to the present day. There is the wreck of the Lituanica, the plane in which Steponas Darius and Stasys Girėnas attempted in 1933 to fly non-stop from New York (*see page 309*). Other exhibits show the history of the Vytautas Magnus University founded in 1922, closed in 1940 and reopened in 1990.

Some of the world's top basketball players were born in Kaunas, including Zydrunas Ilgauskas, Šarūnas Marčiulionis and Arvydas Sabonis. League champions Žalgiris Kaunas can be seen at the Darius and Girėnas Sports Complex (Perkěno 3, tel: 37 20 14 70).

BELOW: Laisves Street.

The **M.K. Čiurlionis Art Gallery** (M.K. Čiurlionis dailės muziejus open Tues–Sun 11am–5pm; admission fee) is situated in the adjoining building and has its entrance at Putvinskio 55. Built in 1936, the gallery has some 360 works of the outstanding Lithuanian painter and composer, and it should not be missed. The mystic and modernist Čiurlionis (1875–1911) saw nature as an inexhaustible source of beauty. Of his musical poem *In the Forest*, he wrote: "It begins with soft and wide chords, as soft and wide as the sighing of our Lithuanian pines." Čiurlionis wrote some 20 preludes, canons and fugues for the organ, and harmonised around 60 folk songs. In a special listening hall, visitors can hear some of his symphonies and orchestral works. (Concerts are also sometimes put on in his former home, now a museum, in the spa town of Druskininkai, 124 km/77 miles to the south, *see page 313*). The museum has an exhibition of Lithuanian crosses and spinning implements.

A few houses away, at Putvinskio 64, is the **A. Žmuidzinavičius Collection**, better known as the **Devil's Museum** (Velnių muziejus; open Tues–Sun 11am–5pm; admission fee) for its impressive number of wooden devil statues amassed by the folk artist (1876–1966). It has grown over the years as new foreign devils have been added, and there are now more than 1,700, including Hitler and Stalin dancing over the bones of Lithuania.

Zaliakalnis District

From Putvinskio you can either take the funicular or climb 231 steps up to the Žaliakalnis district which offers a splendid view of the city. One of the most interesting architectural monuments is the **Church of Christ's Resurrection ⓗ** (Prisikelimo bažnyčia) at Aukštaičių 4, near the funbicular terminal. It was

Look out for concerts and choral works at Kaunas Philharmonic (Kanuno Filharmonia, Sapiegps 5), which start at 5–6pm.

BELOW:
Michael Žilinskas
Art Gallery.

Map on page 292

The Ninth Fort where victims from the Kaunas ghetto died.

BELOW: Pažaislis Monastery.
RIGHT: the Open-Air Museum at Rumšiškės.

started in 1932 and an observation platform opens in 2005–6. With the annexation by the USSR in 1940, the unfinished church, rising to 63 metres (205 ft) was confiscated and in 1952 it was incorporated into the Banga radio plant and a workshop was installed. In 1988 the building was given back to the Catholic church and restoration began, which is now complete. Being one of the symbols of national rebirth and liberation, it houses a chapel for those who died in the struggle for independence.

Outside the town

A visit to Kaunas is not complete without a tour of the **Ninth Fort ❶** (Žemaišių plentas 73; open Wed–Mon 10am–4pm; admission fee), on the A1 road towards Klaipėda. It was the ninth fort built at the end of the 19th century as part of the outer town defences on the orders of Tsar Alexander II to strengthen the western border of the Russian Empire. It became infamous as a concentration camp during the Nazi occupation. In the fort you can visit the former prison cells where Jews from all over Europe were herded together awaiting execution. A silent reminder of the horrors are the inscriptions preserved on the walls of the cell. "We are 500 French" (*Nous sommes 500 Français*), wrote Abraham Wechsler from the French town of Limoges before being killed.

The Way of Death (Mirties kelias) leads to the place where some 30,000 Jews were shot. A monumental concrete statue overlooks the mass graves where most of the inhabitants of the Kaunas ghetto were buried. The museum housed in a concrete hall near the fort describes the deportations of Lithuanians by the NKVD (the predecessor of the KGB), the Nazi and the Stalinist terror, and the resistance fighters under the Soviet occupation who fought on until 1952.

Some 7 km (4 miles) to the southeast of the town centre (take bus No. 5) is Lithuania's baroque gem, the **Pažaislis Monastery ❶** (Pažaislis vienuolynas). Isolated in the countryside above a dam on the River Nemumnas, it was built in the 17th century with orchards and gardens that are still cultivated. Entrance is through the Holy Gate and the church has a fine 45-metre (150-ft) cupola, on the inside of which is a painting of the Virgin Mary. The marble and oak interior is enriched with frescoes restored under the aegis of the Čiurlionis Gallery, which became responsible for it in 1966. Built for the Camaldelese Order, it was briefly populated by Lithuanian-American nuns in the early 20th century, and again in 1992.

The reservoir beside the monastery is called the **Kaunas Sea** (Kauno marios) and it is is popular for recreaction.

Some 20 km (12 miles) east of the city, on the A1, is **Rumšiškės**, the site of Lithuania's main **Open-Air Museum** (open May–Oct Tues–Sun 10am–6pm; admission fee). The 176-hectacre (435-acre) grounds make a good half-day out, and gives time to appreciate the collections of old country homes from all over Lithuania. There are also re-creations of schools, pubs and a mill. It becomes quite crowded during holiday weekends, especially those related to pagan feast days, actors dress as peasants inside the houses at work on traditional crafts. ❑

AUKŠTAITIJA

This region follows the Castle Route beside the River Nemunas to the coast and heads north through agricultural land to Kernavė, one of the most important pagan sites in the country

Map on pages 258–9

Vilnius

T he northern part of Lithuania, which lies above Kaunas and Vilnius between the Nemunas and Neris rivers and the Latvian border, is called Aukštaitija, a name first recorded in the 13th century. In the west it borders Žemaitija and it is higher than the coastal region. The communities of Aukštaitija grew up around uniform, one-street villages and small homesteads were created as land was divided among successive generations. The region was once known for growing flax and still has the largest flax mill in the Baltics. Primarily an agricultural area, Aukštaitija – along with the rest of the country – is moving towards more lucrative forms of income. In general, people from this part of the country have a reputation for being talkative, friendly and fond of songs.

Aukštaitija has are two distinct regions: a rather flat western region, accessible from Kaunas, and a hilly eastern region which has the greatest snowfall in the country and is best approached from the direction of Vilnius. The word *aukštaitija* means "uplands".

The castle road

The willow-lined banks beside the 141, which follows the River Nemunas for 229 km (143 miles) from Kaunas to the coast, are dotted with red-brick fortified manor houses looking out over the wide valley towards Lithuania's southern neighbours. Just beyond Jurbarkas the river forms the border with Kaliningrad. Castles were built all along here when the river marked the border between the Grand Duchy and the lands of the Teutonic Order. From the 17th century, merchants and aristocrats made their castle homes here.

The first stretch of the road, from Kaunas to Jurbakas, is a pleasant 86-km (53-mile) drive. The castle at **Raudondvaris** ❹ (Pilies takas 4; open Thur–Sun 10am–5pm; admission fee) on the outskirts of Kaunas was built in the 17th century and remodelled in the 19th century by the Tiškevičiai family, who embellished it with a picture collection and a fine library. In the park there is an old manor and the town is a centre for agricultural research. The 19th-century church was built by Lorenzo Anichini, who is buried here, and the interior statuary is by Lorenzo Pompaloni. There is also a 25-metre (82-ft) tower here overlooking the **Nevėžis Nature Reserve**.

At **Seredžius** there is a hill fort named after a legendary hero, Duke Palemonas, who is supposed to have been descended from Roman nobility. Al Jolson (Asa Yoelson) is said to have been born in this city before emigrating to the United States and performing in the pioneering 1927 "talkie" *The Jazz Singer*.

Nearby is the old Belveder manor on a high slope,

LEFT: Palūšė church near Ignalina.
BELOW: Raudonė Castle.

but it has been rather neglected, as has the park in which it lies. Only the park is open to the public. To the north of the manor there is a plain that served as an airfield during World War II. Many of the aeroplanes that took off from here never returned.

Veliuona is a small town high on the river bank with a park and two hill forts: the Castle Mountain and the Gediminas Grave – it is thought that Lithuania's Grand Duke died here in 1341. The town has a 17th-century Renaissance church restored at the turn of the century and this is the burial place of Juozas Radavičius (1857–1911), a famous organ master, and Antanas and Jonas Juška, Lithuanian folklorists whose remains were brought back here from Kazan in Russia in 1990.

Aukštaitija is famous for its home-brewed beer, and for the songs of the flax and hay harvesters, called "valiavimai".

A few miles further on is **Raudonė**, a town in a similarly elevated position. Its park is full of ancient oaks. The 17th-century red-brick castle (open daily 10am–5pm; admission fee), a mix of Renaissance and neo-Gothic, was built for a Prussian merchant, Krispin Kirschenstein. It was rebuilt in the 19th century and today it houses a school. There is a wonderful view from its tower, which is open to visitors.

The 17th-century **Panemune Castle** in the village of **Vytėnai** ❺ was also built by a merchant, Janush Eperjesh, who came from Hungary. It is sometimes called Gelgaudai Castle after its 19th-century owner. Set on a hill with a park, it is surrounded by cascading ponds.

Beyond Skirsnemunė (called Christmemel by the Germans) is **Jurbarkas**. It has a population of 14,000 and the biggest employers are the gravel-extraction company, a logging concern and a flax mill. There is an interesting 19th-century part of the town and the local park has a farmstead museum (Vydūno 31; open

BELOW: farm work for sun seekers.

Tues–Fri 10am–6pm, Sat 10am–4pm; admission fee), devoted to the distinguished Lithuanian sculptor Juozas Grybas, who lived here from 1926 to 1941.

Kaunas to Latvia

The A8 (E67) leaves Kaunas past the Ninth Fort *(see page 298)*. After a few kilometres, the 144 turn-off leads up to **Kėdainiai ❻**, an administrative centre with chemical works and a sugar industry. The Old Town is comparatively large and dates back to the 15th century when it was owned by the dukes of Radvila.

Under their patronage industry expanded, schools and publishing houses grew up and Lutheran, Roman Catholic and Reformed churches and a synagogue, all still standing, were built. The local museum (Didžioji 19; open Tues–Sat 9am–5pm; admission fee) tells the story of the town from ancient times to the present, with particular attention paid to the Nazi and Soviet occupations. The room is furnished with horns.

Up the Via Baltica

From Kėdainiai the A8 (E67) runs to **Panevėžys**, where it becomes the A10 (E67) and eventually makes its way to Rīga. Panevėžys is Lithuania's fifth-largest city with a population of 120,000. It dates from the middle of the 16th century when there was a community and a manor house on the River Nevėžis where a park is laid out today. Its rapid expansion as an industrial centre, including the Baltics' largest textile mill turning flax into linen, has not improved its attractiveness. Since the 1960s its name has been linked with the Panevėžys Drama Theatre, which has built up an impressive reputation. The Ethnographic Museum (Panevėžio kraštotyros muziejus; Vasario 16-osios 23; open Tues–Sat

Map on pages 258–9

The area around Panevėžys is famous for wood carvings, particularly the "small architecture" of roadside shrines. In May there is a special exhibition at the Panevėžys Art Gallery for Lithuania's Union of Art Masters.

BELOW: country picnic.

11am–6pm; admission fee). In the oldest house in the area, dating from 1614, a museum also has a small collection of folk art a block away (Kranto 21; open Thur–Sun 11am–5pm; admission fee).

The karst region around **Pasvalys** ❼, 38 km (24 miles) north of Panevėžys, has underground caverns and in the town park there are signs where some of these have caved in. The less than stable terrain is also marked by sinkholes permanently filled with water; one of the best is the Green Spring (Žalsvasis šaltinis), which is located alongside the Lėvuo river and Kalno street.

Branching off the A10, Road 125 leads up to **Biržai** ❽, where the landscape is pockmarked with small lakes and holes caused by the karst. The old town of Biržai was built up around an artificial lake created in the 16th century at the confluence of the Apaščia and the Agluona. The castle that stood here was destroyed in the 18th century but restored in the 1980s and there is a small museum inside. The newly reconstructed area around **Radvila Palace** is on the edge of a man-made lake. Inside is the beautiful baroque Church of St John the Baptist (Šv Jono bažnyčia) and a monument on the town square to a local poet, Julius Janonis (1896–1917). Also beside the lake is Astravas Manor, with a palace and park now used by a linen enterprise. Try som beer while you are here. There a number of breweries in the town, giving Biržai the reputation as the beer capital of Lithuania.

Kaunas to Rokiškis

This route goes through the eastern edge of the Aukštaitija plains, following the River Šventoji. It leaves Kaunas on the A6 (E262), the former Warsaw to St Petersburg post-road which was paved in the early 19th century.

Tourist groups usually take the train from Panevėžys to Anykščiai, and some extend the trip to Lake Rubikiai.

BELOW: the manor house at Biržai.

As the road enters **Ukmergė** ❾ there is a neoclassical post-house built in 1835 on the right. On the south side of the town at Vaitkuškis is the former country home of the Koskovskiai family, arts patrons with a taste for literature who corresponded with Balzac.

After Ukmergė, Road 120 heads towards **Anykščiai** ❿, where wine is blended from imported grapes and either cherries, apples or blackcurrants. The town is also known for its literary tradition. The most famous work from the town was a lyric poem written by Antanas Baranauskas (1835–1902) in response to the felling by the tsar of Anykščių Šilelis, the 1,812 sq. km (700 sq. mile) pine forest 5 km (3 miles) to the south. The poem became a milestone in the idea of conservation and the countryside. In the forest is the Puntukas boulder, one of the largest in the country, weighing 265 tonnes. These big rocks, brought by glacial drift, are scattered throughout the Baltics, and are sometimes called "presents from Scandinavia". The sculptor Bronius Pundzius turned one boulder into a monument to the transatlantic flyers Darius and Girėnas in 1943 *(see page 309)*.

In the exhibition hall (parodų salė) of the Anykščiai Museum (Vienuolio 4; open Sept–June daily 8am–5pm, July–Aug daily 9am–6pm; admission fee) is the work of Stanislovas Petraska, a folk artist who grinds stones into a paste and then "paints" the remaining powder on to a canvas, with some interesting effects. The Railway Museum (Vilties 2; tel: 381 580 15) is interactive and fun, but can only be viewed by reservation. Organised excursions on an old narrow-gauge railway to a nearby lake, with food, wine and live musicians, are also on offer.

In the village of **Niūronys**, just 8 km (5 miles) outside of the city, the Arklio muziejus or Horse Museum (open Sept–June daily 8am–5pm, July–Aug daily

Map on pages 258–9

LEFT: rich woodland.
BELOW: Juozas Puzinas, local folk artist.

TV sculpture,
Europas Park.

8am–6pm; admission fee) focuses on the role and importance of horses, which are highly regarded in Lithuania. Besides the animals, there are numerous carriages and horse-drawn buggies and agricultural machinery. There are also some areas dedicated to showing homes typical of the region. On a weekend every June there is a lively horse gathering called Bėk, Bėk, Žirgeli (Run, horse, run!) and there are races all day, from donkeys to thoroughbreds.

From **Svėdasai** ⓫ beside a lake 24 km (15 miles) further on, Road 118 goes northwest to **Kupiškis**, which is surrounded by manor houses, windmills and rural churches. Continuing 33 km (20 miles) on Road 120 is **Rokiškis** ⓬, a regional centre with a hotel. Beside the main square is a country estate dating back to the 17th century and now housing a museum of wooden sculpture (Tyzenhauzų 5; open Mon–Fri 8am–5pm; admission fee). The 19th-century church dedicated to the apostle Matthew (Šv Mato bažnyčia) on the opposite side of the square is richly decorated thanks to the Tyzenhauzai family.

The Aukštaitija Uplands

The main A2 highway runs northwest from Vilnius towards Rīga and Tallinn until it reaches **Panevėžys**. On its western side, on the banks of the Neris 32 km (20 miles) from Vilnius, is the town of **Kernavė**, which can be reached by following Road 108 to Road 116. Forming a triangle with Vilnius and Trakai, this was the capital and the major trading centre of Lithuania in the 13th and 14th centuries. Now a village of just 200, the site includes five hill-fort earthworks built to repel the crusaders and probably used by Mindaugas. Settlement here has been found to go back 10,000 years and it developed into an exceptionally large defence system. It was an important feudal town until the Teutonic Order

BELOW:
chair sculpture in
Europas Park.

destroyed it in the late 14th century. The area is considered such an important pagan monument that it was designated a Unesco World Heritage Site in 2004. Its prehistoric flavour and perfect setting, with a beautiful view over the Neris valley, make it a popular gathering spot on midsummer's eve when there are bonfires and all sorts of merry-making.

The **Green Lakes** ⓭ (Žalieji ežerai) lie off the A14 due north from Vilnius. The area is a popular, hilly collection of summer homes, where the deep lake waters, tinted green, are a place for people from Vilnius to cool off.

After 26 km (16 miles) up the A14 there is a signpost directing you to the **Centre of Europe** ⓮. At longitude 25° 19', latitude 50° 54', members of the French National Geographic Institute "discovered" this fact in 1989, though few seem to have recognised it. More remarkable is the Europos Parkas Museum (open daily 9am–sunset; admission fee) just south of Road 108. The area covers nearly 55 hectares (136 acres) of land and has a growing number of sculptures by various artists who depict what Europe and its centre mean to them. The grounds also have a post office and restaurant. (A speedier way to Europos Parkas from Vilnius is to take Kalvarijų Street veering right at the roundabout in Santariškės and following the Europos Parkas signs; this road passes Verkių Rūmai (Verkiai Palace) and the Green Lakes.)

Road 102 continues north into the **Aukštaitijos National Park**, an area of 4,530 sq. km (1,750 sq. miles) of which 15 percent is lakes. Around three-quarters of the land is forested and there is a great diversity of flora and fauna, with more than 700 species of plants, 100 species of mammals – including boar, elk, martens and beaver – and 78 species of fish. Canoeing and other water activities are popular and there are many nature trails. The best way to

Map on pages 258–9

TIP

A detailed map is absolutely essential for navigating through the area and can be obtained from the Aukštaitijos National Park Authority in Ignalina (tel: 386 525 97; tel/fax: 836 531 35; www.ignalina.lt).

BELOW: Aukštaitijos National Park.

Map
on pages
258–9

explore the park is to start in **Palūšė** ⓑ, where there is a handsome 19th-century wooden church and belfry. The park has an additional administrative centre at **Meironys**. Perhaps one of the coolest museums in the country is the folksy Beekeeper's Museum in the village of **Stripeikiai** (Bitininkystės muziejus; open 1 May–15 Oct daily 10am–7pm; admission fee). There are various hives in the shapes of pagan gods along with wood carvings of bee-related deities. The area surrounding the cottage is where the actual beekeeping takes place. Honey, of course, can be procured and boats can be hired for a better view of the surrounding lakes. **Ginučiai**, **Šuminai**, **Strazdai** and **Salos** are all pleasant villages in the vicinity.

Ignalina ⓰, the main town close to Palūšė, is a centre for the area and the **Švenčionys Uplands** on its eastern side are an attractive hilly area. It snows more in Ignalina than anywhere else in the country and the snow stays longer, which make it popular for winter sports.

To the north is **Visaginas** ⓱. Most of the 33,700 who live here are Slavs and its main street, Taikos prospektas, looks more like a boulevard in Moscow than anything found in a small Baltic town. The town is situated in a picturesque area of pine forests near a lake, but to the east is the Ignalina Atomic Power Plant on the south bank of Lake Drūkšiai. It was built in 1974, to the same design as Chernobyl, and is scheduled to be fully decommissioned by 2009.

BELOW: carved
figure at the
Beekeeper's
Museum in
Stripeikiai.

On Belarus's border

Vilnius is only 24 km (15 miles) from the Belarus border and there are several places of interest in between. It is tempting to follow the roads into the neighbouring country, but the border has become closely guarded since Lithuania joined the EU and most visitors will need a visa. The A3 has been the main highway to the east since the Middle Ages, and it goes to the Belarus capital of Minsk. **Nemėžis** is the first village on the road, settled by Tatars in Vytautas's time, and they have their own chapel and cemetery here. On the opposite side of the valley are the remains of a 19th-century country estate and park.

The road is now in the **Medininkai Uplands**, an area of wide valleys, fewer depressions and fewer forests, formed in an earlier glacial age than other uplands in the country. At the frontier customs post are seven crosses in memory of the young Lithuanian border guards killed in July 1991. Just before the border an old track goes down to the right to **Medininkai** and the remains of Medininkai Castle, a stone defence work from the 14th century, where Lithuania's patron St Casimir spent part of his childhood. The castle is in ruins, and the surrounding area has some spectacular walks.

Just over 3 km (1 mile) to the south there is a signpost to **Juozapinės Mountain**, the highest point in Lithuania above sea level, at a meagre 293.7 metres (963 ft). Just over the border there are castles of ancient Lithuania at **Lyda**, and at **Navagrudak** (Naugardukas in Lithuanian), where there is an exhibition about the history of the two countries. The poet Adam Mickiewicz was born here in 1798. ❏

Basketball Flyers

The game at which Lithuania excels is baskctball. Seven Lithuanians have Olympic gold medals and the national team took home a bronze in each of the last three Games. A few were even drafted into the NBA, including most notably Šarūnas Marčiulionis, who has put his money into a successful hotel and other businesses in Vilnius. Arvydas Sabonis, another legend, has followed suit; he owns a hotel in Palanga and in 2003 bought a major stake in the Kaunas-based Žalgiris team.

The history of the game here begins with one of the country's great heroes, Steponas Darius. The village of Rubiškė on the coast where he was born in 1896 has since changed its name to Darius. With his mother and stepfather in 1907, he emigrated to the US and as a student he excelled at baseball and football as well as basketball. He signed up for the army in 1917 and fought in France where he was wounded and decorated.

In 1920 he was one of the US volunteers for the Lithuanian Army and as a pilot he took part in the liberation of occupied Klaipėda. As a champion sportsman he introduced basketball into his home country and laid down a sporting tradition that has continued since.

He returned to the US in 1927 and founded a Lithuanian flying club, called Vytis. Five years later he and a colleague and mechanic, Stasys Girėnas, set out to bring fame and glory to their newly independent nation by embarking on an epic flight from New York to Lithuania. They found enough to buy an old plane they called Lituanica but there was no money for radio equipment.

The plane left New York on 15 July 1933 and flew across the Atlantic, covering 6,411 km (3,984 miles) in 37 hours 11 minutes. Nobody knows exactly why but it never reached Lithuania and crashed at Soldin in Germany. At the time there was friction between the two countries, and rumours that the plane might have deliberately been brought down did not improve relations. Their bodies were brought to Kaunas, then the pro-visional capital, and 60,000 turned out for their funeral. Their death was not in vain: many felt the flight had put Lithuania on the map. The duo's portraits appeared on postage stamps and 300 streets, 18 bridges and eight schools were named after them.

The most popular monument to the heroes is near Anykščiai (between Panevėžys and Ignalina) on a huge boulder called Puntukus that has been a landmark from time immemorial. In 1943 a Lithuanian sculptor, Bronius Pundzius, was in hiding from the Germans and he made himself a shelter beside the boulder. To while away his vigil, he sculpted a relief of the faces of the pilots in the stone, adding the text of their will, written before they embarked on the historic flight.

Remnants of the aeroplane and some personal effects are on display in the Historical Military Museum in Kaunas, in the same building as the M.K. Čiurlionis Art Gallery. On the main road from Klaipėda, there is a signpost marked "S. Darius tėviškė" leading 9 km (6 miles) to the village of Darius and a memorial museum. ❑

RIGHT: Darius memorial in the village that has taken its most celebrated son's name.

THE SOUTH

Map on pages 258–9

In the attractive south lies the spa town of Druskininkai, for ever associated with the talented composer and artist, M.K. Čiurlionis, as well as the outrageous Grūtas Soviet theme park

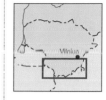

South of Kaunas and Vilnius, the country is split in two by the River Nemunas, which flows down the middle from the Belarus border just beyond Druskininkai. To the west is the region of **Suvalkija**. To the east is **Dzūkija**. Suvalkija was the land of the Sūduva and Jotvingiai tribes until it was joined to the Grand Duchy of Lithuania after the Teutonic Order was crushed in 1410. In the following years of peace, people from Žemaitija and other neighbouring regions came to settle here, but the main villages and townships were not founded until the 17th and 18th centuries.

From 1867 to 1915 the area was part of the Russian province of Suvalkai and although the region still bears the name, the town of Suvalkai is in Poland today and the capital of the province is now Marijampole. After serfdom was abolished in the 19th century, peasants settled in farmsteads and a great number were able to afford to educate their own children. Since the bulk of the first group of educated people in the country came from here, their local dialect became the basis of the modern Lithuanian literary language.

People of Suvalkija have a reputation of being stingy and thrifty, prompting their less well-off neighbours in Žemaitija and Dzūkija to come up with the saying that anybody travelling through Suvalkija would be charged double the prices for necessities, such as bread and milk. They also have a reputation for hard work, summed up in the expression, "It would be better if father fell off the roof than a grain or a drop is lost."

LEFT: wood carving at Makniūnai.
BELOW: Witch's House at Merkinė.

The Suvalkija plain

Marijampolė ⑱ (pop. 48,600), the principal city of the region, is 150 km (94 miles) west of Vilnius and 60 km (38 miles) south of Kaunas across one of the most fertile plains in the country. It lies in a rather dull plain relieved only by the Šešupė, the region's main river. The town manufactures car parts and has one of the largest car markets in the country. The related transport and freighting businesses also generate a great deal of the city's wealth. The town takes its name from an 18th-century Marian monastery and in the 19th century it was a centre of enlightenment.

Among half a dozen local museums is the local ethnographic museum (Marijampolė etnografijos muziejus; Vytauto 29; open Mon–Fri 8am–noon and 1–5pm; admission fee), which has a collection of local history.

Further up the Šešupė river on the A5 (E67) is **Kalvarija** ⑲, the last town before Poland. The old part is attractive with a post-house (1820) and the remains of a large jail built in 1810 to contain 1,000 prisoners. The classical-style church was built in 1840 and rebuilt in 1908 and it has some good paintings

*Composer
M.K. Čiurlionis.
Recitals are given at
his Druskininkai
house every Sunday
in summer.*

BELOW:
Druskininkai Lake.
RIGHT: Liškiava
church nearby.

inside. A large Jewish community settled here in the 17th century but most were exterminated by the Nazis. Their burial place is near Orija Square.

To the west of Marijampolė, the A7 (E28) leads to the Polish border, passing through **Vilkaviškis** ⑳, a local centre that was burnt to the ground in World War II. Nearer the frontier is the **Paežeriai Manor**, a 18–19th century palace set in a park with a lake. It contains a regional museum and there are plans to turn it into a cultural centre. Beyond it is **Kiršai** ㉑, birthplace of the poet Salomėja Nėris (1904–45).

To the south is a hilly, attractive corner of the country. In the southwest corner on Road 186 is **Vištytis**, a border town by a 180-sq. km (70-sq. mile) lake of the same name. Vincas Kudirka (1858–99), author of the Lithuanian national anthem, was born and buried in **Kudirkos Naumiestis**, further north on Road 186.

Suduva land

The southern part of Suvalkija, often called Sūduva, is a picturesque region of lakes and hills, centred on **Lazdijai** ㉒. Road 134 continues for 18 km (11 miles) towards hills, forests, valleys and a lovely labyrinth of lakes around **Veisiejai**, which has a number of pleasant corners to stop for a rest. The old part of the town has a beautiful park and an early 19th-century church. Lazar Zamenhof (1859–1917), the Białystok-born physician who devised Esperanto, lived here in 1886–7.

To the east of Lazdijai is **Seirijai** ㉓, from where Road 181 goes through forests and around the largest lakes in the region. The biggest of these is the 139-sq. km (50-sq. mile) **Lake Metelys**, which has clear water up to 15 metres (50 ft) deep and is teeming with fish. **Meteliai**, near the lake, has a 19th-century

church with good interior decoration, as does the 16th-century church in nearby **Simnas**. To the north is the 100-sq. km (40-sq. mile) **Lake Žuvintas**, surrounded by a large nature reserve, a boggy area which supports more than 600 species of plants and more than 250 species of birds. The Museum Ežero evoliucija (Evolution of the Lake; tel: 315 495 40; open Mon–Fri 8am–5pm; admission fee) in the village of Aleknonių organises tours in the swamps and around the lake. This is a special treat for ornithologists.

Alytus ㉔, 24 km (15 miles) east of Simnas on Road 131, lies in a deep valley of the Nemunas, surrounded by dry forests and deciduous woods on the heights above. Its attractive position has led to the development of good hotels and visitors' facilities. Because the ancient town straddled the river, it developed slowly. Half of it belonged to the province of Suvalkai and half to Vilnius, and in the late 19th century the Russians turned it into a frontier fortress.

Today it has a population of 70,000 and up-to-date industries in building materials, machinery, textiles and food processing. It is also the cultural centre of Dzūkija. There is a local museum, two 18th- and 19th-century churches and a third being built. In Vidugiris, a forest in the southern part of the city, a monument has been erected to 35,000 Nazi victims. The bridge over the Nemunas is called after Antanas Juozapavičius, an officer killed here during the battle for independence in 1919. During World War II a French airforce squadron, Normandy-Neman, was stationed nearby.

Composer's town

Lithuania's best-known artist and composer, Mikalojus Konstantinas Čiurlionis (1875–1911), grew up in **Druskininkai** ㉕, the first main town on this road, 150 km (96 miles) south of Vilnius. It is a spa town and resort of wide boulevards and old and new villas. Around 100,000 people visit each, many of them Poles. The spa opened in 1832 when salty mineral water was first used for treatment: the name Druskininkai comes from *druska* meaning salt. Every litre of water contains 3 grams (0.1 oz) of minerals and it arrives at the surface, both tepid and hot, from a depth of 72 metres (235 ft).

There are several parks, and treatments are offered in the Remedial Gymnastics and Climatotherapy Park, where visitors queue up with their special cups to sample the waters in doses often prescribed by their doctors. Near the health park is a wonderful riverside walk, which traces the Ratnyčia river for 7 km (4 miles) past carved seats and follies inscribed with poems and sayings. At one point the river is wide and deep enough to swim.

The middle of the town has a 20th-century neo-Gothic church and nearby is a memorial to Čiurlionis. His family came here when he was three and until the age of 14 he lived in the family home in the street named after him (No. 41) to the south of the town. This timbered, single-storey buidling is now preserved as a museum (open Tues–Sun 11am–5pm; admission fee). Concerts are held around the piano in the sitting room, while the audience sits outside in the shade of the pretty garden. Further along at No. 102 there is

Raižiai is a small village of 100 Tatars just northeast of Alytus. These Turkic-speaking Asian people began to settle in Lithuania in the 14th century after serving Grand Duke Vytautas who gave them privileges.

BELOW: musician accompanists on Čiurlionis Way.

an installation entitled "Echo of the Forest" (Miško aidas; open Wed–Sun 10am–6pm; admission fee) where a building in the forest has "the forest inside of it," which basically means an oak tree coming up through the building. This is Frank Lloyd Wright's ideas of architecture taken to an extreme.

Tucked in the woodlands around Druskininkai, which are abundant with mushrooms in autumn, there are some ancient farmsteads: at **Latežeris**, for example, just to the east. Nearby is the town of **Grūtas**, which has Lithuania's Soviet sculpture park (Grūto Parkas, *see box on opposite page*; tel: 313 55 511; open daily Oct–Apr 9am–5pm, May–Sep 9am–8pm; admission fee). A controversial and rather startling place, it has collections of former Soviet leaders acquired from the scrapheaps of the early independence years.

Dzukija National park,

Merkinė ㉖, 27 km (17 miles) to the northeast, is at the confluence of the rivers Nemunas and Merkys. Russia's Peter I stayed here and Vladislovas Vaza, the King of Poland, fell ill and died here in 1648. North of Merkinė, forests cover the light plains on both sides of the road from Druskininkai. The route, lined with more than 20 traditional wooden sculptures, is called the **Čiurlionis Way**, since it leads 50 km (31 miles) from the family home to Varėna, the artist's birthplace. The sculptures, based on ideas from his 0music and paintings, were erected on the centenary of his birth, in 1975.

Merkinė also has a small museum of local lore opposite the visitor centre for the 560-sq. km (215-sq, mile) **Dzūkija National Park** (open Mon–Fri 8am–noon and 1–5pm), where you can walk, ride and canoe on the tributaries of the Nemunas. There is another visitor centre in the woodlands at **Marcinkonys** to

Folk totem, Dzūkija National Park.

BELOW:
Grūtas Soviet Sculpture Park.

the southeast near the Cepkeliu Marshes. The woodland of Dzūkija is often called Dainava (from *dainuoti*, meaning to sing). The Dzūkai who live here are known for their cheerfulness and their great singing voices, as well as for an ability to scratch a living out of poor soil. They used to be said to have no saws, only axes; no bricks, only clay. One saying that still persists is "If it weren't for the mushrooms and berries, Dzūkai girls would walk around naked." These berries and mushrooms that keep clothes on the women's back are often sold along the highways.

Continuing east on the A4, just outside the national park in woodland beside the River Merkys, is the small town of **Perloja** ㉗ (pop. 100), a place of independent-minded people. It declared itself the Perloja Republic in 1918, a status it stubbornly maintained for five years, with a government and an armed guard of 50 men, defiant against Russians, Poles, Germans and both red and white Lithuanian factions. In the centre of the town square is a hugely patriotic statue to Vytautas, Grand Duke of Lithuania, sculpted by Petras Tarabilda in 1930.

The old town of **Varėna** ㉘, which also lies on the River Merkys, was burnt down during World War II, and a church is now being built to mark its site. The modern town, the administrative centre of this woodland area, is 5 km (2 miles) to the south. Heading towards Vilnius, the road passes more hilly, sandy woodland and the resurrected village of **Pirčiupiai** ㉙, where there is a monument called *The Sad Mother*, by Gediminas Jokūbonis. It was installed in remembrance of the village that was totally burnt, along with all 119 inhabitants, on 3 June 1944 by the Nazis. The memorial is inscribed with each of the victims' names and the village has since been restored. ❑

Traditional crafts such as weaving, wood carving and pottery are still carried on in the old villages of Dzūkija National Park. Look out for mushrooms and berries, too.

BELOW: Lenin and Stalin in Grūtas Park.

"STALIN WORLD"

Grūtas Park is the world's first — and perhaps last — Soviet theme park. It is the audacious idea of Viliumas Malinauskas, one of Lithuania's wealthiest businessmen who got rich with canned mushrooms. This is a $1-million mock-up of a Soviet prison camp, surrounded by barbed wire and watchtowers and populated by around 70 bronze and granite statues of former Soviet leaders Vladimir Lenin, Josef Stalin and various communist bigwigs that Malinauskas has collected from all over the country.

Visitors can drink shots of vodka and eat cold borscht from tin bowls while loud speakers broadcast old communist hymns. Important days in the Soviet calendar are celebrated and there are said to be plans to build a railway for cattle wagons from Vilnius to give younger Lithuanians an idea of what it would feel like to be deported. Not surprisingly, the project has attracted some criticism.

ZEMAITIJA AND THE COAST

The Amber Coast includes the Curonian Spit, one of the world's great sand-dune nature areas, while inland is the man-made Hill of Crosses, a place of extraordinary devotion

Map on pages 258–9

The province of Žemaitija (pronounced *zhe-may-tee-ya*) covers about a quarter of Lithuania, and roughly corresponds with the Žemaitija Upland. The adjacent coastal area is known as Mažoji Lietuva or Lithuania Minor. Although the ancient tribes probably took their names from the places they came from, the Žemaičiai lived not in the Upland but around the mouth of the Nemunas, trading with the Aukštaičiai towards the river's source. On this coast there is also archaeological evidence of Romans and Vikings, and of Bronze-age trade with Britain and the Mediterranean.

For 200 years the Žemaičiai had a running battle with the German crusaders of the Livonian Order who had established their Baltic base in Rīga, and with the Teutonic Order who harried them from the west. Between 1382 and 1404 the Dukes of Lithuania ceded Žemaitija to the Order, but in the 15th century it became a self-governing district and duchy, known in the west as Samogitia. To outsiders it long seemed a rather mysterious, wild and pagan land, an image enforced by Prosper Mérimée's novel *Lokis*.

The Žemaičiai maintain a strong regional dialect and keep their links with the past. Inhabited by men of few words, this is not a land of songs. Most of the countryside is rather severe, and the western slope of the Upland is windier, foggier and wetter than elsewhere. The trees are mostly firs and once-sacred oaks, and the landscape is dotted with old wooden crucifixes in roadside shrines and cemeteries. The main motorway from Vilnius to Klaipėda via Kaunas is the well-maintained A1 (E85) dual-carriageway. To the north and somewhat parallel of the A1 runs the A9 (E272) from Panevėžys, which becomes the A11 (E272) after Šiauliai. The A12 (E77) runs horizontally to these roads and connects Šiauliai with Tauragė. Connecting Mažeikiai and Tauragė (via Plungė) is the 164.

LEFT: the endless sands of Neringa Spit.
BELOW: Nida holidaymakers.

The Kaunas–Klaipėda Highway

The A1(E85) motorway from Vilnius via Kaunas to the coast is a lovely 311-km (193-mile) stretch. There are a number of diversions not far from the main road should you want to explore lesser-known parts of the country. The first of these that falls within the Žemaitija region is **Raseiniai ㉚**, 86 km (53 miles) west of Kaunas and about 5 km (3 miles) off the A1 on Route 146. The town is historically significant as one of the focal points of the 1831 rebellion against the tsar. The 17th-century church and abbey is dedicated to the Assumption of the Holy Virgin (Švč Mergelės Marijos Ėmimo ī Dangų bažnyčia; Bažnyčios 2). Also of interest further into town and past the city's park is the Raseiniai Area History Museum (Raseinių istorijos muziejus; Muziejaus 3;

*Memorial carvings to
the massacre at
Ablinga.*

open Mon–Fri 8am–5pm, Sat 9am–3pm; admission fee) in a former prison building, which includes photographs of prisoners from 1940–52 and exhibits about the area and the diaspora from this region. There is also an area dedicated to flax, national patterns, ceramics, early 20th-century household utensils and folk art.

About 17 km (10 miles) north of Raseiniai on Route 148 is **Šiluva** ③, which has the beautiful Basilica of the Birth of the Blessed Virgin (Švč Mergelės Marijos gimimo bazilika; Jurgaičio 2), a baroque building dedicated to the "Lourdes of Lithuania". It is believed that in the mid-17th century the Virgin Mary appeared on a rock near the the site of a former church, which had been seized by Calvinists, and she wept for its destruction. Moved by these tears a passing blind man was able to remember that a former church had stood on the grounds and he was able to locate both an icon of the Virgin and the original deed to the land, and through this apparent miracle he regained his sight. The existing church was returned to the Catholics. Although this miracle was historically advantageous many still come here to worship. Large congregations attend services on major holidays to see both the icon, which is now partially covered in gold, and the holy rock.

Tytuvėnai ② is about 10 km (6 miles) north on Route 148. The area surrounding the town is popular due to its lakes and forested areas. There is also an 18th-century church dedicated to the Holy Virgin Mary (Švč Mergelės Marijos bažnyčia; Piliakalnio 1).

Heading out of Raseiniai, Route 196 runs parallel to the significantly faster A1 or you can return to the A1 via Route 146. About 5 km (3 miles) outside of the town of **Kryžkalnis** there is a small sign for **Bijotai** village. Follow the

BELOW: wooden houses in Klaipėda.

signs towards D. Poška Baubliai (open Mon–Fri 10am–7pm, Sat & Sun 11am–3pm; admission fee) in order to find Dionizas Poška's hollowed-out oak tree trunks with pagan carvings in them. Along the same road heading away from the A1 is the town of **Girdiškė**. Its church, dedicated to the Virgin, has an oak altar with six main branches shooting upward and intertwined. Continue along the road and circle around the church in the village of **Upyna** to return to the A1 at the town of Prienai via Gudirvės. Stasys Girėnas, the doomed transatlantic aviator, was born in a peasant family in 1893 in **Vytogana** a little further on. He was the youngest of 16 children.

Another detour from the A1 is along Route 164 towards the town of **Rietavas**, an ancient settlement (pop. 3,979) centred around an old square. The main attraction is the manor house and estate of the Oginskiai family (Parko 10; open Tues–Fri 9am–5pm, Sat & Sun 10am–3pm; admission fee). From 1812 to 1909 they ruled over their own autonomous domain, with their own laws and even their own currency. In 1835 they granted civil rights to their peasants, organised agricultural exhibitions, promoted Lithuanian culture and written language, and started publishing the Lithuanian calendar. They established a music school in the town and in 1872 mustered a famous brass band. They helped introduce electricity and the telephone system to the town of Plungė, to the north, and it was Irenejus Oginskis who in 1951 started building the main Žemaičiai road.

In 1874 a beautiful church in the Venetian style was built on their orders by the German architect Friedrich August Stüler. Today the manor is an agricultural college. The road continues through 50 km (30 miles) of uninhabited forest. At Endriejavas there is a small lake and 8 km (4 miles) to the north is the former village of Ablinga. On 23 July 1841 it was burnt down and obliterated by the Nazis and its 42 inhabitants perished. A wooden sculpture has been erected to each of the dead.

Klaipėda and the coast

The coastal plain, Pajūris, is 15–20 km (10–13 miles) wide and rises to around 40 metres (132 ft). The landscape is diverse, consisting of fertile clay soils, dunes, sandy forests and wet bogs. In the south is the swampy Nemunas delta and the 1,600-sq. km (618-sq. mile) and 4-metre (13-ft) deep **Curonian Lagoon** (Kuršių marios). The coastline has urbanised resorts, around Palanga in the north, and in Neringa along the Kuršių Nerija, or Curonian Spit (Kurische Nehrung in German), which like much of the area was part of Germany's Memelland. Neringa is not actually a town, but an administrative area with its capital at Nida, near the border with Kaliningrad at the southern end of the spit. The area has many miles of empty beaches and some nature reserves.

Klaipėda ③③ is the main town on the coast, situated at the mouth of the Danė river on the Kuršių marios lagoon. It suffered heavy damage during World War II when it was used by the Germans as a submarine base. Since the 1970s when investment was ploughed into local industry, its population has dramatically grown to 193,000, making it the third-largest city in Lithuania. In 1252 the Livonian Order built a castle here, called Memelburg, and the city

Map on pages 258–9

TIP

When in Klaipėda have a glass of Svyturys beer. The brewery has been here since 1784, and its reputation in recent years has been spreading.

BELOW: the Danė river at Klaipėda.

became known as Memel in German. Klaipėda, according to local linguists, finds its etymology in the dialect words of *klaips*, meaning loaf of bread, and the verb *eda* to eat, as the locals would refer to Memel Castle (and by extension their city) as a "place eating bread" or otherwise the place where German knights were gorging themselves on the locals' bread. Today none of this sentiment can be found in this port city, which has a flourishing shipbuilding industry and ferry service to Germany and other Baltic harbours.

Klaipėda claims to be the northernmost ice-free port in Europe.

What is left of the old town is strung out along a couple of cobbled streets running along the left bank of the Danė, where there are some attractive bars and a floating restaurant, the three-masted *Meridianas*. There are a few remaining half-timbered *(Fachwerk)* buildings. The old post office, rebuilt with German bells in 1987, is now a concert venue. The city also has two theatres (Hitler spoke from the balcony of the one in Theatre Squares where the resurrected Annchen von Tarau statue now stands. The original, erected in 1912, was dedicated to the German poet Simon Dach; it is still debated whether it fell into the hands of the Nazis or Soviets.

Also of interest in the old town is the History of Lithuania Minor Museum (Mažosios Lietuvos istorijos muziejus; Didžioji Vandens 6; open Sept–June Tues–Sat 10am–6pm; July–Aug Tues–Sun 10am–6pm; admission fee), which houses all sorts of ethnic, archaeological and historical pieces related to this area. Most attention-grabbing are the eerie photographs of the city during World War II. South of the old town is the Blacksmith's Museum (Kalvystės muziejus; Saltkalvių 2a; open Tues–Sat 10am–5.30pm; admission fee), which is a working smithy, with perspiring blacksmiths forging all types of ironwork.

BELOW: by the river in Klaipėda.

On the other side of the Danė, the Clock Museum (Klaipėdos laikrodžių

muziejus; Liepų 12; open Tues–Sat noon–6pm, Sun noon 5pm; admission fee)
is another strangely satisfying museum. Centred around clocks and how they are
made, it displays mechanism s from sundials to atomic clocks. In the rear courtyard of the museum carillon concerts are often held although the 48 bells are
actually housed in the nearby post office.

Continuing along Liepų leads to the Mažvydos Sculpture Park (Mažvydos
skulptūrų parkas), which is bordered by Daukanto, Liepų and Trilapio streets.
The park was the city's main cemetery until the 1970s when it was closed.
Some of the crosses were salvaged and arc now housed in the Blacksmith's
Museum *(see above)*. The large park is a nice way to come across many and dis-
parate styles of sculpture, most with more than a touch of whimsy.

The northern coast

Some 40 km (25 miles) north of Klaipėda on the A13 are the two resorts of
Palanga and Šventoji. An old settlement of fishermen and amber-gatherers,
Palanga ③④ became popular in the early 19th century when it developed as a spa
and health resort. Considered the wilder resort on the Lithuanian coast, Palanga
still manages to maintain its charm even with the heavy influx of new hotels,
restaurants and bars that sprout up the moment the weather turns warm. Meilės
alėja (Lover's Lane), which runs parallel to the Baltic Sea, and Basanavičiaus,
which leads into the pier, are the two most popular places to stroll, especially as
the sun is setting. A trip to Palanga without watching the sun set (or rise should
you have stayed out all night) along with everyone else is a wasted trip indeed.

Despite the bars and cafés touting karaoke, drinking contests or just playing
loud thumping music so the sound of the ocean is left unheard, peace still

**Map
on pages
258–9**

 TIP

Voted the "best
architectural work
of 2003", the
five-storey Palanga
Hotel in Tiškevičius
Park has a restaurant
terrace with generous
views.

BELOW: Lithuania's
favourite sport,
in Klaipėda.

Amber

There is amber everywhere in the Baltics. At any opportunity, stalls are set up to sell bargain bracelets, necklaces, earrings, keyrings and brooches. In its raw state, buffeted by tides and exposed to the elements, these are dull stones, scattered like pebbles the length of the beaches. People are always on the lookout for them, particularly after storms, though most of the amber bought today will have been dug out of the ground by excavators in Kaliningrad.

Amber is not in fact a stone, but fossilised resin of primeval pine trees. The amber deposit, dating back 40 million years, forms a seam 60–90-cm (2–3-ft) thick beneath the clay surface of the seabed. The jagged bottom of icebergs are thought to plough up the seabed and chunks of amber then become caught up in seaweed which is ripped out and dragged ashore by storms. In spring, fishermen in waders used to comb the beaches with what look like large shrimping nets to pull in flotsam that might contain amber. The Kuršių Lagoon was also a great source of it and in the 19th century Juodkrantė was known as Amber Cove: the Stantien and Becker company used to dredge up to 85 tons of it here every year.

The stone's peculiarity is that, while it was sticky resin, insects were attracted to it, and it often solidified while they were trapped by its surface. The result is that you can hold an opaque, polished stone to the light and see flies, mosquitoes or gnats perfectly preserved inside. They intrigued the 18th-century English poet Alexander Pope, who wrote:

> Pretty! in amber, to observe the forms
> Of hairs, or straws, or dirt, or grubs or
> worms;
> The things, we know, are neither rich
> nor rare,
> But wonder how the devil they got there.

Amber was a commodity that the earliest tribes could easily trade: according to Tacitus, the price it fetched astonished them. It has been found in the tombs of the Mycenae and Tutankhamen's treasure included an amber necklace. The Baltic shoreline was first called the Amber Coast by the ancient Greek poet Homer, who was probably thinking of the material when he described the brilliant "electron" on his warriors' shields.

The best place to see amber in the Baltics is at the Amber Museum in Palanga.

A local legend tells how "Lithuanian gold" was created. There was once a Baltic queen named Jūratė who lived in a submarine palace made of amber. She was to be the bride of Patrimpas, god of water, but she fell for a mortal fisherman called Kastytis whom she visited in his hut on the banks of the Nemunas near Klaipėda at sunset every night for a year. The liaison came to the attention of Perkūnas, god of thunder, and in a rage he threw down bolts of lightning, killing Jūratė and shattering her amber palace into 10,000 pieces. Perkūnas then punished Kastytis by binding him to a rock on the seabed. Now when the west wind blows Kastytis can be heard moaning for his love, and when the wind dies the shore is strewn with fragments of Jūratė's palace. ❑

LEFT: a beachcomber's delight – a hoard of "Lithuanian gold".

Map on pages 258–9

reigns in some parts of the resort. One of the best places to visit besides the beaches is the 110-hectare (272-acre) Botanical Park, which lies alongside the Baltic Sea. In summer, concerts take place regularly throughout the park where there are more than 500 plant species, dominated by pine trees.

In the centre of the park is Count Tiškevičius's mansion, which is now home to the Amber Museum (Gintaro muziejus; Vytauto 17; open Sept–May Tues–Sat 11am–5pm; June–Aug Tues–Sat 10am–8pm, Sun 10am–7pm; admission fee). After touring the museum there will be no question left unanswered about Baltic gold *(see page 322)*. Numerous pieces of amber contain particles of animal or vegetable life, which adss to their fascintion. Behind the mansion is a garden full of fragrant roses.

Also in the park is Birutė's Hill, the tallest point in town and on which a small chapel now stands. The hill is considered to be a former pagan shrine and the presence of a large oak – sacred in local pagan tradition – at the foot of the hill supports this theory. On the edge of the park sits one of the most famous statues in town, of the mythical Eglė. According to the legend, Eglė met an enchanted lake-living prince during a swim. The two married, had children and tried to live happily ever after in their lake. However, when Eglė brought her children to meet their grandparents her brothers killed her husband. In despair Eglė turned herself and her children into trees.

Another worthwhile stop is the Antanas Mončys House Museum (Daukanto 16; open Sept–May Thur–Sun noon–5pm; June–Aug Tues–Sun 3pm–9pm; admission fee). All the wooden pieces by the sculptor can be handled by visitors; in fact the artist requested this in his will.

No trip to Palanga in summer would be complete without a trip to the beach. Nudity is more common than not on public beaches, although in Palanga most tend to cluster around where the River Ràžė meets the sea, or further out towards Šventoji. **Šventoji ㉟**, 18 km (12 miles) north on the A13, is a quieter resort is. On the mouth of the small River Šventoji, it is famous for its sand dunes, beach and bogs. It is shown on Hansa maps and it became a resort at the beginning of the 20th century. A community of small cottages and simple houses, this is the place to go if you want peace and quiet.

Palanga Airport opened in 1939 and was the base of the Lithuanian Airforce. Today it offers direct flights to Scandinavia and Germany.

BELOW:
Nida lighthouse.

The Curonian Spit

The Curonian Spit, which is called Kuršių Nerija in Lithuanian, is named after the Curi who came here from Latvia. It was formed about 5,000 years ago and geologically it is the youngest part of the country. It has no rivers, a few lagoons and along its shore lies a chain of man-made beaches and dunes. A bird's-eye view is a wonderful picture of white, sandy hills against a dark blue background, and it was the sight of these extraordinary dunes that inspired the German naturalist Alexander von Humboldt to write in 1809: "Curonian Spit is such a peculiar place as Italy or Spain. One must see it to give pleasure to one's soul." It was made a Unesco World Heritage Site in 2000.

Winds formed the long, narrow coastal spit no more than a mile wide and 60 metres (200 ft) high. It runs 98 km (60 miles) from just north of Klaipėda down to

TIP

To rent a boat for the lagoon or for the open sea, with or without a skipper, contact the Klaipėda Yacht Club Smiltyne 25, Klaipėda (tel: 39 11 31).

Kaliningrad; 51 km (32 miles) of the spit are in Lithuania. The lagoon on the inland side is formed by the mouth of the Nemunas. On the tip of the spit opposite Klaipėda is **Smiltynė**, reached by regular ferries from the port. This is a popular spot, centred on Kopgalis Castle, where seals glide round the moat.

The Lithuanian Sea Museum (Lietuvos Jūrų muziejus; Smiltynė 3; open Oct–Apr Sat & Sun 10.30am–5.30pm; May & Sept Wed–Sun 10.30am–5.30pm; June–Aug Tues–Sun 10.30am–5.30pm; admission fee) is home to a number of seals, penguins and dolphins. The dolphin show is especially enjoyable for younger visitors. Nearby is Klaipėda Yacht Club, where every June a traditional sea festival takes place.

But most of the peninsula lies to the south, where tourist traffic is curtailed by a toll. All the little villages along here face the lagoon. Until 1992, the white sandy coast, now deserted, was occupied by the Soviet Army. Shifting sands have meant many of the villages have constantly been on the move. During the 18th and 19th centuries more than a dozen were affected, some of them covered over by sand. **Pervalka** and **Preila** are typical seaside communities with signs for *žuvis* (fish) and locals quietly going about their business. **Juodkrantė** is larger and has a harbour once known as Amber Cove because of the amount of the material that was dredged up for the local industry.

Also of note when driving through town is **Witches' Hill** (Raganų kalnas), which was established in the 1980s by a group of local sculptors. This large wooden sculpture park filled with fabled figures – such as the main pagan god, Perkūnas, and Neringa, a local girl who became a giant and helped sailors in trouble – is a pleasant excursion through the pine trees. This spot is especially appreciated by children, as some of the sculptures double as slides and see-

BELOW: making a splash in a safe sea.

saws. Look for the sign on your right as you are heading through town. A walk beside the lagoon path with its stone sculptures provides a pleasant contrast.

At the southern end of the spit, just before the border with Russian Kaliningrad, is **Nida** ❸❻, which has moved several times to escape the mobile sand. This is the largest of the resorts (pop. 1,500, rising to more than 10,000 in summer), with the best facilities. It is the sunniest and most famous place on the Lithuanian part of the peninsula.

Nida has a distinctive landscape, created by the wind and the sea. White sand dunes stretch away like a desert to the south, and trunks of trees show where ancient forests once flourished. It is known among Lithuanians as a place where the landscape forces you to take stock of your life. The area is fantastic and exploring the dunes is an integral part of any visit. Because of the fragile ecosystem, however, it is forbidden just to traipse through them. Instead, visitors are asked to walk through the forest at the end of Naglių to view them or to walk alongside the beach and then climb the steps.

Those who plan on visiting the area's beaches should pay particular attention to the signposting as some are women-only, others are men-only. According to local custom, however, men are allowed to cross women-only beaches if they are close to the water and not disruptive.

To find out more about local life, there is a small re-created fisherman's house (open May–Aug Tues–Sun 11am–5pm; admission fee) from the 19th century at Naglių 4. For some local shopping and further information, head for the Amber Museum and Gallery (Pamario 20; open 10am–7pm). Further along is the Neringa Historical Museum (Pamario 53; open Tues–Sat 10am–5pm; admission fee), which houses amber figures from the Stone Age as well as numerous exhi-

Map on pages 258–9

Note the signposts indicating that some beaches are for women only, some only for men, and others are for both. Men caught loitering on the women-only beaches will often be chastised and herded off by a group of half-naked grannies.

BELOW: Neringa Spit, a World Heritage Site.

bitions chronicling life on the spit. Thomas Mann lived in Nida for three consecutive summers between 1930 and 1933. There is a museum in the house he had specially built (Skruzdynės 17; open June–Sept daily 10am–6pm; Oct–May Tues–Sat 10am–5pm; admission fee). Information is in Lithuanian and German.

Lithuania's national bird is the stork, seen in large numbers from April to September. Every spring and autumn around a million birds of many species pass over the Nemunas delta.

The Nemunas delta

From Klaipėda Road 141 runs southeast through Šilutė and Pagėgiai, following the north bank of the Nemunas all the way to Kaunas. From the typical small town of **Priekulė** Road 221 goes south, past the fishing village of **Kintai**, as it enters the **Nemunas Delta Regional Park** (Nemuno Deltos Regioninis Parkas), an area of islands and waterways teaming with fish, and a main port of call for migrating birds. Among its typical fishing villages here are **Mingė**, the "Venice of Litjuania", where the River Minija serves as its main street, and **Skirvytėlė**, whose traditional houses are made of timber and reeds and include an ethnological farm museum here.

At the western edge of the designated park is the **Ventės Ragas Peninsula** ❸, marked by a lighthouse built in 1863. The main reason for coming to this backwater is the wildlife. An important bird-ringing centre, the Ventė Horn Ornithological Station, which keeps track of the many coastal migrants, has been operating here since 1929. It has vast bird-catching nets, which were used to some effect in the closing programme of Tiniklai, Lithuania's short-film festival, held here in 2001.

From Saugos the 141 falls down into the Nemunas delta plain, passing through **Šilutė** ❸ on the River Šyša. The town of Šilutė spent most of its time under German rule and was only integrated into Lithuania in 1923. Most of its

BELOW: Witches' Museum, Neringa.
RIGHT: a tidy house.

economy centres on textiles, livestock and machinery plants. The city has its own museum (Šilutės muziejus; Lietuvininkų 36; open Tues–Fri 9am–5pm, Sat 9am–4pm; admission fee), which displays a vast amount of ethnic costumes, weaponry, folk art and photographs.

In the village of **Macikai**, just off the 141 past Šilutė, a former concentration camp (1939–48) and later a KGB prison for Lithuanian dissidents was opened to the public in 1995. There are photographs and lists of prisoners along with their journals and drawings. The eerie and harrowing museum (open only 15 May–1 Oct Tues–Fri 10am–4pm, Sat 10am–3pm) is not suitable for youngsters.

Just west of Šilutė in the Nemunas delta is the 45-sq. km (17-sq. mile) **Rusnė Island ③**, which rises just 1.5 metres (5 ft) above sea level. It has a community of around 3,000 who earn a living by fishing and breeding cattle. South of the island is the town of **Rusnė**, the main town for the Nemunas Delta Regional Park, where you can find information on hiring boats and bikes. There is also an ethnographic farmstead (Skirvytėlės 8; open 15 May–15 Sept daily 10am–6pm; admission fee) which shows an authentic farm house of Lithuania Minor.

The next town of any size on the 141 is **Pagėgiai**, 38 km (22 miles) beyond Šilutė. During World War II, in the forest to the west behind a tangle of barbed-wire, the Germans kept prisoners of war under the open sky: 10,000 of them died. The ground is very hilly because the prisoners tried to bury themselves to escape the cold. From Pagėgiai the A12 (E77) goes 32 km (20 miles) northeast to **Tauragė**, which gave its name to the Tauragė Convention, signed in 1812 between General Yorch for Prussia and General Diebitsch for Russia in Požeronys Mill: a monument records the event. The A12 joins with the Kaunas-Klaipėda (A1) highway.

Map on pages 258–9

BELOW: still life in the lagoon.

North Zemaitija

One of the most interesting diversions in northern Žemaitija is the town of **Kretinga** ❹ (pop. 22,000). Although parts of the city are not particularly eye-catching, all is made up for by the Kretinga Museum (Kretingos muziejus; Vilnaus 20; open Wed–Sun 10am–6pm, Tues noon–6pm; admission fee). It is housed in a former mansion of Count Tiškevičius and has collections of numerous Žemaitija craftwork and articles belonging to the count and his family. There are also objects found from archaeological digs displayed in the cellar. The winter garden is perhaps one of the most spectacular displays in the area; it is covered by plants, many of which will have ladies tending to the dust on the leaves. The indoor non-smoking café only makes the experience better. The town, capital of the region, also has an important Franciscan monastery, founded in 1602. Concerts are sometimes given in its courtyard.

On the A11 (E272) between Kretinga and the next main town of Plungė is **Kartena** ❹ in the beautiful valley of the Minija. It has a 19th-century wooden church dedicated to the Assumption of the Virgin (Kretingos 4).

Before reaching Plungė an interesting diversion can be found by turning north on Route 169 towards Salantai. Here in the village of **Gargždelė** ❹ is the Orvydas Farmstead Museum (open daily sunrise–sunset; admission fee), a tribute to all things wacky, serious and religious. The owner, Vilius Orvydas, is part of the Lithuanian naive artist movement. This open-air museum is an arresting amount of stones, boulders, crosses and other pieces of art – many saved from Soviet destruction by the owner. An even more bizarre diversion is to be found further north in the town of **Mosėdis** ❹ at the Museum of Unique Rocks (Salantų 2; open May–Aug daily 8am–6pm; Sept–Apr 8am–noon & 1–5pm; admission

TIP

You can hunt, fish and go horse riding in Žemaitija National Park, or rent boats and catamarans from the yacht club in Plateliai.

BELOW:
a family outing.

fee), which is a collection of more than 20,000 boulders from all countries bordering the Baltic Sea. The point of this rock gathering may have most scratching their heads, but the sheer willpower inherent in this museum's existence does have a certain appeal. Interestingly, many of the rocks have not enjoyed their captivity and spilled out over the town.

Plungė ㊹ (pop 23,000) is a little larger than Kretinga and a centre of light industry and administration, with a long tradition of folk art. It became rich after the Oginskiai family arrived to buy up the local manor. They enlarged and cultivated the 18th-century "Thunder Oak" park still surrounding the manor today and in 1879 entrusted the architect Karl Lorens with the building of a neo-Renaissance palace imitating the 15th-century Palazzo Vecchio in Florence. In 1889 they also sponsored the education of the painter and musician M.K. Čiurlionis. Today the building is the Žemaitija Art Museum (Žemaičių dailės muziejus; Parko 1; open 15 May–Oct Wed–Sun 10am–6pm; Nov–15 May Wed–Sun 10am–5pm; admission fee), which houses mostly paintings executed by Samogitian artists either living in Lithuania or abroad. There is also a small area dedicated to the folk art of the region.

Zemaitija National Park

Due east of Salantai is **Plateliai**, the heart of the **Žemaitija National Park** and its main tourist information centre (Didžioji 10, www.zemaitijosnp.lt). Though 146 metres (480 ft) above sea level, there is a large lake beside it: Lake Plateliai is nearly 12 sq. km (5 sq. miles) in size and 46 metres (150 ft) deep and it has seven islands. There are boating facilities on its western side near the town, where there is an 18th-century wooden church and a ruined manor. Other attrac-

Map on pages 258–9

BELOW: Plateliai.

Map on pages 258–9

tive small towns in this region, which is rich with festivals and calendar customs, include Alsėdžiai and Seda and Žemaičių Kalvarija, a pretty village that has 10 days of pilgrimage celebration every July.

Telšiai is an industrial town with a population of 30,000, but before the war it was an important religious and cultural centre with a bishop's see and seminaries for priests and Jewish teachers. It still has a school of applied art and the Alka Museum of Žemaitija Culture, which is being renovated. A re-created Samogitian village covering 15 hectares (37 acres) can be found in Telšiai (Parko 8a; open May–Oct Wed–Sat 9am–5pm, Sun 10am–4pm; admission fee) and is a fun way to duck in and out of homes and see the tools and modes of living from the early part of the 20th century. The atmosphere is livelier and the amount of visitors larger during holidays.

On the southeast of the town is **Rainiai Forest** where 73 people were executed by the KGB in 1941; 50 years later a chapel was built in their remembrance. East from here is **Luokė**, famous for its folklore festivals, and **Lake Germantas**, where there are holiday facilities and an airfield for pleasure flights.

Place of pilgrimage

Šiauliai ⑮ (pop. 134,000), Lithuania's fourth-largest town, is an industrial centre of shoes, textiles and, notably, bicycles and there is a Bicycle Museum (Dviračių muziejus; Vilniaus 139; open Tues–Fri 10am–6pm, Sat 11am–4pm; admission fee). There is also a Museum of Photography and Radio (Radio ir Televizijos muziejus; Vilnaus 174; open Tues–Fri 10am–6pm, Sat 11am–4pm; admission fee). Another attraction in the town is Venklauskis House (Vytauto 89; open Tues–Fri 9am–5pm, Sat 11am–4pm; admission fee), the home of a lawyer who collected furniture and porcelain. Šiauliai's cathedral was rebuilt in 1954, as, like most other buildings in the town, it was flattened in World War II. Its spire is the tallest in the country.

BELOW: street corner in Šiauliai. **RIGHT:** the Hill of Crosses.

To the south are picturesque hills and lakes around **Bubiai** and **Kurtuvėnai**. Šiauliai is most famous for the **Hill of Crosses** ⑯ (Kryžių kalnas), which lies in the countryside about 14 km (9 miles) to the northeast on the A12 (E77). Nobody is sure of its origins, but for centuries it has been a religious site. People come from all over the world to add their crosses to the thousands already here. The sight is nothing short of awe-inspiring. The hill itself is only a small hump and it used to be much larger. This is because the Soviets bulldozed it three times, the first time in 1960, destroying an estimated 5,000 crosses. Each time they reappeared and today there are thousands of crosses, rosaries, pebbles, branches and other offerings.

The large statue of Jesus at the entrance was a present of Pope John Paul II during his visit in 1993. The Pope subsequently encouraged Italian Franciscans to build a monastery for Lithuanian novitiates, and this opened in 2001 on the north side of the hill. It is also open to pilgrims. A further convent, of St Clara, is planned. The annual pilgrimage to the hill takes place on the third Sunday in July. ❑

In this ever changing world,
Singapore Girl, you're a great way to fly.

SINGAPORE
AIRLINES

A STAR ALLIANCE MEMBER

First to Fly **A380** in 2006

singaporeair.com

BANGKOK · TOKYO · AMSTERDAM · AUCKLAND · NEW DELHI · LOS ANGELES · OVER 55 MAJOR CITIES

TRAVEL TIPS

GETTING THERE AND GETTING AROUND

By Air

Estonia

The national carrier, Estonian Air, and the discount airline easyJet.com both offer direct service from London. Other airlines such as SAS and Finnair offer flights that connect through Copenhagen and Helsinki, though these routes are usually more expensive. CSA, the Czech airline, flies to all three capitals from Glasgow, Manchester, Birmingham and London via Prague. If all else fails, you can try to find a cheap flight to Helsinki and take a ferry south to Tallinn.

Tallinn Airport (TLL) is one of Europe's most modern. With just six gates, it is also one of Europe's smallest, which means it's easy to find your way around, and you can be out of the door almost immediately after you leave the plane.

Taxis and buses wait just outside the arrivals area's main door. The airport is remarkably close to the centre of the capital, and a taxi can take as little as 10 minutes. The fare should be around 70–80kr. City bus No. 2, which will take you to a stop next to the Viru shopping mall in the centre, departs from the airport roughly every 20–30 minutes. Its timetable is posted under the blue-and-white bus sign outside. The journey takes about 10 minutes and costs 15kr. Pay the conductor as you board or buy tickets at the airport shop for 10kr, or 85kr for a book of 10.

The helicopter is also an option for those coming via Finland. Copterline offers an hourly service from the

Hernesaari port near downtown Helsinki to Tallinn's Linnahall. The trip takes only 18 minutes, and boarding/disembarking is quite fast.

Latvia

The national carrier airBaltic is partially owned by Scandinavian Airlines-SAS, its representative abroad. The airline offers affordable direct flights to Rīga from London, Manchester, Dublin, Brussels, Berlin, Stockholm and several other cities in Europe.

Ryanair www.ryanair.com also flies direct from the UK to Rīga and booking is by internet only. Uzbekistan Air operates the only direct flight to Rīga from New York twice weekly.

Rīga International Airport (RIX) is a shiny modern complex 8 km (5 miles) outside the city centre and is easily accessed by taxi or bus. Flights arrive and depart from only three small terminals, so getting lost is impossible. In addition to airBaltic, Rīga is served by Aeroflot, and several other major European airlines, as well as easyJet and Ryanair. For more information visit www.riga-airport.com.

A queue of reputable taxis is always available outside and the trip to the city centre takes roughly 20 minutes and should cost no more than 7Ls. The only other option is the bus that picks up passengers on the far side of the car park when leaving the arrivals hall. Tickets are 0.20Ls, and another may be required for luggage.

Lithuania

The Lithuanian national carrier Lietuvos avialinijos, or FlyLAL (LAL on the website), offers direct flights to and from some major European

points of departure, including London, Dublin, Paris, Frankfurt, Copenhagen, Stockholm and Warsaw. Air Baltic and BA fly from Gatwick.

Vilnius International Airport (VNO) is 5 km (3 miles) south of the capital. The cheapest way into town is bus No. 1 to the train station or No. 2, which stops at both Gedimino and Konstitucijos avenues. Both can be picked up right outside the arrivals hall. For one litas more you can also take minibus Nos 15, 21, 23 or 47, all of which stop in the city centre on Gedimino. Bus drivers will not speak English.

The easiest and fastest way is to hail a taxi from the ranks outside. Your trip into the centre should not cost you more than 30Lt under any circumstances, and should usually be about 20Lt. To ensure that your ride is what it should be, call a taxi. Two companies with good reputations and the occasional English-speaking operator are Martono taksi (tel: 240 00 44) and Vilniaus taxi (tel: 212 88 88).

From outside Europe

The only direct flight to the Baltic states from outside Europe is from New York to Rīga, so in most cases you must link with one of the carriers from the Baltic states (see panel) or from neighbouring countries: Aeroflot, British Airways, Czech Ailrlines, Finnair, KLM, Lufthansa, LOT Polish Airlines or Scandinavian Airlines-SAS. Connections from the US are possible with SAS, Finnair, Uzbekistan Air, American Airlines, Continental Airlines, Delta Airlines, Northwest Airlines and United Airlines, although many will require at least two stop-overs. From Australia and New Zealand it is cheapest to fly to London and connect to a budget flight.

Flight Contacts

Estonia

Tallinn airport
Tel: (+372) 6058 888
www.tallinn-airport.ee
Estonian Air
Tel: (+372) 6 401 233 160
www.estonian-air.ee
UK Ticket Office, London.
Tel: 020-7333 0196
Email: lon@maersk-air.com
Gatwick Airport: Skybreak
(Departure Hall, Zone H)
Tel: 01293 555 700
Email: reps@skybreak.co.uk
In US. Tel: 1-800-397-1354
Email: us@estonian-air.ee
Copterline (Helsinki)
Tel: +358 (0)200 19191
www.copterline.com

Latvia

Rīga airport
Tel: (+371) 720 7009
www.riga-airport.com
AirBaltic
www.airbaltic.com
85a Elizabetes Street, Rīga
Tel: (+371) 900 6006
Fax: (+371) 722 4282
AirBaltic is represented by SAS
Scandinavian Airlines abroad.
In UK: Tel: 0870 600727.

Lithuania

Vilnius airport
Tel: (+370) 5203 6666
www.vilnius-airport.lt
LAL (Lietuvos avialinijos)
Tel: (+370) 5275 2588
Fax: (+370) 5272 4852
www.lal.lt
In UK: Gatwick Airport
Tel: 01293-579900
Email: info-greatbritain@lal.lt
Heathrow Airport:
Tel: 020-8759 7323

UK Airlines

Easyjet www.easyjet.com
Ryanair www.ryanair.com
British Airways, tel: 0870-8509850
www.britishairways.com

By Rail

There are some new local first-class trains, such as the three-times daily train from Tallin to Tartu (free tea/coffee, computer access) but services through the region tend to be cumbersome, with a change of trains in the border towns. For long-distances travel, however, trains can provide a far better level of comfort than road transport and a greater chance of getting some sleep. A luxury express train from Berlin to St

Petersburg has been talked about for years but has yet to come to fruition.
Estonia There is an overnight train from Tallinn to Moscow. Contact: EVR Express, Tallinn Train Station, Toompuiestee 37, tel: 6156 722. Email: evrexpress@evrexpress.ee; www.evrexpress.ee.
Latvia There are two daily convenient and comfortable overnight trains from Moscow to Rīga and one from St Petersburg. For more information contact: Latvian Railways, tel: 723 1181, www.ldz.lv.
Lithuania Lietuvos Gele7+inkeliai, the Lithuanian rail network, connects with Poland and Germany. Train timetables and other useful information in English can be viewed on the Lithuanian rail website, www.litrail.lt.

By Car

At the borders you will be asked to show a valid driver's licence, vehicle registration and/or ownership documents and a Green Card extending your regular car insurance. Vehicles are required to carry a fluorescent warning triangle, fire extinguisher and first-aid kit. You must also have a national identity sticker on the rear of your vehicle. Breakdown insurance is advisable; consult your insurer before travelling.

The three counties are linked by the Via Baltica (E-67), the main highway that runs 670 km (416 miles) from the Lithuanian border with Poland to Tallinn.

Customs posts at the borders should present no problems to visitors, and the roads are generally good. High-grade petrol is available and garages also sell maps (Regio produce good maps for Estonia, Jana Seta for Latvia and Lithuania), which are essential for getting around.

There are a number of hotels and rest stops en route.

The speed limit on motorways is 90 kph (55 mph) and 60 kph (37 mph) in residential areas.

Headlights must be turned on all the time.

See Rules of the Road, page 338.

By Bus

Travelling by bus can be significantly cheaper and faster than travelling by train. From London, Eurolines (www.eurolines.com) offers a service from numerous destinations in Europe to the major Baltic cities and are the main means of transport between the countries.

By Sea

Estonia

In summer, dozens of ships make the quick, 85-km (53-mile) crossing from Helsinki to Tallinn throughout the day, and larger ferries bring in passengers from other cities across the Baltic. There are several hydrofoils making regular crossings from Helsinki to Tallinn with a journey time of between one and two hours depending on the particular craft and the weather. In winter, the route is restricted to ferries, which take between three and four hours. Overnight ferries make slow but inexpensive connections from Stockholm.

Tallinn harbour *(sadam)* is a 15-minute walk from the Old Town. On trams 1 or 2 coming from the Old Town or the centre, the harbour is the next stop after Mere Puiestee, or from the opposite direction, two stops after the railway station.
Main operators:
Nordic Jet Line, Kanavaterminaali K5, PL 134, Helsinki, tel: (+358) 0 9 681 770; and Passenger Port, C-Terminal, Tallinn, tel: 6137 000; www.njl.ee. Large catamarans from Helsinki to Tallinn.
Silja Line, Mannerheimintie 2, Helsinki, tel: (+358) 0 918 041, fax: (+358) 0 9 180 4279; and Passenger Port, C-Terminal, Tallinn, tel: 6116 661; www.silja.ee. Regular Helsinki-Tallinn service; overnight services from Rostok to Tallinn in summer.
Tallink, Erottajankatu 19, Helsinki, tel: (+358) 0 9 228 311; and A. Laikmaa 5, Tallinn, tel: 6409 808; fax: 6409 815; www.tallink.ee. Numerous daily express services and larger ferries from Helsinki to Tallinn; overnight services from Stockholm to Tallinn.
Viking Line, Mannerheimintie 14, Helsinki, tel: (+358) 9 12 351; and Ahtri 12, Tallinn, tel: 6663 966; www.vikingline.fi. Viking Line operates ferries from Stockholm to Helsinki, and Helsinki to Tallinn.

Latvia

The Regina Battica ferry departs from Rīga to Stockholm every other day. For more information visit www.tallink.lv. Ferries from Rīga to Rostock and Lübeck in Germany depart twice weekly. The cities of Nynashamn (near Stockholm) and Karlshamn, Sweden as well as Lübeck and Travemunde in Germany are serviced by regular ferries from the western Latvian cities of Liepāja and Ventspils. There is a service from Ventspils to Saaremaa in

Estonia. Tallinn and Rīga are major ports of call on Baltic cruises.
The main operators are:
DFDS Tor Line, Zivju 1, tel: 735 3523, <www.dfdstorline.com>. Passenger and cargo service between Riga and Lubeck, Germany.
Scandlines, Ventspils, Plostu 7, tel: 360 7358, <www.scandlines.lv>. Passenger and cargo links from Ventspils to Rostock, Germany, Karlshamn, Sweden and Nynashamn, Sweden (60 km/37 miles from Stockholm).
Tallink, Eksporta 3a, tel. 709 9700, <www.tallink.lv>. Regular ferry service between Riga and Stockholm, via the Estonian island of Saaremaa.

Lithuania

Several ferry lines link the Lithuanian port of Klaipėda to Kiel and Sassnitz/Mukran (the shortest sea route from Germany, covering the 520 km/325 miles in less than a day), Åhus in Sweden and Åbenrå and Århus in Denmark.
The main operators are:
DFDS Tor Line, tel: (+370) 46 496 446, fax: (+370) 46 496 498, www.dfdstorline.com. Klaipėda to Copenhagen and Fredericia in Denmark. The company also owns **Lisco Baltic Service**, tel: (+370) 46 393 600, www.lisco.lt, which operates from Klaipėda to Mukran and Karlshamn in Sweden.
Krantas Shipping, Pylimo 4, Vilnius, tel: (+370) 5 231 3314; and Teatro Square 5, Klaipėda, tel: (+370) 46 395 211. Regular sailings to Keil and Sassnitz/Mukran, Germany. The company also acts as local agents for ferries to Kiel and Karlshamn in Sweden and Åbenrå and Århus in Denmark.

Tour Operators

Because of the special rates they enjoy from airlines and hotels, prices for holidays booked through tour operators should cost little or no more than those booked direct.
Baltic Holidays
Individual and group arrangements. 40 Princess St, Manchester M1 6DE, tel: 0870-757 9233, www.balticholidays.com.
Martin Randall Travel
A regular programme of group tours specialising in art, architecture and music festivals.
Voysey House, Barley Mow Passage, London W4 4GF, tel: 020-8742 3355, www.martinrandall.com.
Naturetrek
Specialists for bird-watching tours in the Baltics.
Cheriton Mill, Cheriton, Alresford,

Hants SO24 ONG, tel: 01962-733051, www.naturetrek.co.uk
Operas Abroad
Individual arrangements to opera and musical concerts; part of Regent Holidays. www.operasabroad.com
Regent Holidays
Specialists in the Baltic states since 1992, both with group tours and individuals. They also organise city breaks throughout the year.
15 John Street, Bristol BS1 2HR, tel: 0117-921 1711, www.regent-holidays.co.uk.

Entry Requirements

Citizens of the EU, US, Canada, Australia and New Zealand need only a valid passport. Citizens of South Africa need a visa to visit the Baltic states, but can enter Estonia if they have a valid visa for Latvia or Lithuania.

Customs & Export

Individuals entering and leaving the Baltic states may carry with them most articles, personal property and other valuables in unlimited quantities. However, weapons and ammunition of any kind, drugs and psychotropic substances are not allowed. Lithuania also forbids the import of meat, dairy products, eggs and sausages and the export of more than 10 kg of fresh and 5 kg of dried mushrooms or berries.

GETTING AROUND

Public Transport

Estonia

A system of **buses, trams** and **electric trolleybuses** makes up Tallinn's public transit system. The trams mainly service the centre of town whereas the buses are for reaching outlying areas. Detailed maps posted on most bus stops will show you how to make your journey. (You can also buy good transport maps published by Regio.) All three modes of transit use the same ticket, available from a kiosk for 10kr (a book of 10 is 85kr), which you must punch after you board. Each ticket is good for one ride.
Taxis The biggest complaint among tourists in Tallinn is taxi drivers who overcharge. Even locals have the same difficulty. Most of the city is walkable, but if you do need a taxi, it is best to order one by phone. Dispatchers at Linnatakso, tel: 1242, and Tulika Takso, tel: 1200, usually speak some English. Standard rates

for taxis are 10–35kr starting fee, then 7kr/km. If in doubt, ask a driver for an estimate before starting out.
Buses Long-distance buses are the most convenient and widely used method of getting from city to city in Estonia. In Tallinn, the bus station is located at Lastekodu 46, tel: 6800 900. Bussireisid has complete bus timetables in English on its website, www.bussireisid.ee. It also offers online booking.
Internal flights The private Avies air company offers regular services to Kuressaare on Saaremaa six days a week and to Kärdla on Hiiumaa five days a week.
Avies: Tallinn Airport, tel: 6058 022, www.avies.ee.

Latvia

All public transport in Rīga, including **trams**, **buses**, and **trolleybuses**, costs a flat fee of 0.20Ls for the duration of your trip, regardless of how far you travel. If you get off a tram and hop on the next available one you will have to pay for another ticket. Large pieces of luggage as well as bicycles may be subject to an additional 0.20Ls. Tickets are purchased from the conductors on board who run around like madmen trying to check if everyone has paid in full. For more information in English visit the Tram and Trolleybus Authority's excellent site, www.ttp.lv.
Minibuses called *mikroautobusi*, or *mikriņi* for short, can also be a convenient way of travelling as they will stop at any point along a given route, and are a fast way of getting

BELOW: tourist transport, Tallinn.

TRANSPORT

around, though they are often packed.

Trams Electric trams have been in use in Rīga since 1901. Today, there are 11 different tram lines numbered 1–11, which operate from 5.30am to midnight, and night trams are in service roughly every hour on weekend nights. There are also 21 trolleybus routes for which the same rules for trams apply.

Taxis Rīga's taxis should charge the official tariff, which is 0.40Ls for pick up and 0.30Ls per each additional kilometre during the day or 0.60Ls plus an additional 0.40Ls per kilometre between midnight and 6am. Rīga Taxi, tel: 800 10 10, and Rīgas Taksometru Parks, tel: 800 13 13, are highly regarded and will pick up passengers anywhere in Rīga. Their numbers are toll-free and they won't start the meter until you have boarded their vehicle, even if they had to drive across town to pick you up. You can also wave down taxis on any street.

All official taxis in Latvia have a yellow number plate, run meters and will print out a receipt. Tips are expected.

Internal flights Air Baltic offers only one domestic destination, Liepāja, and only during the summer months.

Lithuania

Public transport has never been the most pleasant part of a stay in Vilnius but the smelly old buses and trolleybuses have now largely been replaced. Most systems operate from 5.30am–11pm, so late-night travel is by foot or taxi. Public transport is, however, inexpensive and covers most of the city, excluding the Old Town.

City buses The newer-looking buses are state-owned. Tickets can be purchased at a *Lietuva spauda* kiosk (0.80lt) or on board the bus (1lt). Once on the bus you must validate your ticket in one of the boxes provided. Failure to do so will result in a fine by the ticket inspectors who constantly patrol. Private bus company tickets can only be bought onboard buses.

Trolleybuses Riding a trolleybus in Vilnius is the easiest way to travel back in time to the Soviet era. As on the city's buses, tickets can be purchased on board or from *Lietuva spauda* kiosks, but must be validated on board.

Microbuses This is the newest and cleanest form of transport through the city. Microbus routes are subject to change as they are privately owned and operated. Most have signs in their front windows giving a general

Car Rental Firms

Tallinn

Avis: at the airport, tel: 6058 222; in the city at Liivalaia 13/15, tel: 6671 500; www.avis.ee.
Budget: at the airport, tel: 6058 600; www.budget.ee.
Hertz: at the airport, tel: 6058 923; in the city at Ahtri 12, tel: 6116 333; www.hertz.ee.
R-Rent: at the airport, tel: 6058 929; in the city at Rävala pst. 4, tel: 6612 400; www.rrent.ee.
Sir Rent: Juhkentali 11, tel: 6614 353; www.sirrent.ee.
Sixt: at the airport, tel: 6058 148; in the city at Rävala 5, tel: 6133 660; www.sixt.ee.

Riga

Avis: at the airport, tel: 720 73 53; in the city at Krasta 3, tel: 722 58 76, fax: 782 04 41; www.avis.lv.
Baltic Car Lease: at the airport, tel: 720 71 21, fax: 720 71 31; in the city at Kaļķu 28 (Hotel de Rome), tel: 722 40 22; www.e-sixt.lv.
Budget Rent A Car: at the airport,

tel: 720 73 27, fax: 720 70 27; www.budget.lv.
Europcar: at the airport, tel: 720 78 25; in the city at Basteja bulvāris 10, tel: 721 26 52, fax: 782 03 60; www.europcar.lv.
Hertz: at the airport, tel: 720 79 80, fax: 720 79 81; in the city at Aspazijas bulvāris 24, tel: 722 42 23; www.hertz.lv.
National Car Rental: at the airport, tel: 720 77 10.

Lithuania

Avis: at the airport, tel: 232 93 16, fax: 232 93 16; www.avis.com.
Budget: at the airport, tel: 230 67 08, fax: 230 67 09; www.budget.com.
Europcar: at the airport, tel/fax: 216 34 42; in the city at Stuokos-Gucevižiaus 9-1, tel: 212 02 07, fax: 212 04 39; www.europcar.lt.
Hertz: at the airport, tel/fax: 232 93 01; in the city at Kalvarijų 14, tel: 272 69 40, fax: 272 69 70; www.hertz.com.
Sixt: at the airport, tel: 239 56 36, fax: 239 56 35; www.sixt.lt.

idea of their trajectory. To get on one, just flag it down, get in, sit down and tell the driver where you would like to be dropped off. As no one usually speaks English, it is best to have decent Lithuanian pronunciation skills or have your destination written down *(see Language, page 373)*.

Taxis Generally, taxi drivers will not take advantage of foreigners as long as they seem to be vigilant. Most horror stories of inflated taxi prices occur when foreigners are inebriated or when the meter clicks away at a super-fast rate and goes unnoticed until the arrival at the destination. Your best bet for not getting ripped off is merely to pay attention to your surroundings. If possible, always try to call for a taxi instead of hailing one off the street as the price will be significantly cheaper.

Two reputable firms that occasionally have English-speakers on their staff are Martono taksi (tel: 240 00 44) and Vilniaus taxi (tel: 212 88 88).

Long-distance buses Buses are more popular than trains for most domestic destinations. The bus station is at Sodų 22, www.toks.lt, across from the train station.

Trains Tickets can be purchased at the train station, www.litrail.lt, located at Geležinkelio 16. On overnight trains to Russia or Belarus there are three different classes of tickets. The cheapest is *obschii*, which is a

sitting place only. *Platzkart* is a bed in a four-person compartment and *coupe* is a softer bed in a four-person compartment with a door that locks. Women travelling alone should be aware that it is not uncommon for them to end up in a *coupe* with three men overnight, although a word in the ear of the train compartment manager once on board can sometimes result in the sleeping arrangements being changed. Only two routes within Lithuania have first and second class – Vilnius–Klaipėda and Vilnius–Šiauliai.

Internal flights In summer, LAL operates flights between Vilnius and Palanga, the seaside resort near the port of Klaipėda. Kaunas-based Air Lithuania operates international flights from Kaunas to Cologne and Hamburg (Germany), Billund (Denmark), Kristianstad and Malmö (Sweden) and Oslo (Norway) via Palanga. Air Lithuania, Kastučio 69, tel: 22 97 06; fax 22 85 04; www.airlithuania.lt.

Car Rental

Renting a car is generally the best way to explore the three countries. Hiring a car is simple and relatively inexpensive. You must be at least 21 years of age and must possess a valid driving licence, passport and major credit card, and must have had

ACCOMMODATION · EATING OUT · ACTIVITIES · A - Z · LANGUAGE

a licence for at least two years. Most of the major international rental agencies operate in the cities and have desks at the airports. In most cases cars can be delivered to your hotel.

Cars with automatic transmission are a rarity, as is air conditioning, and should be requested in advance. Mileage is unlimited but renters are expected to fill the tank just before returning the car. Otherwise a top-up fee will be added to the bill, along with the price of the fuel. Prices in comparison tend to be lower than in Western Europe and the US. Pricing structures are the same as in most countries with added fees for an additional driver, insurance, mileage and the like. If you plan to take your rental car outside the country, you will need special documents for the border. However, many rental companies have special deals even for one-way travel within all three Baltic states.

Driving

Road conditions vary from good to poor. Estonians drivers range from the careless to the aggressive, while Latvians are not above passing on blind turns or suddenly driving in the opposite lane of oncoming traffic to avoid a pothole. Your only recourse is to drive

Take it Easy

Latvia has the highest proportion of road-accident casualties in Europe with around 44,000 traffic accidents each year in which nearly 7,000 are injured and around 500 killed. With a population of just over 2.3 million, 800,000 in Rīga, the statistics are staggering.

defensively. Weather is an issue, particularly in winter when patches of ice appear on roads. If you don't know how to drive in winter conditions, this is not the place to learn.

Also, because markings on rural routes can often be confusing, a good road atlas is essential.

Parking

Parking in the centre of the three capitals can be a battle. Most street parking is paid parking and tickets are sold in vending machines

In **Tallinn** car parks can be found downtown on Freedom Square (Vabaduse väljak), on Rävala 5, and at the corner of Maakri and Rävala. The cost is typically 20kr/h.

To enter **Old Rīga** via its many automated checkpoints, you must first purchase a plastic entry card with a magnetic strip called a *viedkarte* available at Statoil petrol stations or at Parex Bank, smilšu 3. Open 9.30am–8.30pm, Sat, Sun 9am–8pm. Entry fees are a steep 5Ls per hour. For more information visit www.satdep.lv. Once in the old city you can park at any kerb not painted yellow. Rīga has plenty of guarded and multi-storey car parks.

Parking in **Vilnius** is paid by the hour, 8am–8pm Mon–Sat. In Vilnius there are human ticket takers, tickets should be displayed on the dashboard along with a marking clock (usually provided by car-hire companies) or a note indicating the time you parked.

Some **national parks** and the Latvian seaside of Jūrmala charge drivers a small entrance fee.

Rules of the Road

Traffic signs and symbols follow the European standard.
● Drive on the right and overtake on the left.

In Case of a Breakdown

Estonia: call the Estonian Automobile Club, tel: 1888, for 24-hour towing services.
Latvia: LAMB, tel: 800 0000, offers a 24-hour service
Lithuania: Mototuras (tel: 880 000 000, www.mototuras.lt), a private company opened by the Lithuanian Automobile Association (LAS), provides emergency road-side assistance.

● Headlights must be kept on at all times, day and night, even in the city.
● Passengers in both front seats must wear seatbelts at all times; on the highway, the same rule applies to backseat passengers.
● Children under 12 are not allowed in the front seat.
● Winter tyres must be used from October to April.
● The use of mobile phones by drivers is prohibited without hands-free equipment.
● Drivers are considered under the influence and therefore subject to arrest if they have a 0.4 percent alcohol level in their blood – about a half litre of beer. It is best not to drink at all if you are driving.
● The basic speed limit outside built-up areas is 90 km/h (55 mph), in built-up areas 50–60 km/h (31–37 mph), and in residential areas 20 km/h (13 mph). Some roads are marked with their own limits, particularly large motorways, where cars are permitted to go 110 km/h (69 mph) in summer. On the Vilnius-Kaunas motorway speed limits are 100 km/h (62 mph). On all other Lithuanian motorways the limits from 1 October to 1 April are 110 km/h (68 mph) and during the rest of the year 130 km/h (80 mph).
● Drivers must have a valid driving licence and car documents with them at all times.

Police are stationed at most major thoroughfares and most drivers opt to pay their fines in cash on the spot in order to avoid having to go to a particular police station to pay the fine. Even if you are driving by lakes and forests, the town's limits extend up to the point where the sign of the town with a cross through it stands. Often police will have speed traps in these non-populated areas that are still within the town or city limits. Fines may also be imposed on drivers who fail to stop at pedestrian crossings.

If you have an accident, you are not supposed to move your vehicle until the police have arrived.

BELOW: biking is easy in countries where there are so few hills.

A CCOMMODATION

HOTELS, SPAS, HOSTELS, BED & BREAKFASTS

There have been a large number of three- and four-star hotels built throughout the region from around the turn of the millennium and all three capitals offer a choice of world class hotels, with stylish rooms, in-room Internet connections, business centres, top-notch restaurants and other luxury amenities, including health spas

and saunas, both of which are specialities of the Baltics. Most larger hotels also have rooms or entire floors designated for non-smokers, as well as rooms equipped for disabled guests. A growing number of cosy boutique hotels, often built into refurbished Old Town buildings and rural manor houses, offer the same level of luxury in a

more intimate environment. Hotels in smaller cities and the countryside tend to be more basic, but even here, standards of quality are usually at Western European levels. Travellers on a tight budget should consider bed & breakfast, home stay, or tourist farm accommodation. All hotels take credit cards unless otherwise noted.

ACCOMMODATION LISTINGS

ESTONIA

The first rule of Estonian travel is: book early. Hotels in Tallinn, Pärnu, Kuressaare and other popular destinations fill up during the high season (May to August). Tallinn offers the best range of hotels, from medieval-style luxury to millennium-era cracker boxes, and some have sauna and spa treatment facilities, too. With such a range of accommodation, most travellers are happy to stay in hotels, but anyone spending any length of time in the capital, renting a flat is worth considering; an increasing number of firms specialise in rentals. Anyone visiting Tallinn on a tight budget should first try to find space in one the few Old Town guesthouses and hostels, then look to the outskirts for super-cheap accommodation.

Prices for rooms elsewhere in Estonia are

usually drastically lower, but even here there are ways to economise.

Tourist farms (rural B&Bs) offer simple double rooms at hostel prices, though your hosts may not speak English. Many tourist farms, and even a few guesthouses in the city suburbs, will also let you pitch a tent in their yard – and use their facilities – for a small fee.

A database listing every registered accommodation facility in Estonia, with prices and links to web pages, can be found at the Tourism Board's website: www.visitestonia.com. Rooms in private homes in Tallinn, Tartu, Pärnu and Viljandi can be booked through Rasastra (tel: 6616 291, www.bedbreakfast.ee).

Campers should note that at Estonia's official "Kämping" sites you won't even need a tent. These are typically patches of

forest filled with simple little camp huts. All you need is a sleeping bag and lots of mosquito repellent.

HOTELS

Tallinn

Barons
Suur-Karja 7/Väike-Karja 2
Tel: 6999 700
Fax: 6999 710
barons@baronshotel.ee
www.baronshotel.ee
Steeped with elegance, this small luxury hotel is housed in a 1912-era bank building and with original vaults. Amenities include Internet connection, mini-bar, hairdryer, bathrobe and slippers. €€€€
City Hotel Portus
Uus-Sadama 23
Tel: 6806 600
Fax: 6806 601
tallinnhotels@tallinnhotels.ee
www.tallinnhotels.ee

Located in the passenger port area, this modern, 107-room hotel offers colourful rooms and an overall cheerful ambience. Plusses include free WiFi, free parking, a kids' playroom and a retro-style café. €€
Domina City
Vana-Posti 11
Tel: 6813 900
Fax: 6813 901
city@domina.ee

PRICE CATEGORIES

Price ratings, which are given as a guide only, reflect the price of a double room for one night. These are the ratings of the researcher and are not related to the official star ratings issued by the tourist office:
€€€€ = over 2,500kr
€€€ = 1,500–2,500kr
€€ = 750–1,500kr
€ = below 750kr

TRANSPORT
ACCOMMODATION
EATING OUT
ACTIVITIES
A – Z
LANGUAGE

www.dominahotels.ee
A chic, Italian-owned establishment in Old Town with marble columns and grand chandeliers. Rooms are decorated in a smart, old-fashioned style, but each comes with its own computer and high-speed Internet connection. €€€
Imperial
Nunne 14
Tel: 6274 800
Fax: 6274 801
info@imperial.ee
www.imperial.e
Part of the city's medieval wall runs right through this 19th-century building, but the Imperial creates most of its historic ambience with the exposed brick and antique photos. Pride and joy is a magnificent, old-fashioned pub. €€€
Meriton Grand Hotel Tallinn
Toompuiestee 27
Tel: 6677 000
Fax: 6677 555
grandhotel@meritonhotels.com
www.meriton.ee
Considered one of Tallinn's finest, the Grand is in easy walking distance of the main sights and has some excellent views of nearby Toompea Castle. It also has a top-notch restaurant and a busy café. €€€
Meriton Old Town Hotel
Lai 49
Tel: 6141 300
Fax: 6141 311
oldtown@meritonhotels.com
www.meriton.ee
Good-value hotel, built into a 19th-century office building at the edge of Old Town. Rooms are cramped, but decor is cheerful, and lobby cleverly incorporates part of the old city wall. €€
OldHouse Guesthouse/ OldHouse Hostel
Uus 22/Uus 26
Tel: 6411 464
Fax: 6411 604
info@oldhouse.ee
www.oldhouse.ee
Both the guesthouse and hostel offer a handful of simple, modern single and double rooms, as well as larger "dorm-style" rooms, all with shared baths. Price includes breakfast and use of guest kitchen. €
Peoleo
Pänu mnt. 555, Laagri

Tel: 6503 965
Fax: 6503 900
hotel@peoleo.ee
www.peoleo.ee
This roadside hotel on the Pärnu highway 15 km (9 miles) from the centre of Tallinn offers economy rooms, as well as facilities for those who want to park a caravan or to pitch a tent. €€
Radisson SAS
Rävala pst. 3
Tel: 6823 000
Fax: 6823 001
tallinn@radissonsas.com
www.radissonsas.com
Everything one would expect from a world-class chain hotel. A five-minute walk from Old Town, the building is one of the city's tallest; request a room on the town side for the best views. €€€
Reval Hotel Olümpia
Liivalaia 33
Tel: 6315 333
Fax: 6315 325
olympia.sales@revalhotels.com
www.revalhotels.com
Contemporary four-star monolith offering business facilities, a comfortable restaurant, lunch café, English-style pub, and nightclub. €€€
Schlössle
Pühavaimu 13/15
Tel: 6997 700
Fax: 6997 777
schlossle.reservations@schlossle-hotels.com
www.schlossle-hotels.com
Impressive ambience and impeccable service. Ancient stone and heavy wooden beams give the lobby its medieval look, while rooms are furnished in a lavish, antique style. €€€€
Scandic Palace
Vabaduse väljak 3
Tel: 6407 300
Fax: 6407 299
palace@scandic-hotels.com
www.scandic-hotels.com
1930s-style class has worked its way into every corner of this historic building. Few can beat its location or welcoming lobby bar. It has a sauna, conference facilities and, in some rooms, air conditioning. €€€€
Sokos Viru Hotel
Viru väljak 4
Tel: 6809 300

Fax: 6809 236
viru.reservation@sok.fi
www.viru.ee
Tallinn's most famous Soviet-era high-rise hotel has evolved into a quality, international-style establishment popular with Finns. Adjacent to Old Town and attached to downtown's largest shopping complex. €€€
St Petersbourg
Rataskaevu 7
Tel: 6286 500
Fax: 6286 565
stpetersbourg.reservations@schlossle-hotels.com
www.schlossle-hotels.com
Run by the same group as the Schlössle (above), this hotel spoils its guests with similar, old-fashioned comforts, with upmarket Russian restaurant and a simpler Estonian restaurant. Rooms are on the small side. €€€€
The Three Sisters
Pikk 71/Tolli 2
Tel: 6306 300
Fax: 6306 301
info@threesistershotel.com
www.threesistershotel.com
Built inside Tallinn's famous Three Sisters, a trio of 14–15th-century houses, this five-star hotel offers unmatched lavishness from the candles in the lobby chandelier to the amazing room decor. €€€€
Uniquestay
Paldiski mnt. 1
Tel: 6600 700
Fax: 6616 176
info@uniquestay.com
www.uniquestay.com
A trendy hotel in two brick buildings not far from Toompea Castle. Guests can opt for pricier "Zen" rooms with NASA-designed gravity free chairs and aromatherapy. €€
Viimsi Tervis Spa Hotell
Randvere tee 11, Viimsi
Tel: 6061 000
Fax: 6061 010
viimsitervis@viimsitervis.ee
www.viimsitervis.ee
Nestling the bay in Viimsi, 20 minutes by taxi from central Tallinn, Viimsi Tervis is a spa hotel offering beauty packages, plastic surgery and a full range of health and hotel services. €€

Haapsalu

Fra Mare
Ranna tee 2
Tel: 4724 600
Fax: 4724 601
framare@framare.ee
www.framare.ee
Haapsalu's best-equipped hotel is beside the town's swimming beach. The 72-room facility offers modern accommodation, spa-treatment packages, beauty parlour, restaurant and a seawater pool. €€
Kongo
Kalda 19
Tel: 4724 800
Fax: 4724 809
kongohotel@hot.ee
www.kongohotel.ee
A cosy, 21-room hotel in the quaint wooden-house district of Haapsalu. The location, near the castle and city attractions, is a plus, as are the restaurant and sauna. €€
Promenaadi
Sadama 22
Tel/fax: 4737 250
hotell@promenaadi.ee
www.promenaadi.ee
Part new and part built into a 19th-century villa, Promenaadi offers decent rooms and a restaurant café overlooking the waterfront. €€

Kuressaare

Arensburg
Lossi 15
Tel: 4524 700
Fax: 4524 727
terje@tt.ee
www.sivainvest.ee
Built in 2002, this 25-room hotel has cheerful pink and green rooms, sauna and restaurant (with wireless Internet), in an historic building in the heart of Saaremaa's main town. €€
Georg Ots Spa Hotel
Tori 2
Tel: 4550 000
Fax: 4550 001
info@gospa.ee
www.gospa.ee
A large, state-of-the-art spa hotel right on the water. Facials to foot massage, swimming pools, in-room stereo systems. €€€
SPA Hotel Rüütli
Pargi 12
Tel: 4548 100

Fax: 4548 199
sanatoorium@sanatoorium.ee
www.sanatoorium.ee
Most modern and luxurious of the three Saaremaa Spa Hotels, Rüütli has an indoor shopping "street", multiple restaurants and bars, squash court, pool and concert stage. Many rooms have castle or sea views. €€€

Narva

Hotel Narva
Pushkini 6
Tel: 3599 600
Fax: 3599 603
hotel@narvahotell.ee
An old four-storey standby completely revamped in 2004 is now Narva's town's nicest hotel. Rooms are decorated with natural materials, and many have excellent views of Ivangorod castle. €€

Otepää

Bernhard
Kolga tee 22A
Tel: 7669 600
Fax: 7669 601
hotell@bernhard.ee
www.bernhard.ee
A 32-room hotel in a peaceful, lakeside setting. Bernhard is a good choice both in summer and during ski season, with a number of packages available. Restaurant, sauna and fireplace hall. €€

Karupesa
Tehvandi 1a
Tel: 7661 500
Fax: 7661 601
karupesa@karupesa.ee
www.karupesa.ee
A lodge-like hotel next to the ski track, the "Bear's Den" is considered the best place to stay in Estonia's winter capital. Ski rental shop attached. €€

Pärnu

Ammende Villa
Mere pst. 7
Tel: 4473 888
Fax: 4473 887
ammende@ammende.ee
www.ammende.ee
Pärnu's most luxurious hotel opened in 2000 in a stunning 1905 Art Nouveau villa. Pricier suites

are in the main house, plainer doubles at the back. €€

Best Western Hotel Pärnu
Rüütli 44
Tel: 4478 911
Fax: 4478 905
hotparnu@pergohotelswww.ee
www.pergohotels.ee
The centrally located hotel block has been extensively refurbished and offers just the kind of decent service and amenities one would expect from the Best Western hotel chain. €€

Konse Holiday Village
Suur-Jõe 44a
Tel: 53 435 095
Fax: 4475 561
info@konse.ee
www.konse.ee
A riverside guesthouse/campground offering basic double rooms and a café, as well as places for caravans and tents. About 10 minutes' walk from the centre. Credit cards not accepted. €

Lõuna Hostel
Lõuna 2
Tel: 4430 943
Fax: 4430 944
hostellouna@hot.ee
www.hot.ee/hostellouna
Bare-bones hostel accommodation in the centre. Double rooms with TVs also available. Credit cards not accepted. €

Scandic Hotel Rannahotell
Ranna pst. 5
Tel: 4432 950
Fax: 4432 918
rannahotell@scandic-hotels.com
www.scandic-hotels.com
An amazing example of functionalism from 1937 (pictured on page 339) , the beautiful and stylish Rannahotell sits right on the beach. Ask for a sea-facing room with a balcony. €€€

St Peterburg
Hospidali 6
Tel: 4430 555
Fax: 4430 556
stpcterburg@hot.ee
www.seegimaja.ee
A history-themed hotel in Pärnu's Old Town. Some rooms are decorated in tsarist-era style, others reflect the 17th-century Swedish decor. €€€€

Tervise Paradis
Side 14
Tel: 4451 606
Fax: 4451 601

sales@spa.ee
www.terviseparadiis.ee
A full-service spa, the "Health Paradise" is a very family-oriented hotel near the beach, with several restaurants, a casino, bowling alley and a huge indoor water park. €€€

Tartu

Barclay
Ülikooli 8
Tel: 7447 100
Fax: 7447 101
barclay@barclay.ee
www.barclay.ee
Set in what was once the local headquarters of the Soviet Army, the reconstructed Barclay Hotel exudes early 19th-century elegance. Ask for the Dzhokhar Dudayev room, named after the first president of Chechnya, who was stationed here from 1987–1991 while an officer in the Soviet Army. €€€

Draakon
Raekoja plats 2
Tel: 7442 045
Fax: 7423 300
tonyas@solo.delfi.ee
www.draakon.ee
Set right next to the Town Hall, this fairly new, elegant hotel is decorated in a vaguely 1930s' style. It also has a dark, baroque-style restaurant and a beer cellar. €€€

London
Rüütli 9
Tel: 7305 555
Fax: 7305 565
london@londonhotel.ee
www.londonhotel.ee
This modern, luxury hotel opened in the heart of Tartu's Old Town in 2002. Count on stylish rooms and a high-quality restaurant. €€€

Pallas
Riia 4
Tel: 7301 200
Fax: 7301 201
pallas@kodu.eepallas.ee
www.pallas.ee
On top of a business centre overlooking the city, the hotel has 43 rooms and the luxurious suites are wonderfully decorated according to the designs of Estonian 20th-century painters, all of whom were

students of the Pallas Art School, located here before World War II. €€€

Tartu
Soola 3
Tel: 7314 300
Fax: 7314 301
info@tartuhotell.ee
www.tartuhotell.ee
Situated next to the bus station, this friendly, newly renovated hotel has cheaper rooms than elsewhere in town, particularly its bargain-priced hostel rooms. Fifteen percent discount for students and 10 percent for Internet bookings. €

Tartu Student Village Hostels
Raatuse 22, Pepleri 14 and Narva mnt. 27
Tel: 7409 955
Fax: 7409 958
hotel@kyla.ee
www.kyla.ee
These three hostels offer surprisingly modern single and twin rooms in new dormitory buildings. Kitchenette, WC and shower are either in-room or shared with two others. Credit cards not accepted. €

Viljandi

Grand Hotel Viljandi
Tartu 11/Lossi 29
Tel: 4355 800
Fax: 4355 805
info@ghv.ee
www.ghv.ee
Opened in 2002 in a late-1930s building, the stylish, 49-room hotel offers Art-Deco furnishings, a restaurant, gym, sauna and beauty salon. €€€

HOSTELS

Part of the International Youth Hostel Federation, the

PRICE CATEGORIES

Price ratings, which are given as a guide only, reflect the price of a double room per night:
€€€€ = over 2,500kr
€€€ = 1,500–2,500kr
€€ = 750–1,500kr
€ = below 750kr

TRANSPORT

ACCOMMODATION

EATING OUT

ACTIVITIES

A – Z

LANGUAGE

Estonian Youth Hostel Association has given its stamp of membership to ten (mainly privately run) hostels and guesthouses in Tallinn, as well as other establishments in Tartu, Haapsalu and in rural Estonia. Booking and information can be found at www.hotels.ee. All these hostels supply sheets, though not all have kitchen or laundry facilities. Be warned that most have only private double rooms (ranging 230 – 600kr) rather than cheaper dorm beds (125 – 280kr). You do not have to be a member of a hostelling association to stay at them.

Estonian Youth Hostel Association
Narva mnt. 16-25
Tel: 646 1455
Fax: 646 1595
info@hostels.ee
www.hostels.ee
Also in Tallinn is:

Vana Tom Hostel
Väike-Karja 1
Tel/fax: 631 3252
Formerly known as "The Barn", this hostel is the backpacker's favourite, located in the Old Town below a striptease joint. Shared showers, no cards accepted. €

LATVIA

Rīga has many expensive luxury hotels as well as many medium-range hotels, but only old town hotels need to be booked well in advance. When travelling throughout the country, you will find the majority of towns have at least one good hotel where facilities are usually basic but acceptable. Large towns have at least one three- or four-star hotel, ands several have more.

Private bed and breakfast accommodation is becoming increasingly popular and usually costs around half the price of a hotel room. Farmhouse and cottage accommodation can be arranged through Lauku ceļotājs (Country Traveller), Kuģu 11, Rīga. Tel: 761 7600; www.celotajs.lv.

For Rīga hotels visit www.hostal.lv. For self-catering apartments visit www.touristapartments.lv.

Rīga

City Hotel Bruninieks
Bruņinieku 6
Tel: 731 5140
Fax: 731 4310
www.cityhotel.lv
Located just off the main Brīvības Street 15 minutes' walk to Old Town but prices are cheaper than for Old Town hotels. Stylish and recently renovated, it is ideal for families since it also offers triple rooms and junior suites with sofas and kitchenettes. €€

Grand Palace Hotel
Pils 12
Tel: 704 4000
Fax: 704 4001
hotel@grandpalace.lv
grandpalace@consul-hotels.com
www.consul-hotels.com
Rīga's most luxurious hotel, based in the heart of the old town. €€€€

Hotel Bergs
Berga Bazārs
Tel: 777 0900
Fax: 777 0940
www.hotelbergs.lv
Five minutes' walk to Old Town, this fanstastic work of design by architect Zaiga Gaile was among Conde Nast Traveler's Best Hotels of the World, 2004. Rooms are spacious and light. Family apartments with small kitchens also available. €€€

Hotel Centra
Audēju 1
Tel: 770 2718
Fax: 770 2708
www.centra.lv
Located in the Old Town but the interior is modern and minimalist. Rooms are spacious with high ceilings and offer great view over the Old Town from the top floors. €€

Hotel de Rome
Kaļķu 28
Tel: 708 7600
Fax: 708 7606
reservation@derome.lv
www.derome.lv
One of the smartest places to stay in Latvia, this hotel is centrally located on the edge of the Old Town facing the Freedom monument. Treat yourself to a nibble in the Otto Schwarz restaurant if your budget stretches to it. €€€€

Hotel Viesturs
Mucenieku 5
Tel: 735 6060
Fax: 735 6061
www.hotelviesturs.lv
New Old Town hotel. Each room is individually decorated, keeping some original details of the medieval building. Unique lighting fixtures and designers bathrooms. €€

Islande
Ķīpsalas 20
Tel: 760 8000
Fax: 760 8001
www.islandehotel.lv
Scandinavian minimalist design, excellent service and a top-floor restaurant with fantastic views of Old Rīga are just a few reasons to stay here. Bowling alley also available. €€€

Konventa Sēta
Kalēju 9/11
Tel: 708 7501
Fax: 708 7515
reservation@konventa.lv
www.derome.lv
Housed in a medieval convent in the heart of town, the "Convent Courtyard" (Konventhof) is run by the same team as the Hotel de Rome and is definitely one of the best hotels in the Baltics. €€€

Metropole
Aspazijas bulv. 36–38
Tel: 722 5411
Fax: 721 6140
metropole@brovi.lv
www.eunet.lv/metropole
A Swedish-run top-quality hotel on the edge of the Old Town. €€€€

Radisson-SAS Daugava
Kuģu 24
Tel: 706 1111
Fax: 706 1100
radisson@com.latnet.lv
www.radissonsas-riga.lv
The Radisson has 361 rooms and offers the Radisson comfort and service with the price tag to match. Its major drawback, the location on the southern bank of the River Daugava, is tempered by the beautiful views it offers of Rīga's skyline. €€€

Radi un Draugi
Mārstaļu 1/3
Tel: 722 0372
Fax: 724 2239
This British-Latvian joint venture has been booked up ever since it opened and with good reason: it offers moderately priced accommodation in the heart of the Old Town. Reservations are essential. €€€

Reval Hotel Rīdzene
Reimersa 1
Tel: 732 4433
Fax: 728 2100
park.hotel@ridzene.lv
www.parkhotelridzene.com
This former Communist Party hotel, which is in a lovely setting in the garden ring behind the US embassy, has everything you'd expect from a world-class hotel including Piramida, an up-market restaurant in the glass pyramid. €€€

Bed & Breakfast

B&B Rīga
Ģertrūdes 43
Tel: 2652 6400
Fax: 729 7594
www.bb-riga.lv
Small family B&B in a quiet courtyard in central Rīga. Spacious rooms with en-suite bathrooms, TV, fridge and microwave. €

Hostels

Riga Old Town Hostel
Vaļņu 43
Tel: 722 3406
www.rigaoldtownhostel.lv
The first "real" hostel to open in Riga, it's a haven for students and budget-minded backpackers who can often be seen enjoying a beer at the bar, that also serves as a reception area. €

Profitcamp
Teātra 12
Tel: 721 6361
Fax: 721 6362
www.profitcamp.lv
Even the staff can't seem to figure out what Profitcamp means, but backpackers don't seem to mind. Clean, comfortable and safe, it's also located in the heart of Old Rīga. €

Knight's Court
Bruņinieku 75B
Tel: 784 6400
Fax: 784 64 01
www.knightscourt.lv
Cheap and quiet, the Knight's Court is a good place to avoid the often crowded, noisy hostels of old Rīga. €

Riga Backpackers
Mārstaļu 6
Tel: 722 9922
Fax: 722 1023
www.riga-backpackers.com
Located in a medieval building in Old Rīga, its opulent rooms with gilt ceilings and crystal chandeliers are in stark contrast to its youthful, unshaven clientele. €

Cēsis

Kolonna Hotel Cēsis
Vienības laukums
Tel: 412 0122
Fax: 412 0121
www.hotelkolonna.com
Comfortable three-star hotel in the centre of this popular town. €€

Gulbene

Cesu Cottage
Liela Skola 7
Tel: 267 26443
Lovely 200-year-old building with self catering. €

Daugavpils

Park Hotel Latgola
Ģimnāzijas 46
Tel: 542 0932
www.hoteldaugavpils.lv
Recently renovated three-star hotel. Comfortable rooms, sauna, beauty treatments, guarded parking. €€

Jūrmala

Baltic Beach Hotel
23/25 Jūras iela, Majori
Tel: 777 1400
Fax: 777 1410
www.balticbeach.lv
One of the latest four-star spa hotels in Jūrmala has 165 spacious rooms with balconies, spa facilities, swimming pool with sea water, terrace restaurant and guarded parking. Practically on the beach. €€€

Guest House Vēja Roze
41 Bulduru prosp. Bulduri
Tel: 775 1752
Fax: 775 1746
vejuroze@inbox.lv
Small, 100 metres/yds from beach, among centuries old pine trees. All rooms en-suite. Prices depend on season and room size. €

Hotel Eiropa
56 Jūras iela, Majori
Tel: 776 2211
Fax: 776 2299
www.eiropahotel.lv
New elegant four-star hotel in traditional wooden cottage-style building 100 metres/yds from the beach and five minutes' walk from the main Jūrmala restaurant and shopping street. Cosy rooms, spa facilities, facilities for children. Room price includes breakfast, saunas and fitness hall. Parking. €€

Hotel Jūrmala Spa
Majori, Jomas 47/49
Tel: 778 4400
Fax: 778 4411
www.hoteljurmala.com
Located on Jūrmala's bustling pedestrian street, this is without a doubt the resort's best and most stylish hotel. €€

Hotel Pegasa Pils
60 Juras iela, Majori
Tel: 776 1149
Fax: 776 1169
www.pegasapils.lv
Quirky hotel in 19th-century wooden building. All rooms with French balconies, 100 metres/yds to the beach. Bridal suites available. Tennis courts, children's facilities, parking. €€

Majori
Jomas 29, Majori
Tel: 776 1380/1390
Fax: 776 1394
Although a Jūrmala landmark, this ageing Art Nouveau building has seen better days. €€

Villa Joma
90 Joma iela, Majori
Tel: 777 1999
Fax: 777 1990
www.villajoma.lv
Family-run small hotel in historical wooden building on the main Jūrmala promenade. A lot of character. Two minutes to beach. Parking. €€

Bauska

Brencis Motel
On the M12 just north of Bauska, 38 km (22 miles) from Rīga.
Tel: 392 8033
Unusual and welcome motel accommodation in rural setting. €

Kungu Ligzda
Rīgas 41
Tel: 392 4000
Fax: 392 4000
A renovated 18th century building on a bank of the River Mēmele is the perfect place to rest your head in Bauska. Don't leave without trying a local brew in its beer cellar. €

Mežotne Manor House
Mežotne
Tel: 396 0711
Fax: 396 0725
www.mezotnespils.lv
Splendidly renovated historic building, comfortable rooms with modern facilities, beautiful countryside around. Near Rundāle Palace. €€

Kuldīga

Hotel Aleksis
Pasta 5
Tel: 332 2153
A small, cosy family-run hotel. €

Jāņa Nams
Liepājas 36
Tel: 332 3456
Fax: 332 3785
www.jananams.lv
Quaint two-storey hotel with a sauna in the centre of town.€€

Liepāja

Amrita
Rīgas 7/9
Tel: 348 0888/340 3434
Fax: 348 0444
info@amrita.lv
www.amrita.lv
This 83-room hotel is the best address in Liepāja and popular with businessmen. €€€

Fontaine Hotel
Jūras 24
Tel: 342 0956
Fax: 342 0956
www.fontaine.lv
Located in a renovated 100-year-old wooden house, this is most likely the hippest boutique hotel in the Baltics. €

Libeva
Veca ostmala 29
Tel: 342 5319
www.libeva.lv
Centrally situated, with boat pier, lake and spa complex. €€

Madona

Jumurda Country Hotel
Jumurda, Madona distr.
Tel: 651 4457
www.jumurda.lv
Beautiful and quiet location by the lake. All rooms have lake view. Boats, bicycles for hire.

Marciena Manor
Marcienas pagasts
Madona distr
Tel: 480 7300
www.marciena.com
Spa resort in a large estate with delightful farm buildings, with outdoor bath tubs and a lake for swimming. €€€

Sigulda

Aparjods
Ventas 1b
Tel: 797 2230
Fax: 797 2230
www.aparjods.lv
A fantastic Latvian timber building with a thatch roof and modern amenities not far from the city centre. €€

Guest House Līvkalns
3 Peteralas iela
Tel: 797 0916

PRICE CATEGORIES

The price ratings beside hotel names are those of the researcher and not official star ratings. The ranges given, intended as a guide only, are for a double room for one night:
€€€€ = over 80Ls
€€€ = 60–80Ls
€€ = 30–60Ls
€ = below 30Ls

Fax: 797 0919
www.livkalns.lv
Lots of character, with
swimming pool, sauna,
horse riding, bicycle hire
and walking trails. €€
Hotel Santa
Kaljani
Tel: 770 5271
Fax: 770 5278
www.hotelsanta.lv
Beautiful and peaceful
location by the lake. A bit
away from the centre. €€
Sigulda
Pils 6
Tel: 797 2263
www.hotelsigulda.lv
A small modern hotel in a
red-brick building in the
centre of this popular
town.€€

Talsi

Hotel Rezidence
Vandzane distr.
Tel: 329 1170
www.hotelrezidence.lv
This renovated hotel
located between the sea
and Talsi offers cheap
rooms, billiards and a
sauna with a small pool.
Hotel Roja
6 Juras iela
Tel: 323 2226,
rojahotel@inbox.lv
Small, cosy hotel by the

sea. Fishing trips and
beach sports available.

Ventspils

Guest House Sãrnate
Uzava, Ventspils distr
Tel: 591 5519
www.sarnate.lv
On the Baltic coast,
offering a variety
of activities including
boating and cycle hire. A
beautiful and quiet place.
€€
Hotel Ostina
32 Dzintaru iela
Tel: 360 7810
Fax: 360 7814
Recently renovated hotel
with spacious rooms in the
residential area. €€
Kupfernams
5 Karla
Tel: 362 6999
Pleasant guest house in the
city centre with restaurant-
café. €€

CAMPING

Rīga

Rīga City Camping
Kipsalas 8
Tel: 706 5000
www.bt1.lv/camping

Located on an island
overlooking Old Town.
Offers modern facilities as
well as rental of equipment
including tents, bicycles,
barbecues. Laundry service
is available too.

Cēsis

Camping Unguri
Raiskums
Tel: 413 4402
By the Unguri lake. Cabins,
tent and caravan places.

Ludza

**Guest House &
Camping Meldri**
Nirza, Ludza distr.
Tel: 2948 5444
meldri@one.lv
Recreation centre by Lake
Nirza. Cottages, tent sites,
country sauna, picnic
spots, a garden fireplace,
sports grounds and boat
hire. Traditional Latgale
meals available.
**Guest House &
Camping Akmeņi**
Tel: 2645 4793
By Lake Akmeņi. There are
a few rooms at the guest
house, plus tent sites.
Sports grounds, boat,
bicycle hire, visits to
Latgale potters workshops.

Ventspils

Camping PieJuras
Vasarnicu 56
Tel: 362 7991
Surrounded by pine forest,
next door to the Open-Air
Ethnographic Museum and
500 metres/yds to beach.
Excellent facilities, cosy
cabins, places for tents and
caravans. Book ahead.
Usmas Camping
Usma
Tel: 2916 3264
www.usma.lv
On the shores of Lake
Usma. New camping with
comfortable cabins. Boats,
paddle boats, wind surfing
boards and bicycles for
rent. Sailing lessons
available.

RURAL LIVING

Countryside Holidays,
www.traveller.lv have a
catalogue and on-line
reservation system for a
variety of countryside
accommodation in all
three Baltic states.
They have more than 300
guest houses, castle
hotels, self-catering
apartments, cottages,
farmhouses and camp
sites to chose from.

LITHUANIA

A great deal of time, effort
and money has been spent
to produce some swishy
establishments in which
the visitor can rest his or
her weary head. Most
hotels are child-friendly, but
not pet-friendly. Rates in
Vilnius, as opposed to the
coastal regions, tend not to
fluctuate seasonally.
However, hotel prices can
sometimes be lower in
winter as hotels scramble
to fill up their empty rooms.
Breakfast is usually
included in smaller and
mid-price range hotels, but
will cost extra at the more
upmarket ones.
It is always best to have
a reservation before
entering the country. Many
of the newer hotels have
online booking systems,
making the experience

hassle-free. Large hotels
are hardly ever booked to
capacity, but the cosier bed
and breakfast or cheaper
options can be filled in the
summer. If you arrive
without a reservation, there
is a Vilnius Tourist
Information Centre in the
train station that can give
you listings of
accommodation in the city.
All hotels are graded by the
Lithuanian Tourism Board
but the star system is
based on the amount of
amenities on offer, not by
the level of service.
Most hotels do not have
facilities for wheelchair-
bound customers. It is best
to ask pointed and
numerous questions about
the facilities if you are
disabled. Those travelling
with these sorts of

concerns should check out
newer hotels, as zoning
laws tend to make them
more wheelchair-friendly.

HOTELS

Vilnius

Atrium
Pilies 10
Tel: (5) 210 77 77
Fax: (5) 210 77 70
<www.atrium.lt>
The rooms are more than
ample and the leather
couches and cordless
phones are noteworthy
touches. Restaurant and
Sauna. €€€
Centro Kubas
Stiklių 3
Tel: (5) 266 08 60
Fax: (5) 266 08 63

<www.centrokubas.lt>
Small but charmingly
decorated with antiques
and all conveniences. One
room is specifically
designed for wheelchair-
bound guests. €€€
City Park
Stuokos-Gucevičiaus 3
Tel: (5) 212 35 15
Fax: (5) 210 74 60
<www.citypark.lt>
Modern and lovely, the
77-room City Park is one of
the few truly wheelchair
accessible hotels. Free in-
room internet access, mini-
bar and TV. Breakfast not
included. €€€
Crowne Plaza Vilnius
Čiurlionio 84
Tel: (5) 274 34 00
Fax: (5) 274 34 11
<www.cpvilnius.com>
This new hotel near Vingis
Park is exceptionally

soothing. Lovely touches are to be found throughout their 108 rooms; 24-hour room service; 16th-floor bar with views. €€€€

Domus Maria
Aušros Vartų 12
Tel: (5) 264 48 80
Fax: (5) 264 48 78
<domusmaria.vilnesis.lt>
Rooms in this renovated monastery are basic and a bit small, but the location alongside the gates of Dawn and the windows looking out onto the city make this a sound option for inexpensive accommodation. Breakfast included. Parking. €€

Europa Royale Vilnius
Aušros Vartų 6
Tel: (5) 266 07 70
Fax 261 20 00
<www.hoteleuropa.lt>
The ground-zero locale and the abundance of windows add distinctiveness to this mid-sized hotel. Some rooms have balconies right over The Gate of Dawn, others have views onto the Old Town. Breakfast included. Restaurant and parking. €€€

Grotthuss
Ligoninės 7
Tel: (5) 266 03 22
Fax: (5) 266 02 23
<www.grotthushotel.com>
Absolutely charming, with attentive staff. Try to book a room overlooking the garden. Breakfast included. Restaurant, parking and conference facilities. €€€

Mabre Residence
Maironio 13
Tel: (5) 212 20 87
Fax: (5) 212 22 40
<www.mabre.lt>
Situated around a courtyard at the edge of the Old Town, this former Orthodox monastery has pleasant, insular surroundings. Breakfast is not included. Restaurant, sauna, parking. €€€

Novotel
Gedimino 16
Tel: (5) 266 62 00
Fax: (5) 266 62 01
<www.novotel.com>
Clean and crisp, the Novotel has jazzed up the otherwise drab Gedimino hotel options. Works of art in the rooms add a delightful quirkiness. All the

amenities – mini-bars, satellite TV, fitness and business centres – plus wheelchair accessy. €€€

Radisson SAS Astorija
Didžioji 35/2
Tel: (5)212 01 10
Fax: (5) 212 17 62
<www.radissonsas.com>
Geared to an international business clientele, so expect all comforts, including in-room safes, modem points and mini-bars. Restaurant. €€€€

Relais & Chateaux Stikliai
Gaono 7
Tel: (5) 264 95 95
Fax: (5) 212 38 70
<www.stikliaihotel.lt>
This lovely upscale hotel has been setting the standards for class in this town for decades. A truly exceptional experience. Staff wait on you hand and foot. Apartment rentals are also available in the building. Restaurant, sauna and pool. €€€€

Reval Hotel Lietuva
Konstitucijos 20
Tel: (5) 272 62 72
Fax: (5) 272 62 70
<www.revalhotel.com>
Just across the pedestrian White Bridge (Baltasis tiltas), this beautiful new 300-room hotel has a restaurant, 22nd floor bar and casino. Executive-class rooms have balconies. €€€

Shakespeare Boutique Hotel
Bernardinų 8/8
Tel: (5) 266 58 85
Fax: (5) 266 58 86
<www.shakespeare.lt>
The city's original boutique hotel, with each room devoted to a literary genius. Their second hotel, Shakespeare Too (Pilies 34) pays homage to painters. All rooms have an touch of decadence. Restaurant. €€€€

Guest Houses

Bernadinč Guest House
Bernardinų 5
Tel: (5) 261 51 34
Fax: (5) 260 84 21.
A good option for the budget traveller, the guest house is located in the Old Town and rooms, though small, are clean and comfortable. Parking. €

Litinterp
Bernardinų 7–2
Tel: (5) 212 38 50
Fax: (5) 212 35 59
<www.litinterp.lt>
In the old town. Litinterp is known throughout Lithuania, offering the best range of accommodation with extremely reasonable pricing. B&b and rooms with or without hosts are available also in Kaunas, Klaipėda, Nida and Palanga. €

Outside Vilnius

Le Méridien Villon Resort
A-2 motorway 19km (12 miles) north of Vilnius
Tel: (5) 273 97 00
Fax: (5) 265 97 30
<www.lemeridien.com>
A short car ride from the city, this spa-hotel has some of the most luxurious rooms in the country. Most overlook the lake or near-by forested area. Amenities are plentiful. €€€

Trakai

Trakai
Trakų viešbutis
Ežero 7
Tel/fax: (528) 55 505/55 503.
hotel.traku@takas.lt
http://members.hotels.lt/traku
Trakai's best hotel is set on the shores of Lake Totoriškės. €€€

Druskininkai

Druskininkai
Kudirkos 43
Tel: (313) 525 66
Fax: (313) 513 45
<www.hotel-druskininkai.lt>
This spa and hotel combination has been the most well-known hotel in the area for decades. Although not entirely swishy, the place does manage to soothe. Breakfast included. €€€

Regina
Kosciuškos 3
Tel: (313) 590 60
Fax: (313) 590 61
<www.regina.lt>
The Regina is a very classy full-service hotel. Numerous weekend packages are available to entice reticent visitors. €€

Kaunas

Apple Economy Hotel
Valančiaus 19
Tel: (37) 321 404
Fax: (37) 321 404
<www.applehotel.lt>
An absolute delight. Rooms are bright, non-smoking and previous guests send along toys and trinkets which make up the lobby décor. Parking available. €

B&B Litinterp
Gedimino 28–7
Tel: (37) 228 718
Fax: (37) 421 520
<www.litinterp.lt>
Offers bed and breakfast in the city centre and the old town. Also rent cars. €

Best Western Santakos
Gruodžio 21
Tel: (37) 302 702
Fax: (37) 302 700
<www.santaka.lt>
Lithuania's first Best Western hotel is set in an old red-brick warehouse in a side street. The 40 rooms are refurbished and comfortable. €€€

Kaunas
Laisvės 79
Tel: (37) 750 850
Fax: (37) 750 851
www.kaunashotel.lt
This is the most luxury hotel in the city centre. The less modern rooms are overlook the bustle of Laisvės, but the more modern rooms are further into the building. €€€

Minotel
Kuzmos 8
Tel: (37) 203 759/229 981
Fax: (37) 220 355
<www.minotel.lt>
Right off Vilniaus, this cosy, 23-room hotel offers clean and comfortable surroundings. €€

Perkūno Namai
Perkūno 61

PRICE CATEGORIES

The price ratings beside hotel names are those of the researcher and not official star ratings. The ranges given, intended as a guide only, are for a double room for one night:
€€€€ = over 500Lt
€€€ = 300–500Lt
€€ = 200–300Lt
€ = below 200Lt

TRANSPORT

ACCOMMODATION

EATING OUT

ACTIVITIES

A – Z

LANGUAGE

CAMPING

Official campsites in Lithuania are:

Rukainiai
Rytų Kempingas (off the highway to Minsk)
Tel: 651 195
Some 25 km (15 miles) east of Vilnius, Rukainiai comprises small summer lodgings for three to four people, with communal showers and kitchens. Tents can be pitched on this riverside campsite with a sauna and video-café.

Trakai
Totoriškės, Kempingas Slònyje
Tel: 38 51 387
The campsite is on the northern shore of Lake Galvò around 4 km (2 miles) from Trakai on the road to Vievis. €

Tel: (37) 320 230
Fax: (37) 323 678
<www.perkuno-namai.lt>
What this hotel lacks in centrality it makes up for in gorgeous furnishings and exquisite attention to detail. Rooms with a balcony on this hilltop hotel situated near a park are spectacular. €€€

Takioji Neris
Donelaičio 27
Tel: (37) 306 100
Fax: (37) 306 221
<www.takiojineris.com>
This large, central hotel is popular with groups and businessmen. Swishier business class rooms are on offer. €€

Klaipėda and the coast

Baltpark
Minijos 119
Tel: (46) 482 020
Fax: (46) 380 803
<www.baltpark.com>
Located in an industrial district alongside the Curonian lagoon, this hotel offers comfortable and clean surroundings. €€

Europa Royale Klaipėda
Žvejų 21/1
Tel: (46) 404 444
Fax: (46) 404 445
<www.hoteleuropa.lt>
This 50-room hotel straddles the fine line between opulent and overdone. The Friendly staff and ll manner of amenities are available. €€€

Klaipėda
Naujoji Sodo 1
Tel: (46) 404 372
Fax: (46) 404 373
<www.klaipedahotel.lt>
This 220-room red-brick monster has been gutted and brought into this century to great effect. Expect comfort and anonymity. €€

Litinterp
Puodžių 17
Tel: (46) 410 644
Fax: (46) 420 176
<www.litinterp.lt>
Organises b&b rooms, flats and car rental in Klaipėda, Nida and Palanga. €

Lūgnė
Galinio Pylimo 16
Tel/Fax: (46) 411 884
<www.lugne.com>
Right outside the Old Town, this 26-room hotel provides a marvellously funky atmosphere. Each room comes with two TVs. Lovely staff. Parking. €

Radisson SAS
Šaulių 28
Tel: (46) 490 800
Fax: (46) 490 815
<www.radissonsas.com>
Leave it to the Radisson people to class up a drab hotel scene. The lovely nautical themed hotel, in a central location, has beautiful rooms. Expect all the pleasant trappings of a large hotel.€€€

Neringa

Ažuolynas
Rėzos 54 (Juodkrantė)
Tel: (469) 533 10
Fax: (469) 533 16
www.hotelazuolynas.lt
The large waterslide is the first clue that this place is geared toward the happy-go-lucky. The 52 rooms, doubles or apartment, are comfy and spacious. €€

Auksinės Kopos
Kuverto 17 (Nida)
Tel: (469) 52 390
Fax: (469)52 947
The "Golden Dunes" hotel is the largest on the spit with 96 rooms, but is tucked away in the woods above Nida. €€

Inkaro Kaimas
Naglių 26-1
Tel: (469) 52 123
<www.inkarokaimas.lt>
Three spare apartments make up this lodging. It's location right on the main street and in spitting distance of the water make it a fabulous option for those not fussed by less than noble surroundings. €€

Linėja
Taikos 18 (Nida)
Tel: (469)52 390
Fax: (469) 52 718
www.lineja-hotel.lt
This is one of the better establishments in Nida. Its main claim to fame is its bowling lane. €€

Rasytė
Lotmiškio 11
Tel: (469) 52 592
The rooms in this traditional fisherman's house are spartan and basic. Reservations are nevertheless essential. €

Santauta
Kalno 36 (Juodkrantė)
Tel: (469) 53 346
By far the cheapest option in town, this hotel has both shared dorm rooms and some private rooms. €

Villa Banga
Pamario 2 (Nida)
Tel: (469) 51 139
Fax: (469) 52 762
smilte@is.lt
A seven-room house that looks like something out of a fairytale. Privacy is in lieu of amenities. €€

Palanga

Mama Rosa Villa
Jūratės 28a
Tel: (460) 48 581
<www.mamarosa.lt>
Palanga's prime villa has eight rooms. It's popular, so book ahead. €€€

Palanga
Birutės 60
Tel: (460) 41 414
Fax: (460) 41 415
<www.palangahotel.lt>
A better location and better view onto the pine tree forests is hard to find. The rooms are extremely stylish. €€€

Pušų Paunksnėje
Darius ir Girėno 25
Tel: (460) 49 080
Fax: (460) 49 081
<www.pusupaunksneje>
Owned by the world-class basketball player Arvydas Sabonis, this hotel is pure luxury with (unsurprisingly) high ceiling. Fireplaces and wooden décor insure a romantic feel in every room. €€€€

Šachmatinò
Basanavičiaus 45
Tel: (460) 51 655
<www.sachmatine.lt>
This flashy eleven-room hotel is set right behind the dunes next to the beach. €€

Villa Ramybė
Vytauto 54
Tel: (460) 54 124
<www.vilaramybe.lt>
Few people can run an adorable 12-room hotel so perfectly. Reservations are an absolute must. €

Voveraitė vardu Salvadoras
Meilės 24
Tel: (460) 52 532
Fax: (460) 534 22.
The "Squirrel named Salvador" is as quirky as its name and Salvador Dalí has left an indelible imprint on the décor. Some of the rooms have balconies. €€€

Siauliai

Šaulys
Vasario 16-osios 40
Tel: (41) 520 812/520 844
Fax: (41) 520 911
<www.saulys.lt>
This mid-sized hotel is the best hotel in town. Breakfast included. €€

Turnė
Rūdė s 9
Tel: (41) 500 150
Fax: (41) 429 201
<www.turne.lt>
A bit on the drab-side, but the attentive staff makes up for any decor faux-pas. Breakfast included. €

PRICE CATEGORIES

Price ratings, which are given as a guide only, reflect the price of a double room per night:
€€€€ = over 500Lt
€€€ = 300–500Lt
€€ = 200–300Lt
€ = below 200Lt

E ATING OUT

RECOMMENDED RESTAURANTS, CAFÉS & BARS

One new establishment opens every month in each of the capital cities and you can feast on French haute cuisine, sample Japanese sushi or Armenian shashlik and wolf down vegetarian dishes. In the main cities, some of the bars and clubs here are so funky that they would stand out in Paris, London or New York. Most waiting staff speak English – if they don't speak English, the menu will certainly be in either English, German, French or Russian. The best hotels and restaurants have imported top international chefs, serving first-class international food. Most restaurants accept Visa and MasterCard unless otherwise noted. As there is not enough room here to give a full list of restaurants, we have tried to recommend the most notable establishements, with the stress on local cuisine.

Tipping: service is not included in most bills. Round up the sum of the bill and add a little if service was appreciated. No more than 5 percent is expected.

For an informed, general read about what to eat, see pages 77–82.

RESTAURANT LISTINGS

ESTONIA

Fuelled by its recent prosperity, and in no small way due to tourism, Estonia's restaurant scene is blossoming. Diners can today find anything from medieval fare to cutting-edge fusion cuisine. Tallinn's Old Town in particular is awash with theme restaurants, and it is not uncommon to see waiters in elaborate costumes roaming the streets, handing out coupons and flyers.

One thing that is surprisingly hard to find in the city, however, is a restaurant that serves Estonian food. Even at the casual lunch cafés and pubs favoured by locals, the choices are typically *seljanka* (a thick, Russian soup) or *schnitzel*, which are not originally Estonian. The reason for this conspicuous absence of traditional fare is that Estonian cuisine is for the most part a simple – some would say bland – affair with country roots. Favourites are *sült* (jellied meat), *mulgikapsas* (fatty sauerkraut), rollmops (soused herrings) and *kama* (a mixture of ground cereals taken as dessert). Estonians think of this cuisine as something they make at home, but wouldn't necessarily look for when they go out, hence its scarcity in the restaurant world. That said, visitors who know where to look can find one or two decent places to sample the local food. Not surprisingly, however, these are mainly aimed at tourists.

Out in the country it is different, and this is the place to head for if you really want to find more of the local flavour, especially locally smoked fish and meat, which you should definitely try.

RESTAURANTS

Tallinn

Admiral
Lootsi 15
Tel: 6623 777
Fax: 6318 444
admiral@estpak.ee
www.aurulaev-admiral.ee
Open daily noon–11pm
A 1950s-era steamship that's been cleverly rebuilt into an elegant, romantic restaurant. The menu is a wide-ranging mix that includes several Balkan specialities and a few Russian favourites. €€€

Controvento
Vene 12
Tel: 6440 470
Fax: 6464 677
info@controvento.ee
www.controvento.ee
Open daily noon–11pm
Set in a cosy medieval building in the Katariina passageway, this Italian restaurant is a long-time favourite of Tallinn's expatriate elite. Consistently high-quality cuisine and professional service. Reservations essential. €€–€€€

Eesti Maja
Lauteri 1
Tel: 6455 252
Fax: 6998 809
eneken@eestimaja.ee
www.eestimaja.ee
Open daily 11am–midnight
Specialising in Estonian national cuisine, this is the

PRICE CATEGORIES

These prices are for a starter, main dish and dessert for one person (without drinks) and should be taken as a guide only. A glass of wine or beer will add 30–60kr to the bill.
€€€€ = over 350kr
€€€ = 250–350kr
€€ = 150–250kr
€ = below 150kr

best place in town to try local favourites like Baltic sprats, *mulgikapsad* (saurkraut stew) and *sült* (jellied pork). The casual, folksy atmosphere makes this a good choice for families. **€€**

Gloria
Müürivahe 2
Tel: 6446 950
Fax: 6446 180
gloria@gloria.ee
www.gloria.ee
Open daily noon–midnight
This luxuriously decadent restaurant has hosted a number of statesmen, dignitaries and even Pope John Paul II. An interesting mix of French, Italian, Baltic and Russian creations makes up the menu. **€€€€**

Mõõkkala
Kuninga 4
Tel: 6418 288
Fax: 6448 930
info@mookkala.com
www.mookkala.com
Open daily noon–midnight
Mõõkkala (swordfish) is both fish-lover's paradise and a long-time Tallinn favourite. Delicacies of the sea, not to mention the restaurant's signature swordfish dish, are all expertly prepared and served with flair. **€€–€€€**

Olde Hansa
Vana turg 1
Tel: 6279 020
Fax: 6279 021
reserve@oldehansa.ee
www.oldehansa.ee
Open daily 11am–midnight
A visit to Tallinn wouldn't be complete without experiencing this medieval-style restaurant. Far more intricate and authentic than a typical theme restaurant, it offers an intriguing menu, costumed waitresses, candlelight and minstrels. Reserve on weekends. **€€€**

Pegasus
Harju 1
Tel: 6314 040
pegasus@restoranpegasus.ee
www.restoranpegasus.ee
Open Mon–Thur 8am–1am, Fri 8am–2am, Sat 10am–2am
Top-notch world cuisine prepared under the strict direction of an experienced London chef. The bar on the ground floor is

considered one of Tallinn's most sophisticated places to mingle. Closes early on Sundays. **€€€€**

Troika
Raekoja plats 15
Tel: 6276 245
Fax: 6314 091
restoran@troika.ee
www.troika.ee
Open daily noon–midnight
A lavishly decorated Russian restaurant resembling something out of a Tsarist-era fairy tale. The menu ranges from blinis to Tver mutton and even includes bear Stroganoff. Reserve in advance. **€€€**

Vanaema Juures
Rataskaevu 10
Tel: 6269 080
vanaema.juures@mail.ee
Open Mon–Sat noon–10pm, Sun noon–6pm
Just as you might expect from a restaurant called Grandmother's Place, this cosy cellar venue is bursting with antiques, old photos and friendly attitudes. An excellent place to try Estonian national dishes. **€€€**

Zebra Cafe
Narva mnt. 7
Tel: 6109 230
info@zebracafe.ee
www.zebracafe.ee
Open daily 11am–midnight
Set in a futuristic-looking structure, this casual-chic restaurant sits at the trendier edge of Tallinn's dining spectrum. Order salads and fillets from the menu, or just pick out sushi, pastries and deserts from the counter. **€€€€**

BELOW: staff dress adds to the flavour.

Tartu

Gruusia Saatkond
Rüütli 8
Tel: 7441 386
gruusiasaatkond@gruusiasaatkond.ee
www.gruusiasaatkond.ee
Open daily noon–midnight
The comfortable Georgian Embassy, right next to Tartu's Town Hall Square, is an excellent place to get acquainted with Georgian cuisine. Try *shashlyk* (kebab) and *hatchapuri* (cheese-filled bread). **€**

La Dolce Vita
Kompanii 10
Tel: 7407 545
ladolcevita@ladolcevita.ee
www.ladolcevita.ee
Open Mon–Thur 11.30am–10pm, Fri and Sat 11.30am–midnight, Sun noon–10pm.
Run by Italians, this cosy, Old Town cellar restaurant serves up a huge variety of tasty pizzas and pastas. A local favourite. **€–€€**

Maailm
Rüütli 12
Tel: 7429 099
restoran@klubimaailm.ee
www.klubimaailm.ee
Open daily 11.30am–1am (kitchen closes 11pm)
This funky club-restaurant is a wonderful example of Tartu's brand of eccentricity. The menu ranges from African salad to cheeseburgers, and the artsy interior borders on the odd. **€**

Rasputin
Ülikooli 10
Tel: 7305 997
Fax: 7305 996
venetrahter@hot.ee

www.rasputin.ee
Open Sun–Thur 11am–1am, Fri & Sat 11am–3am
With its colourful and deliberately exaggerated decor, this lively Russian tavern/restaurant isn't one to miss. Musicians play accordion and guitar on Saturdays. **€–€€**

Tsink Plekk Pang
Küütri 6
Tel: 7303 415
Fax: 7313 410
pang@pang.ee
www.pang.ee
Open Tues–Sat noon–midnight, Sun & Mon noon–11pm
Though it bills itself as a Chinese restaurant, the cleverly decorated Tsink Plekk Pang (Zinc-plated Bucket) also has an Indian menu and a sushi room. It's something of a nightspot, with DJs playing late on weekends. **€€**

Pärnu

Ammende Villa
Mere pst. 7
Tel: 4473 888
Fax: 4473 887
ammende@ammende.ee
www.ammende.ee
Open daily noon–11pm
Pärnu's finest hotel is also home to its most upscale restaurant. Fine French and Mediterranean cuisine is served in the Art Nouveau mansion's three elegant, old-fashioned dining rooms. **€€€€**

Munga Kohvik
Munga 9
Tel: 4431 099
cinteras@hot.ee
Open daily 11am–11.30pm
A cosy café/restaurant set in an authentic 19th-century cottage. Antique furniture and classic dishes give it the right touch of charm. **€€**

Seegi Maja
Hospidali 1
Tel: 4430 550
Fax: 4430 556
seegimaja@hot.ee
www.seegimaja.ee
Open daily noon–midnight
This somewhat cheeky, Hanseatic-themed restaurant is appropriately located in what was Pärnu's 17th-century almshouse. The inventive

DRINKING NOTES

Although vodka (viin) has a strong presence in Estonian drinking culture, its proliferation is actually due to last century's Russian influence. Without question, Estonia's national drink is beer (õlu), brewed at home by farmers since time immemorial. The most popular brands are Saku and A. Le Coq, which are served on tap throughout the country.

In the past few years, cider (siider) has become popular. For urbanites,

wine (vein) has also held a growing sway, giving rise to several swanky wine bars in the capital. Mostly, however, drinking establishments come in three varieties: old-fashioned cellar bars or trahters (taverns), a few 1990s-era Irish-style pubs and, more recently, trendy, cosmopolitan lounges.

During the all-too-brief summer season Estonians will drink at any establishment, just so long as it has an outdoor table.

menu includes choices like stewed venison and roast boar. €€

Islands

Seahouse Pub & Terrace
Pädaste Manor
Muhu Island
Tel: 4548 800
Fax: 4548 811
info@padaste.ee
www.padaste.ee
Open daily noon–3pm & 6pm–10pm; closed in winter
A highly respected, gourmet restaurant built into a restored manor house on the road to Kuressaare. Guests can sit inside by the fireplace or dine on the terrace and watch the sunset over the sea. Reservations strongly recommended. €€€€

FAST FOOD

International burger barons McDonald's (Viru 24) and the Finnish chain Hesburger (Viru 27) have both staked out territory in and around Tallinn. For pizza on the run, try the thin-crust Peetri Pizza (Mere pst. 6) or the thick, deep-dish variety at Pizza Americana (Müürivahe 2). For a more Estonian option, order filled pancakes, which are available in meat or dessert varieties at most cafés and pubs.

CAFÉS

Estonian urban café culture is very much alive with a new breed of entrepreneurs competing to supply caffeine – and ambience – to discerning city dwellers.

Tallinn

Basso
Pikk 13
Tel: 6419 312
Fax: 6419 311
basso@basso.ee
www.basso.ee
Open Sun and Mon 11am–midnight, Tues–Thur 11am–1am, Fri and Sat 11am–3am
Located in the heart of Old Town, this modern, comfortable lounge is a sophisticated place to stop for tea or light meals. During the evenings the emphasis turns to jazz, wine and cocktails.

Bogapott
Pikk jalg 9
Tel: 6313 181
www.bogapott.ee
Open daily 10am–6pm
A charming old favourite built into the back of a pottery shop and incorporating a medieval city wall. Upstairs you can sip coffee under the gaze of ceramic angels.

Kehrwieder
Saiakang 1
www.kehrwieder.ee
Open daily 11am–midnight

Three artfully decorated, cave-like rooms make up this popular café on Town Hall Square. Its main features are excellent gourmet coffee, eclectic furniture and a hip, young clientele. No credit cards accepted.

Moskva
Vabaduse väljak 10
Tel: 6404 694
moskva@moskva.ee
www.moskva.ee
Open Mon–Thur 9am–midnight, Fri 9am–1am, Sat 11am–4am, Sun 11am–midnight
Moskva's ultra-cool, ground floor café is a good introduction to the trendiest end of Tallinn's social scale. Its upstairs restaurant provides more space in an equally chic environment.

Tartu

Werner
Ülikooli 11
Tel: 7426 377
caf@werner.ee
www.werner.ee
Open Mon–Thur 7.30am–11pm, Fri and Sat 8am–1pm, Sun 9am–9pm
Its interior may be ultra-modern, but this historic bakery-café has been providing caffeine and cheap meals to students since the early 20th century. Gourmet restaurant upstairs.

Wilde
Vallikraavi 4
Tel: 7309 764
Fax: 7309 761
wilde@wilde.ee
www.wilde.ee
Open Mon–Sat 9am–9pm, Sun 10am–7pm
This combination of pub, café and bookshop has become a Tartu landmark, and is worth seeing for its elaborate decor alone. The art-filled café serves excellent cakes, and the pub upstairs (open later) is also a worthy nightspot.

Pärnu

Jazz Café
Ringi 11
Tel: 4427 546
jazzcafe@hot.ee
www.hot.ee/jazzcafe
Open Mon–Wed 9am–10pm,

Thur–Sat 9am–midnight, Sun 10am–8pm
Changing art exhibitions and terrace concerts in summer make Jazz Café one of Pärnu's most sophisticated coffee destinations.

Teatrikohvik
Keskväljak 1
Tel: 4420 664
kohvik@endla.ee
www.endla.ee
Open Mon–Thur 8.30am–10pm, Fri 8.30am–midnight, Sat 11am–midnight, Sun 11am–10pm
A favourite of the local cultural elite, the upstairs section of the Endla Theatre's modern café is also known for its summer terrace.

BARS

Tallinn

Hell Hunt
Pikk 39
Tel: 631 37236818 333
hellhunt@hellhunt.ee
www.hellhunt.ee
Expats and locals gather in the Gentle Wolf to sip drinks in a comfortable, relaxed milieu. The tasty Hell Hunt beer served here is brewed on Saaremaa Island, exclusively for this pub.

Karja Kelder
Väike-Karja 1
Tel: 6441 008
karjakelder@hot.ee
www.karjakelder.ee
Open Sun & Mon 11am–1am, Tues–Thur 11am–2am, Fri & Sat 11am–4am
This lively cellar pub is the only truly Estonian place to drink in Tallinn's Old Town. Karja Kelder gets crowded in the evenings so arrive early and be

PRICE CATEGORIES

These prices are for a starter, main dish and dessert for one person (without drinks) and should be taken as a guide only. A glass of wine or beer will add 30–60kr to the bill.
€€€€ = over 350kr
€€€ = 250–350kr
€€ = 150–250kr
€ = below 150kr

prepared to pay 6kr for the coat check.

Lounge 8
Vana-Posti 8
Tel: 6274 770
kaheksa@bdg.ee
Open Sun–Tues noon–midnight, Wed–Thur noon–2am, Fri & Sat noon–4am
Lounge 8, or Kaheksa as it's called in Estonian, is a trendy, tropical-style lounge where wine and cocktails, rather than beer, are the order of the day. Excellent smoothies.

Molly Malone's
Müündi 2
Tel: 631 3016
molly.malones@jjj-bars.com
www.jjj-bars.com
Sun–Thur 11am–2am, Fri & Sat 11am–4am
Situated in a prime location overlooking Town Hall Square, this spacious Irish pub is a favourite with

expats and tourists. Football matches are shown on a multiple screens here.

Tartu

Püsirohu Kelder
Lossi 28
Tel: 7303 555
Fax: 7303 560
pyss@pyss.ee
www.pyss.ee
Open Mon–Thur noon–2am, Fri & Sat noon–3am, Sun noon–midnight
The spacious 18th-century Gunpowder Cellar is now

famed as a beer-hall/ restaurant, as well as a live music venue. Plenty of outside seating in summer.

Ristiisa
Küüni 7
Tel: 7303 970
Fax: 7303 974
ristiisapubi@hot.ee
www.ristiisapubi.ee
Open Sun & Mon 11am–midnight, Tues–Thur 11am–1am, Fri & Sat 11am–3am
A truly unexpected find in downtown Tartu, the popular Godfather Pub is decorated in an Al Capone theme and filled with mobster memorabilia.

Pärnu

Pärnu Kuursaal
Mere pst. 22
Tel: 4420 367
Fax: 4420 366
info@kuur.ee

www.kuur.ee
Open Sun–Thur noon–2am, Fri & Sat noon–4am (shorter hours in winter)
Dubbed "Estonia's biggest tavern", this is a vast beer hall built inside Pärnu's century-old resort hall adjacent to the beach. In summer, live bands keep it buzzing late into the night.

Postipoiss
Vee 12
Tel: 4464 864
Fax: 4464 861
postipoiss@ag.ee
www.restaurant.ee
Open Sun–Thur noon–midnight, Fri & Sat noon–2am
What was an old post station is now a casual Russian (actually "Slavic") theme restaurant. In the evenings, it turns into a hotspot for drinking and dancing. Try their Emperor beer.

LATVIA

Being a nation of farmers for so many years, Latvia's national foods are, to put it mildly, rustic in nature. *Pīrāgi* are small pastry buns traditionally, although not exclusively, filled with chopped ham and onions. A bowl of boiled grey peas fried with bacon and onions is also a favourite treat often topped with *kefirs*, a dairy drink similar to yoghurt.

Latvians also pride themselves on a wide variety of sausages, which, when compared to German *bratwurst* or *knockwurst*, sadly, just don't cut the mustard. However, the thin *mednieku desiņas*, or hunters' sausages, are definitely worth a try.

Although difficult to find in Rīga, *grūdenis* is a thick country stew that uses half a pig's head as a base. The pork chop or *karbonāde* is the most ubiquitous national dish usually complemented by potatoes, *saurkraut* and a slice of delicious rye or black bread baked only with natural ingredients. Due to so many years of culinary isolation, dill and

caraway seeds are often the only seasonings used by chefs at Latvian restaurants.

Rīga is a food haven with ethnic cuisines from Tex-Mex to Korean. There are excellent (and expensive) upmarket restaurants in the Hotel de Rome, Konventa Sēta, Hotel Bergs and the Park Hotel Rīdzene.

Good Latvian home-cooking is served in a number of Lido establishments, notably at Alus Sēta, Dzirnavas, Lido Atpūtas Centrs, Staburags or Vērmanītis *(further details are given below).* These places have made country cooking their trademark, but do not accept credit cards.

RESTAURANTS

Rīga

Alus Sēta
Tirgoņu 6
Tel: 722 2431
Open daily 11am–1am
Latvian home-cooking in a self-service cafeteria-style establishment. Help

yourself to the grey peas and ribs that are grilled in front of you. Fine views of Dome Square from the seats outside. **€**

Bergs
Elizabetes 83/85
Tel: 777 0949
www.hotelbergs.lv
Open daily noon–midnight
Without doubt the best restaurant in Rīga. A unique interior and plenty of open space mask its location in the hotel of the same name, listed in the top 100 hotels of the world by *Conde Nast Traveler.* **€€€**

Charlestons
Blaumaņa 38/40
Tel: 777 0573
Fax: 777 0571
www.charlestons.lv
Open daily noon–midnight
Charlestons is a classy and trendy – albeit expensive – restaurant with a beautiful outside terrace. It's popular, especially in the summer, so reservations are recommended. **€€**

Fabrikas
Balasta dambis 70
Tel: 787 3804
Open 11am–midnight
Trendy restaurant on Kipsala island in restored

wooden building with views of the old town. **€€**

Lido Atpūtas Centrs
Krasta 76
Tel: 750 44 20
Open daily 10am–11pm
This vast food court on three levels serves only Latvian fare. The Lido Leisure Centre, slightly out of town, is packed to the rafters on weekends with Latvian families out for a cheap and hearty meal. Beer is brewed on the premises. **€**

Melnie mūki
Jāņa sēta 1
Tel: 721 5006
Open daily noon–2am
The Black Monks, which is situated in the heart of the Old Town, has quickly become Rīga's most popular modestly priced restaurant, which means

PRICE CATEGORIES

These prices are for the average cost of a main dish for one person and should be taken as a guide only:
€€€ = over 7 Ls
€€ = 4–7 Ls
€ = below 4 Ls
Drinks will double the bill.

FAST FOOD

McDonalds followed swiftly after independence, opening in the heart of the city. Scandinavia's most beloved burger joint **Hesburger** also opened its doors in Rīga at the Olympia Shopping Centre, Āzenes 5.

Copycats of KFC such as **Chicko Chicken** (Kr. Barona 44) and **Southern Fried Chicken**, (Ieriśu 3 at the Domina Shopping Centre) are also in business.

Russian-style meat dumplings can be had at **Pelmeņi XL** (Kaļķu 7; open daily 9am–4am). For cheap pancakes of all sorts look no further than **Šefpavārs Vilhelms** (Šķūņu 6; open daily 9am–10pm). For an inexpensive buffet of delicious food try **Olé** (Audēju 1; open Mon–Fri 7.30am–5pm).

Pizzerias can be found all over town, most with their own delivery services. For American-style pizza try **Pizza Lulū** (Ģertrūdes 27; tel: 800 5858; www.lulu.lv; open 24hrs). **Čili Pica** (Brīvības 26; tel: 800 3355; open Sun–Wed 8am–3am, Thur–Sat 8am–6am) and **Vairāk saules** (Dzirnavu 60; tel: 728 2878; open daily 9am–11pm) serve dozens of delicious thin-crust pizzas.

that reservations for dinner are essential. €€
Staburags
Čaka 55
Tel: 729 9787
Open daily noon–midnight
The best place for hearty Latvian fodder served in oversized portions. Get a big party together and go for the roast pig. The only sit-down restaurant in the Lido chain. €€
Vērmanītis
Elizabetes 65
Tel: 728 6289
Open daily 8am–11pm
Set next to Vērmanes Park, this Lido restaurant offers Latvian and international cuisine in a wonderful rustic atmosphere. €
Vincents
Elizabetes 19
Tel: 733 2634
Open daily noon–11pm
This culinary institution made popular by the renowned local chef Martins Ritins, is a favourite with the rich and famous. Sushi menu and business lunch deals. €€€

Cēsis

Café Popular
Vienības laukums 1
Tel: 412 0122
Open Mon–Thur 11am–11pm, Fri & Sat 11am–midnight, Sun noon–10pm
This cosy cellar restaurant specialising in pizzas has long been a favourite with locals and tourists. €
Sarunas
Rigas iela 4
Tel: 410 7173
Open daily 10am–midnight
Stylish bar with a variety of dishes including a full breakfast. €

Daugavpils

Gubernators
Lāčplēša 10
Tel: 542 2455
Open Sun–Thur 11am–midnight, Fri & Sat 11am–1am
Part beer hall, part restaurant, The Governor offers a good selection of brews, good atmosphere and sports via satellite TV. €

Ikšķile

Meidrops
Rīgas 18
Tel: 503 0466
www.meidrops.lv
Open daily 11am–midnight
Sandwiched between the highway and the River Daugava, this huge log cabin offers great food and good service, not to mention a beach volleyball court, sauna and excellent views. €€

Jelgava

Tami-Tami
Lielā 19a
Tel: 302 5378
Open Sun–Tues 11am–3am, Wed–Sat 11am–5am

Jelgava's most popular pizzeria decorated with black-and-white photographs and funky modern paintings is also a cocktail bar with a wide selection of drinks. €–€€

Jūrmala

Al Tohme
Pilsoņu 2, Majori
Tel: 775 5755
Open daily 11am–11pm
Perched on a hill above the white sandy beach at Majori, this Lebanese restaurant serves up authentic Middle Eastern cuisine, hookahs and excellent views. €€
Haizivs un bullis
Dulduru prospekts 31, Dulduri
Tel: 775 3371
Open daily noon–midnight
The Shark and Bull, which, not surprisingly, specialises in seafood and steaks, has a unique interior inspired by American Southwest architecture. €€

BELOW: dinner awaits in Rīga.

Slāvu restorāns
Jomas 57, Majori
Tel: 776 1401
Open daily noon–11pm
Sample Slavic cuisine here as diverse as meat dumplings, grilled sturgeon and borsch. Don't leave without trying one of their vodkas flavoured with garlic or horseradish. €€
Sue's Asia
Jomas 88a, Majori
Tel: 775 5900
Open daily noon–11pm
One of the country's few Indian restaurants also serves delicious Thai food on Jūrmala's most popular pedestrian street. €€–€€€

Kuldīga

Stenders
Liepājas 3
Tel: 332 2703
Open Sun–Thur 11am–11pm, Fri & Sat 11am–4am
Take the stairs to the second floor of this wooden building to find the city's best bar/café. It's also a favourite

TRANSPORT

ACCOMMODATION

EATING OUT

ACTIVITIES

A – Z

LANGUAGE

evening hangout attracting crowds of locals at the weekends. €–€€

Lielvārde

Kante
Laimdotas 1 (A6)
Tel: 507 1829
Open daily 11am–midnight
Friendly service, inexpensive Latvian food and local Lāčplēša beer on draught make this a popular stop on the way to Daugavpils. €

Liepāja

Latvia's 1st Rock Café
Zivju 3
Tel: 348 1555
www.pablo.lv
Open daily 9am–7am
Covering three floors and a cellar, this huge bar, club and restaurant is one of the largest entertainment complexes in Latvia. It also boasts live music every night and is open 24 hours during the summer. €€

Pastnieka māja
Brīvzemnieka 53
Tel: 340 7521
Open Mon–Thur noon–midnight, Fri & Sat noon–2am,
Sun 11am–midnight
This historic building is now the setting for the Postman's House, one of the city's best restaurants that serves its menu inside an envelope. €

Ragana

Raganas Ķēķis
Ragana A3, Rīga–Valmiera highway
Tel: 797 2266
Open Sun–Thur 9am–11pm, Fri & Sat 9am–midnight
Undoubtedly the best place to eat in the area, this charming roadside tavern offers typical Latvian dishes like pork chops and potatoes at cheap prices. €

Rēzekne

Mols
Latgales 22/24
Tel: 462 5353
Open Sun–Thur 9am–10pm, Fri & Sat 9am–midnight
Part art gallery, part café, Mols offers unique Latgalian cuisine and an interesting interior decorated with ceramics

and paintings that are all for sale. €

Rubene

Mazais Ansis
A3 Rubene, Rīga–Valmiera highway
Tel: 424 8400
www.mazais-ansis.lv
Only 6 km (4 miles) southwest of Valmiera this beautiful log cabin-style building offers excellent food and atmosphere as well as a playground, outdoor barbecue, boat hire on the lake and accommodation above the bar. €

Sigulda

Aparjods
Ventas 1a
Tel: 770 5242
www.aparjods.lv
Open daily noon–1am
Housed in a rustic building

with a wood-shingled roof, this charming restaurant decorated with antiques is the best place to eat in Sigulda. €€

Kropotkins
Pils 6
Tel: 797 2263
www.hotelsigulda.lv
Open Tues–Sun noon–11pm
Named after the family that once ruled this ancient town, this upmarket restaurant serves international cuisine in an ivy-draped fieldstone building. €€

Ventspils

ANRI
Tirgus laukums 1
Tel: 362 7155
Open daily 11am–2am
Just off the market square, ANRI is not only popular due to its large selection of international cuisine, but also because of its bowling alley on the ground floor. €€

Melnais sivēns
Jāņa 17
Tel: 362 2396
Open daily 10am–midnight
Located in the restored Livonian Order castle, this medieval-style restaurant specialises in its namesake – roast suckling pig. €€

CAFÉS

Rīga

Ai Karamba!
Pulkveža Brieža 2
Tel: 733 4672
www.aikaramba.com
Open Sun–Thur 8am–midnight, Fri & Sat 8am–1am.
An authentic American diner in the Art Nouveau quarter, which is also the best place in the city for an early or late breakfast. €

A. Suns
Elizabetes 83/85
Tel: 728 8418
Open Mon–Wed 10am–1am, Thur–Fri 10am–3am, Sat 11am–3am, Sun 11am–1am
Funky arty hangout located in a former workshop with a small cinema upstairs. €€

Lidojošā varde
Elizabetes 31a
Tel: 732 1184
Open daily 10am–midnight
A staple of the Rīga dining scene for several years, the Flying Frog is often frequented by expatriates from surrounding embassies.
€€

Salt 'n' Pepper
13 janvāra 33
Tel: 722 6835
Open Mon–Fri 8.30am–midnight, Sat & Sun 9am–midnight
This bright atrium café and bar has become popular due to its funky décor, cheap breakfast buffet and a long wooden table with its own beer tap.
€€

V. Kruse
Jekaba 20/22
Tel: 732 2943
Open 8am–10pm
Small Art Deco cafe in the Old Town, selling handmade cakes and chocolates.
€

BARS

Rīga

Četri Balti Krekli
Vecpilsētas 12
Tel: 721 3885
www.krekli.lv
The best place to see local acts perform on weekend nights. All of the music played here is Latvian and the lively crowds often include a number of poets and politicians.

Dickens
Grēcinieku 9/1
Tel: 721 3087
Open Sun–Thur 11am–1am, Fri & Sat 11am–2am
This plush English pub has good food and a great beer selection and is popular among Rīga's expatriate boozers.

Paddy Whelan's
Grēcinieku 4
Tel: 721 0249
Open Sun–Thur 10am–midnight, Fri & Sat 10am–2am
Rīga's first Irish pub has changed owners several times over the years, but you're always guaranteed good service and a decent selection of beers. The

second floor has been transformed into a cosy sports bar.

Paldies Dievam Piektdiena ir klāt
11 novembra krastmala 9
Tel: 750 3964
Open Mon–Thur 9am–1am,
Fri 9am–2am, Sat 9am–4am,
Sun noon–1am
Perhaps the best drinks to be had in town, served in a bright, lively Caribbean atmosphere where staff

wear tropical gear and dancers in bikinis delight audiences on the bar on weekends.

Pulkvedim Neviens Neraksta
Peldu 26/28
Tel: 721 3886
Open Sun–Thur noon–3am,
Fri & Sat noon–5am
Riga's hippest restaurant/bar/club in the Old Town is named after Gabriel García Marquéz's book *Nobody*

Writes to the Colonel and draws an artsy, intellectual crowd. An admission fee of 3Ls operates on weekends.

Rīgas Balzama bārs
Torņa 4
Tel: 721 4494
Open Sun–Thur 8.30am–midnight,
Fri & Sat 8.30am–1am
Award-winning bartenders serve drinks with flair at this cosy cellar bar that specialises in cocktails

made with Latvia's national drink.

LITHUANIA

In Lithuania's cities you can find almost all major cuisines. Top hotels often have some of the city's best restaurants and often are a safe bet for those who wish to slowly ease themselves into the local cuisine.

Lithuanian cuisine, which is mainly based on potatoes, is rich and rather fatty. The national dish, *cepelinai* (mashed potato rolls filled with meat and dripping in a buttery bacon sauce), is quite a mouthful. Although traditional Lithuanian food tends to be some combination of meat (usually pork), cabbage and potatoes there are many pleasant exceptions to the rule. Lighter eaters will enjoy the array of salads and soups, which usually are more than just a fair sprinkling on the menu. Most menus are written in Lithuanian, Russian, English, German or French.

RESTAURANTS

Vilnius

Balti Drambliai
Vilniaus 41
Tel: 262 0875
Open Mon–Fri 11am–midnight, Sat & Sun noon–midnight
As the only completely non-smoking vegetarian restaurant in town, with a lovely courtyard, the "White Elephants" deserves a large stamp of approval.

Laid back service, so stay cool. €

Čagino
Basanavičiaus 11
Tel: 261 5555
Open daily noon–midnight
The only centrally located Russian restaurant in the city serves up some fabulous fare. Impromptu singing by inebriated Russian men adds an extra touch of authenticity. €€

Čili Kaimas
Vokiečių 8
Tel: 231 2536
Open Mon–Thur & Sun 10am–midnight, Fri & Sat 10am–4am
Wood and hearty potions are in abundance at this large, somewhat Disney-fied version of a traditional Lithuanian restaurant. Queuing up is not unusual at weekends. €€

Forto Dvaras
Pilies 16
Tel : 261 10 70
Open daily :10am–midnight
Upstairs is a faux cottage, downstairs a cellar and everywhere the music is loud. Music and sound are core Lithuanian, with regional varieties of cepelinai. The meals are great value and the service sort of friendly and efficient. €€

Pegasus
Didžioji 11
Tel: 260 9430
www.restaurant-pegasus.lt
Open daily 11.30am–midnight
European food with an Asian twist is in swishy surroundings. Exclusive

crowd on the late evening cocktail circuit. €€€

Lokys
Stiklių 8
Tel: 262 5267
www.lokys.lt
Open daily noon–1am
Through the courtyard and down a narrow staircase find this cellar where local game dishes abound. Tamer types may opt for the handful of vegetarian dishes. €€€

Markus ir Ko
Antokolskio 11
Tel: 262 3185
Open daily noon–midnight
Located on a small street off Stiklių is one of the oldest steakhouses in the city. Customers are guaranteed to get exactly what they want as they must choose their sauce, cut of beef and accompanying side dishes. €€€€

Neringa
Gedimino 23
Tel: 261 4058
Open Mon–Wed & Sun 7am–11pm, Thur–Sat 7am–midnight
A giant mural of hard-working peasants fits Neringa's former glorious past as the elite meeting spot during Soviet times. The butter sputtering around is from their signature dish, the chicken Kiev. Live music at the weekend ensures the middle-aged crowd gets exercise. €€€

La Provence
Vokiečių 22
Tel: 261 6573
www.laprovence.lt
Open daily 11am–midnight
The cellar interior belies

the *haute cuisine* within this French restaurant. Lovely service and outrageously good food. €€€€€

Riverside restaurant
Konstitucijos 20
Tel: 272 6272
Open Mon–Fri 6.30am–11.30pm, Sat & Sun 7am–11.30pm
Inside the Reval Hotel, the chefs here respect food in a way not entirely common to the Baltics. Expect light flavours and a dining experience. €€€€

Stikliai
Gaono 7
Tel: 264 9580
Open daily noon–midnight
Lithuanian and French food form a happy marriage in this well-known spot for Vilnius's elite. (Next door is their old-fashioned and still upscale beer cellar, Stiklių Aludė, which serves more traditional fare for a third of the price.) €€€€€

Tores
Užupio 40
Tel: 262 9309
Open Mon–Thur & Sun 11am–midnight, Fri & Sat 11am–2am
Although named after a Spanish wine, the kitchen

mostly sends out plates of Lithuanian cuisine. Summer days on their terrace overlooking the Old Town will make you feel like everything is right in the world. Reservations are usually a must, especially in summer. €€–€€€

Ukrainos Vakarai
Algirdo 5
Tel: 265 0302
Open Mon–Thur 11am–10pm, Fri & Sat noon–midnight, Sun noon–10pm
Just a short walk from the Old Town, this is the place to sample the Ukrainian take on the medley of potatoes, meat and cabbage – not completely dissimilar to Lithuanian. Their selection of vodkas makes the occasionally loud Ukrainian pop music less irritating. €€

Vandens Malūnas
Verkių 100
Tel: 271 1666
www.vandensmalunas.lt
Open daily noon–midnight
The Water Mill makes the trip north from Vilnius worthwhile. Its huge terrace is appreciated in summer, its fireplace-warmed interior in winter. The menu is varied, but stays somewhat run-of-the-mill. Great for children. €€–€€€

Žemaičių Smuklė
Vokiečių 24
Tel: 261 6573
Open daily 11am–midnight
This traditional cellar tavern/outdoor beer garden is great fun. The food is a delectable array of national dishes that are complemented best by their strong homemade brew. Highly recommended. €€€

Kaunas

Bernelių Užeiga
Valančiaus 9
Tel: 200 913

ABOVE: Lithuanian restaurant sign.

www.berneliuuziega.lt
Open Sun–Thur 9am–midnight, Fri & Sat 11am–1am
All the delightful trappings of a "Lithuanian" restaurant – the staff and the food are all dressed traditionally. Occasional live music. €€

Medžiotojų Užeiga
Rotušės 10
Tel: 320 956
Open 11am–midnight
The Hunter's Tavern serves up all manner of local game dishes right on Town Hall Square. Look for the door with the antler handles. A bit on the stiff side. €€€–€€€€

Miesto Sodas
Laisvės 93
Tel: 424 424
Open 11am–11pm
One of the loveliest places to sit in Kaunas as the

dining room is partially enclosed by glass, ensuring a good view onto the City Gardens or the people walking past. Food is exceptionally good. €€–€€€

Pas Prancišką
Zamenhofo 11
Tel: 203 875
Open 10am–10pm (closed sun)
No one will be blowing smoke rings on to you in this no-smoking establishment, but the menu is only in Lithuanian. This is the only trade-off, as the food is excellent. €€

Pizzeria Milano
Mickevičiaus 19
Tel: 206 382
Open Sun–Thur 9am–1am, Fri & Sat 9am–2.30am
Some of the best pizza can be found inside the Kaunas Army Officer's Club. When crowded, expect to share your red-and-white checked tablecloth. €€

Unija
Kiškių Takas 20
Tel: 749 544
Open Sun–Thur noon–midnight, Fri & Sat 11am–2am
As the kids re-enact the battle of Žalgiris in the medieval castle outside the

restaurant, adults can enjoy the huge dining hall with stone fireplace. €€–€€€

Viva Blynai-Viva Koldunai
Laisves 53
Tel: 42 52 37
Open 10am–9pm, Sat 10am–8pm, Sun 11am–7pm
A great place for a snack. Self-service specialising in *blynai* (rolled pancakes) and *koldunai* (Lithuanian ravioli) where you can eat as much as you can fit onto your plate. €

Žalias Ratas
Laisvės 36b
Tel: 200 071
Open 11am–midnight
The huge fireplace in the centre of this thatched-roof restaurant aids in the "step back in time" feel of this place. One of the better places in town. €€

Outside Kaunas

Bajorkiemis
Vilnius–Kaunas highway
Tel: 440 770
www.berneliuuziega.lt
Open Mon 10am–10pm, Tues–Thur 10am–midnight, Fri & Sat 10am–1am
This place somehow manages to attract all sorts of visitors. This huge roadside restaurant serves up hearty portions of Lithuanian standards. A lake, a petting zoo and crafts workshops round out the experience. €€–€€€

Klaipėda

Boogie Woogie
H. Manto 5
Tel: 411 844
Fax: 213 894
Open Mon–Thur 11am–midnight, Fri & Sat 11am–2am, Sun noon–midnight
The original Boogie Woogie (there is also one in Kaunas) is still one of the hippest places to have a solid meal. €€–€€€

Memelis
Žvejų 4
Tel: 403 040
www.memelis.lt
Open Mon 11am–midnight, Tues–Thur 11am–2am, Fri & Sat 11am–3am, Sun noon–midnight
This brewery/restaurant is a popular haunt usually filled with tourists. The Lithuanian menu has a German influence. €€€

FAST FOOD

McDonalds' Baltic headquarters is in Lithuania, and there are outlets in every major town in the country. In Vilnius, the opening of their drive-in went hand-in-hand with a

thorough clean-up of the entire train station area. For inexpensive local food see the café section on the next page.

For cheap pizza look out for the ubiquitous **Čili Pizza** outlets.

DRINKING SNACKS

Lithuania has some excellent beers. The main brands are Horn, Kalnapilis, Švyturys, Utenos and Tauras. Along with a beer-drinking culture the Lithuanians have also perfected the beer snack. The most common is *kepta duona* (fried bread), which are pieces of dark bread deep-fried and accompanied by a massive amount of garlic. Some enjoy it *su sūriu* (with cheese) melted on top. Meat products like smoked pig's ears (*rūkytos kiaulių ausys*), pig's leg (*kiaulės koja*), dried meats similar to jerky (*basturma*) and beef tongue (*jautienos liežuvis*) are also common.

Anikės Kursiai
Sukilėlių 8
Tel: 314 471
Open daily 11am–midnight
This is perhaps the finest dining in the city with quality dishes. Expect to see the city's well-heeled spending their riches. €€€€
Ferdinandas
Naujoji Uosto 10
Tel: 313 681
Open Mon–Fri 10am–midnight, Sat & Sun noon–midnight
Authentic Russian cuisine in swishy surroundings. Recommended. Occasional live music. €€€
Metų Laikai
Donelaičio 6b
Tel: 410 373
Open daily 11am–midnight
Quite possibly the classiest restaurant in town, "Seasons of the Year" always seems to impress. If the weather allows, their patio is a superb place to enjoy your meal. €€€€
Trys Mylimos
Taikos 23
Tel: 411 479
Open 11am–midnight
This quaint ode to olde Lithuania has linen-clad waitresses serving up national dishes to hungry locals and tourists alike. Pleasant. Occasional, traditional live music. €€€

Palanga

The pulse of Palanga is along Basanavičiaus and as such the street is crammed with numerous restaurants, bars and cafés. With such competition, establishments tend not to slack on atmosphere, food or service.

Baltoji Žuvėdra
Dariaus ir Girėno 1
Tel: 484 15
Open daily 8am–7pm
Inside the Baltoji Žuvėdra Hotel is a glass-enclosed dining room looking out to the sea. More romance than some can handle. €€€–€€€€
Pušų Paunksnėje
Dariaus ir Girėno 25
www.pusupaunksneje.lt
Open daily 8am–midnight
A pleasant medley of European and Lithuanian food can be found inside this unpretentious but upscale hotel restaurant. €€€–€€€€
Vila Ramybė
Vytauto 54
Tel: 541 24
Open 9am–midnight
The proprietor's love for food and music is undeniable. The attractiveness of this restaurant, where ordering anything from a full meal to just a drink is acceptable, is in its accommodating ambience. €€

Outside Palanga

HBH Brewery
Žibininkų village
Tel: (8-445) 446 78
Open Tues–Sun 10am–midnight, Mon noon–midnight
A good old-fashioned brewery serving Lithuanian food and some Chinese flavours too. Although a bit odd, the brewery usually proves fun, especially for Sunday outings and for children, as its large grounds and play structures can keep them entertained. €€

Nida

Ešerinė
Naglių 2
Tel: 527 57

Open 10am–midnight
Sitting in a hut alongside the water while eating fish will make you wonder if you should just move here. €€
Seklyčia
Lotmiškio 1
Tel: 529 45
Open 9am–midnight
The most upscale dining in this sleepy village. Their rooftop terrace has unbeatable views. €€€
Sena Sodyba
Naglių 6-2
Tel: 527 82
Open daily 10am–10pm
This tiny garden makes the most charming "dining room". The menu, although diminutive, augments the delightful atmosphere. €€

CAFÉS

Vilnius

Mano Kavinė
Bokšto 7
Open daily 11am–2am, Fri–Sat 11am–4am
A good selection of light snacks and a few heartier meals along with charming staff makes the somewhat student hang-out of "My Café" welcoming to all. €
Ponių Laimė
Stiklių 14/1
Tel: 264 9581
Open Mon–Fri 9am–8pm, Sat 10am–8pm, Sun 11am–6pm
Coffee, cakes and a few savoury dishes is what the proprietors must think brings the "ladies' happiness" as that is how the name translates. The same Stikliai group also own the similar **Pauzė Café** at Aušros Vartų 5. No credit cards. €
Skonis ir Kvapas
Trakų 8
Tel: 212 2803
Open Mon–Fri & Sun 8.30am–11pm, Sat 8.30am–11pm
Walk through the marked courtyard to find this delightful café. Food is superb and tea is fit for a queen. Two non-smoking rooms at the back. €€

Kaunas

Pas Gertrūdą
Laisvės 101A
Tel: 200 486

Open Tues–Sun 9.30am–11pm, Mon 9.30am–10pm
Get a tray, get in line and point to what you want to eat. Lovely in its simplicity. No credit cards. €

Klaipėda

12 Kėdžių
Kanto 21
Tel: 219 343
Open 9am–11pm
Named after the popular Russian story, this café has more charm than a school of Southern belles. Waiting times for service can be lengthy.

BARS

Vilnius

Amatininkų Užeiga
Didžioji 19
Open 10am–5pm
A good central meeting spot on the Town Square, and popular with locals. Several rooms and good snacks.
Šoulalkinio Meno Centras
Vokiečiu 2
Open 11am–midnight
In the Contemporary Arts Centre, this is a bar where the arty crowd meets.
Užupio Kavinė
Užupio 2
Open 10am–11pm
The breakaway republic's favourite spot, with a terrace overlooking the river. Good snacks, too.

Kaunas

Avilys
Vilniaus gatvė
Open 11am–midnight
Beer is brewed on the premises of this attactive cellar bar.

PRICE CATEGORIES

These prices are for a starter, main dish and dessert for one person and should be taken as a guide only:
€€€€€ = over 75Lt
€€€€ = 60–75Lt
€€€ = 45–60Lt
€€ = 30–45Lt
€ = below 30Lt
Drinks will double the bill.

TRANSPORT · ACCOMMODATION · EATING OUT · ACTIVITIES · A–Z · LANGUAGE

ACTIVITIES

FESTIVALS, THE ARTS, NIGHTLIFE, SHOPPING AND SPECTATOR SPORTS

FESTIVALS

For Public Holidays, see A–Z, Page 366. For background information, see Folklore chapter, page 59.

January

New Year is celebrated throughout the Baltics, with fireworks and gatherings in town squares.
The Magi (6th) The Magi arrive in Vilnius Cathedral Square.
OpeNBaroque: (late January or early February) long-standing series of concerts in Tallinn centred on baroque and other early music.

February

Shrovetide. In Estonia, this day is called Vastlapäev, and is the day when children go sledding. In Lithuinia on the weekend before Lent Užgavėnės takes place in Vilnius Old Town when people wear costumes and masks; in the evening a large effigy of a woman is burned.
Rīga Fashion Week. This annual showcase features new talents from the whole of Europe.
International Ice-sculpture Festival and art symposium (first week), Jelgava, Latvia.

March

St Casimir (4th, or closest weekend). The patron saint of Lithuania is celebrated with a large fair, Kaziukas, in Vilnius Old Town. Everyone carries *verbos*, a long stick of colourful dried flowers, grasses and/or herbs, used later at Palm Sunday services.

April

Jazzkaar international jazz festival in Tallinn, with world-class performers.
International Baltic Ballet Festival is held in Rīga and features the best performers from the Baltic Sea region.
Bimini International Animated Film Festival, Rīga.

May

Spring Student Days (early May), Tartu. Thousands of Tartu's students take part in creative and often silly competitions, including river races in bizarre, homemade boats.
Museum Day (May 24), all museums free, with interactive night tours.
Grillfest (May–June, weekend and location vary). Casual, two-day event involving barbecues, games and rock music.
International Folklore Festival, Vilnius.

June

Old Town Days Festival (first week). Entertaining mix of medieval tournaments, markets and concerts all over Tallinn's Old Town.
Annual Crafts Fair (first weekend) at Rīga's Ethnographic Museum.
Annual Dome Square Crafts Fair (22nd), Rīga. Large event with many stalls anticipating midsummer.
Midsummer's Eve (23rd–24th). The Baltic states' favourite national holiday is always celebrated on the actual date and never moved to the closest weekend for sake of convenience. The pagan fertility celebrations consist of singing, dancing, lots of beer and bonfires in the countryside. Called Jaanipäev in Estonia, Jāņi in Latvia and Joninės in Lithuania, it is a festival of pagan origins, deeply rooted in peasant culture. The date marks the end of spring labours in the fields and used to be seen as a night of omens and sorcery. One tradition that still exists is that of leaping over bonfires. A successful clearance of the flames used to indicate similar success for the year ahead. On the days leading up to this festival Tallinn is drained of people, as everyones heads for the countryside. At Jāņi in Latvia special beers and cheeses are made for the occasion and citizens sport floral wreathes. In Lithuania, the town of Kernavė, a small village about 24 km (15 miles) north of Vilnius off the A2 motorway is the best place to enjoy the festivities. The highlight of the evening is when young girls take off the wreaths from their heads, surround them with candles and set them afloat along the Neris and the water, half-lit by moonlight and far-off bonfires, carries the hundreds of candles downstream.
Rīga Opera Festival (lasts two weeks). Celebrities have included Warren Mok, Inese Galante and other international stars.
Rīgas Ritmi Rhythmic Music Festival R&B and Latin bands from around the world take part in this annual festival in Rīga.
Vilnius Festival celebrates the classical music in many of Vilnius's venues and is overseen by the Vilnius Philharmonic

July

Beer Summer (early July). Estonia's largest outdoor party. Five days of beer tasting, concerts, carnival rides and games for children.
Mindaugas Coronation Day (6th). A Lithuanian national holiday; a large festival takes place in Kernavė.
Watergate Water Festival (mid-July) Pärnu. Boat races, flotillas, water sports and a number of other water-related activities (as well as pop concerts) take over Estonia's "Summer Capital".
Baltic Beach Party Annual International Rock Festival on the beach in Liepāja, Latvia.

Open-air Opera Festival, Sigulda Castle ruins, Latvia.

St Christopher Festival A large music festival throughout Vilnius. See www.kristupofestivaliai.lt for exact dates and venues.

International Organ Festival (late July or early August), Tallinn.

Viljandi Folk Music Festival (late July), Viljandi. In one of the largest events of the Estonian summer, folk music groups, both Estonian and international, gather to perform.

Song and Dance Festival

The next Song and Dance Festival will take place in the summer of 2008 in Latvia, and in 2009 in Estonia. The festival has been held roughly every five years since 1873 and its highlight is the final concert during which hundreds of choirs from around the country sing together in front of tens of thousands of spectators who often join in on the most popular songs.

August

August Dance, Tallinn. Modern dance performances by cutting-edge groups from Estonia and abroad.

Banitis Festival (first weekend). Narrow-gauge railway festival at Ates Mills Gulbene, Latvia. www.banitis.lv

Rīga Sacred Music Festival (Aug–Sept). Musicians from around Europe converge on Rīga to play religious music.

Annual Organ Music Festival at Dome Cathedral, Rīga (when restoration is completed).

Visagino Country International country music and bluegrass festival in Visaginas, Lithuania. Dates change annually. For details see the website web.sugardas.lt/country.

Feast of the Assumption (Šolinė, 15th). A Lithuanian public holiday with activities throughout the country. The Rumšiškės Open Air Museum of Lithuania also hosts a celebration.

September

Homo Novus (Sept–Dec). International Festival of Contemporary Theatre takes place every two years in Rīga.

Vilnius Capital Days is a week of folk concerts and fairs. For more information and latest dates see www.vilniusfestivals.lt

Vilnius Jazz Festival when music is heard throughout the city. See www.vilniusjazz.lt for more information and latest dates.

Old Music Festival (Sept–Oct). Medieval and baroque church music

played in many of the city's churches.

November

All Saint's Day (1st). People visit cemeteries, placing candles around graves.

Black Nights Film Festival (two weeks, beginning late Nov or early Dec), Tallinn. International feature films, with sub-festivals for student films, children's films and animation.

December

Christmas Jazz (early December), Tallinn. An event similar to the April Jazzkaar but less ambitious in scale.

Christmas is celebrated throughout the Baltics with concerts, decorated trees and craft markets.

THE ARTS

The admission price to most **museums** is nominal. Irrespective of the collection, it's often worth paying this fee just to look inside the building. Several of the main museums are located in beautifully preserved medieval guild houses or merchants' buildings, while manor houses and churches provide other venues of architectural interest. Many museums close on Mondays, or sometimes Tuesdays, and they may have a free day of the week (usually Wednesday in Lithuania).

Information on current exhibitions can be found in the local *In Your Pocket* guides and most galleries promote their exhibitions with posters around the town.

Estonia

Theatre

Theatre has enjoyed enormous popularity in this country since the 19th century when the first Estonian plays arose out of the National Awakening. The centre of the nation's theatrical activity has traditionally been Tallinn, including several small experimental theatres, but there are well-established houses in Tartu, Pärnu and Viljandi too. Note that all performances, except those at the Russian Drama Theatre, are in Estonian. Full information on Estonia's theatre scene, as well as programmes, can be found at www.teater.ee.

Eesti Draamateater (Estonian Drama Theatre), Pärnu mnt. 5, tel: 6805 555; www.draamateater.ee. Tallinn's pre-eminent theatre since the 1950s, it has a repertoire stretching from Shakespeare to modern Estonian

comedy. It is housed in a beautiful, Art Nouveau building in central Tallinn.

Tallinna Linnateater (Tallinn City Theatre), Lai 23, tel: 6650 850; www.linnateater.ee. Three medieval buildings in Old Town make up the City Theatre's house. In summer, plays are staged in the outdoor arena, in back.

Endla Teater, Keskväljak 1, Pärnu, tel: 44 42 4804420 000, www.endla.ee. A time-honoured institution playing in a very modern house in central Pärnu.

Vanemuine Theatre, Vanemuine 6, Tartu, tel: 7440 167, www.vanemuine.ee. Tartu's all-in-one theatre is also the city's main venue for ballet, opera and classical music.

Music and Dance

Virtually every night from September to May, a classical performance is held at the Estonia Theatre and Concert Hall. More often than not the performances are given by the Estonian National Symphony or the Estonian National Opera. Guest orchestras, choirs and ensembles are also invited from around the world. These performances usually transfer to other concert halls, notably to Tartu's Vanemuine Theatre and the Pärnu Concert Hall. Churches, guild halls and other historic buildings also frequently serve as classical concert venues. Details of performances are posted on notice boards outside the concert halls and around city centres.

Estonia Concert Hall, Estonia pst. 4, tel: 6147 760, www.concert.ee, www.opera.ee. There are operas and ballets here as well as classical concerts. Look out for performances by the Tallinn Philharmonic Society (tel: 6613 757; www.filharmoonia.ee) and for Tallinn's early-music ensemble, Hortus Musicus, whose repertoire of baroque and Renaissance music fits in well with the city's historic ambience.

Other venues in Estonia include: **Mustpeade Maja** (House of the Brotherhood of the Blackheads), Pikk 26, tel/fax: 6313 199, www.mustpeademaja.ee. The medieval Guild Hall is an intimate venue for smaller classical events.

Niguliste (St Nicholas') Church, Niguliste 3, tel: 6449 911, www.ekm.ee. Organ concerts are held every Saturday and Sunday afternoon in a casual atmosphere. Concert times are posted outside.

Väravatorn, Lühike jalg 9, tel: 6147 760. The early-music ensemble, Hortus Musicus, occasionally performs in this 15th-century tower.

Vanemuine Theatre. *See "Theatre" above.*
Pärnu Kontserdimaja (Pärnu Concert Hall), Aida 4, tel: 4455 810, www.concert.ee. Built in 2003, the high-tech, towering concert hall also serves as a catch-all cultural centre and houses the city's art gallery.

Latvia

Theatre

Latvians have traditionally been seen as a nation of theatregoers and hundreds of people from the countryside take buses to Rīga for the premieres of new plays:
Latvian National Theatre (Nacionālais teātris), Kronvalda bulv. 2, tel: 732 2759, www.teatris.lv. This fantastic theatre was completely renovated in 2004 and continues to draw crowds for traditional Latvian plays.
Russian Drama Theatre (Krievu drāmas teātris), Kaļķu 16, tel: 722 4660. New and classic plays in Russian.
New Rīga Theatre (Jaunais Rīgas teātris), Lāčplēša 25, tel: 728 0765, www.jrt.lv. Avant-garde plays are often sold out at Rīga's most popular theatre.
Dailes Theatre (Dailes teātris), Brīvības 75, tel: 727 0278. This large theatre shows classic plays from around the world in Latvian.
Valmiera Drama Theatre (Valmieras drāmas teātris), Lāčplēša 1, tel: 420 7334, www.vdt.lv. This renowned theatre has been in operation under various names since 1919 and its extensive repertoire includes plays from Chechov and Ibsen as well as Latvian classics and new drama.
Liepaja Theatre (Liepājas teātris), Teātra 4, tel: 340 7811, http://teatris.liepajanet.lv. One of Latvia's oldest theatres still has regular performances of classic plays in autumn and winter.

Music and Dance

With such native sons as Mikhail Baryshnikov and Alexander Gudunov, it's no surprise that Rīga's ballet and opera draw crowds from around Europe. The city is never short of concerts and festivals, but organisers seldom know exact dates until only weeks and sometimes even days before an event.
Dome Cathedral (Doma baznīca), Doma laukums 1, tel: 721 3213. Professionals from around the globe often waive their fees just to play on the magnificent organ, which has 6,718 pipes and is one of the world's largest.
House of Blackheads (Melngalvju nams), Rātslaukums 7, tel: 704

Cinema

Cinema is an easy entertainment option in the Baltic countries as films are nearly always shown in their original language, with subtitles. The Forums Coca-Cola Plaza (www.forumcinemas.lv) in Riga offers 14 cinema halls and a 260 square metre film screen, the second largest in Northern Europe.

4300. Venue of frequent chamber music concerts.
Latvian National Opera House (Latvijas Nacionālā opera), Aspazijas bulvāris 3, tel: 707 3777, ww.opera.lv. Opulently decorated with gilded ceilings, crystal chandeliers and priceless works of art.
Wagner Hall (Vāgnera zāle), Vāgnera 4, tel: 721 0817. Concert hall named after the famous composer who conducted there.
The Great Guild (Lielā Ģilde), Amatu 6, tel: 721 3798. Home to the Latvian Philharmonic Orchestra, which has a host of national and international concert events.
The Small Guild (Mazā Ģilde), Amatu 3/5, tel: 722 3772. Across the street from the Great Guild, it often hosts chamber-music concerts and special events.

Lithuania

Theatre

In spite of funding difficulties the main theatres in Vilnius show a broad range of plays. The country has a strong acting tradition and many players enjoy excellent reputations. Look out for performances at the university and by troupes such as the 15-strong Lithuanian National Theatre, which are particularly good. Performances usually start at 6 or 7pm, and resumés are sometimes available in English.
National Drama Theatre (Lietuvos nacionalinis dramos teatras), Gedimino pr. 4, tel: 262 97 71, www.teatras.lt. The theatre has two stages – a main one and a small platform located round the back of the building.
Vilnius Small Theatre (Vilniaus mažasis teatras), Gedimino pr. 4, tel/fax: 261 31 95, www.vmt.lt.
Russian Drama Theatre (Rusų dramos teatras), Basanavičiaus 13, tel: 262 71 33/262 05 52. Puts on Russian-language plays.
Youth Theatre (Jaunimo teatras), Arklių 5, tel: 261 61 26. Ambitious

productions of classical and modern works.
OKT (Oskaro Koršunovo teatras), Gedimino 4, tel: 261 00 15, www.okt.lt. The theatre director Oskaras Koršunovas's troupe performs more contemporary works at National Theatre stage.

Music and Dance

The new **Siemens Arena** (Ozo 14, tel: 1653) is in the northwest section of the city. In summer many concerts, from classical to metal, take place in **Vingis Park**'s amphitheatre. All tickets to events in Vilnius can be purchased at the kiosk at Gedimino 9A (tel: 212 11 81; open daily 10am–8pm) or online: www.bilietai.lt or www.tiketa.lt.
Tickets for most classical concerts in Vilnius can be purchased beforehand at the central ticket office of the National Philharmonic, where one of the country's leading concert halls is also found.
National Philharmonic Aušros Vartų 5, tel: 627 165/222 290, fax: 622 859, info@ filharmonija.lt, www.filharmonija.lt
Opera and Ballet Theatre (Operos ir baleto teatras), Vienuolio 1, tel: 620 636, www.opera.lt. Opera and ballet productions are wide ranging but on the whole are classical and conservative.
Vilnius Congressional Palace. Tel: 261 88 28, www.lvso.lt. One of the best venues for classical music in the city with excellent acoustics and a large stage. Often plays host to large orchestra performances.

NIGHTLIFE

Summer nights are long in the Baltic states and there are few better ways to relax than to sit in an outdoor café, beer in hand, watching the world slowly meander past. When the day gets late, however, most people like to head for more social surroundings. The capitals in particular have a wide spectrum of nightlife to explore – everything from quiet, sophisticated lounges to pulsing dance clubs.

Estonia

Tallinn
Like everything else in Tallinn, most of the nightlife is squeezed into a few Old Town streets, giving rise to the custom of frequent bar-hopping. Since the bars are literally only a few paces apart, locals (and savvy visitors) will often change locations

after every single drink, exploring all the options until they finally find the place they want to settle in.

Bars and pubs are easy to find in Old Town – just follow the crowds and the noise. Beware, though, that annoying groups of British stag weekenders (bachelor partiers) infiltrate many of the central pubs, so the saner crowds tend to go elsewhere. **Molly Malone's** (Mündi 2, tel: 6313 016) on the square is still a safe bet and has good live music most weekends. **Hell Hunt** (Pikk 39, tel: 6818 333) has a good atmosphere and its own brand of beer. Local flavour can be found in the crowded **Karja-Kelder** (Väike Karja 1, tel: 6441 008).

For more cosmopolitan, lounge-type surroundings, **Lounge 8** (Vana-Posti 8, tel: 6274 770) and **Pegasus** (Harju 1, tel: 6314 040) are both good choices. Cosy wine bars are also fashionable. Two highly recommended wine bars are **Kolme Näoga Mees** (Kuninga 1, tel: 6484 261) and **Gloria Veinikelder** (Müürivahe 2, tel: 6448 846).

Tallinn has an active, local band scene, and many of the larger bars and pubs offer live music on weekends. A couple of these, such as **Von Krahli Baar** (Rataskaevu 10, tel: 6269 096) and the cop-themed **Scotland Yard** (Mere pst. 6e, tel: 6535 190) build much of their business on live performance. The free mini-magazine *Heat*, distributed in bars, has the most complete schedule of who is playing where. Ask locals which of the bands are their favourites.

Nightclubs are also easy to find in Tallinn, but hard to recommend. Crowds are fickle, so what could be full of life on one night could be desolate the next. One that's always enormously popular, however, is the huge, central **Club Hollywood** (Vana-Posti 8, tel: 6274 770), which draws a young crowd. The scene at nearby **Club Privé** (Harju 6, tel: 6310 545) is more exclusive and mature.

Tartu

Tartu's student crowds give that city's nightlife a younger, more casual energy. The Irish-style **Wilde Pub** (Vallikraavi 4, tel: 7309 764) and the historic **Püssirohu Kelder** (Lossi 28, tel: 7303 560) are both popular live-music venues. **Nightclubs Atlantis** (Narva mnt. 2, tel: 7385 584) and **Pattaya Club** (Turu 21, tel: 7303 400) play mainstream dance hits. Those seeking more "club-style" sounds head to the trendy **Club Tallinn** (Narva mnt. 27, tel: 7403 157).

Pärnu

For the summer season, the same Club Tallinn packs up and moves to the "summer capital", Pärnu, where it sets up in the **Pärnu Kuursaal** (Mere pst. 22). Other notable clubs in Pärnu are the downtown **Mirage** (Rüütli 40: tel. 4472 04) and the beachside **Sunset Club** (Ranna pst. 3, tel: 4430 670). Generally though, Pärnu's nightlife is more rustic and down-to-earth than that of the larger cities. Pubs such as **Viies Villem** (Kuninga 11, tel: 4427 999) and **Postipoiss** (Vee 12, tel: 4464 864) offer live bands and an old-fashioned feel.

Latvia

Rīga

Trendy cocktail bars, chic clubs, 24-hour casinos and down-to-earth pubs occupy nearly every street corner in Rīga and, best of all, they seldom close their doors before everyone's had their fill.

For cosy, dimly lit atmosphere and expertly poured mixed drinks with the potent national elixir, take the steps down to the cellar of **Rigas Balzams** (Torņa 4, tel: 721 44 94). Nearly its exact opposite is the bright, modern **Skyline Bar** on the 26th floor of the Reval Hotel Latvia, which has the most spectacular views of the city (*see pages 180–181*).

For live blues music on weekends visit **Bites Blues Club** (Dzirnavu 34a, tel: 733 31 25), but those out for a more local experience should take in a concert by a Latvian band at the popular **Četri Balti Krekli** (Vecpilsētas 12, tel: 721 38 85). For dancing and seeing how the young and fashionable dress, try the huge techno club **La Rocca** (Brīvības 96, www.larocca.lv) or a hip alternative popular with Bohemians, **Pulkvedim Neviens Neraksta** (Peldu 26/28, tel: 721 38 86). The **Olympic Voodoo Casino** at the Reval Hotel Latvia is stylish and is open 24 hours.

Liepaja

In this coastal town, **First Rock Café** is a large friendly club decorated with the posters and photographs of Latvian rock legents and different festivals. During the day it is a favourite place for families to have a meal. It's on three floors and there is an outdoor terrace in summer. Live concerts on Fridays in the basement. The **Fontain Club** has a big stage and regular live bands, bar and dancing area, plus the biggest drum machine in the world – the owner's own invention.

Lithuania

Vilnius

Most bars in Vilnius are open until the early hours of the morning and it is not uncommon to feel as though most people have been consuming high amounts of alcohol when roaming the streets after 10pm. Visitors should be more aware of their personal belongings in nightlife establishments and should stick to well-lit areas walking home.

Any time before midnight is a good time to visit one of the many beer tents that spring up along Pilies or Vokiečių. Later in the evening most patrons move inside for further drinking and discussion, or on to some of the city's clubs. New clubs practising face-control and charging exorbitant covers are rare. Many of the hotels across the river have entire complexes with nightclub, bar and casino as part of their repertoire.

For a quiet drink you can't beat **Būsi Trečias** (Totorių 18, tel: 231 26 98), with their home-made beer and wooden benches. Just down from the Gates of Dawn two particularly good places to have drinks are **Soho** (Aušros Vartų 7, tel: 212 12 10) and **Iki Aušros** (Aušros Vartų 15, tel: 8-610 041 31) as their cocktail selection will be appreciated by those with a more discerning palate. For a livelier atmosphere **Mano Kavinė** and **Mano Klubas** (Bokšto 7, tel: 215 30 00, www.manoklubas.com) are a café and adjacent club; both are exceptionally laid-back and comfortable even amid the occasional rowdiness of their patrons. **Brodvėjus** (Mėsinių 4, tel: 210 72 08, www.brodvejus.lt) is a large high-energy place for dancing at the weekends and often hosts live music shows. An unpretentious but sophisticated lounge/club can be found at **Cozy** (Dominikonų 10, tel: 261 11 37, www.cozy.lt). At Gedimino No. 46 is the ex-pat stand-by combination of **Prie Parlamento**, the bar, and the cellar dance club **Ministerija** (tel: 249 66 06), which tends to stick to safer beats. Across the river in the Reval Hotel Lietuva the **SkyBar** (Konstitucijos 20; tel: 272 62 72) serves up cocktails and an amazing view in swishy surroundings. Another club option, **Gravity** (Jasinskio 16, tel: 249 79 66, www.clubgravity.lt) is housed in a former bomb shelter and picks up a more eclectic crowd.

Kaunas

One of the best places to visit is **Miesto Sodas** (Laisvės 93, tel: 42

44 24), as the restaurant/bar's glass windows look out onto the city garden. There is also a nightclub, **Siena**, located downstairs.

Klaipėda
Kurpiai (Kurpių 1a, tel: 41 05 55) is considered one of the country's top venues for live jazz performances.

CHILDREN

Estonia

Tallinn
The most fun way to tour Tallinn's Old Town in summer is hitching a ride on **Toomas the Train**. The red-and-black electric locomotive departs from Vana-Turg Street (near Olde Hansa restaurant) and makes a 20-minute circuit through the cobblestone streets. Other entertainment in Tallinn includes:
The Doll Museum, Kotzebue 16, tel: 6413 491. Filled with teddy bears, dolls and other toys.
The Tallinn Science and Technology Centre, Põhja pst. 29, tel: 7152 650. Young audiences are dazzled with lighting displays and hands-on activities such as making giant soap bubbles.
The Kalev Confectionery Museum, Pikk 16. Discover the secrets of making traditional marzipan.
The Estonian Puppet Theatre, Lai 1, tel: 6679 550. Short performances for tots. The language is Estonian, but the colourful action is universal.
Indoor play centres: Jõmmi mängutuba, Narva mnt. 31, tel: 6558 358, and Riki-Tiki, Pärnu mnt. 59, tel: 6461 025. These offer ball pools, trampolines, climbing walls, crafts and organised entertainment. Here parents typically attend, but

BELOW: Tallinn Zoo.

the Reds play centres in the Kristiine Keskus and Ülemiste Keskus shopping malls are designed to watch your children while you shop.
Tallinn Zoo, Paldiski mnt. 145, tel: 6943 300. More than 350 species of animals, including wolves, tigers, bears, elephants and lynx, make their home here. An essential stop is the zoo's popular Tropical House, which simulates rainforest conditions for alligators and chimpanzees.
FK Centre, Paldiski mnt. 229a, tel: 6870 101. Engage in a laser shoot-out or live out Formula 1 fantasies on the high-speed, motorised go-cart track.

Pärnu
With its beach and parks, Pärnu is more naturally set up for children's enjoyment. The beachside promenades offer playgrounds, mini-golf, roller-skate rental and electric cars for tots.
Amusement Park, Remmeiga 5, tel: 4474 491. A Ferris wheel and other attractions, adjacent to Pärnu's beach.
Tervise Paradiis, Side 14, tel: 4451 606. This indoor water park is great for kids with its numerous waterslides, climbing wall and a variety of swimming pools.

Tartu
Tartu has its own indoor water park, albeit small. It's the **Aura Keskus** (Turu 10, tel: 7300 280). For outdoor fun, there is a playground on Toomimägi, and the well-developed **Kaubamaja Mänguplats** along Küüni Street.
Tartu Mänguasjamuuseum (Tartu Toy Museum), Lutsu 8, tel: 7461 777. An amazing collection of toys, as well as a playroom.
Atlantis Club, Narva mnt. 2, tel: 7385 584. Holds discos for kids every Sunday afternoon.

Latvia

Rīga
Vairak Saules (Dzirnavu 60, tel: 728 2878) and **B-Bars** (Doma laukums 2, tel: 722 8842) offer special games rooms for kids.
No trip to Rīga would be complete without a short trip to the kitschy **Lido Recreation Centre** (Krasta 76, tel: 750 4420). The complex's main attraction is a huge log cabin which offers three floors of Latvian restaurants and beer halls with live music and a supervised children's room with interactive games, colouring books and other activities. Outside is an amusement park that offers slides,

games, pony rides, skating and ice-skating in the winter.
State Puppet Theatre K. Barona 16/18, tel: 728 5418, www.puppet.lv. An excellent place for children to spend time and although the plays are performed in either Latvian or Russian, the plot is generally easy enough to follow. The theatre is usually closed July and August.
The Open-Air Ethnographic Museum, Brīvības gatve 440, tel: 799 4515 *(see Around Rīga chapter)*.
The Museum of Natural History *(see Rīga chapter)* has interactive computer learning games in English on the top floor past the bizarre specimens in formaldehyde.
The **Rīga National Zoo** *(see Around Rīga chapter)*. A quick tram ride from the centre will bring you in sight of lion, leopard, musk ox, alligator and other beasts.
Rīga Circus, Merķeļa 4, tel: 722 0272, www.circusriga.lv. Not quite what P.T. Barnum envisaged but a good place to view animals. The circus is seasonal and is closed each year from Easter until the third Friday in October.
Līvu Akvaparks water park, Lielupe, Vienības gatve 36, tel: 775 5640, www.akvaparks.lv. Six water slides, a wave pool, children's pool, a tubing river and various other attractions guaranteed to keep the kids engaged for several hours.
Akvalande water park (Mūkusalas 45/47, tel: 762 9700), close to the centre of Rīga, doesn't offer as many attractions as Līvu Akvaparks.

The coast
Latvia's coastal resorts are ideal for children. **Ventspils** is particularly well suited for families. The beach is well eqipped and there are lots of festivals throughout the summer. The Open Air Museum has has children's play area and a working steam train, and Children's World is dedicated to keeping them happy.
Cesis, There are lots of things for families to see and do in this popular outdoor area.

Lithuania

Vilnius
By far the most exciting place for children in the city is any of the outdoor festivals. During summer the occasional carnival or circus comes to town. If all else fails, take them to the mall. In both of the city's two large shopping centres, Akropolis (Ozo 25, tel: 248 4848) and Europa (Konstitucijos 7a, tel: 248 7070), there are play areas for children.

Iele Puppet Theatre, Aiklių 5, tel: 262 8678, has adorable shows that will engage younger guests despite language barriers.

The Outdoor Ethnographic Museum, Rumšiškės *(see page XX)* is littered with children's play structures made from wood. The kids might also learn something about farm life and crafts.

Pavilnys (Džiaugsmo 44, tel: 267 4873). A small petting zoo outside town. Opening times can be erratic so it is best to call ahead.

Kaunas
Ažuolynas Park, Kaunas (tel: 332 540). The only real zoo in the country is unremarkable (open Apr–Sept 9am–7pm, Oct–Mar 9am 5pm; admission fee).

SHOPPING

Estonia

Estonia is a great place to shop. Notable local products include art, knitwear, linen and a wide selection of handicrafts. Much of the delight of casual shopping here is not the goods but rather the shops themselves, many of which, particularly those in Tallinn's Old Town, possess great character. All shops listed here are in Tallinn unless otherwise stated.

Antiques
Antique shops seem to be everywhere, selling everything from 19th-century furniture, gramophones and jewellery to Soviet-era trinkets and military memorabilia. The trade in religious icons is still active here, although this has dropped off because it encourages their removal from isolated country churches.
Antikvaar, Rataskaevu 20, tel: 6418 269. A large shop with a varied assortment of furniture and distinctive, metal-worked items.
Reval Antiik, Pikk 31, tel: 6440 747. Every item you can imagine, from Russian samovars to ceiling lamps.

Fine Art & Graphics
From its very beginnings, Estonian fine art has spanned a number of different media, and many of its brightest stars expressed themselves with applied art and graphics even more so than painting. These days it's just as common, if not more common, to see art shops selling innovative works in ceramics, jewellery, glass, metal and textiles, rather than framed pictures. That said, painters such as Jüri Arrak

(1936) and a younger generation of oil-on-canvas innovators have become well-known internationally since independence was re-established.
Galerii 2, Lühike jalg 1, tel: 6418 308. Exquisitely made jewellery, ceramics, etched glasses and other items.
Haus Galerii, Uus 17, tel: 6419 471. Haus is a commercial gallery that features changing exhibitions of works by Estonia's finest painters.
Keraamikaa Ateljee, Pikk 33, tel: 6464 006. Part shop, part art studio, this is the best source for off-beat, whimsical ceramics.
Lühikese Jala Galerii, Lühike jalg 6, tel: 6314 720. An interesting place to shop, not only because it supplies such a range of fun, fresh artistic gifts, but because it has a natural spring running through the wall in the back room.
Navitrolla Galerii, Pikk jalg 7, tel: 6313 716. Contemporary Estonian artist Navitrolla has become known for his strange animal creations. Prints are sold in his shop, as are T-shirts, coffee mugs, etc.

Books
The selection of English-language books in Estonia leaves something to be desired, but there are usually a few travel and gift books about Tallinn and Estonia in the shops. Books by Estonian author Jaan Kross can often be found in English.
Allecto, Juhkentali 8, tel: 6277 230. Specialising in foreign-language books, this shop has a small but respectable collection of novels and travel books.
Apollo Ramatumaja, Viru 23, tel: 6548 486. Books on Tallinn and Estonia, as well as novels in English, are on the ground floor. Technical books and dictionaries are upstairs.
Raamatukoi, Voorimehe 9, tel: 6442 633. A squirrel's nest of second-hand and antiquarian books, maps, postcards, magazines, etc.
Rahva Raamat, Viru väljak 4/6, on the 4th floor of the Viru Centre. It probably has the largest collection of English-language books in Tallinn.

Handicrafts
You can find the best hand-made sweaters, mittens and caps at the knitwear market on Tallinn's Müürivahe Street, Tallinn *(see Markets, below)*. An equally fascinating place to pick up a gift or two is the **Katariina Guild**, in the Katariina Passage that runs from the knitwear market to Vene Street. In this string of small workshops, visitors can watch craftswomen at

work creating quilts, ceramics, glass items, hand-painted silk, jewellery and even hats. While the artists use time-honoured methods, their products are usually modern, even avant-garde.
Kodukäsitöö, Müürivahe 17, tel: 6314 076, also at Kuninga 1, Viru 2 and in the Viru Centre. These four shops run by the Estonian Handicraft Union sell traditional and authentic handicraft products, from toys to entire folk costumes.
Nukupood, Raekoja plats 18, tel: 6443 058. This tiny shop specialises in hand-made dolls and toys.
Puupood, Lai 5, tel: 6412 473. A cellar shop specialising in all things made of wood, including tankards and toys.
VeTa, Pikk 8, tel: 6464 142. One of several shops on this stretch of Pikk Street selling woollens and linen.

Markets
Outdoor markets, while not common in Tallinn, present the most interesting shopping experience. First and foremost is the much-loved knitwear market along the old city wall on Müürivahe Street, near the Viru Gates. Since it doesn't have an official name, most foreigners simply refer to it as the **Wall of Sweaters**. Here local women sell just about every kind of knitted item you can imagine, with a better variation in styles than in most shops. A similar, but less spectacular craft market operates nearby on Mere Puiestee, just north of Vana-Viru Street. In summer, temporary markets also appear from week to week on or near Town Hall Square, where there is an enchanting Christmas Market.

Latvia

Latvians are renowned for their craftsmanship and there is a wide range of paintings, ceramics, jewellery, glassware, porcelain, textiles, amber, leather, wooden crafts and locally made clothes. Shops listed are in Rīga unless otherwise stated.

Antikvariats Del Arte, Barona 16/18. Open Mon–Fri 11am–7pm, Sat 11am–4pm. Paintings, porcelain, instruments, books, Soviet medals and antique postcards.
Berga Bazaar, good for boutique shopping, in the middle of Rīga.
Galerija, Dzirnavu 53. Open Mon–Fri 10am–7pm, Sat 11am–5pm. Books, Soviet memorabilia, coins and knick-knacks.
Konvents, Kaļķu 9/11. Open daily

10am–8pm. Mostly furniture, books, icons and porcelain.

Raritets, Čaka 45. Open Mon–Fri 10am–6pm, Sat 10am–5pm. Religious icons, local porcelain, paintings, coins, stamps, silverware and furniture.

Retro A, Tallinas 54. Open Mon–Fri 10am–5pm, Sat 10am–2pm.

Volmar, Šķūņu 6. Open Mon–Sat 10am–8pm, Sun 11am–6pm. Upmarket antiques shop specialising in religious icons.

Folk Art & Souvenirs

Best buys are the locally made woollen mittens and socks in bright patterns. Some lovely shawls are also available. Linen is a speciality – it comes in all shapes and sizes and is usually of especially high quality. Traditional leather shoes with long thong laces make good slippers.

Art Nouveau Rīga, Strēlnieku 9. Open 8am–7pm. The only shop in Rīga completely dedicated to Art Nouveau merchandise.

Grieži, Mazā Miesnieku 1. Open Mon–Fri 11am–7pm, Sat 11am–6pm. Stylish, hand-made non-traditional souvenirs.

Sena Klēts, Merķeļa 13. Open Mon–Fri 10am–6pm, Sat 10am–4pm. The only shop in Rīga that specialises in Latvian folk costumes is worth a visit even if you don't intend to buy anything.

Tine, Vaļņu 2. Open Mon–Sat 9am–7pm, Sun 10am–5pm. The city's best selection of traditional gifts and souvenirs.

Upe, Vāgnera 5, www.upe.parks.lv. Open Mon–Fri 11am–7pm, Sat 10am–3pm. The best shop for traditional Latvian music, instruments and wooden folk souvenirs.

Jewellery

There are well-designed, locally made pieces available in Latvian shops usually made of silver. The most interesting jewellery incorporates ancient pagan styles, including the distinctive designs of the interlocking Latvian ring, the Namejs. Amber is also relatively cheap.

A&E, Jauniela 17. Open 10am–6pm. Hillary Clinton shopped here for designer Baltic jewellery.

Līvs, Kalēju 7. Open Mon–Fri 10am–6pm, Sat 10am–4pm. This shop specialises in jewellery based on ancient Baltic designs.

Romuls, Jaunavu 1 (Rātsnams). Open Mon–Sat 11am–6pm. Exclusive amber jewellery.

Books

You can find picture books, guides and maps in the following shops:

Globuss, Vaļņu 26. Open daily 8am–10pm.

Jaņa Rozes, Barona 5. Open Mon–Fri 10am–7pm, Sat 10am–6pm.

Jaņa Sēta, Elizabetes 83/85, www.kartes.lv/veikals. Open Mon–Fri 10am–7pm, Sat 11am–5pm.

Jumava, Dzirnavu 73, www.jumava.lv. Open Mon–Fri 10am–7pm, Sat 11am–5pm.

Valters un Rapa, Aspazijas 24. Open Mon–Fri 9am–9pm, Sat 10am–9pm, Sun 10am–4pm.

Flowers

The best place to buy flowers in Rīga is the flower market on Tērbatas next to Vērmanes garden. The market is open 24 hours. Note that a small bunch of flowers traditionally makes a very welcome gift if you are visiting a Latvian home. Always buy an odd number of flowers unless attending a funeral or sad occasion.

Markets

Every town has its market, selling a wide selection of food and other trinkets and providing a fascinating view of local life. As in any market, watch out for pickpockets. In Rīga the main venues are:

Central Market (Centrālais tirgus), Prāgas 1. Open daily 8am–6pm. This vast market in five old Zeppelin hangars spills down across a flea market towards the river. Friday and Saturday are its busiest days.

Latgales Market, Sadovņikova 9a. Open Mon–Sat 8am–4.30pm, Sun 8am–3pm. You can buy anything here from tools to pirated CDs.

Vidzemes Market Vidzemes tirgus, Matīsa 2. Open Mon–Sat 8am–6pm, Sun 8am–4pm. Like the central market but smaller.

Āgenskalna Market Āgenskalna tirgus, Nometņu 64. Open Tues–Sat 8am–5pm, Sun and Mon 8am–3pm. Rīga's oldest market.

BELOW: knitwear.

Lithuania

It is impossible to walk down a street in Vilnius's Old Town without being made aware of local amber, linen goods or woodcarvings for sale. Most can be found right on Pilies and Didžioji. There is a small market where street vendors sell similar items usually for a bit less. In the Old Town, Žydų and Stiklių streets also have shops that are worth looking around. Gedimino Avenue is geared to those wanting to purchase clothing or shoes. As a rule, shops in Lithuania are not open on Sundays; however, tourist-based shops in the Old Town tend to be open everyday. All shops listed here are in Vilnius unless otherwise stated.

Antiques

Bear in mind customs regulations when buying items made pre-1945. An export licence is needed for antiques produced before this date.

Antikvaras, Pilies 32-4. Open Mon–Sat 11am–6pm, Sun 11am–5pm. Walk through the courtyard to find this shop full to the brim with all sorts of antiques. Most notable are its selection of musical instruments.

Dominikonų Antiques, Dominikonų 3-2. A few pieces of furniture crowd the interior of the shop, but mostly smaller items like books and postcards can be found here.

Maldis, Basanavičiaus 4a. Although more spare in its use of space than its counterparts, Maldis focuses a lot of its inventory on jewellery. The selection tends to be of a high quality.

Senasis Kuparas, Dominikonų 14. Open daily. An impressive collection of paintings, furniture, icons and Russian samovars makes this shop look almost like a museum. The staff is very knowledgeable and helpful.

Books

Foreign-language literature and guides are fairly easy to find

Akademinų Knyga, Universiteto 4. The first stop for those looking for reference books although they have a small selection of paperbacks.

Humanitas, Vokiečių 2. The English-language section tends towards books on art.

Littera, Universiteto 3. Inside Vilnius University, this campus bookshop has a fairly varied selection of English-language titles.

Oxford Centre, Trakų 5. The perfect place to find the next great paperback you'll need for the overnight bus or train trip.

Prie Halės, Pylimo 53. Their buyers are aware of what is selling abroad

Buying Amber

Baltic amber is believed to have begun forming about 30–40 million years ago. It is fossilised tree resin, which dripped down the bark, perhaps caught a few insects or leaves, and hardened. It is rare to find bugs or leaves, called inclusions, inside an amber piece sold in one of the shops. Numerous types exist. Often the classification is by colour. In Vilnius you can find white, yellow, orange/red, and green amber.

White amber, called King's amber, is usually off-white with some yellow accents. Similarly, yellow amber is typically yellow with white swathes of colour throughout. The orange/red varieties are the most

common and green amber is the rarest, commanding a higher price.

The only real ways to tell if amber is not plastic is to see if it floats in seawater or turns to powder when scraped with a knife; neither of which any right-minded street vendor will allow you to do. The two best streets in Vilnius to search for amber are Pilies and Aušros Vartų.

Most amber is converted into jewellery, polished or left natural and strung as necklaces or inlaid with silver, or made into rings or bracelets. Houseware, such as glasses and cups, with amber decoration is becoming more popular.

io a smaller version with a less arresting variety of goods, though occasionally a rummage can produce some exceptionally good Soviet-made cameras and lenses.

The **Flower Market** in Vilnius is on Basanavičiaus 42. Lithuanians offer flowers on many occasions and for almost any reason. You can find flowers here around the clock.

On weekends from 10am–3pm the building at Pamėnkalnio No. 7 plays host to a CD and DVD market.

SPORT

See the Outdoor Activites chapter, pages 72–5, for what's on generally in the three countries.

Estonia
Spectator Sports
Basketball has long been the spectator sport of choice in Estonia. Tallinn's Kalev is the most recognised of the handful of teams based around the country. The national team plays tournaments in the Saku Suurhall stadium (Paldiski mnt. 104B, tel: 6600 200).
Football Though the Estonian team doesn't excel compared to its neighbours, soccer is fast catching up to basketball in popularity. Major games are held in A. Le Coq Arena (Asula 4c, Tallinn, tel: 6279 940).
Horse racing On some weekends, weather permitting, horse racing takes place in Tallinn's Hipodroom (Paldiski mnt. 50, tel: 6771 677).

Participation Sports
Golf Tallinn's only golf course is the 18-hole Niitvälja Golf (tel: 6780 110) located in Niitvälja, about 30 minutes from town. There are a number of new courses being developed elsewhere in Estonia, most notably White Beach Golf (Valgeranna, tel: 4443 453) near Pärnu.
Squash addicts can satisfy their needs at Metro Squash in Tallinn (Tondi 17, tel: 6556 392), which will also rent equipment. In Pärnu, try Mai Squash (Papiniidu 50, tel: 4420 103).
Tennis clubs in Estonia are visitor-friendly. Good choices in Tallinn are the Rocca-al-Mare Onistar Tennis Centre (Haabersti 5, tel: 6600 520), and the Kalevi Tenniseklubi (Herne 28, tel: 6459 229). In Tartu, there's the Tamme Indoors Tennis Hall (Tamme pst. 1, tel: 7428 194) and in Pärnu, the Pärnu Tennisehall (Tammsaare pst. 39, tel: 4427 246). Reserve courts beforehand.

and the stock has the latest English-language fiction.
Vaga, Gedimino 50/2. Open daily. Climb up to the top floor and then look for the English-language section in a back room. There you will find a satisfying amount of books.

Records
It is worth hunting out records of äiurlionis's work, as well as local jazz and folk music for souvenirs. The largest label in the country is **Garsų Pasaulis** (Pamėnkalnio 14, tel: 262 2551, www.gp.lt) and their shop is chock full of most major Lithuanian records. **Muzikos bomba** (Jakšto 24/3, tel: 262 4557) has a shop located right off of Gedimino. **Thelonious** (Stiklių 12, tel: 221 076; www.thelonious.lt) is the best place to find independent and rare LPs in the Old Town.

Amber
The walk from Aušros Vartų through Didžioji and onto Pilies guarantees at least seven billion chances to purchase amber. The street hawkers tend to have less ornate items, but they all sell the real deal because it is more difficult to create amber-like plastics than it is to collect the fossilised tree resin. For decidedly more unique pieces it is best to stop by the **Mažasis Gintaro Muziejus** (Didžioji 5, 6, 10 and 11), which straddles both sides of the street, or the **Amber Museum Gallery** (Šv Mykolo 8) where the staff will walk you through the 40-billion-year history of amber in about half an hour.

Souvenirs
There are countless souvenir shops along Pilies Street, the main tourist

road in Vilnius. Look out for *verba*, dried-flower and twig willow, and yew bouquets, which are especially popular on Palm Sunday.
Linen & Amber Studio (open Mon–Sat 10am–7pm, Sun 10am–5pm) has somewhat taken over the Old Town. Located at Didžioji Nos 5, 6, 10 and 11 along with two other Old Town locales ensures the most confused tourist is likely to step into their shops. Waiting in the wings is the **Sauluva** company, which also has shops dotting the Old Town (Literatų 3, Totorių 20, Šv Mykolo 4). Both sell a variety of amber, linen and wood sculptures. For something different check out **Dailininkų Sajungos Parodu Salė**, Vokiečių 2, in the Contemporary Arts Centre and find some original paintings, drawings and jewellery. **Dailė** (Stiklių 16) sells the same linen goods found elsewhere, with a less corporate touch, plus hand-painted mugs and dolls.

Markets
All markets are closed on Mondays and open sunrise to mid-afternoon unless otherwise noted. Do be aware that markets are easy places to be pick-pocketed and be especially alert when moving through large crowds.
Gariūnai, the biggest market in Lithuania, is outside Vilnius along the A1 where large number of shacks are strung along the right side of the highway. Everything can be found here: cars, food items, household goods, tools, wedding dresses, wigs and much more. The magic of this place is in its intensity and high amount of traffic.
Kalvarijų Market, across the river in the northern suburb of Šnipiškės,

Windsurfing is practised by enthusiasts at just about every beach in the country. Lessons for beginners are held weekly at Tallinn's Pirita Beach: contact Hawaii Express (Regati 1, tel: 6398 508).

Swimming The Kalev SPA's water park (Aia 18, tel: 6493 300) offers 25m and 50m pools right in the centre of Tallinn. The water centres in Pärnu and Tartu *(see Children, page 360)* also have pools for adults.

Ice skating is popular in winter. In Tallinn, you can head to indoor rinks like the one in the Linnahall Ice Hall (Mere pst. 20, tel: 6412 266) or, if it's cold enough, try the Schnelli Pond, in the small park between Old Town and the train station.

Latvia

Spectator Sports

Ice hockey is a national obsession and Latvians worship their hip-checking heroes, especially the ones that play in the National Hockey League. Each year at the end of April businesses close early and locals head out to their favourite pubs to watch their team strive for glory in the World Hockey Championship. A victory often leads to gatherings of hundreds of fans in Rīga who parade about the city shouting slogans and singing songs often ending their wanderings at the embassy of their vanquished foes.

A new arena was built in Rīga for the hockey championship in 2006 (Arena Rīga, skanstes 13, www.arenariga.com). Eastern European Hockey League matches are most commonly played just outside the city limits at the modern Siemens Ledushalle, Piņķi, Jūrmalas šoseja, tel: 714 7000, www.bhh.lv, in Liepāja at the Liepāja Olympic Ice Rink, Brīvības 3/7, tel: 348 1840, www.liepaja-online.lv/icehall and in Ogre at the Ogre Ice Hall, tel: 505 5132, www.vidzemesledus.lv.

Football doesn't command the same amount of respect that hockey does, but it is increasingly popular, especially with Latvia's surprising victory over mighty Turkey to qualify for the Euro 2004 Football Championship in Portugal. Latvia didn't make it past the group stage but was narrowly defeated (2–1) by a mighty Czech Republic and drew (0–0) with Germany. Latvia's best team was FC Skonto which won the Latvian Championship every year since the club's founding in 1991 until 2005, a *Guinness Book* world record. Ventspils were the 2006 champions. Matches in Rīga are held at the Skonto Stadium,

E. Melngaiļa 1a, www.fcskonto.lv, at the Ventspils Olympic Centre in Ventspils, Sporta 7/9, tel: 362 2587, www.ocventspils.lv and in Liepāja at the Daugava Stadium in the Seaside Park.

Participation Sports

Bobsleigh and luge The run at Sigulda, just a short ride from Rīga, hosts international events that draw huge numbers of spectators. When professionals aren't training at the difficult run on weekends, an instructor will take you for a quick run down the mountain year-round at speeds in excess of 125 km/h (80 mph) for only 5Ls/person

Golf Choose from an exclusive 18-hole lakeside course (OZO, Mielgrāvja 16, tel: 739 4399, www.ozogolf.lv) owned by millionaire hockey star Sandis Ozoliņš, the second Latvian to play in the NHL, and a less challenging 9-hole course by the airport (Viesturi, tel: 644 4390, www.golfsviesturi.lv).

Shooting Visitors can fire off rounds from weapons as diverse as World War II-era Lugers and AK-47s (Kalashnikovs) at the Reast rifle range, Daugavgrīvas 23a, Rīga, tel: 760 1705. Ex-military staff know enough English from their fairly frequent encounters with foreign tourists. It also has the added benefit of being located in an underground Cold War bomb shelter on the Pārdaugava side of the river.

Skiing and Snowboarding Latvia's tiny hills won't challenge your downhill skills, but many resorts have created special parks for snowboarders with half pipes and other attractions.

The best are: Baiļi (Valmiera, 107 km/65 miles from Rīga), tel: 422 1861, www.baili.lv; Gaiziņkalns (Madona county, 120 km/75 miles from Rīga), tel: 761 9335 www.gaizins.lv; Kaķīšu Trase (Sigulda, 50 km/30 miles from Rīga), tel: 657 9939; žagarkalns (Cēsis, 90 km/ 55 miles from Rīga), tel: 412 5225, www.zagarkalns.lv; Zviedru Cepure (Baiļi, 120 km/75 miles from Rīga), tel: 919 8283, www.zviedrucepure.lv.

Lithuania

Spectator Sports

Basketball is the national pastime and arguments over teams are more likely to turn violent then ones over political issues. The Lithuanian Olympic basketball team regularly wins medals and their winning of the European championships in 2004 guaranteed their place at the Athens Olympic Games. The best-known

national team is the Kaunas-based Žalgiris team, but the Vilnius Lietuvos Rytas have begun to make a name for themselves outside the country. The Lietuvos Rytas (also the name of a popular Lithuanian daily), team's stadium should be contacted for ticket sales (Olimpiečių 3; tel: 272 1845). Major local (for example Žalgiris versus Rytas) or international basketball events are held at Vilnius's Siemens Arena (Ozo 14, tel. 1567). To see league champions Žalgiris Kaunas requires a drive to Kaunas's Darius and Girėnas Sports Complex (Perkūno 3, tel: 3720 1470).

Football is also a popular sport with games often shown in a few of the city's establishments.

Participation Sports

Bicycling, though not too popular, tends to see a rise in summertime, especially along the coast. For information about routes and how to meet other serious cyclists check out the Lithuanian-based BalticCycle site, www.balticcycle.lt.

Bowling has taken off. Vilnius's bowling alleys include the small but pleasant Boulingo Klubas (Jasinskio 16; tel: 249 6600), the spacious and modern Cosmic Bowling Center (Vytenio 6; tel: 233 9909) and Ten Pin (Žirmūnų 68; tel: 277 0760).

Bungee jumping from the Television Tower in Vilnius is possible at weekends. Contact the Latvia-based LGK company (tel: 6002 3210, www.atrakcionai.lt) for details.

Go-karting (Savanorių 178, tel: 231 1507) is one of the more popular ways to pass the time.

Golf is still nascent in its popularity. The only course in the entire country, Elnias, is a nine-hole course located about 15 km (9 miles) from Kaunas (Didžiosios Lapės, tel: 470 237).

Flight is a national obsession. Visitors can get in on the act by learning to fly a glider or light aircraft or by parachuting out of a plane at the Kaunas Acrobatic Flying Club (Kauno aeroklubas; Veiverių 132, tel: 391 553, open Mon–Fri 9am–5pm) inside the city airport. Also, for a fee, you can fly in a fighter jet. Contact www.activeholidays.lt for more information.

Ice sports are perennially popular. Although not always the safest option, sledding attracts fair numbers to Vilnius's hills. The lack of mountains ensures that skiing is only of the cross-country variety. Ice rinks can be found inside the large shopping complex Akropolis (Ozo 25; tel: 248 4848) northwest of the city centre or at the Ice Palace (Ažuolyno 9; tel: 242 4212) in the northwest suburb of Viršuliškės, which is open to the public at different times, depending on whether the Vilnius city hockey team is using the facilities.

Countryside By far the best way to stay active is by cycling through the countryside or swimming or canoeing in the numerous lakes. For information about national parks contact the Vilnius Tourist Information centres at either Vilniaus 22 (tel: 262 9660, fax: 262 8169) or the Town Hall (tel: 262 6470, fax: 262 0762).

TOURS

Estonia

Around Tallinn
Tourism in Tallinn is heavily oriented towards groups, who tend to arrange their own excursions, but the city does offer a couple of tours that individuals can join. The most popular is the Tallinn Official Sightseeing Tour operated by Reisiekspert (tel: 6108 634), a combination bus and walking tour that covers all the city's major sights. It runs three times daily and costs 250kr (free with Tallinn Card). Phone for schedules and meeting places.

A more adventurous option is the Welcome to Tallinn bicycle tour organised by City Bike (tel: 5111 819). It departs from the City Bike Hostel (Uus 33) at 11am and 5pm daily in the warmer months. Phone ahead during the off-season. The tour covers the city's outlying green districts, the beach area and the Old Town. The 250kr tour price includes bicycle rental and mineral water. Book at least one hour in advance.

You can also book your own, private guide through Tourist Information *(see page 372)*. Guides cost 350kr per hour, irrespective of the size of the group, and have to be hired for a minimum of 1½ hours. Book 48 hours ahead.

Around Estonia
There are a number of travel companies that will organise pre-packaged or tailor-made trips to the various regions of the country, including the islands. Among these are Baltic Tours (Pikk 31, tel: 6300 460, www.baltictours.com), who offer tours from the standard sightseeing to adventure trips with off-roading and ice climbing, Via Hansa (Rüütli 13, tel: 6277 870, www.viahansa.com), who also have thematic tours as well as the all-inclusive country tours. In all cases, tours should be booked well in advance. Nature and rural tours have become particularly

popular in the past few years. The non-profit Estonian Rural Tourism Organisation, Eesti Maaturism, lists over a hundred specific tours and packages on their website, www.maaturism.ee. For bog-walking, canoeing or tracking wolves in Soomaa National Park, contact Soomaa.com (tel: 5061 896).

Latvia

Around Rīga
Latvia Tours, Kaļķu 8, tel: 708 5057, www.latviatours.lv, provides regular tours in English of Rīga, Rundāle Palace and Sigulda for groups of at least five people. They can also organise excursions to the cities of Jūrmala, Cēsis and Liepāja upon request. Amber Way, tel: 727 1915, specialises in English-language tours of Rīga on foot, bus and boat. Tickets can be bought at the Rīga Information Centre, Rātslaukums 6. Tours are also offered from outside the Opera House, Stabu iela 19-20, Visit www.sightseeing.lv.

Boat tours depart nearly every hour from the Old Rīga bank of the River Daugava in the summer and usually cost no more than 3–4Ls. Longer boat rides may also include trips to Mežaparks and Jūrmala.

Bike Tours, for cycling around Rīga and beyond, tel: 622 5437, www.bicycle.lv,

Nature Tours
Latvia is famous for its rich nature and fauna and its great outdoors. The following two addresses are for travel agents, who arrange tailor-made nature/outdoor packages. Eastbird Tours, tel: 616 1077, eastbird@latnet.lv. Small firm running birdwatching tours. Makars Tourism Agency, Sigulda, Peldu 2, tel: 924 4948, fax: 797 0164, www.makars.lv. For boat, rafting, bike and horse-riding tours.

Beer Tours
There are many breweries around the country to visit, with tasting. For details contact TAS, www.tas.lv

Castle and Manor House Tours
Latvia's countryside is dotted with

castles, palaces and elegant manor houses, many offering hotel rooms. For routes and descriptions, visit www.pilis.lv.

Soviet Charm Show
This living museum takes participants through different stages of Soviet life from Pioneer marches to fire-brigade competitions, shooting Kalishnikovs, helping at a collective farm and driving old Soviet cars vehicles. Visit www.kuldiga.lv

Lithuania

Around Vilnius
Most Vilnius hotels have an arrangement with a tour company for specialised or even run-of-the-mill tours of the city or surroundings. Bus tours of the Old Town with explanations in English are also available. In good weather look for the open-top bus parked at the end of Didžioji, otherwise a US-style child's school bus will be there.

Trips to Trakai and walking tours of the Old Town are the most popular and are offered by almost all agencies. Individual tours of specific interest such as a tour of Jewish Vilnius are also offered but usually by only a handful of people.

You can also take one-day cycling or canoe excursions.

Around Lithuania
Cultural, fishing and horse-riding tours are offered by Lithuanian Tours, Šeimyniškių str. 18, LT-2005 Vilnius, tel: 272 4154, www.lithuaniantours.com

Nature Tours
A number of companies offer nature tours in the countryside, such as Ave Vita (Daukanto sq 2/10, Vilnius, tel: 260 8410, fax: 260 8421, www.avevita.lt.

The Lithuanian Ornithological Association (Naugarduko 47–3, Vilnius, tel: 230 498, birdlife@post.5ci.lt) offers bird escorts every October.

For a list of tour companies and operators contact the local tourist information centre.

BELOW: Daugava riverboat, Latvia.

A – Z

A HANDY SUMMARY OF PRACTICAL INFORMATION, ARRANGED ALPHABETICALLY

Accidents & Emergencies

An all-encompassing emergency number, **112**, works in all three countries. They try to staff with English-speaking personnel at all times, though a non-English speaker may get your call.

You can also call:

Police in Estonia, **110**. In Latvia and Lithuania, **02**

Paramedics in Latvia and Lithuania, **03**.

Budgeting for your Trip

Food, transport and entertainment are all relatively inexpensive. Lithuania is the cheapest of the three countries, Latvia the most expensive, with Estonia in between. A meal, without drinks, will typically cost from £3 to £8. In the capitals' most expensive restaurants, it will be from £10 to £25 respectively. A large beer in a local pub costs 80p–£1.10, and in a touristy café £1.20–£2.60. Soft drinks are 50p–£1.

The rate for a double room in a mid-range hotel is from £45 in Latvia to £90 in Estonia, with Lithuania in

between, but quite decent rooms can be found for under £35 in Lithuania and £50 in Estonia.

Museum tickets are nominal and one- to three-day tourist cards, available at tourist offices, give discounts in the capitals.

Childcare

Children take a central part in Baltic life and are welcomed in restaurants and other outings. Parks in the cities cater for children, but don't expect Disneyworld. *(For children's activities see Activities, page 360.)*

Some hotels offer child-care facilities.

Children under seven travel half price or free on public transport.

Climate & Clothing

June is by far the best time to visit. This is when the days are longest, with the most hours of sunlight. Rain often comes in July and it may increase as the summer progresses. In June the temperature is usually mild: the last of spring's icy spells having ended in May in Estonia and earlier in

Lithuania. July is the hottest month, when mid-summer temperatures can reach up to 30°C (86°F). The average for the month is a pleasant 17°C (63°F).

In winter, temperatures as low as –30°C (–22°F) have been recorded in Estonia and –20°C (–4°F) in Lithuania. In recent years winter temperatures have tended to be milder, seldom falling below around the –5°C (23°F) mark, and temperatures inland are generally lower than near the coast. Despite this, winters can often seem extremely cold because of the piercing coastal winds.

Snow is most prolonged in Estonia where it can fall from January through to March. In recent years, however, the average fall has been decreasing and there is often no lasting snow cover.

The biggest drawback for visitors in winter is generally not the cold or the snow but the lack of sunlight. From early November through until late March darkness never seems to completely lift, and the six or seven hours of daylight are often marred by overcast, misty conditions.

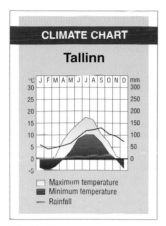

CLIMATE CHART
Tallinn

☐ Maximum temperature
■ Minimum temperature
— Rainfall

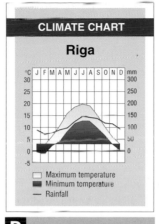

CLIMATE CHART
Riga

☐ Maximum temperature
■ Minimum temperature
— Rainfall

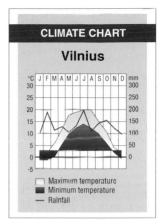

CLIMATE CHART
Vilnius

☐ Maximum temperature
■ Minimum temperature
— Rainfall

What to Wear

Although people tend to dress up for concerts, the theatre and official business, the dress code on all three countries is otherwise fairly informal. When packing, bear in mind how cold the winter climate can be. From November to April minimum requirements are a heavy woollen jumper, leggings and something thick soled and waterproof on your feet. Thermal underwear can also be welcome. From January to March it is highly advisable to wear gloves and a hat and scarf.

In summer, lightweight garments and even shorts and T-shirts are adequate. Evenings can turn chilly, so bring a sweater and jacket to keep you warm. It is also advisable to pack waterproof clothing and an umbrella. Sensible, comfortable footwear is highly recommended as the cities' cobbled streets are uncomfortable in thin-soled shoes and treacherous in high heels.

Crime

Economic hardship and chronically understaffed and ill-equipped police forces have contributed to urban crime. Violent crime tends to be gangland related and assaults on foreigners are rare. Take the usual precautions against theft that you would when travelling anywhere – anything that you are not physically attached to is liable to walk, so be watchful. This applies equally to valuables left in hotel rooms, which should be kept out of site, or in the safes provided. Further good advice is to remain sober; nothing could present a more appealing target than an inebriated tourist staggering through dimly lit streets.

D isabled Travellers

The medieval Baltic capitals are a headache for anyone in a wheelchair. Pavements can be rocky, kerbs steep, and many restaurants, cafés, shops and museums can only be accessed via cramped, narrow staircases. On the positive side, traffic in the Old Towns is usually restricted, leaving the streets wide open for pedestrian explorers. Wheelchair-bound visitors will need to ask numerous, pointed and direct questions about a hotel's facilities in order to ensure they can be accommodated. The largest and newest hotels are fairly accessible, and almost always have rooms specially equipped for disabled guests. Buses and trams don't yet have equipment to aid in boarding, but phone around the major taxi companies and you're likely to find a car that's designed for disabled passengers.

The situation gets progressively worse as you leave the capitals and go into more rural regions.

E lectricity

The electricity in all three countries is 220 volts AC, 50Hz. Plugs are the round, two-pinned variety used in continental Europe. In Estonia, adaptors can be found in electronic shops and in department stores such as Tallinna Kaubamaja, but these are harder to find in Latvia and Lithuania, so it's best to bring one with you.

Embassies & Consulates

The embassies are all in the capital cities. When there is no local embassy, Australians, Irish, New Zealanders and South Africans

should contact the UK Embassy, or their own embassy in a neighbouring country.
Tallinn
Canada (Representative office only), Toomkooli 13, tel: 6273 311.
Ireland Vene 2, tel: 6811 888.
UK Wismari 6, tel: 6674 700.
US Kentmanni 20, tel: 6688 100.
Riga
Canada Baznīcas 20/22, tel: 781 3945, fax: 781 3960.
Ireland (Honorary Consulate), Brīvības 54, tel: 702 5259, fax: 702 5222.
UK Alunāna 5, tel: 777 4700, fax: 777 4707.
US Raiņa bulvāris 7, tel: 703 6200, fax: 782 0047.
Vilnius
Australia Vilniaus 23, tel: 212 3369, fax: 212 3369
Canada Jogailos 4, tel: 249 0950, fax: 249 7865.
UK Antakalnio 2, tel: 246 2900, fax: 246 2901.
US Akmenų 6, tel: 266 5500, fax: 266 5510.

G ays & Lesbians

Though the situation is generally improving, especially in the cities, attitudes in the Baltic states toward homosexuality are not as liberal as those elsewhere in the West. Overt displays, such as holding hands, are not yet socially acceptable and may attract the wrong sort of attention.

Tallinn has a small but active gay night scene, which encompasses a handful of bars and clubs. The very central X-Baar (Sauna 1) is the most established of these, but Angel, next door, is newer and more club-like.

In **Latvia** the only local website available in English, www.xxl.lv, is operated by the nightclub XXL.

A small male gay scene does exist in Vilnius but most gay organisations are underground and often geared simply towards providing a social and dating scene.

Genealogy

Those wanting to track down information about their Baltic ancestry can get help from several agencies who specialise in such matters.

Estonia

Estonian Genealogical Society (Eesti Genealoogia Selts), www.genealoogia.ee. The society doesn't have an office, but its extensive website in English is an excellent starting point for research.
Estonian Biographical Centre (Eesti Isikuloo Keskus), Tiigi 10-51, Tartu, tel: 7420 882, www.isik.ee. The centre specialises in genealogical research and, for a fee, will track down relatives and create a family tree.
Estonian Historical Archives (Eesti Ajalooarhiiv), Liivi 4, Tartu, tel: 7387 500, fax: 7387 510, www.eha.ee. Archivists charge an hourly rate for researching and creating a family tree, but visitors can look through the archives at no expense.

Latvia

In Latvia contact the **State History Archive** (Valsts Vēstures Arhīvs) in Rīga, at Slokas 16, tel: 761 3118.

Lithuania

In Lithuania there are several specialist agencies.
Lithuanian Central State Archive (Lietuvos centrinis valstybės archyvas), Milašiaus 21, tel: 276 5290, fax: 276 5318. A directory of people living in Lithuania during the Nazi occupation (1941–1942).
Lithuanian State Historical Archive (Lietuvos valstybės istorijos archyvas), Gerosios Vilties 10, tel: 213 7482, fax: 213 7612. A church registry from 1940 to the present.
Vilnius Civilian Archive (Vilnaus civilinės metrikacijos dokumentų archyvas), Kalinausko 21, tel: 233 7846. Birth, death and marriage certificates from 1940 to the present.

Government

The Baltic republics are all parliamentary democracies with a president as the head of state, and the elected governents are led by prime ministers who are responsible for the day-to-day running of the country.

The president of the **Republic of Estonia** (Eesti Vabariik) is called the Riigivanem, meaning "state elder". The parliament, the Riigikogu, is responsible for all national legislative matters.

In the **Republic of Latvia** (Latvijas Republika) a 100-member parliament, the Saeima, elects government personnel, from the head of state to the 12 ministers and the prime minister. The Saeima can approve or reject the appointment of ministers, as well as government decrees and resolutions.

In the **Republic of Lithuania** (Lietuvos Respublika) the government is also subordinate to the unicameral parliament, the Seimas, which has 141 seats, of which 71 members are directly elected by popular vote and 70 by proportional representation. The prime minister is appointed by the president on the approval of parliament. Elections are every four years, presidential elections every five years.

Health & Medical Care

No vaccinations are required. One concern, however, only applies to visitors who plan to spend time deep in the Estonian wilderness or in the wilds of the Latvian countryside, in which case a vaccination against tick-borne encephalitis is recommended. People are advised to check themselves for ticks – tiny black mites in the skin – after tramping through tall brush.

There are no real problems with medical care and most Western medicines are available in all three countries. If you feel unwell, your best first stop is a pharmacy, where you can often find most of what you might need to cure common, temporary ailments. Many pharmacies carry everything from Pepto Bismol, Advil and antibiotics to such goods as Visine, condoms and Slim Fast.

If over-the-counter medicines do not do the trick, it is advisable to seek help from a qualified doctor.

With the European reciprocation of treatment, UK visitors should theoretically need only to present an E111 form, available from post offices, for free treatment, but you are strongly advised to take out private insurance, too.

Although health-care systems are undergoing crises due to budget cuts, foreigners are generally well-treated. Doctors and nurses are grossly underpaid but still try to provide an adequate service. If you want to, you can show your appreciation by giving a gift after you have been treated. Hospitals are usually spartan, but sanitary, and the health care is generally good.

For an ambulance in all the countries, dial 112.

Tallinn

Pharmacies (apteek)
Tõnismäe Apteek, Tõnismägi 21, tel: 6442 282 in central Tallinn runs an all-night pharmacy window.
Hospitals (haigla)
Tallinn Central Hospital, Ravi 18, tel: 1900 or 6207 040. Open 24 hours. The paramedic service in Tallinn runs a first-aid hotline (tel: 6971 145) that can give you advice or direct you to a hospital.
Dentists (hambaravi)
Baltic Medical Partners, Tartu mnt. 32, tel: 601 0550, fax: 601 0549.
Kaarli Hambapolikliinik, Toompuiestee 4. Tel: 611 9119.
Sexually Transmitted Diseases
Aids Information and Support Centre, Kopli 32, tel: 6413 165.

Rīga

Pharmacies (aptiekas)
Tallinas aptieka, Tallinas 57b, tel: 731 4211. Open 24 hours.
Vecpilsētas aptieka, Audēju 20, tel: 721 3340. In Old Rīga. Open 24 hours.
Hospitals (slimnīcas)
ARS, Skolas 5, tel: 720 1001/1007/1003/1005. For all emergencies.
Diplomatic Service Medical Centre, Elizabetes 57, tel: 728 2534. Full English-speaking staff.
Paediatrics
Dr Zālītis, Skolas 2, tel: 724 0202. Harvard-educated paediatrician.
Sexually Transmitted Diseases
Aids Centre, Krijānu iela, tel: 737 2275, www.aids.lv.
Dentists (zobārsti)
A+S Health Centre, Lāčplēša 60, tel: 728 9516.
Diplomatic Service Medical Centre, Elizabetes 57, tel: 722 9942, fax: 728 9413.

Vilnius

Pharmacies (vaistinė)
Gedimino Vaistinė, Gedimino pr. 27, tel: 624 930/610 135.
The only central pharmacy in Vilnius. Open 24 hours.
Hospitals
Baltic–American Medical & Surgical Clinic, Nemenčinės Road 54a, tel: 234 2020, www.bak.com.
In Vilnius's northeast suburb of Antakalnis, the clinic is open 24 hours and is by far the most recommended and well-known.
Emergency Hospital, Šiltnamių 29, tel: 269 069/269 140.

Dentists (stomatologos or dantistas)

Dr Sidaravičius Dental Clinic, Klaipėdos 2/14-3, tel: 262 9760, Open Mon–Fri 7am–8pm.
Stomatologijos Gydykla, Dominikonų 3-45, tel: 262 8482. Open 8am–8pm.
Gidenta, Vienuolio 14-3, tel: 261 7143, www.gidenta.lt. Open Mon–Fri 9am–7pm.

Sexually Transmitted Diseases

Lithuanian Aids Centre, Vytenio 59/37, tel/fax: 233 0111, www.aids.lt Open 8am–5pm.

L eft Luggage

Estonia

In cities, left-luggage services can be found at all the major transportation hubs. In Tallinn Airport, it is in the main departure hall, next to the information desk. At the train station, the room is in the centre rear of the main hall, closest to the tracks. The passenger port's A and D terminals have both luggage rooms and lockers.

At the bus station, luggage lockers are immediately to the right of the ticket windows. The lockers use 5kr coins, which usually have to be obtained from a change machine or requested specially.

Latvia

Although many small stations in the Latvian countryside may lack left-luggage rooms or lockers, Rīga has proper facilities in each of its major transportation hubs. At the airport, store luggage for 1Ls per item per day in the arrivals hall at the end of the corridor to the left of the exit (open 24 hours). The luggage room at the bus station is located on the left side when entering from the platforms and storage costs 0.30Ls for the first hour and 0.20Ls for each additional hour (open 5am–midnight). A luggage room for 0.50–1.50Ls per day are available in the basement of the train station (open 4.30am–midnight).

Lithuania

Most major transit points in Lithuania have left-luggage facilities. In Vilnius there are 24-hour left-luggage facilities at the airport and in the train station. Left-luggage facilities in the Vilnius bus station (open Mon–Sat 5.30am–9pm, Sun 7am–9pm) are also available.

M aps

In **Estonia**, free maps of Tallinn's Old Town are readily available in passenger ferries, hotel receptions and the tourist information office. More complete city maps, as well as maps of other cities and regions, produced by Regio at Narva mnt 13a and can be bought everywhere.

In **Latvia**, city maps are readily available at the Rīga Tourist Information Centre. A wide selection of inexpensive maps and guides of Latvia and its other cities can be purchased at the Jāṇa Sēta Map Shop, Elizabetes 83/85, www.kartes.lv.

In **Lithuania** Jāṇa Sēta maps are available at tourist offices, bookshops and petrol stations. There are also maps by the Vilnius publishers, Briedis.

Money

All three countries are tied to the euro, which they aim to adopt in due course.

Estonia's currency is the crown or the kroon, abbreviated kr or EEK. Its value is fixed at 15.6kr to the euro, and there are 23kr to the £. Each kroon is made of 100 senti. Paper bills come in denominations of 500kr, 100kr, 50kr, 25kr, 10kr, 5kr and 2kr. Coins, come in 1kr, 50 senti, 20 senti and 10 senti varieties. There are also 5kr coins, but these are very rare, and used almost exclusively in luggage lockers.

Latvia's lat is worth roughly the same amount as the £ (0.70 euros). One lat consists of 100 santimi, with 1, 2, 5, 10, 20 and 50 santimi and 1 and 2 lat coins. Bank notes are available in denominations of 5, 10, 20, 50, 100 and 500 lats.

Lithuania's litas (Lt) are about 3.45 to the euro. There are 5Lt to £1. Lt comes in denominations of 10, 20, 50, 100, 200 and 500Lt notes. Coins are divided into the valuable – 1, 2 and 5Lt ones – and the nearly worthless centai variety of which there are 50, 20, 10, 5, 2 and 1.

Currency exchange In Tallinn and Vilnius, exchange bureaux are for the most part inside banks. This ensures that changing money between 9am and 5pm is relatively easy, but outside those times it can be a bit more difficult. In a pinch one can turn to receptions at major hotels and a few tourist-targeting, after-hours exchanges. In both cases, rates will be less favourable than in the banks. In Rīga, exchange booths are easier to find. Some may look questionably make-shift, but these are perfectly legitimate and many are open all night.

Credit cards Almost all upmarket or mid-range establishments such as hotels, restaurants, nightclubs, bars and shops, will accept most major credit cards. However, it is always best to double-check before committing to or eating up all of your intended purchase.

ATMs are easy to find in the cities and accept all major credit and bank cards, but before leaving home check with your bank that your card will be acceptable.

Travellers' cheques The number of establishments accepting travellers' cheques are less frequent, but you can cash them at most banks. They cannot be used as currency.

N ewspapers & Magazines

The Baltic Times (Skunu 16, tel: 722 9978, fax: 722 6041, editorial@ baltictimes.com; www.baltictimes.com), printed in Rīga, is the only pan-Baltic English-language newspaper covering all three states. The paper is sold in kiosks for US$1.50 but you can find it for free in major hotels around the Baltics.

Tallinn In Your Pocket, *Rīga In Your Pocket* and *Vilnius In Your Pocket* are handy city guides, published six times a year with an updated calendar of events, full reviews about the cities' ever-changing restaurants, cafés and bars, and a selection of tourist sites. Once a year, the In Your Pocket team also publishes *Pärnu In Your Pocket*, *Klaipėda In Your Pocket*, *Kaunas In Your Pocket* and *Tartu In Your Pocket*.

Tallinn's *City Paper* (www.balticsworldwide.com) is a bi-monthly colour publication with news features covering all three capital cities.

The International Herald Tribune, *The Financial Times*, *The Times* and the *New York Times* are also on sale in the main hotels.

O pening Hours

With the exception of major shopping centres, which usually open Mon–Fri 10am–10pm (9pm in Estonia), most shops open 10am–7pm (6pm in Estonia), Sat 10am–5pm, and close on Sundays. Banks and government offices are generally open weekdays 9am–5pm. Most museums are open 11am–5pm (6pm in Estonia) and many are closed on Mondays and Tuesdays. Typical office hours are Mon–Fri 9am–5pm.

P opulation & Size

Estonia, the northernmost of the three Baltic states, is also the smallest, but at 45,227 sq. km (17,375 sq. miles) it is larger than either Denmark, The

Netherlands or Switzerland. The country is pocked with lakes and the surrounding coastline is dotted with more than a thousand islands. The landscape is remarkably flat and over 40 percent of the country is covered with dense forest.

Estonia has a population of 1,356,045 of which almost a third (397,150) live in and around Tallinn. Other major settlements include Tartu (pop. 101,190), Narva (pop. 67,752), Kohtla-Järva (pop. 46,765) and Pärnu (pop. 44,781). Estonia is 68 percent Estonian, 26 percent Russian, with most of the remainder composed of other ex-Soviet nationalities such as Ukrainians and Belarusians. The composition of the populace in any particular region varies from the industrial towns of northeastern Estonia, where Russians account for some 95 percent of the population, to rural areas where Estonians form over 90 percent of the population.

The state church is the Estonian Evangelical Lutheran Church, which has held sway since the Reformation in the 16th century. Orthodox and Baptist churches also draw large congregations, mainly from the Russian community. Estonians have never been a particularly religious people. However, since independence there has been a renewed interest in the church and attendances have risen.

Latvia, the middle of the three states, lies on the eastern coast of the Baltic Sea, less than an hour's flight from Stockholm or Helsinki. It is bounded by Estonia to the north, Lithuania to the south and Russia and Belarus to the east. The territory covers 64,589 sq. km (24,950 sq. miles). The average north-south distance is 210 km (130 miles) and the greatest east-west distance in a straight line is 410 km (255 miles). The 1,030-km (640-mile) River Daugava enters the Baltic Sea in Rīga Bay and the dune-backed coast runs for more than 500 km (310 miles). The country is generally flat and forested, with uplands in the northwest and in the east, where most of the lakes lie. The highest point in Latvia is Galziņkalns, which reaches just 312 metres (1,025 ft).

The population of Latvia is 2,387,470, of whom 769,500 live in Rīga. Latvia's second city is Daugavpils (pop. 115,590), followed by Liepāja (pop. 89,515), Jelgava (pop. 63,915), Jūrmala (pop. 55,570) and Ventspils (pop. 44,050). Latvians make up 58 percent of the population, while Russians account for 30 percent

of the total. Belarusians number 4 percent and Ukrainians form 3 percent of the population. Latvians are a minority in the country's two largest cities, but a majority in the smaller towns and countryside.

Prior to World War II, 55 percent of Latvia's population was Lutheran and 24 percent was Catholic (concentrated in Latgale, the eastern region). The rest of the people were Russian Orthodox, Baptist or Jewish. A religious revival in 1988 has since abated.

Lithuania is the largest of the three Baltic countries, covering 65,302 sq. km (25,213 sq. miles), twice the size of Belgium. It borders Latvia in the north, Belarus in the east and south and Poland and the Russian enclave of Kaliningrad in the southwest. Its claim to fame is that it is the centre of Europe: the dead centre of the continent lies near Bernotai, 25 km (15 miles) north of Vilnius. The countryside is slightly more undulating than its northern neighbours and it is covered with rivers and lakes, 2,833 of which exceed an acre. It has the shortest coastline of the three states, covering 99 km (60 miles), much of which is taken up by the extraordinary sand dunes of Neringa Spit, where the 937-km (582-mile) River Nemunas reaches the sea via a large lagoon.

Lithuania's population is almost 3.5 million. Vilnius, the capital, is the biggest city with 542,000 inhabitants, followed by Kaunas (pop. 374,000), Klaipėda (pop. 192,000), Šiauliai (pop. 133,000) and Panevėžys (pop. 119,000). Lithuanians make up just over 83 percent of the total population. The second-largest ethnic group is Polish (6.7 percent) followed by Russians (6.3 percent).

Predominantly Catholic, Lithuania could be described as the most religious of the three countries – the flame of religion having been kept alive throughout the communist era by the church in Rome. A lot of money has been poured into churches, monasteries and seminaries to re-establish Vilnius in particular as a major Catholic centre in Europe.

Postal Services

There are good international postal links. Letters generally take about five days to reach the rest of Europe and around seven days to arrive in the US. Stamps can be bought at post offices or hotels, which are also the best places to post your letters.

Tallinn
Tallinn Central Post Office: Narva mnt. 1 (opposite the Viru Centre), tel: 625 7300/661 6616, fax: 661 6047; post@tallpost.ee; www.post.ee. Open Mon–Fri 7.30am–8pm, Sat 9am–6pm. Most services are handled in the main hall, upstairs. Packages, including those sent by EMS courier service, are sent and received in an office with an entrance around the left side of the building (open also Sunday 9am–3pm).
DHL Express Centre, Hobujaama 4, tel: 6652 555.
Federal Express, Narva mnt.13, tel: 6143 301, fax: 6143 300.
TNT Express Worldwide, Kesk-Sõjamäe 10a, tel: 627 1900, fax: 627 1901, kliendi.teenindus@tnt.com
UPS, Suve 5, tel: 6664 700, fax: 6664 701, customer.service@upspartner.ee.
Riga
Riga Central Post Office, Stacijas laukums 1, tel: 701 8804, www.pasts.lv. Open Mon–Fri 8am–8pm, Sat & Sun 8am–4pm.
Express Mail: Stacijas laukums 1 (near the central railway station), tel: 701 8804. Open Mon–Fri 8am–7pm, Sat 8am–4pm, Sun 10am–4pm.
DHL, Airport, tel: 771 5500, www.dhl.lv.
FedEx, Zemitana 2b, tel 732 6067.
TNT Express Worldwide, Airport, tel: 713 8432.
UPS, Ulmaņa 2, tel: 780 5650.
Vilnius
Vilnius Central Post Office, Gedimino pr. 7, tel: 262 5468. Open Mon–Fri 7am–7pm, Sat 9am–4pm.
Old Town Post Office, Vokiečių 7, tel: 619 960. Open Mon–Fri 8am–7pm, Sat 8am–3pm.
DHL, Dariaus ir Girėno 40, tel: (8-800) 223 45, www.dhl.lt. Open Mon–Fri 8am–5.30pm, Sat 8am–noon.
Express Mail Service, Geležinkelio 6, tel: 239 8334. Open Mon–Fri 8am–6pm.
FedEx, Verkių 29, tel: (8-800) 202 00; www.fedex.com. Open Mon–Fri 8am–5pm.
TNT, Dariaus ir Girėno 42, tel: 239 7555, www.tnt.com. Open Mon–Fri 8am–6pm.
UPS, Eigulių 15, tel: 247 2222; www.ups.com. Open Mon–Fri 8am–6pm, Sat 8am–2pm.

Public Holidays

Public holidays are cause for great celebration in the Baltics. Each state flies the flags of the other two nations on these special days, as well as their own flag – in Latvia the national flag must, by law, be

displayed prominently on facades by the front door on public holidays.
(See also Festivals, pages 356–7.)

Estonia
January New Year's Day (1)
February Independence Day (24)
March/April Good Friday and Easter Sunday
May Spring Day (1)
June Victory Day (23), Midsummer (24)
August Day of Restoration of Independence (20)
December Christmas (25/26)
Memorial Day
January Holocaust Memorial Day (27)

Latvia
January New Year's Day (1)
March/April Good Friday and Easter Monday
May May Day (1)
May Proclamation of Independence (4)
June Līgo Day (23), Jāņi summer solstice (24)
November Independence Day (18)
December Christmas (24/25/26)
Memorial Days
March mass deportation of Balts to Siberia in 1949 (25)
May World War II Memorial Day (9)

BELOW: phone home – from Latvia.

June first mass deportation of Balts to Siberia, 1941 (14)
July Jewish Genocide Day (4)
November 1919 battle, during which invading German forces were repulsed from Rīga (11)

Lithuania
January New Year (1)
February Independence Day (1918) (16)
March Restoration of Lithuania's statehood (11)
March/April Easter
May Labour Day (1), Mothers' Day (first Sunday)
June St John's Day/Joninės (23–24)
July Crowning of Mindaugas, Day of Statehood (6)
August Feast of the Assumption (15)
November All Saints' Day (1)
December Christmas (25–26)

T elephones

You can direct dial to any country on the globe from almost any phone in the Baltic states. Public phones are card-operated. Colourful chip-cards can be bought from post offices, kiosks, shops and hotels. Some card phones can also be used with your credit card and all of them accept incoming calls. To call anywhere within each country just dial the full seven-digit number. To call any of the countries from abroad, dial your country's international dialling code (00 in Europe) and the country code:

Estonia 372
Latvia 371
Lithuania 370

followed by the number.

To call abroad dial 00, followed by the country code and then the number. You can call abroad from any phone. Calls cost around 15p minute to the rest of Europe and 20p to the US, a little more from call boxes and much more from hotels – check first.

Operator: 115/116.

Fax and Telegrams
Faxes and telegrams can be sent from central post offices. Faxes can also be sent from major hotels.

Mobile Phones
Mobile phones are popular in the Baltics, and the same GSM phone you use in Europe and the UK will also work here. You will automatically be switched over to a local service once you arrive. Check with your own provider at home to see if there are partnership agreements that will make roaming cheaper. To avoid roaming charges altogether, you can

get a local number by buying an inexpensive starter kit, sold in kiosks and shops, which comes with pre-paid credit.

Estonian mobile numbers start with 50–57. To call a mobile phone, simply dial the subscriber's number. From abroad, dial Estonia's country code (372), followed by the subscriber's number. Some older advertisements and business cards may still list mobile numbers beginning with 0. In this case, ignore the 0 and dial the rest of the number.

Latvian mobile phone numbers have eight digits starting with 2. Digital rules apply *(see above)*. From abroad, dial Latvia's country code (371), followed by the subscriber's mobile-phone number.

Lithuanian mobile phone numbers always begin with an 8. To dial a mobile phone, dial 8, wait for the changed tone, then dial the number. When calling a Lithuanian mobile from abroad, dial the country code (370), but drop the 8 so that the number begins with 6. All cities in Lithuania have a code. When calling from abroad or from one city to another the code must be dialled. For example, when calling from Kaunas to Vilnius one must press 8, wait for the changed tone and then dial 5 (Vilnius city code) followed by the number. A pre-paid SIM card can be purchased in order to use your own mobile phone in the country. The three largest companies, Bitė (Gedimino 39, www.bite.lt), Omnitel (Gedimino 12, www.omnitel.lt) and TELE2 (Vienuolio 12, www.tele2.lt) provide such services.

Internet
Most hotels have email addresses and accept reservations via their websites. Public internet access points and Internet cafés charge about £1–£1.50 per hour of surfing time.

Television & Radio

Most major hotels have rooms with radios and satellite televisions; the majority of them will come with BBC World, CNN, SkyNews, plus a clutch of other channels such as Eurosport, Discovery and Cartoon Network. Much of the entertainment programming on local channels is in English with subtitles in Estonia, but not not so often the case in Latvia or Lithuania. You may also be able to pick up channels from the neighbouring countries.

Television stations
Estonia There are three terrestrial broadcasters. Eesti Televisioon (ETV),

TRANSPORT
ACCOMMODATION
EATING OUT
ACTIVITIES
A – Z
LANGUAGE

the public channel, broadcasts mainly cultural and documentary programming. Kanal 2 is a commercial station whose programming leans heavily towards soap operas and reality TV. Higher-quality entertainment programmes appear on TV3. Four Finnish stations, YLE TV1, YLE TV2, MTV3 and Nelonen can also be received off the air in northern Estonia. Cable and satellite TV are widespread.

Latvia The two state-owned channels LTV1 and 7 show a variety of dated sitcoms from the US as well as local programming which is rarely of interest, even to Latvians and Russians. Privately owned LNT, TV3 and TV5 often broadcast good films, reality shows and even sporting events, but most are dubbed in Latvian with Russian subtitles.

Lithuania The three local channels are LTV (the national broadcasting station) and the privately owned and more popular LNK and TV3. Foreign movies or television shows are almost always dubbed into Lithuanian.

Radio

Estonia There are 18–21 radio stations on Tallinn's FM band. The state-owned Eesti Raadio airs the BBC World Service on 103.5FM every day midnight–6am, 7am–8am and 6.30pm–8pm.
Latvia There are 15 FM radio stations in the capital, notably Radio Latvia (Latvijas Radio), which has three channels including Klasiska radio, a classical radio station on 103.7FM. The BBC World Service can be picked up 24 hours a day on 100.5FM. Of the private music and news radios SWH on 105.2FM and SWH Rock on 89.2FM are well worth a listen.
Lithuania You can pick up 15 different FM radio stations in Vilnius. For news in English tune to the BBC World Service on 100.1 FM, VOA Europe on 105.6 FM or the French Radio France Internationale on 98.3 FM.

Time Zone

The Baltic states are in the Eastern European time zone which is GMT +2 hours. An hour is added between the end of March and October for daylight savings, so during the summer local time is GMT +3 hours, known as Eastern European Summer Time or EEST for short.

Tourist Information Centres

Note that tourist office opening hours often vary from year to year.

Estonia

Tallinn
Tallinn City Tourist Office & Convention Bureau, Vabaduse Väljak 7, 15199 Tallinn, tel: 6457 777; fax 6404 208; www.tourism.tallinn.ee for conference organisers.
Tallinn Tourist Information Centre, Niguliste 2/Kullaseppa 4, 10146 Tallinn, tel: 645 7777; fax: 645 7778; turismiinfo@tallinn.ee; www.tourism.tallinn.ee. Open May–June Mon–Fri 9am–7pm, Sat–Sun 10am–5pm; July–Aug Mon–Fri 9am–8pm, Sat & Sun 10am–6pm; Sept Mon–Fri 9am–6pm, Sat & Sun 10am–5pm; Oct–Apr Mon–Fri 9am–5pm, Sat 10am–3pm.
Tourist Information at Tallinn Passenger Port, A-Terminal, Sadama 25, tel: 6318 321.
Elsewhere in Estonia
Hiiumaa Island, Hiiu tn 1, Kärdla, tel/fax: 462 2232; hiiumaa@visitestonia.com; www.hiiumaa.ee.
Kuressaare (Saaremaa Island), Tallinna 2, tel/fax: 453 3120; tourism@kuressaare.ee; www.saaremaa.ee.
Narva, Puškini 13, tel: 356 0184; fax: 356 0186; narva@visitestonia.com.
Pärnu, Rüütli 16, tel: 447 3000; fax: 447 3001; tourism@parnu.info, www.parnu.ee.
Tartu, Raekoja plats 14, tel/fax: 7442 111; info@turism.tartu.ee; www.tartu.ee.
Võru, Tartu mnt 31, tel/fax: 7821 881; www.vorulinn.ee.

Latvia

Rīga Information Centre, Rātslaukums 6, Rīga, tel: 703 7900; fax: 703 7910; www.rigatourism.lv. Lativa TIC, Smilsu 4, tel: 722 4664; www.lativatourism.lv.
Elsewhere in Latvia
Balvi, Bērzpils1a, tel: 458 1195; fax: 458 1195.
Bauska, Rātslaukums 1, tel: 392 3797; fax: 392 3797; www.bauska.lv.
Cesis, Pils lank 1, tel: 412 1815, www.cesis.lv.
Daugavpils, Rīgas 22a, tel: 542 2818; fax: 542 2818; www.daugavpils.lv.
Dundaga, Pils 14, tel: 323 7860; www.dundaga.lv.
Jelgava, Pasta 37, tel/fax: 302 2751; www.jelgava.lv
Jūrmala, Lienes 5, tel: 714 7900; www.jurmala.lv.
Kandava, Talsu 11, tel: 318 1150; fax: 318 1194; www.kandava.lv.
Kolka Liv Centre, tel: 327 7267.
Kuldīga, Baznīcas 5, tel/fax: 332 2259; www.kuldiga.lv.
Liepaja & Southern Kurzeme, Roža laukums 5/6, tel: 348 0807; fax: 348 0808; www.liepaja.lv.
Roja, Selgas 33, tel: 326 9594; www.roja.lv.

Sabile, Pilskalna 6, tel: 325 2344; www.sabile.lv.
Sigulda, Valdemāra 1a, tel: 797 1335; fax 797 1372; www.sigulda.lv.
Talsi, Lielā 19/21, tel: 322 4165; www.talsi.lv.
Tukums, Pils 3, tel: 312 4451; fax: 312 2237; www.tukums.lv.
Valmiera, Rīgas 10, tel/fax: 420 7177; www.valmiera.lv.
Ventspils, Tirgus 7, tel: 362 2263; fax: 360 7665; www.tourism.ventspils.lv.

Lithuania

Lithuanian State Department of Tourism, Juozapavičiaus 13, Rīga, tel: 210 8796; fax 210 8753; www.tourism.lt.
Vilnius Tourist Information Centres. Two of the three information centres – the one at the train station and the other at Vilniaus 22 – have the same working hours (Mon–Fri 9am–6pm, Sat & Sun 10am–4pm). The third one is inside the Town Hall at Didžioji 31 (open Mon–Fri 10am–6pm).
Elsewhere in Lithuania
Kaunas, Kaunas Region Tourist Information Centre, Laisvės al. 36, tel: 323 436; www.kaunas.lt. Open Oct–Apr Mon–Thur 9am–6pm, Fri 9am–5pm; May & Sept Mon–Fri 9am–6pm, Sat 9am–3pm; June–Aug daily 9am–6pm.
Kaunas, "Mūsų Odisėja" Tourist Information Centre, M.K. Čiurlionio 15, tel: 220 426; fax: 408 411; www.turinfo.lt. Open Mon–Fri 9am–6pm.
Klaipėda Tourist Information Centre, Turgaus 5 and 7, tel: 412 186; fax: 412 185; tic@one.lt. Open Mon–Sat 9am–7pm.
Palanga Tourist Information Centre, Kretingos 1, tel: 488 11; fax: 488 22; www.palangatic.lt. Open daily 8am–8pm.
Nida Tourist Information Centre, Taikos 4, tel: 523 45; fax: 523 44; agilainfo@is.lt. Open June–Sept Mon–Fri 10am–8pm, Sat 10am–6pm, Sun 10am–3pm; Oct–May Mon–Fri 10am–1pm & 2pm–6pm, Sat 10am–3pm.
Trakai, Vytauto 69, tel: 519 34; trakaitic@is.lt; www.trakai.lt. Open Mon 8.30am–4pm, Tues–Fri 8.30am–5.30pm, Sat 9am–3pm.

Websites

The best Baltic-related Internet resources are:
www.ee (search the Estonian-wide web);
www.lv (search the Latvian web);
www.all.lv (all Latvian links);
www.on.lt (Lithuanian links);
www.inyourpocket.com (the entire contents of the print guides are available online; information on events is updated monthly).

LANGUAGE

UNDERSTANDING THE LANGUAGE

ESTONIAN

Estonian, the official language of the Republic of Estonia, is closely related to Finnish and Hungarian. Although it uses a Latin alphabet, and each letter represents only one sound, it is a difficult language to master. There are 14 different cases of any noun, verb conjugation is complex and the verb's meaning may also change according to how its root is pronounced. There are, however, no articles or genders in Estonian. If you can manage to pick up a few of the words listed below, this will be appreciated by the locals.

Numbers

1	üks
2	kaks
3	kolm
4	neli
5	viis
6	kuus
7	seitse
8	kaheksa
9	üheksa
10	kümme
11	üksteist
12	kaksteist
13	kolmteist
20	kakskümmend
21	kakskümmend-üks
30	kolmkümmend
100	sada
200	kaksada
1,000	tuhat

Days of the Week

Sunday pühapäev
Monday esmaspäev
Tuesday teisipäev
Wednesday kolmapäev
Thursday neljapäev
Friday reede
Saturday laupäev

Estonian Sounds

Vowels
a – as in car
e – as in bed
i – as in beet
o – as in on
u – as in up
ä – a as in cat
ö – o as in hurt
õ – as in girl
ü – oo as in shoot.
When a vowel is doubled its sound is lengthened.

Consonants
These have the same sound values as in English, except:
g – always hard, as in gate
j – as the y in yet
š – tch as in match
ž – as in pleasure

Common Expressions

hello tere
good morning tere hommikust
good evening tere õhtust
goodbye head aega
see you nägemist
thanks aitäh or tänan
please palun
sorry vabandust
excuse me vabandage palun
yes/no jah/ei
fine hästi
a greeting or a toast tervist
bon appetit head isu
The general purpose negative – ei ole – is used to encompass every inconvenience from "**we're sold out**" to "**she's not here**".

Useful Words

airport lennujaam
train station raudteejaam
(in Tallinn the station is known as Balti jaam)
harbour sadam
shop kauplus/pood
town centre kesklinn
market turg
hairdresser juuksur
pharmacy apteek
street/road maantee mnt./ puiestee pst.
every day äga päev
holiday puhkepa&&ev

LATVIAN

Latvian is the native language of about 60 percent of the 2.3 million people living in Latvia and one of the world's endangered languages. It is one of two surviving Baltic languages of the Indo-European language group, the other being Lithuanian. Remotely related to the Slavic languages Russian, Polish and Ukranian, Latvian has 48 phonemes – speech sounds distinguishing one word from another – 12 vowels, 10 diphthongs and 26 consonants. Stress is placed on the first syllable.

Numbers

1	viens
2	divi
3	trīs
4	četri
5	pieci
6	seši
7	septiņi
8	astoņi
9	deviņi
10	desmit

Latvian Sounds

Vowels
These have the same sound values as in English, with several additions:
a – as in cat
e – as in bed
i – as in hit
o – as in floor
u – as in good
a line over a vowel lengthens it:
ā – as in car
ē – as in there
ī – as in bee (Riga = Rīga)
ū – oo as in cool

Diphthongs
au – ow as in pout
ie – e as in here
ai – I as in sight
ei – ay as in sway

Consonants
Consonants have the same sound values as in English with the following exceptions:
c – ts as in tsar
č – ch as in chin
g – always hard, as in gate
ģ – as in logical. The accent can also be a "tail" under the letter.
j – as the y in yet
ķ – tch as in hatch
ļ – as in failure
ņ – as in onion
r – always rolled as in Spanish
š – sh as in shoe
ž – as in pleasure

11	vienpadsmit
12	divpadsmit
20	divdesmit
30	trīsdesmit
100	simts
200	divi simti
1,000	tūkstotis

Days of the Week
Sunday svētdiena
Monday pirmdiena
Tuesday otrdiena
Wednesday trešdiena
Thursday ceturtdiena
Friday piektdiena
Saturday sestdiena

Common Expressions
hello, hi sveiki
good morning labrīt
good afternoon labdien
good evening labvakar
goodbye uz redzēšanso/visu labu
yes jā
no nē
Please; You're welcome lūdzu
Thank you paldies

I am sorry! Excuse me Atvainojiet!
That's all right Nekas
May I ask a question? Vai drīkstu jautāt?
May I come in? Vai drīkstu ienākt?
Where can... be found? Kur atrodas...?
How much is it? Cik tas maksā?
Would you please tell me/show me Vai Jūs lūdzu mannepateiktu/neparādītū?
Pleased to meet you. Patīkami ar Jums iepazīties.
Let me introduce myself. Atļaujiet stādīties priekšā.
My name is... Mani sauc...
Do you speak English? Vai Jūs runājat angliski?
I don't understand/speak Latvian Es nesaprotu/nerunāju latviski.
We need an interpreter Mums ir vajadzīgs tulks.

Useful Words
doctor ārsts
hospital slimnīca
first aid ātrā palīdzība
hotel viesnīca
restaurant restorāns
shop veikals
airport lidosta
bus station autoosta
railway station dzelzceļa stacija
petrol station degvielas uzpildes stacija
post office pasts
street iela
boulevard bulvāris
square laukums
closed slēgts
open atvērts

LITHUANIAN

Lithuanian and Latvian both belong to the Baltic family of the Indo-European languages. Lithuanian is one of the oldest surviving languages related to Sanskrit and it has kept its sound system and many archaic forms and sentence structures. When the language was first formalised in 1918, there were a variety of distinctive dialects across the country and Suvalkiecių. The southern "sub-dialect" of Western High Lithuania was adopted as the official dialect. Today, local dialects have been largely assimilated. There are 32 letters in the alphabet. One of Lithuanian's idiosyncrasies is the tail that appears beneath its vowels.

Numbers
1	vienas
2	du
3	trys
4	keturi
5	penki
6	šeši
7	septyni
8	aštuoni
9	devyni
10	dešimt
11	vienuolika
12	dvylika
20	dvidešimt
30	trisdešimt
100	šimtas
200	du šimtas
1,000	tūkstantis

Common Expressions
hello laba diena
hello Mr... laba diena, pone...
hi sveikas
please prasom
excuse me atsiprašau
sorry apgailestauju
good morning labas rytas
good evening labas vakaras
good night abanakt
goodbye Sudiev viso gero
welcome sveiki atvykò
How are you? Kaip sekasi?
Pleased to meet you Malonu su jumis susipaēnti
See you later Iki pasimatymo
yes/no taip/ne
okay gerai
perhaps galbūt
when? kada?
where? kur?

Lithuanian Sounds

Vowels
a – as in arm
e – as in there
i – as in sit
o – as in shot
u – as in should
ė – as in make
ū – oo as in stool
y – ee as in see
ą, ė, į and ų appear in special cases and are slightly longer than the equivalent letters without a "tail".

Diphthongs
ai – as in i
au – as in now
ei – as in make
ie – as in yellow
uo – as in wonder

Consonants
c – ts as in tickets
č – ch as in chin
j – as in yes
š – sh as in she
z – as in zoo
ž – as in vision

Who? *kas?*
why? *kodėl?*
Do you understand me?
Ar mane suprantate?
I don't speak Lithuanian
Aš nekalbu lietuviškai
I understand Lithuanian
Aš suprantu lietuviškai
**Do you speak English, German,
French, Russian, Polish?** *Kalbate
angleškai, vokiškai, pranc?ziskai,
rusiškai, lenkiškai?*

I speak English, German...
Aš kalbu angliškai, vokiškai...
May I have...? *Prašyālau...?*
May I smoke? *Ar galima uzsirūkyti?*
What time is it? *Kelinta dabar
valanda?*
How much is it? *Kiek kainuoja?*
**Where is the nearest shop, hotel,
restaurant, café, bar, toilet?** *Kur
artimiausia parduotuvė, viešbutis,
restoranas, kavinė, baras, tualetas?*
thank you (very much) *(labai) aci?*

Useful Words

left *kaire*
right *dešine*
straight *tiesiai*
bread *duona*
butter *sviestas*
cheese *sūris*
beer *alus*
wine *vynas*
tea *arbata*
coffee *kava*

FURTHER READING

General

Baltic Countdown, by Peggie Benton. Centaur Press, 1985. An extraordinary account of the wife of a British diplomat caught up in Rīga at the outbreak of World War II.
The Baltic Nations and Europe, by John Hiden & Patrick Salman. Longman, 1995. A history of the 20th century in the three countries.
The Baltic Revolution, by Anatol Lieven. Yale, 1993. A fine background to the cultural, economic and political life in the region by a member of one of the foremost Baltic families, and a contributor to this book.
The Baltic States: Years of Dependence (1940–1990), by Romanuld J. Misiunas, Rein Taagepera. C. Hurst & Co, London; and University of California Press, 1983. This is a follow up to the classic Years of Independence (1917–1940) by Georg von Rauch.
The Czar's Madman, by Jaan Kross. Harvill, 2001. Estonia's premier writer brilliantly evokes life in the times of the Russian occupation in the 19th century. Also by Kross:
Professor Marten's Departure, 1994; **Treading Air**, 2003.
The Good Republic, by William Palmer. Minerva, 1990. An excellent and imaginative novel about an emigre returning to the Baltic city he fled during World War II and encountering some ghosts on his return 40 years later.
The Singing Revolution, by Clare Thompson. Michael Joseph, 1992. Personal account of the rebirth of the Baltics by a British journalist who was there in 1989–90.
To the Baltic with Bob: An Epic Misadventure, by Griff Rhys Jones. Penguin, 2003. The humorist's adventures from the Thames to St Petersburg.
Racundra's First Cruise and **Racundra's Third Cruise**, by Arthur

Ransome, Brian Hammett (Editor). Fernhurst Books, 2003. Reprint of 1920s boating tales from the Baltic – the first around Estonia's islands, the third upriver in Latvia – from the creator of Swallows and Amazons.
Walking since Daybreak, by Modris Eksteins. Papermac, 2000. An account of a Latvian family through the 20th century.
War in the Woods: Estonia's Struggle for Survival, 1944–1956,

by Mart Laar. 1992. The courageous story of the "Forest Brothers", freedom fighters who took to the woods after the second Soviet occupation.

Other Insight Guides

The 190-title Insight Guides series includes eight books on Spain and its islands, all combining the exciting pictures and incisive text associated with this series.

Insight Guides

The major *Insight Guide* series, with top photography and complete background reading, has titles on Scandinavia, as well as one on each individual country, and on Russia, Poland and Eastern Europe.

Insight City Guides

A new series, *Insight City Guides* are written by locally based writers, who show you how to make the most of such destinations as St Petersburg and Prague. Includes detailed listings and a free Restaurant Guide Map to locate the city's favourite restaurants.

Insight Pocket Guides and Insight Compact Guides

Scandinavian and all the European countries and major cities are well covered by these two fact-filled series. Insight Pocket Guides have a local author to guide you to their favourite haunts while Compact Guides are the ultimate "portable encyclopedia" – the ideal easy-reference book.

Feedback

We do our best to ensure the information in our books is as accurate and up-to-date as possible. The books are updated on a regular basis, using local contacts, who painstakingly add, amend and correct as required. However, some mistakes and omissions are inevitable and we are ultimately reliant on our readers to put us in the picture. We would welcome your feedback on any details related to your experiences using the book "on the road". Maybe we recommended a hotel that you liked (or another that you didn't), as well as interesting new attractions, or facts and figures you have found out about the country itself. The more details you can give us (particularly with regard to addresses, e-mails and telephone numbers), the better. We will acknowledge all contributions, and we'll offer an Insight Guide to the best letters received.

Please write to us at:
Insight Guides
PO Box 7910
London SE1 1WE
United Kingdom
Or send e-mail to:
insight@apaguide.co.uk

ART & PHOTO CREDITS

INDEX

Numbers in italics refer to photographs. Abbreviations: Est = Estonia; Lat = Latvia; Lith = Lithuania

Register with
HotelClub.com
and get £15!

At *HotelClub.com*, we reward our Members with discounts and free stays in their favourite hotels. As a Member, every booking made by you through *HotelClub.com* will earn you Member Dollars.

When you register, we will credit your account with **£15** which you can use for your next booking! The equivalent of **£15** will be credited in US$ to your Member account (as *HotelClub Member Dollars*). All you need to do is log on to *www.HotelClub.com/insightguides*. Complete your details, including the Membership Number and Password located on the back of the *HotelClub.com* card.

Over 2.2 million Members already use Member Dollars to pay for all or part of their hotel bookings. Join now and start spending Member Dollars whenever and wherever you want – you are not restricted to specific hotels or dates!

With great savings of up to 60% on over 20,000 hotels across 97 countries, you are sure to find the perfect location for business or pleasure. Happy travels from *HotelClub.com!*

www.insightguides.com

TRULY ADVENTUROUS

TRULY ASIA

In the heart of Asia lies a land of many cultures, wonders and attractions. Especially for the adventure seeker to whom fear is not a factor. There are hundreds of thrills to experience. Mount Kinabalu. Mulu Caves. Taman Negara. These are just a few places where you'll always find that rewarding adrenaline rush. Where is this land, so challenging and exhilarating? It can only be Malaysia, Truly Asia.

Malaysia Truly Asia

KUALA LUMPUR (Head Office): 17th Floor, Menara Dato' Onn, Putra World Trade Centre, 45 Jalan Tun Ismail, 50480 Kuala Lumpur, Malaysia. Tel: +603-2615 8188 Fax: +603-2693 5884 Website: www.tourismmalaysia.gov.my

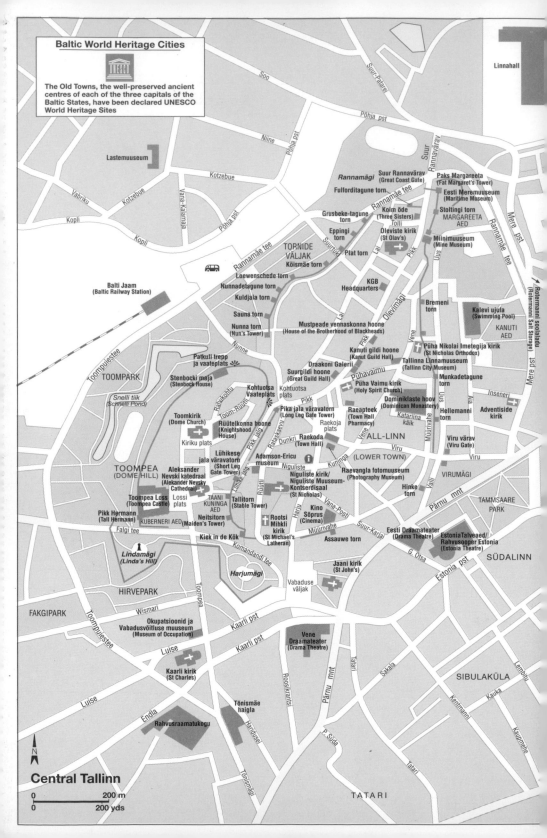

Baltic World Heritage Cities

The Old Towns, the well-preserved ancient centres of each of the three capitals of the Baltic States, have been declared UNESCO World Heritage Sites

Linnahall

Lastemuuseum

Balti Jaam
(Baltic Railway Station)

Rannamägi

Suur Rannavärav
(Great Coast Gate)

Paks Margareeta
(Fat Margaret's Tower)

Fulforditagune torn

Eesti Meremuuseum
(Maritime Museum)

Grusbeke-tagune torn

Kolm õde
(Three Sisters)

Stoltingi torn
MARGAREETA
AED

Eppingi torn

Tolli

Oleviste kirik
(St Olav's)

Miinimuuseum
(Mine Museum)

TORNIDE
VÄLJAK

Plat torn

Köismäe torn

KALEVI AED

Loewenschede torn

KGB
Headquarters

Kalevi ujula
(Swimming Pool)

Nunnadetagune torn

Bremeni
torn

Kuldjala torn

Olevimägi

Sauna torn

Mustpeade vennaskonna hoone
(House of the Brotherhood of Blackheads)

Nunna torn
(Nun's Tower)

Püha Nikolai Imetegija kirik
(St Nicholas Orthodox)

Kanuti gildi hoone
(Kanut Guild Hall)

Tallinna Linnamuuseum
(Tallinn City Museum)

Patkuli trepp
ja vaateplats

Stenbocki maja
(Stenbock House)

Draakoni Galerii

Suurgildi hoone
(Great Guild Hall)

Munkadetagune
torn

TOOMPARK

Püha Vaimu kirik
(Holy Spirit Church)

Snelli tiik
(Schnelli Pond)

Kohtuotsa
Vaateplats

Kohtuotsa
plats

Dominiklaste hoov
(Dominican Monastery)

Hellemanni
torn

Adventiste
kirik

Toomkirik
(Dome Church)

Pika jala väravatorn
(Long Leg Gate Tower)

Raeapteek
(Town Hall
Pharmacy)

Katariina
käik

Rüütelkonna hoone
(Knightshood
House)

Raekoja
plats

ALL-LINN

Viru värav
(Viru Gate)

Kiriku plats

Raekoda
(Town Hall)

Lühikese
jala väravatorn
(Short Leg
Gate Tower)

Adamson-Ericu
museum

(LOWER TOWN)

VIRUMÄGI

TOOMPEA
(DOME HILL)

Aleksander
Nevski katedraal
(Alekander Nevsky
Cathedral)

Niguliste

Raevangla fotomuuseum
(Photography Museum)

Toompea Loss
(Toompea Castle)

Lossi
plats

TAANI
KUNINGA
AED

Tallitorn
(Stable Tower)

Niguliste kirik/
Niguliste Muuseum-
Kontserdisaal
(St Nicholas)

Hinke
torn

TAMMSAARE
PARK

Pikk Hermann
(Tall Hermann)

Neitsitorn
(Maiden's Tower)

Rootsi
Mihkli
kirik
(St Michael's
Latheran)

Kino
Sõprus
(Cinema)

Eesti Draamateater
(Drama Theatre)

Estonia Talveaed/
Rahvusooper Estonia
(Estonia Theatre)

KUBERNERI AED

Kiek in de Kök

Assauwe torn

SÜDALINN

Lindamägi
(Linda's Hill)

Harjumägi

Jaani kirik
(St John's)

HIRVEPARK

Vabaduse
väljak

FAKGIPARK

Okupatsioonid ja
Vabadusvõitluse muuseum
(Museum of Occupation)

Vene
Draamateater
(Drama Theatre)

SIBULAKÜLA

Kaarli kirik
(St Charles)

Tõnismäe
haigla

Rahvusraamatukogu

Central Tallinn

0   200 m
0   200 yds

TATARI